URBAN EXODUS

URBAN EXODUS

Why the Jews Left Boston and the Catholics Stayed

Gerald Gamm

HARVARD UNIVERSITY PRESS

Cambridge, Massachusetts

London, England

First Harvard University Press paperback edition, 2001

Library of Congress Cataloging-in-Publication Data

Gamm, Gerald H.
  Urban exodus : why the Jews left Boston and the Catholics stayed /
Gerald Gamm
      p.   cm.
      Includes bibliographical references and index.
      ISBN 0-674-93070-3 (cloth)
      ISBN 0-674-00558-9 (pbk.)
      1. Boston (Mass.)—Race relations.
      2. Boston (Mass.)—Ethnic relations.
      3. Jews—Massachusetts—Boston—Attitudes—History—20th century.
      4. Catholics—Massachusetts—Boston—Attitudes—History—20th century.
      5. Migration, Internal—Massachusetts—Boston—History—20th century.
      6. Social classes—Massachusetts—Boston—History—20th century.
      I. Title.
F75A1G36   1999
305.8′009744′6109045—dc21   98-39536

In memory of my mother,
Sandra Gamm
1940–1990

Contents

Maps and Figures

Maps

Figures

URBAN EXODUS

People explore the new Seaver Street Temple on a quiet day in September 1925, the month Congregation Mishkan Tefila dedicated the structure. The congregation's decision to build the temple in Roxbury's Elm Hill district reflected and stimulated the migration of its members. However, with the growing popularity of the automobile in the early 1920s, another urban exodus was already under way. The congregation, like many of its members, eventually left this structure behind in its move to suburban Newton. (*Photograph courtesy of the* Boston Herald.)

Prologue:
The Church and the Temple

The temple erected by Congregation Mishkan Tefila still stands on Seaver Street, rising majestically above Franklin Park. It is awesome in its loneliness. Dedicated in 1925, the temple was built in upper Roxbury, Boston's first Jewish suburb. It was built by a congregation that traced its origins to the 1850s and to a few immigrants who had organized a humble synagogue in one of Boston's tenement districts. On the occasion of the Seaver Street Temple's completion, the *Jewish Advocate* devoted an editorial to "this beautiful landmark, the shrine and pride of a prosperous, dignified and cultured Jewish community."[1]

Today the beautiful landmark stands empty, even less than empty. Along the side of the temple, roman letters carefully chiseled in limestone resonate with the voice of Ozymandias, who bid us look on his works and despair: "NOT BY MIGHT NOR BY POWER BUT BY MY SPIRIT, SAITH THE LORD." The words from Zechariah had not been part of the architect's original plan for the temple building but were incorporated at the request of Herman H. Rubenovitz, the rabbi who came to Mishkan Tefila in 1910 and led it into the 1940s, into the postwar era.

The words remain, with the limestone shell and granite steps and marble portico. And when you climb the temple's steps and stand on the portico, you can look up at the terra cotta ceiling and marvel that the colors remain vivid and brilliant. The view from the portico, the view of Frederick Law Olmsted's magnificent Franklin Park, also remains. But that is all that remains. The temple has been three times abandoned—by its congregation, which, with the rest of Boston Jewry, moved long ago to new suburbs; then by a Jewish day school; then by an

1

African-American school for performing arts. There is now nothing left but the husk.

I visited the site for the first time on a crisp fall day in 1991. It was late in the afternoon. I discovered a temple lost in a wilderness, the wide esplanade of grass that once led from the park to the granite steps now overgrown with trees. The thicket of trees has been growing on the old esplanade since the 1960s.[2] Bushes and tufts of weeds now sprout from the cracks and seams of the granite staircase. I found sheets of plywood instead of the two-story-high stained glass windows, and every entrance was boarded up. The engraved Stars of David were intact above each of the side entrances to the temple, but outside two of the entrances were heaps of trash: tree stumps, lumber, a mattress, swatches of fabric and pieces of carpet, broken bottles, and old chairs and sofas.

Finding the boards pried off of one of the side entrances, I made my way through the trash and gingerly walked down into the dark basement. I walked onto a floor of ash and remembered reading that there had been two or three major fires in the building since the early 1970s. I walked farther into the basement, toward light, and then looked up. There was nothing left of the temple: I was standing in basement, vestry, main sanctuary, and balcony all at once. I was in a vast barn. The successive fires had destroyed all the floors, all the walls, all the ceilings, as well as the pulpit and the ark. I looked for the walls but saw only the skeleton that supported the exterior limestone shell. I stood in ash and was sheltered not by a ceiling but by what was left of the old copper roof, which was itself torn through with a gaping hole.

After a few minutes, I left the building the way I had entered it, squeezing through the boards that guarded the side door. I walked slowly back toward my car, stopping at the side of the building to read the inscription again. I saw that some of the plywood was missing from one of the large windows and realized that, from a certain angle, you could look into the building through the window and see the sky through the hole in the roof.

It was beginning to get dark, but I approached the front of the building one more time. I walked up the granite steps and stood on the portico. Looking down the steps, I could see the weeds and bushes and trees and I could see across to Franklin Park. But when I turned my back and looked instead up at the terra cotta ceiling and straight ahead to the carved Italian marble that framed the main entrance, I found myself for an instant back in time. Seeing the sun beginning to set, I realized with a start that it was Friday and that the Jewish Sabbath was being ushered in at synagogues all over the world. I realized that in a different age, men and women and children would be walking through those trees, up these steps, onto this very portico, and through the marble entrance, talking, laughing, and greeting one another. I stood on the portico and tried to hear their voices and see their faces. I tried to see the clothes that they were wearing. I looked at the main entrance, added my voice to theirs as we greeted the dusk and the Sabbath, then, back in the 1990s, I went down the steps, walked through the rubble, and drove back to Cambridge.

My first visit to St. Peter's Church had come a few months earlier. I had an appointment to meet with the pastor of the parish, and Father Sullivan had given me directions to the church over the telephone. I took the subway from Harvard Square out to Fields Corner, in Dorchester. Fields Corner, at the intersection of Dorchester Avenue and Adams Street, is a busy commercial district with insurance agencies, dentists' offices, banks, bars, restaurants, a branch of the city library, a post office, hair salons, a bakery, and a fish market. From Fields Corner I walked up Adams Street, up the steep hill toward the church. On my left I passed Ronan Park, a moderately sized neighborhood park named for the parish's first pastor. Adams Street is lined with three-deckers: the three-story frame structures, with porches on each level, that are ubiquitous in Dorchester. As I walked up Adams Street, I saw men and women sitting on their porches, talking and shouting and listening to music.

At the top of the street I found Dorchester Common. A hillside's distance from the busyness of Fields Corner, Dorchester Common is green and proper, the legacy of a colonial New England town. Large frame homes face the common on three sides. On the fourth side is the First Parish Church, a steepled, white frame meeting-house whose congregation was formed in 1630 by Dorchester's earliest English settlers. I stood at the side of the common and looked anxiously for St. Peter's Church, which I could not see. I continued on Adams Street, to the far side of the common, and found St. Peter's just to my left, one house lot removed from Dorchester Common. The church, on Bowdoin Street, faces a little park at the west side of the common.

St. Peter's Church still stands. The imposing pudding-stone church on Meeting House Hill, begun in 1873 and completed in 1891, is one of the great monuments of Dorchester and of Catholic Boston. Under the leadership of their founding pastor, Rev. Peter Ronan, the men and women of St. Peter's Parish had built the church as well as a rectory, a convent, a school building, and a parish hall. For generations, St. Peter's Parish had been one of the largest parishes in the archdiocese, a stronghold of several thousand Irish Catholics.

The church was smaller than I expected. I had read and heard so much about the grand pudding-stone cathedral that I was disappointed at first. The church seemed somehow cramped on its lot. Its square tower did not soar triumphantly; it seemed squat, even truncated. (Later I found out that the upper half of the tower, which was becoming structurally unsound, had been removed in the early 1980s, when the parish could not raise funds for its restoration.)[3] As I walked around the church, trying to find an unlocked door and the church offices, I began to appreciate the structure. Built of blocks of rough gray stone, St. Peter's Church is a hard building that rewards second and third looks with elegant detail that cascades from its main entrances to its façade to the base of its tower. Its nave is wide and tall. The building and the grounds are well maintained, but, to my frustration, none of the doors was unlocked.

Finally I noticed a large brick home to the right of the church and saw from a sign that it was St. Peter's rectory. I walked up the steps to the rectory, introduced myself to the woman who greeted me at the door, and took a seat in the front parlor, where I waited for Father Sullivan. I had a lot of questions to ask. This was my first visit to a Catholic church in Dorchester or Roxbury, and I was not sure what it was I needed to learn and what documents and papers I could hope to see. Father Sullivan came into the parlor and welcomed me to the rectory, offering to share whatever he knew about the parish. He located some recent papers and an early church history. On the understanding that I would make no use of individual names, he also offered me access to the parish's volumes of sacramental records, which were kept in the rectory, and to the school records, which were kept in the school building. He took time to listen to my questions and, sitting in the parlor of his rectory, to talk with me about life in an urban parish.

After we were done talking, Father Sullivan took me into the church. He showed me first the lower church, a large room that can seat one thousand people, and then the upper church, which can seat twelve hundred. I walked over to the altar, examined it, then sat down in one of the pews. I looked up at the wooden arches and the grand, vaulted ceiling, and thought about what the church must be like on Sundays, when some parishioner sits where I was sitting and Father Sullivan and other priests celebrate Mass. I got up from my seat and walked around the room, examining the pulpit and the baptismal font, and I took one more look at the altar.

Leaving the church, I then walked with Father Sullivan across Bowdoin Street to St. Peter's School. There he introduced me to the school's principal, who agreed to let me sit in the basement and pore through old school reports. I spent two days at the school examining the records, which are kept in a closet in a supply room. Sitting at a small student desk, surrounded by art supplies, I read through minutes of teachers' meetings in the 1940s, counted the numbers of students registered at the school in different years, and looked at photograph albums.

When I walked down the main corridor of St. Peter's School, I could hear teachers lecturing and students answering questions. I stood outside the school auditorium for a few minutes one afternoon, as some kind of assembly was taking place. I took my lunch at the table of the teachers' lounge. I read papers that were taped to one wall of the corridor, discovering that grade school students practiced their penmanship with quizzes on the catechism. I especially enjoyed the moment when a group of eighth-grade girls, passing between classes, discovered me in their supply room. They took a step into the room, hesitantly, giggling, and asked what I was doing. I told them. They wondered why anyone cared about their old school.

The girls, like most of the students now at St. Peter's School, were black. From annual reports that I examined some months later at the Catholic School Office downtown, I found enrollment figures and racial breakdowns for each of Dorchester's and Roxbury's parochial schools. In the spring of 1991, when I was rifling through papers in the school's supply closet, there were 180 students enrolled in St. Peter's in grades one through eight.[4] Of them, sixty-two were classified as African-American, another fifty-one as Haitian, thirty-five as Hispanic, three as Asian, and twenty-nine as "other." Just over two-thirds of the students that year were Catholics. The school, like the parish itself, is no longer an Irish Catholic stronghold.

When I met Father Sullivan again, in August, he told me about a sign that he was having prepared for the front of the church. He wanted the sign to remind those passing by that St. Peter's Church served a diverse body of parishioners. There were still some elderly white parishioners who continued to attend the church, he told me, but there were also many other families now active in the parish: white, black, Vietnamese, Hispanic, Haitian, and Cape Verdean. On Sundays, he told me, Mass was celebrated in three languages. There were four Masses in English, including the Saturday afternoon Mass, and Masses in Spanish and in Vietnamese. Several hundred Vietnamese came to the church every Sunday, arriving at one o'clock for various activities in the school building and staying for the Vietnamese Mass at five o'clock.

The next time I visited the parish I saw the sign that Father Sullivan had told me about. It is painted red, and it hangs to the right of the church's main entrance. Illustrated with a drawing of the bark of Peter, the sign greets visitors to St. Peter's Church. In gold lettering, the sign bids "welcome" five times over, in English, in Spanish, in Vietnamese, in Portuguese (for Cape Verdean parishioners), and in French (for Haitian parishioners).

This, then, is the state of things today in Dorchester and Roxbury. On Meeting House Hill and on Seaver Street, two structures built generations ago—two structures that in the 1930s and 1940s stood as leading institutions in their respective, bustling ethnic communities—still stand today as exemplars, as faithful bearers of distinct institutional traditions and patterns. Each institution in its way has survived and adapted to the exodus of the ethnic community that originally supported it. St. Peter's Church survives as a multiethnic community, sponsoring religious, educational, and social activities for people who have moved into the parish and identify with it. And, equally, Congregation Mishkan Tefila survives in the only way that its institutional rules allow: having moved in the 1920s from an older neighborhood into its magnificent temple on Seaver Street, it moved again in the 1950s out to the affluent suburb of Newton.

In its new suburban temple, Mishkan Tefila remains in the 1990s one of New England's leading congregations. I spent three weeks doing research in the archives of the Newton temple. As I sat in the temple library, I watched various people walk down the main hallway, off to class or a meeting or some other temple activity. On Fridays, the regular week-

It's very journalistic

day activity ended early, in anticipation of the Sabbath and the services that brought hundreds to the temple every Friday night and Saturday morning.

Recently, Mishkan Tefila constructed an addition to its Newton temple, a new youth center to house the congregation's flourishing nursery school. Embedded in an exterior wall of the youth center are two large marble tablets. The two "tablets of Ten Commandments hammered in gold," as they were described in 1926, had originally been set into the pediment of the Seaver Street Temple, directly above the entrance portico. The tablets were removed from the Roxbury structure and buried in a local cemetery in the late 1960s, when the structure was about to be transferred to non-Jewish owners. In the spring of 1992, leaders of Mishkan Tefila returned to the cemetery to retrieve the shattered remains of the two tablets. After stoneworkers carefully reconstructed them, the tablets were installed in the courtyard of the Newton temple's youth center. About three hundred members of the congregation gathered on a Sunday morning in May 1993 to dedicate the addition to the temple and celebrate their congregation's continued vitality.[5]

Mishkan Tefila, like St. Peter's Church, still lives. But the old buildings, reflecting dual modes of survival, offer powerful images of what institutions can mean for the neighborhoods they inhabit. To survive, of course, Mishkan Tefila needed to leave behind a handsome and valuable physical plant. After passing through two more owners, the Seaver Street Temple fell into ruin. One day when I was visiting the site, a woman walking along the sidewalk asked me what the building used to be. She told me that she lived down the street from the structure and had always wondered who had built it and what they had built it for. So I answered her questions. I then asked this woman what, until that moment, she had assumed about the structure. She responded that she had always thought it must have been a great library or museum or something like that, but that she really hadn't known. The only sign on the temple building is one posted by the city to warn off trespassers: it is written in English.

The messages communicated by the old temple and by the old church are clear and distinct. They speak to current residents of upper Roxbury and Dorchester. And they have spoken over the years to the ethnic communities that constructed the buildings. The different messages of the two structures—the posted signs, the condition of the structures, the upkeep of the grounds—have not resulted from good decisions or bad decisions. They are the products of rules. The temple on Seaver Street and the church on Meeting House Hill were created and sustained by institutions bound by two different sets of rules. These rules dictated the actions that each institution could take to survive in the face of suburbanization. Those actions, in turn, have shaped the urban exodus.

journalistic, true, but it draws you in (+ certainly doesn't scare you off)

I

Flight

Preparing to close their Mattapan synagogue in the fall of 1971 and move to a suburban site, members of Congregation Chevra Shas pack sacred books. The Jewish exodus was in its last stages. A year earlier, after arsonists had destroyed a Torah scroll, members had pleaded for assistance. "Our Torah has been *desecrated!* Our Sanctuary has been *vandalized!* Our People have been *dispersed!*" the congregation exclaimed. "If we do not relocate at once, we must close the doors of this sacred house of worship forever." (*Photograph courtesy of the* Boston Globe.)

1

Introduction

Suburbanization has transformed Dorchester and upper Roxbury. This district contains nearly one-third of Boston's population and as much of its land. From the turn of the century through the early 1960s, two separate worlds existed side by side in this area. As Map 1 shows, Jews were concentrated on the western side of the district, following Blue Hill Avenue. Theirs was a large community, numbering at its peak, in the late 1920s and early 1930s, about 77,000 persons—half of the entire Jewish population in the Boston area. To the east of the Jewish district, in Dorchester, and to the north and northwest, in upper Roxbury, lived about 136,000 white Catholics. Through the early 1950s, both communities remained substantially intact.[1] The vast majority of these whites lived in segregated neighborhoods; indeed, the 1950 census counted just six blacks in Jewish Mattapan's population of 10,603 and fourteen blacks in Catholic Savin Hill's population of 12,708.[2]

While a slowly growing black community had existed in upper Roxbury since the 1920s, large-scale racial succession did not begin until the early 1950s. By 1970, as Map 2 illustrates, most of the area's former Jewish neighborhoods had become black neighborhoods. Today, in the 1990s, the area of Dorchester and upper Roxbury is a patchwork of white-ethnic enclaves, racially integrated districts, and African-American, Haitian, Hispanic, and Vietnamese neighborhoods. According to the most recent census, 91,000 blacks, 19,000 Hispanics, and 46,000 whites now live in Dorchester and upper Roxbury.[3] Dorchester's whites, overwhelmingly Catholic, live in Irish-Catholic strongholds like Savin Hill as well as in a large swath of integrated neighborhoods. But there has not

11

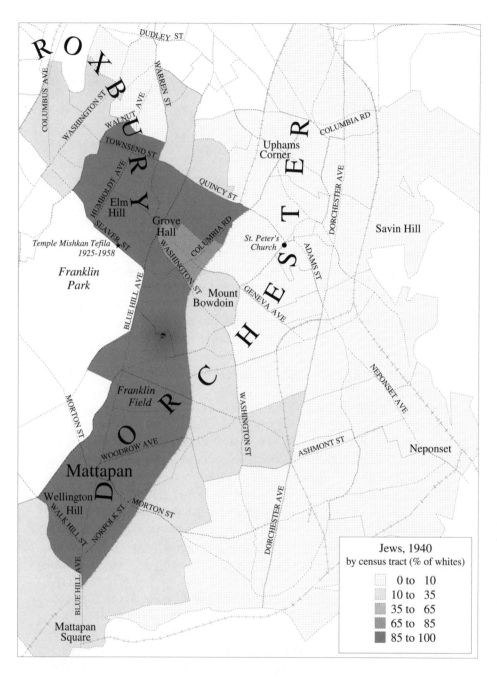

Map 1 Jews, 1940

been a significant Jewish presence in Roxbury and Dorchester since the early 1970s, when, with the collapse of Mattapan Jewry, the exodus of Jews came to an end.

In the fall of 1971, Michigan senator Philip A. Hart convened three days of Senate subcommittee hearings in Boston to investigate the causes of the Jewish exodus from Mattapan and the tense resegregation of the neighborhood. As a subcommittee staff member explained to the *New York Times,* "We believe that the set of events in Boston illustrates what is going on all over America." The rapid white exodus from Boston had become a national symbol of the urban crisis. Three years later, when thousands of white Bostonians violently protested the court-ordered desegregation of the city schools, Boston again became a symbol. Though more restrained than residents of other Boston neighborhoods, members of a Savin Hill neighborhood association vowed angrily in the summer of 1974 to keep their children home rather than allow them to be bused to a distant school. The urban crisis is two stories: in one story whites abandon cities, and in the other story whites refuse to relinquish their old neighborhoods.[4]

Across the country, most dramatically in the Northeast and Midwest, middle-class Americans have fled the great cities. Left behind are the poor who cannot move and those working-class and middle-class families who have chosen not to: among white-ethnic groups, Catholics have been especially likely to remain in traditional urban neighborhoods. "While the proportion of whites in the northern cities has been declining, the proportion of Catholics has been increasing," a member of the Philadelphia Catholic Housing Council asserted in 1959. Between the early 1950s and the early 1970s, the proportion of Catholics in Brooklyn's white population rose from 26 to 44 percent. In the same years— even as the total number of Catholics in Dorchester and upper Roxbury fell from 137,000 to 95,000—the proportion of Catholics in Dorchester and Roxbury's white population rose from 59 to 73 percent. In Boston, as in virtually every major American city, the story of racial succession has differed from neighborhood to neighborhood. But in Boston, as elsewhere, one general theme recurs with striking frequency: the exodus from Jewish neighborhoods occurred earlier, faster, and more thoroughly than the exodus from Catholic neighborhoods—and with much less violence.[5]

"No instance has been noted in the literature where a Negro invasion

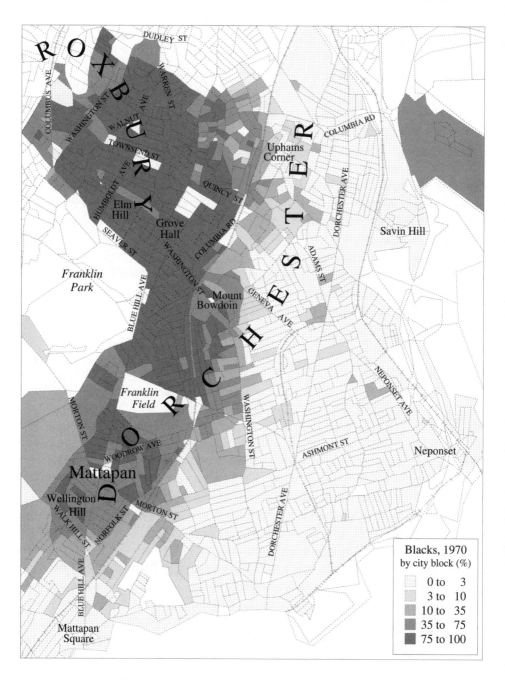

Map 2 Blacks, 1970

succeeded in displacing the Irish in possession of a community. Yet, frequently, as notably in New York and Chicago, Negroes have pushed forward in the wake of retreating Jews," Ernest W. Burgess wrote in 1928. Malcolm X, in his autobiography, emphasized how quickly and completely Jews abandoned neighborhoods in which African Americans had begun settling. "Who would always lead the whites' exodus? The Jews!" he observed. "Generally in these situations, some whites stay put—you just notice who they are: they're Irish Catholics, they're Italians; they're rarely ever any Jews."[6]

If Jews tended to leave their neighborhoods more quickly than Catholics, Jews also tended to greet new African-American neighbors with higher levels of tolerance and with little violence. In Chicago, racial change in the large Jewish district of North Lawndale occurred with none of the antiblack violence that routinely characterized the city's working-class Catholic neighborhoods. The same pattern prevailed in Detroit, where African Americans encountered little resistance in Jewish neighborhoods, but where homeowners' associations, dominated by Catholics, became organized vehicles of rabid, antiblack violence in the 1940s, 1950s, and 1960s. The white battle against busing in Boston was waged overwhelmingly by working-class and lower-middle-class Catholics. Drawing on evidence from various cities, John T. McGreevy notes that, for contemporary observers, "comparisons between the resistance found in heavily Catholic neighborhoods and more peaceful racial transitions in other sections of the city were inevitable."[7]

Residential segregation remains pervasive in late-twentieth-century America, constraining housing choices and contributing to the physical and social isolation of poor inner-city districts.[8] While many other factors have contributed to the urban exodus of middle-class and working-class whites, racism must be counted as a major cause of this exodus. To some extent, racism exists in the rapidity with which Jews have often abandoned newly integrated neighborhoods. And, to some extent, racism exists in the fire bombings, riots, and personal insults that African Americans have often endured when they settle in Catholic neighborhoods.

Yet this contrast between Jewish and Catholic behavior exists even in the absence of racial change: what primarily distinguishes Jews from Catholics is not a different capacity for racist behavior but a different attachment to territory. Catholics have a strong sense of turf, regarding their neighborhoods as defended geographical communities. This territorial understanding of community is evident when Catholics react violently to new African-American neighbors and when Catholics choose to stay in their neighborhood if it is successfully integrated. But it is also evident in the hostility with which Czech Catholics in Cicero, a working-class city near Chicago, greeted the area's first German Catholics in the 1930s, and in the fierceness with which Dorchester's Irish Catholics defended their neighborhood boundaries against Jews in the 1920s, 1930s, and 1940s. Jews, in contrast, are much less likely to defend a neighborhood against outsiders. They offer little resistance, then leave quickly, when African Americans settle in the area. This behavior, too, is neither new nor necessarily driven by race. Louis Wirth, writing in 1928, argued that Jews leaving Chicago's West Side were not "being pressed out by succeeding immigrant groups and Negroes." Rather, he contended, the Jew was eagerly moving out to a higher-status district and "fleeing from his fellow-Jews who remain in the ghetto."[9]

"White flight"—a term that simultaneously names and presumes to solve the riddle of the urban exodus—cannot account for the middle-class abandonment of cities. Many whites did leave neighborhoods that were undergoing racial change, but these whites were relatively few in number compared with the whites who had already left the neighborhood, gradually and over many decades. Only after the urban exodus had nearly run its course, emptying apartments and lowering rents, were blacks able to overcome longstanding barriers to entry. In the main, suburbanization has been sustained by middle-class whites leaving still-white neighborhoods.

In this book I set out to explain why some neighborhoods have persisted relatively unchanged for generations, while others have changed radically. I do not claim to explain the whole phenomenon of urban change—the middle-class abandonment of cities has been a consequence of many factors, including federal and local housing programs, highway projects, public housing, blockbusting, redlining, urban renewal, the deterioration of urban schools, crime, homeowners' associations, and prejudice—but rather to explain divergent patterns of urban change. Both in periods of racial succession and in the times when race has not been an issue, Catholics have been more territorial than Jews. Though explaining this difference is crucial to understanding long-term patterns of neighborhood stability, existing studies offer no satisfactory explanation. Understanding these patterns requires a new approach that takes a long-term perspective on neighborhood change and that places local institutions at the center of the story.

Neighborhood Institutions

Ancient rules binding churches and synagogues have shaped the twentieth-century urban battle of race and housing. Different patterns of neighborhood change have resulted from fundamental differences in Catholic and Jewish institutions. Because of these differences, an institution like St. Peter's Church reassured and anchored its surrounding Catholic neighborhood, while an institution like Mishkan Tefila undermined and exacerbated stresses in its surrounding Jewish neighborhood. Neither St. Peter's Church nor Mishkan Tefila acted in idiosyncratic fashion: the fate of neither facility was determined mainly by the decisions or actions of its own leadership. Rather, both institutions were defined, bound, and ultimately constrained by rules that dictated their own inexorable logic.

St. Peter's Parish and Mishkan Tefila are archetypes of two distinct institutional forms, the Catholic territorial parish and the American synagogue. Measured along a variety of dimensions, the territorial parish and the typical synagogue emerge as opposite types, as nearly ideal expressions of divergent codes of institutional organization and behavior.[10] Protestant churches, national (or ethnic) Catholic churches, and the institutions of Lubavitcher Jews stray in various ways from these ideal types. I focus on the polar types because they represent the most common institutions of American Catholic and Jewish communities; indeed, the two models are sufficient to characterize every Jewish and Catholic institution in Dorchester and upper Roxbury. Other institutions—religious schools, social clubs, community centers—have generally been guided by the rules that govern the typical synagogue and the territorial church. Moreover, focusing on the two ideal types—and on a set of neighborhoods in which they predominate—makes it analytically feasible to investigate the impact of institutional differences on neighborhood stability.

These rules fall into three broad classes: rules of membership, rules of rootedness, and rules of authority. To identify these rules, I not only examined canon law and Talmudic guidelines but also reconstructed the actual practice of Boston's synagogues and parish churches, studying the histories of each of the more than one hundred Jewish and Catholic institutions that have served Dorchester and Roxbury since 1870. Given the remarkable divergence between Jewish and Catholic institutions and given the strong similarities within each of the two groups of institutions, I argue that the rules defining them are widely understood and respected. These rules are real not because they are written down but because they are obeyed.[11]

The first class of rules, which I examine in Chapter 5, are the rules of membership. Jewish institutional membership is entirely voluntary. The typical Jewish synagogue recognizes no geographical barriers to membership, while the territorial parish has historically been defined by strict physical boundaries. Within its boundaries, the parish church exercises monopoly jurisdiction, receiving the loyalty of all Catholics within the parish who identify with a territorial church. Synagogues and other Jewish institutions, in contrast, compete for support and for members. In this regard, the synagogue is bound by rules similar to those defining many Protestant churches. "Unlike the Roman Catholic churches, those of Protestant faith do not mass their adherents in geographical areas distinct from one another," H. Paul Douglass found. "The result is a network of geographical ties between church and home of incredible perplexity and incoherence."[12]

The second class of rules, as I discuss in Chapter 6, are the rules of rootedness. One aspect of rootedness is structural; the other is geographical. The Catholic church is a permanent structure, consecrated to God and built around a permanent altar, and the territorial parish's relationship to its neighborhood is inalienable. "Real-estate agents welcome the coming of a Catholic church into a community," according to a 1934 study, "for it is regarded as an evidence of permanence, and almost invariably it tends to increase the value of the neighboring property." Jewish neighborhoods, in contrast, do not take their identities from religious buildings. In Jewish law, the Torah is holier than any synagogue structure, and Torah scrolls are entirely portable. American Jewish congregations move freely from building to building and from one residential district to another. Like "some of the oldest and most influential" of St. Louis' Protestant churches described by Douglass, most of the nation's oldest Jewish congregations "have reached their present sites as the result of a series of removals following upon large movements of population."[13]

The third class of rules, which I present in Chapter 7, are the rules of authority. In five distinct ways—creation and dissolution of an institution; acquisition, ownership, and disposal of funds and property; determination of policy and doctrinal questions; selection and dismissal of clergy; and prerequisites for congregational worship—a synagogue's rules reflect the authority and autonomy of the individual congregation, while a Catholic church's rules reflect a system of hierarchical authority. Governed by rules that render the rabbi and any religious hierarchy superfluous, the American Jewish synagogue enjoys the purest form of congregational authority. In contrast, a Catholic parish does not exist apart from a priest and a hierarchy. "Catholic lay people cannot start a church on their own, nor can an entrepreneurial priest set up shop without Church approval," Nancy Tatom Ammerman writes. "The diocese draws parish lines and supplies parish priests."[14]

Because they are defined according to specific sets of rules, the two sets of institutions are related in distinct ways to their neighborhoods and to their members. That those distinct relationships actually matter is not self-evident. Other scholars have argued that differences in neighborhood stability have been due to differences in educational levels, incomes, culture, redlining, targeting by real-estate agents, discrimination by banks, or levels of homeownership. But, as I show in Chapter 2, these variables are not sufficient to explain differences in neighborhood stability. The relative strength and stability of neighborhoods is determined not by external pressures but by each neighborhood's internal structure. Institutions play a profound and independent role in the capacity of a neighborhood to resist change and, when change comes, to deal with it in orderly fashion.

The synagogue and territorial parish were created and modified over thousands of years by countless individuals in Europe, Asia, and North Africa, then eventually carried to North America. For at least the last century, however, these institutions have changed little in their basic form: indeed, it is the persistence of these rules that made it possible for American Jews to establish alternatives to traditional Orthodoxy and that has frustrated efforts by American Catholics to create alternatives to the organized Church. Given the constancy of these rules, these institutions must be regarded as exogenous in understanding twentieth-century urban change. Dorchester and Roxbury's Catholics and Jews did not choose and mold their institutions; they inherited them, and these institutions molded and constrained the communities in which they were situated. Rules that had evolved over centuries, rules created in ancient Babylon and medieval Europe, have come to matter, in utterly unanticipated and sometimes undesired ways, in American cities.

Rules of membership, as I show in Chapter 9, allowed Jews to move out of Roxbury and Dorchester without severing institutional ties. Jews settling in Boston's suburbs could remain active in their old synagogues and community centers, easing the transition to a new community. While a member's loyalty to a synagogue does not require a residence in the synagogue's neighborhood, a parishioner's loyalty to a Catholic church does require a home in the parish. Consequently, in moving from their old neighborhood, Catholics have had to leave behind their parish church, their parish grammar school, and their parish social activities. Thus Catholics have faced a much higher exit cost than Jews; following the logic of Thomas C. Schelling's model, the territorial parish reduces the likelihood of a "speculative acceleration of tipping," the point at which resegregation becomes suddenly irreversible.[15] Loyalty, as Albert O. Hirschman suggests, "can serve the socially useful purpose of preventing deterioration from becoming cumulative, as it so often does when there is no barrier to exit."[16] By conditioning institutional loyalty on neighborhood loyalty, the Catholic parish buttresses neighborhood stability and frustrates out-migration.

The rules limiting membership in the church to parish residents are predicated on the rules that keep the church rooted and open. The Catholic church's ability to anchor its parishioners is grounded in the credibility of its continued presence in a neighborhood. As I emphasize in Chapter 10, rules of rootedness have meant that Jewish institutions could survive by moving out of a declining neighborhood and into the suburbs, but Catholic institutions have been permanently tied to their original location. Mishkan Tefila—like many other synagogues, Hebrew schools, and community centers in the 1950s and 1960s—knew that, to survive, it had to relocate. Since successful relocation required a healthy base of members and financial resources, each of these Jewish institutions moved out after many members had left but at a time when tens of thousands of Jews still remained in Roxbury and Dorchester. Jewish institutions that bided their time withered away and died at their old locations. Of the seventeen parishes that once existed in Dorchester and upper Roxbury, sixteen continue to function and to support their churches;

of the thirteen parishes that once supported their own schools, twelve still do.[17] Conversely, every one of the more than fifty Jewish community centers, Hebrew schools, and synagogues that once stood in Roxbury and Dorchester had dissolved or relocated by the early 1970s.[18]

Rules of authority, by forcing Jewish institutions to survive without outside support, ineluctably led these institutions to relocate when large numbers of their members had begun to move. No Jewish hierarchy exists to sustain an institutional presence in urban neighborhoods. But, in accordance with the rules of authority in the Catholic Church, as I discuss in Chapter 11, the archdiocese provides funding and priests for struggling Catholic parishes. Such rules limit and constrain the parish's ability to determine outcomes while strengthening its ability to make credible commitments.[19] Although the parish's continued viability contributes to neighborhood stability, the parish can commit to a long-term presence in its neighborhood only because of the rules establishing the authority of the archdiocese.

This book is about rules that define local institutions, the ways in which these rules constrain and shape the decisions of neighborhood residents, and the implications of this rule-constrained residential behavior for neighborhood stability. I do not argue that Catholics are always more likely than Jews to stay in urban neighborhoods. As I discuss in Chapter 3, there are Catholics who have vacated neighborhoods quickly and Jews who have persisted in their neighborhoods. Any set of people—Catholics or Jews, whites or blacks, villagers or urban residents—bound to an institution characterized by the membership rules, rootedness rules, and authority rules of the territorial parish will demonstrate a tenacious commitment to their local area. And any set of people tied to autonomous, mobile institutions that set no boundaries to membership will be more loosely tied to a given district.

Neighborhood residents make decisions about leaving and staying within an institutional context. In developing a model to explain "tipping points" and "white flight," Schelling emphasizes how individuals behave in the absence of coordinating institutions. Decisions that are individually rational generate perverse collective consequences, according to Schelling: even when white residents prefer an outcome in which they remain in an integrated neighborhood, their individual strategies lead to rapid resegregation.[20] Given the allure of suburbs, the various programs that have encouraged suburbanization, and the black demand for housing, Schelling's model helps explain patterns of racial succession in many postwar neighborhoods. But local institutions must be introduced into this model before it can explain the persistence of many other neighborhoods through decades of urban upheaval.

That Catholics have stayed over the years, while Jews have tended to move, suggests that the territorial parish has effectively solved a coordination problem that remains unresolved in Jewish districts. In assessing the costs of leaving a neighborhood and the risks of staying, a resident considers the likelihood that other long-term residents will remain in the neighborhood. Even for non-Catholics living in a predominantly Catholic district, the local parish church provides an effective coordination mechanism. Because it strengthens the neighborhood attachments of Catholics, all residents of this district—including Jews, Protestants, and nonpracticing Catholics—can reasonably expect their neighbors to confront racial change with greater violence and less panic than residents of a predominantly Jewish neighborhood. And expectations about other people's behavior affect each resident's decision.

Rational-choice approaches to institutions have tended to emphasize the study of national institutions, but a growing number of other scholars have begun calling attention to local institutions. Some have contended that an individual's political preferences are shaped by social contexts, such as the church that he or she attends, while others suggest that church or club membership also provides opportunities for learning civic skills. Still others argue that local institutions are not only arenas for learning civic skills or contexts for forming political views but also repositories of social capital. Indeed, the very existence of local associations, Robert D. Putnam writes, reflects and strengthens trust, cooperation, and civic engagement.[21]

Though Robert E. Park has contended that institutions were crucial elements of "the ecological organization of the community," ecological models of residential change have relegated institutions to the background. Traditional models have regarded institutions in relation to the organic nature of a neighborhood rather than as constraints on individual choices. Consequently, few studies of neighborhood change have analyzed how small-scale local institutions shape the decisions of residents. William Julius Wilson, who discusses local institutions in his analysis of neighborhood change, does not assess how these institutions vary or why variance matters.[22]

To the extent that social scientists have explored variance among churches, they have generally used measures that either are incapable of differentiating among Catholic, Protestant, and Jewish institutions or disconnect the institution from its locality. Some scholars distinguish the horizontally organized Protestant churches from the vertically organized Catholic church, but they draw on those differences to show that the hierarchical Catholic structure leads to depressed levels of political and civic involvement. They do not consider that the same authority structure that limits lay leadership also enables local institutions to make credible commitments to their neighborhoods.[23]

The special ability of the Catholic parish to sustain neighborhood attachments is not widely recognized. Arnold R. Hirsch notes that Monsignor John J. Egan of Chicago complained in the 1950s that "the Catholic Church, unlike more mobile Protestant churches, could not abandon its 'cathedrals' and that Hyde Park's renewal was 'creating too much of a problem for them,'" but Hirsch neither discusses the reasons for that difference in institutional mobility nor considers the consequences of such difference for neighborhood change. Hillel Levine and Lawrence Harmon, while contrasting the movement of two Jewish institutions from Roxbury with the strong territorial commitment of Mattapan's St. Angela's Parish, attribute the actions of the two Jewish institutions wholly to the "methodical and managerial style" of Boston's Jewish leadership in the 1950s. Rather than contending that Roxbury's Jewish institutions were bound by a distinct set of rules, Levine and Harmon argue that the decisions to relocate these institutions reflected a leadership of cramped vision, a leadership pursuing goals that were short-sighted and personalistic.[24]

Indeed, other scholars have suggested that Jewish institutions slow out-migration. "We might expect more rapid change to occur in a predominantly Jewish area," Eleanor K. Caplan and Eleanor P. Wolf have written. "The presence of Jewish institutions in an area, however, might act as a deterring force and thereby slow the rate of transition." Albert J. Mayer has argued that Orthodox Jews were less likely than other groups to move from Detroit's Russell Woods. But "even the Orthodox are beginning to respond to the same pressures as the other white groups," he observed. "One of the most Orthodox organizations—a *yeshivah*—has purchased land in one of the 'Northwest' Jewish neighborhoods," a Detroit suburb. Mayer described the yeshiva's decision as a typical white response to neighborhood change. This assertion, however, cannot hold as a generalization, since Catholic institutions never moved. They could not.[25]

Understanding urban change requires us to examine the ways in which the ordinary institutions of daily life differ from one another. It also requires us to examine the consequences of those differences for localities. McGreevy, examining Catholic responses to racial change, shows how fully urban Catholics fused religion, parish, and neighborhood. "Catholics used the parish to map out—both physically and culturally— space within all of the northern cities," McGreevy argues.[26] Since he presents evidence drawn almost exclusively from Catholic areas, McGreevy can suggest but cannot show that Catholic institutions and Catholic responses to neighborhood change were distinctive. Still, he describes vividly how religious institutions shape patterns of neighborhood resistance and change.

Churches, synagogues, religious schools, and community halls are, above all, local institutions. Analyses that detach them from their neighborhoods, that disregard the extent to which these institutions matter to specific places and people, miss a fundamental attribute of local institutions. Because of differences in their institutional networks, Catholics have tended to be better equipped than Jews to resist and cope with residential succession. Ironically, the very reach and size of these networks may explain why they have been overlooked in earlier studies. A great university or automobile plant can have an impact on a community that is apparent and unusual, but churches and synagogues are so ubiquitous that their impact is universally but more subtly felt. I thought about this as I sat in the supply room at St. Peter's School, thumbing through old yearbooks. Like many students of urban neighborhoods, the girls who discovered me in their supply room take their old school for granted. Not long ago, so did I.

The Transformation of the 1920s

Concentrated in the nation's great cities, working-class Jews and Catholics directly confronted the issues of race and residential succession. These white ethnics were late suburbanizers. Many white-ethnic families had abandoned the city in the 1920s and 1930s and 1940s, leaving predominantly white neighborhoods for predominantly white suburbs, but they had not led the exodus. Nor did other white-ethnic families, leaving or refusing to leave the racially changing neighborhoods of the postwar era, lead the exodus: indeed, they and their fragile white-ethnic neighborhoods have been the residue, the flotsam, of a century-long flight outward. If blacks searched for housing in these neighborhoods and if these neighborhoods became the stage for urban change and racial tension, it is only because these working-class ethnic families had noisily lingered on stage when the rest of the white players had left the theater.

When they left or when they resisted leaving, these working-class Catholics and Jews were simply responding to the example set years earlier by white Protestants. "In the face of the outward march of Hibernian and Jew," two settlement-house workers wrote in the 1910s, describing the recent transformation of a section of Dorchester, "the Yankees have girt their garments well about them, snatched up their skirts that so much as a hem might not be defiled by contact with 'foreigners,' and have betaken them elsewhere in a spirit little and shallow, if not mean and snobbish."[27] It was middle-class white Protestants, joined by smaller numbers of Catholics and Jews, who pioneered the tools of suburbanization and urban residential segregation.

Suburbanization was not a new phenomenon in the 1920s. Since the middle of the nineteenth century, the movement of central- and upper-middle-class residents to the urban periphery had been reconfiguring the American city, separating residential districts from business districts and segregating residential districts by race, ethnicity, and class. But with the popularization of the automobile in the 1920s, the pace of suburbanization quickened. In the 1920s, "new suburbs sprouted on the edges of every major city," Kenneth T. Jackson writes. "Between 1920 and 1930, when automobile registrations rose by more than 150 percent, the suburbs of the nation's 96 largest cities grew twice as fast as the core communities."[28] This wave of middle-class residential expansion created the modern, independent suburb.

That same wave also transformed the central city. The great exodus from white-ethnic neighborhoods, I argue, began in the early 1920s. The white-ethnic neighborhoods of the 1940s and 1950s were not indicators of urban vigor; rather, these neighborhoods were the products of cities that were already coming apart. From the 1870s until the 1920s, the streetcar suburbs of Dorchester and upper Roxbury had attracted large numbers of middle-class ethnic families. But in the 1920s the middle-class presence in many of these ethnic districts had come to an end, most dramatically in Jewish districts. As middle-class Jews moved to suburbs like Brookline and Newton, Jewish districts in Roxbury and Dorchester became dense working-class neighborhoods. The white-ethnic exodus since World War II, though more visible because of its association with racial change, was only the late stage of an exodus that was already under way in the 1920s. And this was an exodus from entirely white neighborhoods: in the early 1920s, racial succession lay three full decades in the future.

Patterns established by the 1920s shaped postwar responses to racial succession. Differences between Jewish and Catholic migration patterns persisted unchanged even in the 1950s and 1960s, with the onset of racial change; throughout this entire period, Catholics were more likely to resist suburbanization. In the 1920s as in the 1960s, rules embedded in local institutions—synagogues, churches, religious schools—created these lasting differences. Moreover, the suburbanization of middle-class Jews in the 1920s and 1930s itself set an example that other Jews in Dorchester and Roxbury followed as they moved into the middle class. Because they moved out in relatively larger numbers and because institutional rules allowed them to remain active as leaders in their old neighborhoods, suburban Jews were much more visible as role models in their former neighborhoods than were suburban Catholics.

Though evidence from other cities is scanty, the transformation of the 1920s appears not to have been peculiar to Boston. Brief remarks in various studies suggest that similar changes occurred in Jewish districts in Philadelphia, Brooklyn, and the Bronx. Marshall Sklare, noting that many middle-class Jews lived in Chicago's Lawndale district from 1900 through the early 1920s, argued that Lawndale declined in status in the middle 1920s. Once considered "a middle-class area," according to Sklare, "the neighborhood dropped to lower class and lower-middle class" in the middle 1920s. The first Jews settling in Lawndale had sought a middle-class suburban district. "In their attempt to flee from the ghetto, the partially assimilated groups have found that the ghetto has followed them to their new quarters . . . Within fifteen years these areas have become overwhelmingly Jewish," Wirth observed in 1928. "Unwittingly the deserters from the ghetto have become the founders of a new ghetto. Scarcely does this consciousness begin to dawn upon them when the flight is resumed, this time to a new frontier."[29]

But the urban transformation of the 1920s is nearly invisible in existing scholarship. The common wisdom embodied in the literature suggests that the African-American migration to northern cities in the 1940s, 1950s, and 1960s represented a sudden intrusion into working-class white neighborhoods that had been stable and secure for many decades. Hirsch and Thomas J. Sugrue document the violence that accompanied racial change in the Catholic neighborhoods of Chicago and Detroit in these years—as whites, according to Hirsch, came to fear "the disintegration of traditional neighborhoods." These old Catholic neighborhoods, McGreevy argues, were "in the midst of a momentous transition" in the 1950s, confronting racial change even as they were losing large numbers of older residents to suburbanization. The same themes resonate in accounts of Jewish neighborhoods. Chicago's Lawndale, Brooklyn's Brownsville, Philadelphia's Strawberry Mansion, and Boston's Roxbury and Dorchester, various scholars suggest, still flourished as Jewish communities in the 1940s, having changed little since the first Jews had settled in the districts.[30]

The urban crisis truly began in the early 1920s. It was in the 1920s—not in the 1960s and 1970s, as Alan Ehrenhalt, Thomas and Mary Edsall, Jonathan Rieder, Allen Matusow, Nicholas Lemann, and William Julius Wilson suggest; not in the 1940s and 1950s, as Hirsch and Sugrue suggest[31]—that middle-class white ethnics forged their paths from urban neighborhoods to the suburbs. It was in the 1920s that Jewish neighborhoods began their long unraveling, and it was in the 1920s that Catholic neighborhoods began their resistance to the new forces promoting suburbanization. Slowly, relentlessly, through out-migration and through violent neighborhood confrontation, cities started to come apart.

Students of suburbanization have emphasized the rise of new suburbs in the 1920s rather than the fate of the old streetcar districts, and students of neighborhood change have focused on racial succession since the 1950s. Lost in this vast scholarship are the intervening decades, the era when old suburban districts like Dorchester and Roxbury became dense, working-class ethnic neighborhoods. This loss has not been trivial. In recovering this urban era, it becomes possible to link the story of suburbanization to the story of the urban crisis: the rise of automobile suburbs in the 1920s, I argue, abruptly set in motion the urban exodus and neighborhood changes that culminated in the 1950s and 1960s.

Many of the secrets of this lost world are embedded in its institutions. The dramatic Jewish exodus of the 1920s and the consistent patterns that bind the Catholics and Jews of the 1920s with their descendants in the postwar era are etched most clearly in the churches and synagogues and community halls that once populated these communities. Aggregate census data do not reveal this story: ethnic and socioeconomic characteristics were not reported at the census-tract level before 1930. While census data and contemporary newspaper accounts buttress the evidence imprinted in these institutions, it is the institutions themselves, always sensitive to changes in their memberships and in their neighborhoods, that yield the greatest secrets. This is fitting, since these same institutions have helped shape the urban exodus.

The neighborhoods of upper Roxbury and Dorchester together form one large, interconnected section of a big city; I report evidence from all of the component neighborhoods, examining neighborhoods that have changed little over the course of the century as well as contiguous neighborhoods that have experienced radical racial and socioeconomic transformation. These neighborhoods are almost wholly residential. With small exceptions, there have been no major universities, hospitals, or industries in Dorchester or upper Roxbury.[32] The principal institutions in these neighborhoods have been ordinary, small-scale community institutions. No map of transportation corridors or natural boundaries can explain different patterns of neighborhood change.

Rarely is it possible, at least in the real world, to test the impact of changes in one variable—in this case, the nature of local institutions—while holding all other relevant variables constant. Here, in neighborhoods where institutional differences generally distinguish Jews from Catholics and even, as I discuss in Chapter 3, distinguish some Catholics from other Catholics, this test becomes possible and compelling. The evidence supports the thesis that institutional rules explain why, in city after city, Catholics and Jews have related differently to their neighborhoods and responded differently to urban change. More broadly, the evidence supports the thesis that institutions of all sorts, but especially locally oriented institutions, affect the behavior of populations.

The urban exodus is one of the great migrations in American history. The story of Dorchester and Roxbury is a window into that urban saga; it is the story told from the church pew, from the stone wall that runs along a ballfield, and from the fraying lawn chair on the front porch of a three-decker. Before Americans can reverse the long flight from cities, they must understand the nature of that flight as well as the sources of neighborhood stability. Strengthening communities means recognizing the particular and different ways that institutions affect community life. Each institution survives according to its own set of rules, and city planners and local leaders must appreciate those different rules. They must reinforce institutional actions that strengthen local community life and compensate for institutional actions and tendencies that weaken it. They must do this because an institution like a church or a school or a state capitol or a ballpark does not just matter for those who identify with the institution. It matters for everyone in the neighborhood.

For three decades, most of the residents of Roxbury and Dorchester's Jewish districts paid little heed to the magnificent temple on Seaver Street. Most of them were indifferent to the large numbers of Jews who attended services every Friday at Temple Mishkan Tefila. Some were indifferent because they were not Jewish, others because they belonged to some other Jewish congregation or to no congregation at all, and still others because they were Orthodox Jews and regarded the more liberal ritual of Mishkan Tefila with suspicion. All of them were indifferent— they were sure they were indifferent—to the thousands of Jews who attended meetings each weeknight in the temple and worshiped there for the Sabbath. But then, in the 1950s, Mishkan Tefila left the old temple behind and relocated to the suburbs, leaving the temple to a Lubavitcher school that could not afford to maintain the facility. Soon the lawn was overgrown with weeds. Abandoned school buses rusted and rotted beneath the stained-glass windows. Day and evening, week after week, the building was empty. Only then did the Jews of Dorchester and Roxbury, and the non-Jews in their midst, understand that their indifference to this institution had been illusory.

true, but how do you keep it? what would we be keeping for + against whom?

2

Class, Crime, Homes, and Banks

Catholics and Jews have responded differently to urban change. This observation is so common that it is generally offered as folk wisdom or simple fact. In exaggerated form, cause and effect become intermingled and muddled in a circular argument: the very presence of Jews becomes an explanation for a neighborhood's vulnerability to change. Scholars have suggested several hypotheses for the differences between Catholic and Jewish behavior, though no one has systematically studied these differences or tested these hypotheses.

Studies of neighborhood change have emphasized the period of racial change that extended from the late 1940s through the 1970s. Consequently, existing explanations—socioeconomic differences, proximity to African-American neighborhoods, levels of arson and other crimes, redlining, blockbusting, discriminatory banking programs, and homeownership levels—generally focus on this specific period. These explanations cannot fully account for long-term trends in the urban exodus, trends that began early in the twentieth century and without relation to race. And even as efforts to explain patterns of racial change in the 1950s, 1960s, and 1970s, these explanations are not sufficient to explain the different neighborhood attachments of Jews and Catholics.

Socioeconomic Status

Geographic mobility is often a function of socioeconomic mobility. Most Jews rose faster and earlier into the middle class than did most Catholics. "Wherever studies have been made," Nathan Glazer and Daniel Patrick

Moynihan write, "Jews have been found to be moving out of the working class into the middle class at a surprising rate."[1] From the early 1920s through the middle 1950s, socioeconomic differences contributed to the more rapid pace of Jewish suburbanization. As I show in Chapter 9, the exodus of Dorchester and Roxbury's middle-class and upper-middle-class Jews began in the early 1920s and never slowed. While institutional membership rules facilitated this exodus—exit costs were lower for Jews than for Catholics—the high rate of Jewish upward mobility was also a factor.

The federal census did not report aggregate data for census tracts or other small territorial areas in 1920, but census-tract data from 1930, 1940, and 1950 suggest that the socioeconomic level of Jewish neighborhoods was higher than that of Catholic neighborhoods through the early 1950s. Maps 3 and 4 show the average rent in each of Dorchester and Roxbury's census tracts in 1930 and 1950, respectively.[2] As a comparison of Map 1 with Maps 3 and 4 illustrates, the census tracts reporting the highest rents corresponded closely to the tracts with the heaviest populations of Jews. (The correlation is less exact in Map 3 because many of the 1930 census tracts were larger than the 1940 and 1950 census tracts.) Just one Jewish tract, in Roxbury's Blue Hill Avenue–Grove Hall district, did not conform to the general pattern. Various other indicators—the number of homes with mechanical refrigerators in 1940, the number of homes with central heating in 1940, the number of homes with televisions in 1950, median education levels in 1950—demonstrate that the socioeconomic advantage of Dorchester and Roxbury's Jews persisted through the early 1950s. This advantage, relative to Catholics, persisted despite the steady Jewish migration to the suburbs and an absolute deterioration in the socioeconomic level of the Jewish community.

But this relative advantage ended in the 1950s. The 1960 census reported no significant socioeconomic differences between Dorchester's Jewish and Catholic districts. As Map 5 shows, median rents in 1960 were no higher in Jewish than in Catholic neighborhoods; the median rent in Mattapan, like rents in Dorchester's other outer neighborhoods, was relatively high, while median rents elsewhere in Dorchester, among both Catholics and Jews, were relatively low. Median levels of education in 1960, as Map 6 shows, were also no higher in Jewish neighborhoods than in Catholic neighborhoods. And, as Map 7 illustrates, median family incomes were significantly lower in 1960 among Dorchester's Jews

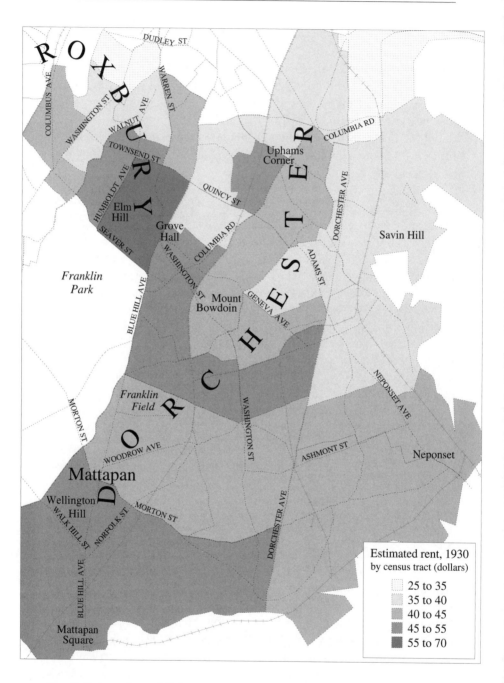

Map 3 Estimated rent, 1930

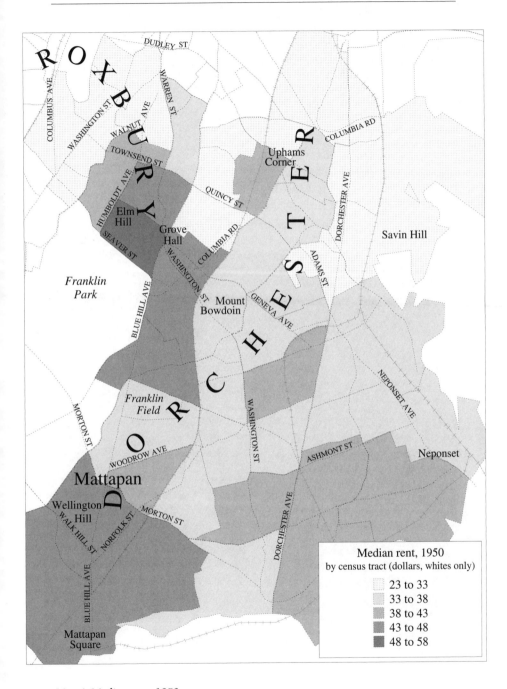

Map 4 Median rent, 1950

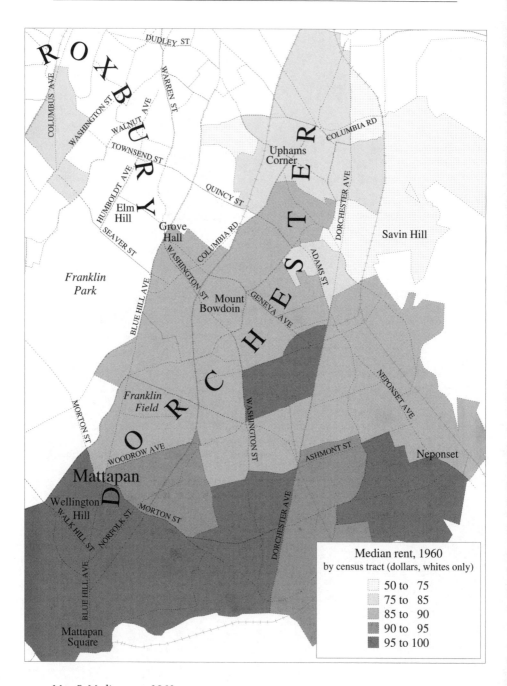

Map 5 Median rent, 1960

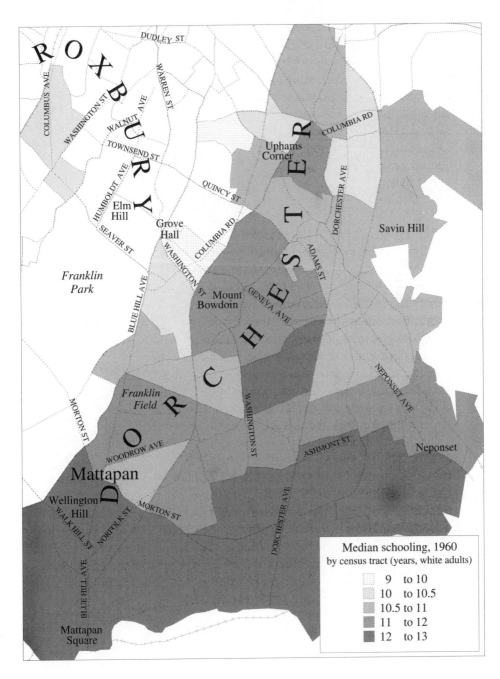

Map 6 Median schooling, 1960

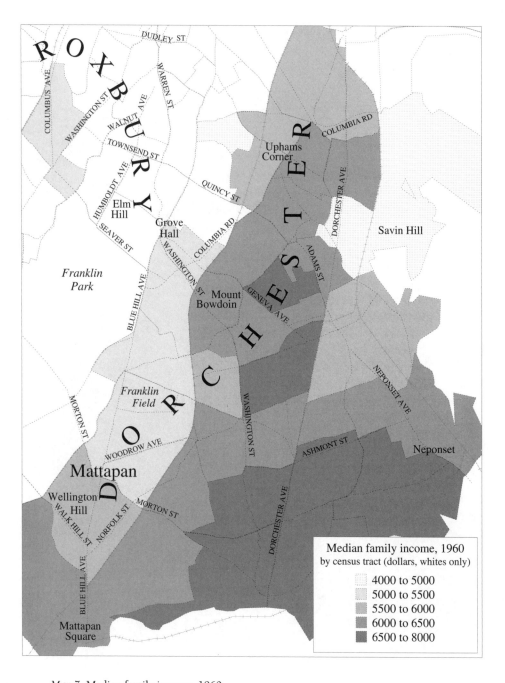

Map 7 Median family income, 1960

than among Dorchester's Catholics; only in Mattapan was median family income at least $5,500, a level exceeded in almost every census tract that was predominantly non-Jewish.[3]

Large numbers of Jews still lived in Dorchester and Roxbury in the late 1950s; indeed, though many tens of thousands of Jews had left these neighborhoods since the 1920s, about 47,000 Jews still remained in 1960. But the Jews who remained in the late 1950s differed profoundly from the Jews who had lived in Dorchester and Roxbury in earlier decades. Once home to Boston Jewry's emerging middle class, Dorchester and Roxbury had become a distinctively working-class enclave. The three-decade-old movement of middle-class Jews to suburban communities had effectively filtered the old neighborhoods.

A study of Boston's Jewish community conducted in the middle 1960s observed that Dorchester's Jews "have the lowest level of education in the metropolitan area (less than 15 per cent went to college) and the highest proportion of blue collar workers." As the study concluded, "The kinds of Jews remaining here are typical of those who do not move."[4] By the late 1950s, Jews possessed no advantages of education or income over Roxbury and Dorchester's Catholics, no set of resources that could facilitate an exceptionally fast rate of suburbanization. Yet it was at this very moment that the Jewish exodus was accelerating, in absolute and in relative terms. At no time were the differences in the Jewish and Catholic exodus sharper than in the 1960s and early 1970s, when urban Jews and Catholics had become indistinguishable on socioeconomic grounds.

Proximity to African-American Neighborhoods

Some scholars have suggested that simple proximity explains differences in neighborhood stability. New areas of black settlement, this hypothesis suggests, develop as extensions of older areas of settlement. Yet, as Map 8 demonstrates, Roxbury and Dorchester's black neighborhoods in 1960 bordered Catholic neighborhoods as well as Jewish neighborhoods. Proximity alone cannot explain why Blue Hill Avenue—rather than, say, Columbia Road or Washington Street or Quincy Street or Geneva Avenue—became the principal route for the expansion of black settlement into Dorchester. It was only because Jews were leaving Dorchester at a more rapid rate than Catholics that black neighborhoods expanded into formerly Jewish districts.

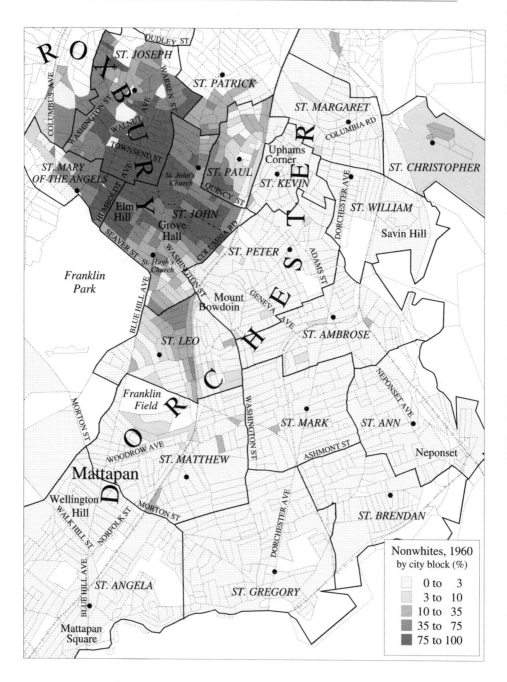

Map 8 Nonwhites, 1960, with parishes

Two miles separated Mattapan's Wellington Hill district in 1960 from well-established areas of African-American residency, and more than one mile of Jewish neighborhoods separated Wellington Hill from even the frontier of racial change. No Catholic enclave in 1960 was farther removed than Jewish Mattapan from African-American neighborhoods. St. Peter's Parish stood at the very edge of the city's burgeoning black district in 1960, and less than a mile separated St. William's Parish from the racial frontier. As Blue Hill Avenue ran from the black settlement in Roxbury straight to Mattapan, so Columbia Road ran from that black settlement directly to St. Margaret's Parish, adjacent to St. William's.

But by 1970, as racial change and panic transformed Mattapan, St. Peter's Parish remained predominantly white and Catholic. In the 1990s, a generation after the collapse of Mattapan Jewry, St. Margaret's Parish and St. William's Parish still contain large white Catholic communities; racial change in those districts has been steady but gradual. The exodus of Jews has long been associated with the influx of African Americans into Mattapan, but it was not Mattapan's nearness to the racial frontier that caused the Jewish exodus. Rather, it was the Jewish exodus itself that brought the frontier down Blue Hill Avenue and into Mattapan.

Arson and Other Crimes

Crime undermined the security of Dorchester's Jews and Catholics alike. The culmination of attacks on Jewish property and persons came in May 1970, when arsonists attacked two synagogues serving Mattapan's Jews. The fires destroyed a Torah at the synagogue of Congregation Chevra Shas and caused $10,000 in damage to the large synagogue structure of Congregation Agudath Israel. According to the *Boston Globe,* "The Jewish community viewed the attacks upon their temples as 'part of a pattern' and a continuation of a campaign to scare the Jewish residents out of the area." One year earlier, two black men had thrown an acid bomb at a Dorchester rabbi.[5]

These attacks on religious leaders and institutions, as well as rising levels of street crime and burglaries, convinced many Jews that they were becoming special targets of urban violence. Alan Mandell, the local leader of the Jewish Defense League, which each night had been patrolling the area near the two synagogues, explained that the patrols had been ending at midnight, forty minutes before the first fire had been set.

"Now the patrols will last all night on staggered shifts, and God help any vandals found in the temples," Mandell stated. "I haven't seen pictures such as this since Germany."[6]

But that violence extended across Dorchester. Catholics, too, were concerned by the prevalence of crime. St. Ann's Church, the central institution of Neponset's Catholics, was attacked by arsonists in May 1970, and again in July. The July fire caused $5,000 in damage to the church. "I have Security Protection, including Police and Dogs, every night and on Sunday mornings," Rev. Ernest P. Pearsall, the pastor of St. Ann's Parish, wrote in October. "I think that the word has gotten around, quietly, about our watchfulness and security. The dogs are trained to attack and knock down but not to kill. God help our enemies." Pearsall regarded attacks on St. Ann's Church as indications of the growing disorder in American cities and in American life. "As you well realize, these are days when we have to keep our eyes peeled, our guts obvious and our guns cocked. It is about time we took the offensive," he wrote to the chancellor of the archdiocese. "Yours in love, courage and calmness to fight the enemies of our Church and our Country."[7]

While arson caused damage to St. Ann's Church as well as to the synagogues of Agudath Israel and Chevra Shas, fires set by arsonists completely destroyed two other Catholic churches in Dorchester. St. William's Church and St. Ambrose' Church, both serving predominantly white neighborhoods near the edge of racially changing areas, were reduced to ruins in the early 1980s. Both churches were rebuilt.

Redlining

Abetted by federal agencies, banks and insurance companies contributed to the destabilization of neighborhoods across Dorchester and Roxbury. Until the middle 1960s, the Federal Housing Administration (FHA) "exhorted segregation and enshrined it as public policy," Kenneth T. Jackson argues. "Whole areas of cities were declared ineligible for loan guarantees."[8] Even after FHA reversed its long-time bias against urban neighborhoods, other institutions continued to undermine those neighborhoods, refusing to extend home mortgages, rejecting applications for property insurance or dramatically increasing premiums for urban policyholders, and denying home-improvement loans.

Throughout Dorchester and Roxbury, Jewish and Catholic neighborhoods contended with the same set of discriminatory practices. In May 1968, the Mattapan Organization stated that it had "received reports that it is difficult to get mortgage loans in Mattapan for home and business improvement"; residents, most of them Jewish, also "reported difficulty in securing home and business insurance in Mattapan." The Columbia–Savin Hill Civic Association, serving a predominantly Catholic neighborhood, expressed its concern in May 1972 over "the cancellation of many Home-owner Insurance policies in this area." Residents of Dorchester's other Catholic neighborhoods reported similar problems. "Homeowners are unable to get mortgages or home improvement loans to keep their houses in livable condition," the *Dorchester Community News* observed in August 1974. "In Dorchester many neighborhoods are on the brink of physical destruction," the newspaper argued a few months later. "Redlining threatens to push Dorchester over that brink."[9]

Blockbusting

Real-estate agents encouraged panic selling and rapid neighborhood upheaval. In July 1967, "real estate agents' tactics of scaring whites into moving" were a primary concern of the Mattapan Organization. "There are persistent reports of 'panic selling' tactics by real estate agents," according to minutes of the Mattapan Organization's steering committee. "The agents reportedly capitalize on fears of neighborhood change and deterioration and urge people to sell their property at low prices. The Real Estate Committee noted that this practice is one of the neighborhood's main enemies, and determined to try to put a stop to it."[10]

Real-estate agents engaged in blockbusting not only in Dorchester's Jewish neighborhoods but also in its Catholic neighborhoods. By 1969, Uphams Corner residents had grown concerned about "Block-busting activity in the area." Five years later, the *Dorchester Community News* reported that Michael F. Kenealy, a real-estate agent who had "made his fortunes by block busting in the Mattapan area," was attempting to disrupt other Dorchester neighborhoods. "The neighborhoods of St. Ann's, St. Mark's, and St. Brendan's parishes have been leafleted. The yellow leaflet says Park Realty will sell your home for you 'discreetly and in strict confidence.' It is not unlike the ones distributed in Mattapan," the *Community News* stated in April 1974. "Kenealy will patiently develop the exodus of whites from Dorchester. There will be more propaganda, *what's normal? no change? no slums? no blacks?*

more terror and more chances to get out, all provided by Kenealy who will milk Dorchester for every penny he can get out of it."[11]

Blockbusting was more successful in Jewish than in white Catholic neighborhoods, but it is clear that real-estate agents also attempted to use these tactics in the latter. That blockbusting was more common and more successful in Jewish neighborhoods suggests that these neighborhoods were especially vulnerable to such tactics. "We have had widespread reports of real estate salesmen's activity designed to scare persons into moving," Mark S. Israel wrote in the summer of 1967, describing Mattapan's Jewish community. "Much of the panic is self-generating, however."[12] Though they took advantage of it, real-estate agents did not create the peculiar vulnerability of Jewish neighborhoods.

Boston Banks Urban Renewal Group

Since 1971—when Senator Philip A. Hart convened Senate subcommittee hearings in Boston and when the *Boston Globe* published the first of its many reports on racial change in Mattapan—every attempt to explain the unraveling of the Roxbury and Dorchester Jewish community has focused on the perniciousness of the program organized by the Boston Banks Urban Renewal Group (BBURG). Established in the summer of 1968 to provide home-mortgage funds to low-income black families, BBURG has been widely criticized for Mattapan's rapid and tense racial transition. "Without the knowledge of the residents, and with funds guaranteed by the federal government," Hillel Levine and Lawrence Harmon write, "2,500 low-income black families were . . . funneled into a small, cohesive Jewish neighborhood by the chairmen of twenty-two Boston savings banks."[13]

Accepting this argument, many scholars have inferred that similar banking programs contributed to the Jewish exodus from other cities. FHA reversed its longstanding bias against mortgages in urban neighborhoods in the middle 1960s; this sudden reversal, many observers argue, only exacerbated the white urban exodus and contributed to the victimization of new black homeowners by real-estate speculators. BBURG is a program often cited as evidence. "The Boston story," Nathan Glazer suggested in the *New Republic*, reveals "the cause, the spring, the hidden works" of neighborhood change.[14]

The case against BBURG rests on three pillars. First, critics of BBURG argue that the Mattapan Jewish community was relatively stable until the fall of 1968, when Wellington Hill—the section of Mattapan that lay within BBURG territory—was suddenly invaded by real-estate agents inspired by quick, BBURG-related profits. Second, critics of BBURG state or imply that the program was restricted to Dorchester's Jewish district. "Incredibly, the area selected for heightened loan activity skirted the predominantly Irish and Italian working-class neighborhoods and, less surprisingly, the suburbs where the bankers themselves lived," Levine and Harmon write. "Falling exclusively within the B-BURG line, however, was almost the entirety of Boston's Jewish community."[15] Third, critics of BBURG assert that the frenzied real-estate activity was confined to the areas within the BBURG line; areas outside the line, according to this assertion, were unaffected by the wave of panic that engulfed the Jewish community in Wellington Hill. These three interconnected assumptions, these three pillars of faith upon which the case against BBURG is based, are pillars of sand. The BBURG program did not target Jewish neighborhoods and it was not responsible for the different reactions of Jews and Catholics to urban change and racial transition.

The Urban Exodus before 1968

In arguing that BBURG caused the collapse of Mattapan Jewry, observers suggest that the Wellington Hill district of Mattapan had been a stable Jewish neighborhood through the summer of 1968. Mattapan, presumably, was immune to the racial change that had already transformed the other Jewish districts of Dorchester and upper Roxbury—and the experience of these other districts was irrelevant to understanding racial change in Mattapan. "The realtors and associates laid out a strategic campaign of blockbusting," Francis Russell writes. "Violence engulfed what had been a quiet Jewish backwater." According to Levine and Harmon, Mattapan was "a small, cohesive Jewish neighborhood," a suburban enclave located "a few blocks" away from Roxbury and Dorchester's main Jewish district.[16]

But the Jewish community in Mattapan had never existed apart from the other Jewish neighborhoods of Dorchester and Roxbury. Jews had begun settling in Mattapan in the 1910s, as early as they had begun settling in Roxbury's Elm Hill district and Dorchester's Mount Bowdoin–Franklin Park district; the only older Jewish settlement in Roxbury and

Dorchester was the district northeast of Grove Hall. In the 1920s, as the original Jewish districts had grown together along the axis of Blue Hill Avenue, Wellington Hill had emerged as the southern anchor of a three-mile-long belt of Jewish neighborhoods. Wellington Hill's Jewish community was bound up, from the start, with the rest of Dorchester and Roxbury's Jewish community.[17]

Panic selling and blockbusting had come to Wellington Hill in the winter of 1966–1967, almost two years before the initiation of BBURG. That winter the Jewish Community Council of Metropolitan Boston assigned Mark S. Israel the task of attempting to stabilize the Mattapan community. "In recent years there has been a precipitous movement of Jews away from the area, as Negroes from Roxbury, and some non-Jewish whites have moved in," Israel wrote in February 1967. "The rapid neighborhood change is hurting all parties. Jewish families flee because of a sense of panic." In a report written a month later, Israel noted, "There is a sense of despair in many residents. Many have given up on the neighborhood and are only awaiting a chance to move out." Israel helped establish the Mattapan Organization in June; according to the draft of a newsletter, "It appeared that Mattapan was being given up to become another 'ghetto.'" The Jewish exodus from Wellington Hill continued throughout 1967, as large numbers of African-American families settled in the area. "The colored are moving in," one white resident of Wellington Hill Street told a *Globe* reporter in August 1967. "I called five real estate people, and they all told me I'd be lucky if I got my price." A black resident of Wellington Hill Street, interviewed for the same article, stated, "We had no trouble buying, but a lot of people are selling. I don't know why they're selling."[18]

About 1,500 blacks lived in Mattapan by the winter of 1967–1968; nearly all of them lived in the census tract dominated by Wellington Hill and nearly all of them had settled there since the early 1960s. Since the beginning of the decade, the Jewish population of Wellington Hill had fallen by almost 2,000—20 percent of the census tract's whole population.[19] A city tax assessor visited "homes in the Wellington Hill section of Mattapan" in March 1968, "telling residents that their property is being reassessed downward because of racial change in the neighborhood."[20] That May, the Mattapan Organization assessed the situation. "Black people have been moving into Mattapan in a wave-like pattern from the North," the group reported. "The committee is trying to slow down the process of change and to prevent spreading ghettoization."[21]

In the first week of September 1968—as BBURG was just beginning to fund mortgages—the president of the Mattapan Organization told her executive board that arresting the panic might soon prove futile. "Our crisis is too critical," she declared. "Whites [are] leaving fast."[22] Map 9 illustrates the extent of racial change by the spring of 1968, before the BBURG program began. By that spring, large numbers of blacks had already settled on Wellington Hill. Change had come to Wellington Hill without BBURG, as change had already come to all of the other Jewish neighborhoods in Roxbury and Dorchester. The Jewish exodus had entered its final stages before the line was drawn.

Catholics and Jews inside the BBURG Line

The first contention made by BBURG's critics is that Wellington Hill remained insulated from panic selling and racial change until BBURG began issuing mortgages in late 1968; the second is that the BBURG line tightly circumscribed Dorchester's Jews. "The white areas within the bounds were Jewish neighborhoods," the *New York Times* reported in 1971, "those immediately outside were Irish." The BBURG line, the *Globe* argued, "pointed like an arrow into the heart of Mattapan." This misconception has been part of the BBURG story for almost three decades. In the statement that she gave to the Senate subcommittee in September 1971, Sadelle R. Sacks, the former director of a Roxbury housing service, noted that "the area defined by the BBURG line was the line of Jewish residents" extending down Blue Hill Avenue into Mattapan. "Outside the 'line,'" according to Sacks, "were the neighborhoods still identified by parish names of Catholic churches." Quoting the subcommittee's counsel, the *New York Times* reported "speculation" that the BBURG line was drawn in conformity with the belief that "the Jews would move but the Irish would fight."[23]

In fact, all of the heavily white neighborhoods within the BBURG territory were Catholic neighborhoods. Map 9 shows the racial composition of census tracts that lay in Roxbury, Dorchester, and the rest of the BBURG area in the spring of 1968, while Map 10 shows the percentage of Jews in each census tract's population. The heavy line on both maps is the BBURG line. The line itself has never been in dispute. It was described in the *Globe* investigative articles of 1971 and 1972, introduced as evidence into the Senate hearings, and illustrated in Levine and Harmon's 1992 book—though none of these sources attempts to reconcile its

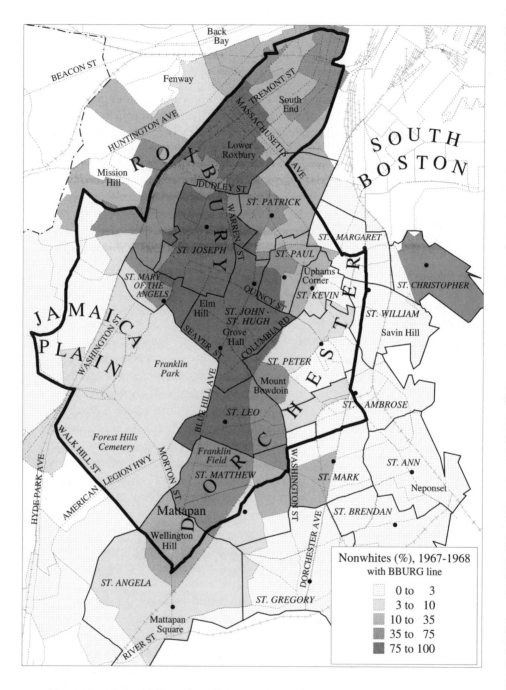

Map 9 Nonwhites, 1967–1968, with BBURG line and parishes

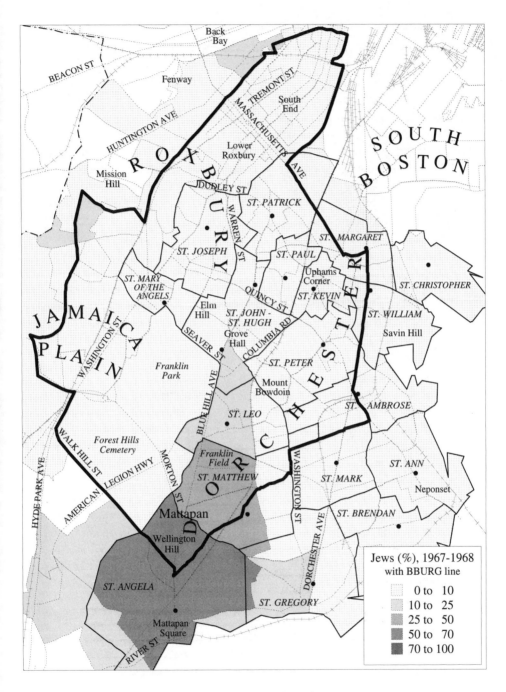

Map 10 Jews, 1967–1968, with BBURG line and parishes

map with its analysis.[24] As Map 9 illustrates, the BBURG area included a large set of white neighborhoods in Dorchester, running south from St. Margaret's to St. Ambrose' Parish. This set of neighborhoods, as Map 10 illustrates, was entirely non-Jewish. This white Catholic district included the commercial center at Uphams Corner as well as the whole of St. Peter's Parish and portions of St. Margaret's, St. William's, St. Kevin's, St. Ambrose', and St. Mark's parishes.

Offering testimony at the 1971 Senate subcommittee hearings, Carl Erickson, the mortgage banker who had drawn the BBURG line, stated matter-of-factly that the white-ethnic neighborhoods inside the line were "predominantly Irish." Astonished, the subcommittee's counsel interrupted, "Irish? Along Blue Hill Avenue?" "No. To the right of Blue Hill," Erickson responded to the more specific question. "Jewish people were living to the south." It was a brief exchange, quickly forgotten in the context of hearings organized to show that BBURG was responsible for racial tension and the Jewish flight from Mattapan. "Almost two decades after drawing a red line on a wall map in order to establish the loan boundaries for the B-BURG consortium," Levine and Harmon report in their 1992 book, Erickson still insisted that "he had no knowledge at the time that he had essentially walled off the city's Jewish community." Of course he had no knowledge; he had never done this.[25]

The BBURG territory was vast. It constituted one-third of the city of Boston, a great swath of lower-class, working-class, and middle-class neighborhoods. Wellington Hill, already undergoing racial change, made up only a small part of the BBURG area. While the mythology of the BBURG line maintains that nearly 100 percent of the residents originally within the line were Jewish and almost none of them were white and Catholic, the truth is different: of those who lived within the boundaries of the BBURG line when it was drawn, half were white Catholics and fewer than 8 percent were Jews. The BBURG line included not only several white Catholic neighborhoods in Dorchester but also the heavily Catholic district of Jamaica Plain. All of these Catholic areas, unlike the Jewish neighborhood on Wellington Hill, were relatively stable and overwhelmingly white when the BBURG line was drawn.

The belief that BBURG made a particular target of Dorchester Jewry has been a product of analysts' confusing causation with correlation. In the late 1960s and early 1970s, when BBURG existed, it was in Mattapan that blockbusting, panic selling, and real-estate transactions were concentrated. Consequently, observers assumed that a logical connection existed between the BBURG line and the Jewish exodus. Although the decision of a banking consortium to dictate boundaries for its loans was patently offensive, it does not follow that the only meaningful section of BBURG territory was the small section in Mattapan.[26] In no way did the BBURG line target Jewish neighborhoods.

The Urban Exodus after 1968

The massive Jewish exodus affected all of Mattapan. It knew no bounds, literally. The third belief surrounding BBURG—that the existence of the line undercut the Jewish community in Mattapan because black families could obtain mortgages only within the BBURG line—is not supported by the evidence. Yet the belief persists that the BBURG program defined the boundaries of racial change. "Real estate brokers just didn't show houses outside of the lines marked on the map by the banks because if they wanted to make a sale, it was fruitless. They knew the banks would reject them," Sadelle Sacks explained to the Senate subcommittee. "In fact, when the line was announced there were many families who were caught in negotiating for houses just outside the line, some even just across the street, who had to give up on the houses. They couldn't buy them. The BBURG coalition had decided where the black communities could live." As the *New York Times* reported in 1971, "Loans from the pool were made to blacks buying homes within the boundary, but no loans were made for homes outside it."[27]

Even as BBURG confined its lending to the area defined by its line, panic selling among Jews was spreading outside the line. As Map 10 demonstrates, the BBURG line did not include the large numbers of Jews who lived in the new houses and apartments south of Wellington Hill. Thus Jews who lived in overwhelmingly white neighborhoods in 1968 were entirely outside the BBURG territory. It was, however, precisely in this area that racial change began after 1968. "There has been a radical shift in the last year and a half" in the Wellington Hill section of Mattapan, according to a September 1969 memorandum prepared for a Jewish community agency, "and the change appears to be a continuing one down along Blue Hill Avenue toward Mattapan Square."[28] In 1969 and 1970, during the heyday of BBURG, it was in the Jewish neighborhoods in southern Mattapan—in the newer, Jewish areas near Mattapan

Square—that blockbusting and panic selling were beginning. Mattapan's racial frontier in 1970 stood entirely outside the BBURG line.

Levine and Harmon open their book with the words of a real-estate agent who encouraged panic selling in the late 1960s. The agent learned "that the banks had decided to take a certain area and designate it with a red pen . . . : Mattapan and parts of Dorchester." By engaging in block-busting, that agent quickly learned how "to make a buck." He believed that the "red pen" of BBURG had made him rich, and Levine and Harmon quote him to demonstrate the power of that "red pen." But the real-estate agent was wrong. His good fortune was not BBURG's doing. As the agent himself recalled, "The big area at that time was River Street (Mattapan). Back towards Woodhaven, Colorado, Alabama Streets, that whole area, it was primarily a Jewish community." It was in that area that he found his first victims and his earliest opportunities in the late 1960s—and that area lay entirely outside the BBURG line. As this real-estate agent vividly recalled and as block-level data from the 1970 census confirm, the BBURG line proved irrelevant to the progress of neighborhood change in Mattapan. "The BBURG boundary line did not seem to have a major effect on where people bought their homes," Rachel G. Bratt concluded in a 1972 report for the Boston Model City Administration. "There is convincing evidence to suggest that, even if boundaries had not existed . . . migration of the black community would have moved in the direction of Mattapan."[29]

Funds available through the BBURG program may have encouraged reckless speculation and accelerated the general process of racial change throughout Dorchester—from St. Peter's to Uphams Corner to Mattapan—but BBURG did not target Mattapan. The existence of BBURG cannot explain why Jews left Dorchester more quickly and with greater panic than Catholics; its existence cannot explain Mattapan's crisis. The BBURG line did not cause the racial transformation of the Jewish neighborhoods that had once run along Blue Hill Avenue from Roxbury through Dorchester. Wellington Hill, which fell inside the BBURG boundary in August 1968, had been experiencing rapid racial change for two or three years before the program began. And Jewish neighborhoods in southern Mattapan, which fell outside the BBURG boundary, proved vulnerable to the same forces that had transformed the rest of Dorchester and Roxbury's formerly Jewish neighborhoods. Evidently, those forces were not rooted in BBURG.

Homeownership

Though redlining, blockbusting, and banking programs cannot account for differences in Jewish and Catholic neighborhood attachments, perhaps homeownership levels can. Two competing arguments, one precisely the opposite of the other, have been offered by scholars. One argument contends that homeowners, concerned about the consequences of racial change for property values, are more likely than renters to panic and flee a changing neighborhood. A second argument contends that renters are more likely than homeowners to leave a neighborhood, since it is easier for renters to move.

In describing the perception among homeowners that racial change is associated with declining property values—a perception that may not, in fact, be accurate—some observers have concluded that high levels of homeownership result in rapid racial succession. "Home ownership," Schelling notes, "should be expected to aggravate speculative departure because it makes shifting of residence more cumbersome and costly."[30] Critics of BBURG emphasize this argument. BBURG was a program for home buyers: thus BBURG directly affected the homeownership market but not the rental market. Warning residents that "the value of your house is dropping $1,000 every month," real-estate agents had a simple objective, according to Levine and Harmon: "scare away the approximately fifteen thousand Jews who were living within the B-BURG line and get as much of the action [as possible] before the $29 million minority mortgage pool dried up."[31] But Wellington Hill, the section of Mattapan supposedly targeted by BBURG, was an area where more than two out of three Jewish families rented rather than owned their housing.[32] Curiously, none of those who have blamed BBURG, a home-mortgage program, for the Jewish exodus from Mattapan has explained how this program disrupted a neighborhood dominated by renter-occupied housing.

Other observers contend that renters, not homeowners, are the leaders of the urban exodus. Noting that Jewish rates of homeownership in urban neighborhoods tended to be unusually low, Arnold R. Hirsch, John T. McGreevy, and Thomas J. Sugrue all argue that the high levels of renter-occupied housing in Jewish neighborhoods explain the vulnerability of these neighborhoods to rapid change. "Homeownership restricted residential mobility," McGreevy asserts. According to Sugrue, describing postwar Detroit, "Jews had a lower rate of homeownership than Catholics and Protestants in the city, making it easier for them to pick up and flee. They did not have the financial or personal stake in their own homes that motivated homeowners to defend their neighborhoods against black newcomers in other parts of the city."[33]

This argument, however, has been difficult to test, since none of these studies analyzes the behavior of Jews and Catholics when levels of homeownership do not differ between the two groups. In most large cities, rates of homeownership were lower among Jews than among Catholics. In Boston, Chicago, Cleveland, Philadelphia, Pittsburgh, and St. Louis, Russian-born residents in 1930 were less likely to own homes than were Irish-born or Italian-born residents.[34] Evidence from most of Dorchester and upper Roxbury is consistent with this national pattern: the level of homeownership tended to be higher in Catholic than in Jewish neighborhoods. It is on the basis of evidence from such cities that scholars have concluded that Jews were less likely to own homes than Catholics—and suggested that this factor explains different patterns of residential change.

Yet there were many cities where Jewish and Catholic rates of homeownership did not differ. According to Stanley Lieberson, levels of homeownership among Russian-born residents in 1930 were no lower than those of other groups in cities like Buffalo, Cincinnati, and Syracuse.[35] Though Jews in these cities were as likely as Catholics to be homeowners, they otherwise acted like Jews in other cities. High levels of homeownership did not frustrate or slow the Jewish flight from urban neighborhoods.

Evidence from Boston strengthens this finding. Homeownership rates, of course, are summary statistics: though the number of renters was relatively high in Boston's Jewish neighborhoods, many thousands of Jews in Dorchester and Roxbury did own homes. Examining the pace of racial change in owner-occupied housing and in renter-occupied housing makes it possible to analyze the relationship between homeowning and neighborhood attachment. Whether Jewish homeowners resisted racial succession longer than Jewish renters is a straightforward empirical question.

The answer is plain: homeowners, not renters, led the Jewish exodus at every stage and in every neighborhood in Dorchester and Roxbury. Figures 1, 2, and 3 illustrate the percentage of nonwhites among both homeowners and renters in each of the once-Jewish census tracts of Dorchester and Roxbury. In 1950, as Figure 1 shows, blacks made up a substantially higher proportion of homeowners than renters in each of the four census tracts with measurable black populations. In 1960, as Figure 2 shows, the same pattern prevailed in six of seven census tracts. Racial succession had ended in much of Dorchester and Roxbury by 1970; in that year, whites made up at least 10 percent of the population in just four census tracts. But again, as Figure 3 shows, white renters proved more persistent than white homeowners in three of those four tracts.

Over two decades of racial change and in virtually every Jewish neighborhood, the Jewish exodus was led by homeowners. Not until the last phases of racial succession, when each census tract was almost fully resegregated, did the proportion of white renters in each census tract decline to levels already established by white homeowners. The rapid flight of Boston's Jews occurred despite, rather than because of, relatively low rates of homeownership.

Levels of homeownership—like class, crime, proximity to black neighborhoods, redlining, blockbusting, and mortgage programs such as

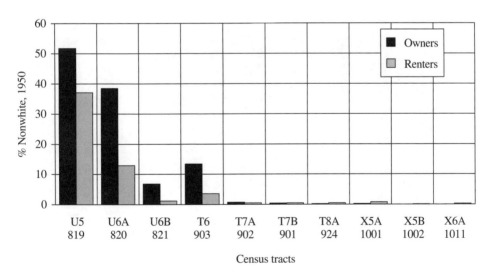

Figure 1 Homeowners and renters, 1950

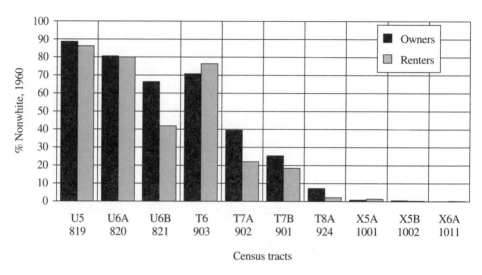

Figure 2 Homeowners and renters, 1960

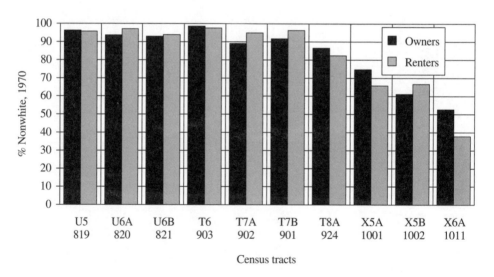

Figure 3 Homeowners and renters, 1970

BBURG—cannot explain why Jews and Catholics have demonstrated different attachments to American urban neighborhoods. When these factors are held constant, the differences in Jewish and Catholic responses to neighborhood change remain profound. None of these factors was more than a proximate cause of the Jewish exodus. Arson, banking programs, and blockbusting targeted Jewish and Catholic neighborhoods without discrimination, but Jewish neighborhoods succumbed to the urban exodus more easily, more rapidly, and more thoroughly than Catholic neighborhoods. Developing a full theory of neighborhood stability requires reckoning with local institutions.

3

Institutions and
Neighborhood Change

Most of the time, and in most of the neighborhoods of Dorchester and upper Roxbury, the differences between Catholic and Jewish residential behavior have been stark. The most dramatic distinctions in behavior have been those that distinguish Catholics from Jews, not those that distinguish some Catholics from other Catholics. Consequently, it is tempting to conclude that cultural differences are sufficient to explain why Catholic attachments to neighborhoods have proven stronger than Jewish attachments.

"It goes back to their tradition: the Jews are wanderers," an Italian resident of Canarsie explained, according to Jonathan Rieder. "They always kept a suitcase packed and close to hand. The wandering Jews were pushed from here to there." In the last days of the Jewish exodus from Dorchester, as crime increased and as arsonists attacked synagogues, Jews felt their vulnerability. "It is like Germany in 1939," State Representative I. Edward Serlin declared in the summer of 1969, in a letter to the *Jewish Advocate*. "Almost every business on Blue Hill Avenue has had its Crystal Night and still the so-called Jewish leaders look the other way." As another Mattapan resident wrote a few months later, "Those Jewish remnants, such as myself, that still remain within the community, feel abandoned and frightened. To live in fear of your neighbor is a terrible thing."[1]

Yet despite their fears many of Dorchester's Jews were determined to remain in their old neighborhoods. "The Jews have a history of running away from persecution. Maybe this time they are tired of running? I could leave Mattapan if I want to, but I prefer to stay and fight as I will not be pushed out of my home. Everything I want is right here," a twenty-six-year-old mother wrote to the *Jewish Advocate* in April 1970. "The plight of Mattapan may very well be in your town next. It does not pay to run. We must fight right here and now and stick together as a people. This is the only answer."[2]

Although such resolve failed to slow the Jewish migration from Mattapan, there have been other times and places when Jews have demonstrated stronger attachments to their neighborhoods. If Jewish mobility were simply a cultural trait, then it becomes difficult to explain why Roxbury Jewry flourished for three decades in close proximity to a growing black community, whereas Mattapan Jewry dissolved in five years. It becomes difficult to explain why some American Jews, such as the Lubavitcher Jews of Crown Heights—who are culturally Jewish, but whose institutions bear closer resemblance to Catholic parishes than to typical synagogues—have been defiantly immobile. And, if Catholic persistence were equally nothing but a product of culture, then the behavior of the Catholics of St. Leo's Parish becomes entirely inexplicable. In an age when most Catholics fought racial succession and successfully defended neighborhood boundaries, St. Leo's Catholics abandoned their neighborhoods quickly and quietly.

When culture is held constant—when we examine, for example, only the behavior of a few thousand Irish Catholics in one or two Dorchester parishes, people who live in similar homes and hold similar jobs—and when systematic differences in neighborhood attachments nevertheless appear, culture cannot explain those differences. And such differences do appear, and often. They appear in the unusual behavior of St. Leo's Catholics. They appear in the prominence of parish boundaries and parish churches in shaping maps of ethnic change. And they appear in the peculiar ways that Jews, then blacks, established their first neighborhoods in Dorchester and Roxbury. Many Catholics have diverged from the general model of resisting change, and, in their settlement patterns, blacks and Jews have shown clear preferences for some neighborhoods over others. Cultural explanations cannot explain these intragroup differences. Institutions can.

In the late 1960s and early 1970s, Mattapan's Jews spoke often of their abandonment. "The letters and numerous telephone calls that have come into the *Advocate* offices," the *Jewish Advocate* stated in a 1969 editorial, "indicate that the Jewish people in this changing neighborhood

of Boston have been hurt many times, physically by attacks and emotionally by the feeling of a sense of isolation from and abandonment by the
Jewish community at large."[3] Abandonment was a Jewish term, and it
resonated in Mattapan in a way that it had not resonated earlier in upper
Roxbury, when blacks had begun settling in once-Jewish enclaves. The
sense of abandonment was acute in Mattapan by the late 1960s because
the collapse of Jewish institutions throughout Dorchester and Roxbury
was nearly complete. Catholic institutions do not easily close and cannot
move; therefore, Dorchester and Roxbury's Catholic residents have never
experienced abandonment.

Because the rules of Catholic institutional life—membership boundaries, rooted churches and parishes, and hierarchical authority—constitute the foundation of Catholic neighborhood attachments, the church
buildings and the parish boundaries themselves explain differences in
Catholic residential behavior. The Catholics who demonstrate the
strongest loyalties to their neighborhood are those who live on the
blocks nearest the church. Parish boundaries distinguish one Catholic
institutional world from another: thus ethnic changes can engulf one
parish while leaving an adjacent parish undisturbed. While synagogues
and black churches can anchor and define Jewish and black settlements,
no institution is so successful in coordinating neighborhood action as
the Catholic parish.

Coordination Problems and Solutions

Analyzing the emergence of Roxbury and Dorchester as streetcar suburbs
in the late nineteenth century, Sam Bass Warner, Jr., argues that suburban
development destroyed traditional centers of residential life. Old town
centers were ignored by the real-estate agents and homebuilders who
were drawing the new suburban maps. "There was nothing in the process of late nineteenth century suburban construction that built communities or neighborhoods: it built streets," Warner writes. "As a result of
the centerless character of most suburbs, community life fell into frag-
ments." Yet local neighborhood institutions did persist as focal points for
ethnic communities, even in neighborhoods that were not ethnically
homogeneous. Churches and synagogues have helped define the centers
of discrete communities.[4]

As members of new ethnic groups searched for homes in Dorchester and Roxbury, they confronted older ethnic communities, and this confrontation was often hostile. "It is within our personal experience that agents have refused Jews in Roxbury and Dorchester," the *Jewish Advocate* reported in 1910, "or that neighbors have made it so unpleasant for Jews that they have been obliged to move away after spending considerable money in fixing up their homes." Francis Russell described the panic that engulfed the white Protestant community of Wellington Hill in the late 1910s, when residents learned that the Robinsons—"suddenly, and in secret"—had sold their home to a Jewish family. "Everyone on the Hill was appalled," Russell recalled. "At the tennis club they talked of nothing but the perfidy of the Robinsons." Blacks, even more than Jews, confronted such bigotry as they moved into new neighborhoods, and Catholics, too, faced hostility when they began settling in Dorchester and Roxbury.[5]

Patterns of ethnic settlement in Dorchester and Roxbury were not preordained. One household at a time, newcomers have searched for places to live. Simple laws of supply and demand have guided this search. In areas where older residents have been firmly rooted, members of new ethnic groups have been more likely to encounter hostility and less likely to find homes on the market. But in areas where older residents have been only weakly attached to their neighborhood, newcomers have been able to purchase or rent homes more easily. Thus the supply of available housing—as well as the likelihood of overt resistance to members of a new ethnic group—is directly related to the strength of older residents' attachments to their district and to the continued appeal of the district for the existing ethnic group. Similarly, the demand for housing in a particular neighborhood is a function of that neighborhood's desirability for new ethnic residents.

By affecting these matters of supply and demand, churches and synagogues have solved coordination problems for potential and current residents. Thomas C. Schelling, characterizing neighborhood change as a collective-action problem, emphasizes the decisions made by individuals who lack means of coordinating their actions. "A moderate urge to avoid small-minority status may cause a nearly integrated pattern to unravel and highly segregated neighborhoods to form," he writes. "The fact that people voluntarily do something, or acquiesce in the consequences, does not mean that they like the results. Often the individual is not free to change the result; he can change only his position within it, and that does him no good."[6] Institutions, however, can affect these individual decisions.

The first synagogues and black churches of Dorchester and Roxbury were erected by ethnic communities that were still small and scattered, but the new buildings themselves became nodes for the nascent ethnic communities. As additional Jewish or black families searched for housing in Dorchester and Roxbury, they were most likely to seek homes in these emerging ethnic centers. In shaping demand for housing, these pioneer institutions helped coordinate the development of Dorchester and Roxbury's new ethnic neighborhoods.

Institutional constraints have proven especially strong in binding Catholics to their neighborhoods. Catholic churches and parishes have not only helped create new Catholic communities but also effectively guided the paths of Jewish and African-American settlement in Dorchester and Roxbury. In making credible commitments to their neighborhoods, in restricting membership to local residents, and in establishing clear boundaries and definite centers, Catholic parishes have sustained strong neighborhood attachments. Because Catholics can be confident in their church's long-term commitment to its neighborhood, they can reasonably expect other Catholics to stay in the district, and those rational expectations are mutually reinforcing. Parishes are the institutional fortresses of "defended neighborhoods."[7] Where Catholic attachments are fiercest—in the blocks surrounding a strong parish church—the housing supply for non-Catholics is sharply limited.

Demand: The Early Settlement of Blacks

In 1926, St. Mark Congregational Church moved to upper Roxbury. It was the first black institution organized in upper Roxbury or Dorchester. Its new home, at the corner of Townsend Street and Humboldt Avenue, stood at the margins of Roxbury's Jewish and Catholic communities—at the northern edge of the Jewish settlement on Elm Hill and near the southern edge of St. Joseph's Parish. Although several hundred blacks had settled in upper Roxbury by the early 1920s, even this marginal area remained contested space. In the fall of 1921, two blocks southeast of the future church site, the Hebrew Educational Alliance had dedicated its new, two-story community hall; within a few months, the group had established a synagogue, Congregation Toras Moshe. Another Jewish congregation, Anshey Amis, organized by about fifteen men in the early

1920s, had purchased a building in September 1924 and opened its synagogue two blocks north of the church site.[8]

Members of St. Mark Congregational Church, which had been located in the South End since the 1890s, recognized that their new church was not in a black district. "Many of the St. Mark members considered this move a mistake," according to the congregation's 1945 history. "They thought that the church was going too far away from the Colored neighborhood." Soon, however, under the leadership of Rev. Samuel Leroy Laviscount, the congregation—and, with it, Elm Hill's middle-class black community—began to prosper and grow. St. Mark Congregational Church and St. Mark Social Center erected a gymnasium building "with game rooms and bowling alleys" in the 1930s. The church and social center organized the first black Cub Scout pack in the country and the first black Boy Scout troop in Boston. "Long before we had a YMCA in the Roxbury community . . . it was the St. Mark Social Center that provided a whole range of recreational sports and educational programs, particularly for young people," Robert C. Hayden recently recalled. "That Social Center was a legend in Boston's black community."[9]

A second black church, Charles Street A.M.E., moved to upper Roxbury in 1939. The congregation, which had been worshiping on Beacon Hill since the early nineteenth century, acquired a stone church at the corner of Warren Street and Elm Hill Avenue. The new church stood a few blocks from St. Mark. "The upper Roxbury district now has a second Colored church of large size," the *Guardian* reported in the summer of 1939. "It is hoped the church will receive new life here and be a factor for good for many years." Charles Street A.M.E. Church did not organize as large a social program as St. Mark. As an African Methodist Episcopal church, however, Charles Street appealed to the many blacks who did not identify with St. Mark's Congregationalist orientation. Until the early 1950s, the two churches and St. Mark Social Center were the only prominent black institutions in upper Roxbury.[10]

Data from the 1940 and 1950 censuses, aggregated at the level of city blocks, suggest that upper Roxbury's African-American community developed as two distinct residential areas. Since no distinct black district existed before the middle 1920s and since the two churches anchored these two districts, the churches themselves appear to have created this residential pattern. By far the larger and denser district in 1940, as Map 11 shows, was centered on Humboldt Avenue, extending north and west from St. Mark Congregational Church. A thin line of predominantly

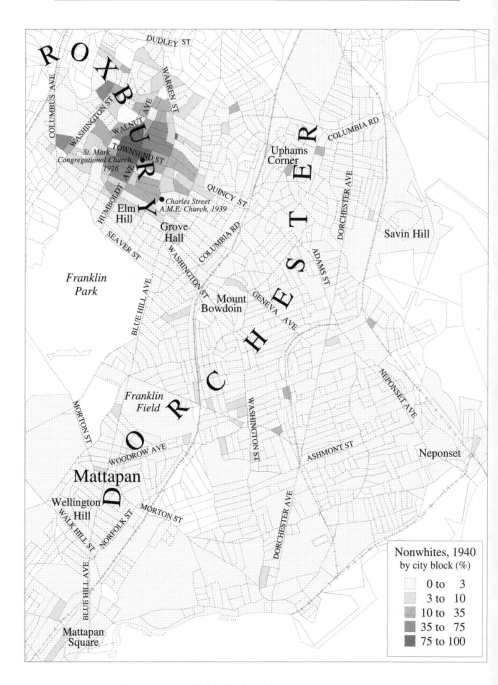

Map 11 Nonwhites, 1940, with black churches

white blocks separated that district from the smaller black district that was forming near Charles Street A.M.E. Church, which had been organized just one year earlier. By 1950, as Map 12 illustrates, the black district centered on Charles Street A.M.E. Church had grown, but it had not fused with the older district that was oriented toward St. Mark. A cluster of seven predominantly white (and Jewish) city blocks—six of them virtually all-white—separated Elm Hill's two black districts. Two churches had defined the first generation of African-American settlement in upper Roxbury, coordinating the formation of the area's black districts by effectively concentrating black demand for homes.

Demand: The Early Settlement of Jews

Congregation Adath Jeshurun was the founding institution of Roxbury and Dorchester's Jewish community. Established in the early 1890s, the congregation rented space for a few years in a building at the corner of Dudley and Washington streets. The Jews who lived in upper Roxbury and Dorchester in the 1890s were few in number and widely dispersed; no significant Jewish neighborhood existed. The Dudley Street location was accessible to a membership that probably came both from older neighborhoods in the South End and lower Roxbury and from the suburban areas of upper Roxbury and Dorchester. In 1897, leaders of Adath Jeshurun attempted to purchase the Boston Highlands Methodist Episcopal Church, near Dudley Street. But the congregation's offer was not accepted, so Adath Jeshurun remained in its rented hall.[11]

Adath Jeshurun left the Dudley Street district in 1900, moving to the Blue Hill Avenue–Grove Hall district, more than one mile away. A few Jewish families lived in the area in 1900, scattered on streets running east from Blue Hill Avenue between Quincy Street and Grove Hall; altogether, perhaps one or two hundred Jewish families lived in all of Dorchester and upper Roxbury. These Jews, according to two settlement-house workers, were "prosperous" and "of a more assimilated type," living on quiet suburban streets far from the city's Jewish neighborhoods.[12]

In the fall of 1900, Adath Jeshurun established its new synagogue, leasing a three-story chapel that stood at the corner of Blue Hill and Lawrence avenues, two blocks beyond Quincy Street and six blocks before Grove Hall. According to Aaron Pinkney, whose family had settled in

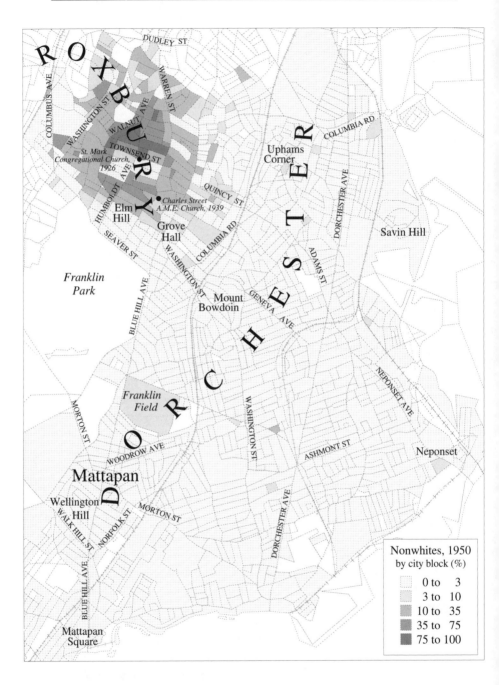

Map 12 Nonwhites, 1950, with black churches

the district that year, High Holy Day services in 1900 "were attended by a large gathering, many coming from quite a distance." In April 1901, the congregation purchased the structure. Adath Jeshurun held regular services in the synagogue on Friday nights and Saturday mornings but had difficulty maintaining weekday services. "There were so few families of the Hebrew faith," the *Jewish Advocate* later wrote, "that it was seldom that a 'minion' could be assembled from the neighborhoods of Roxbury and Dorchester together." Each family in the congregation donated fifty cents each month to support the synagogue.[13]

"This small Chapel" at the corner of Blue Hill and Lawrence avenues, the only Jewish institution in Dorchester and upper Roxbury, "served as the synagogue and communal center of the neighborhood," Pinkney recalled. "The Jewish community grew in leaps and bounds." Nathan Pinanski, who in 1903 moved from East Boston to a home on Lawrence Avenue, quickly became active in the growing congregation. In the fall of 1904, Pinanski organized a campaign for a new synagogue building. George Wyner, another member of the congregation, donated a large lot of land that he had purchased the year before; the property, on Blue Hill Avenue at the corner of Brunswick Street, was located three blocks south of the Lawrence Avenue synagogue. The Jewish community was growing "so rapidly in this district," the *Advocate* reported in May 1905, "that larger and better quarters were needed." By 1905, almost 4,000 Jews— several hundred families—had settled in upper Roxbury and Dorchester, the majority of them in the Blue Hill Avenue–Grove Hall district. With an active membership of ninety families, Adath Jeshurun broke ground for its new synagogue in the spring of 1905.[14]

Adath Jeshurun dedicated the Blue Hill Avenue Synagogue in September 1906. It was an extraordinary achievement. According to the *Boston Journal,* the synagogue was "probably the finest structure of its kind in New England." About 150 families belonged to the congregation that fall, of whom 100 had made "substantial" contributions to the building fund. Estimates of the cost of the Blue Hill Avenue Synagogue ranged from $100,000 to $150,000. "Seven times the collector of the church has come to the handful of rich citizens and asked them to give more money, and each time they have given up without a murmur," the *Journal* reported. "Owing to the small number in the congregation, the achievement of building this magnificent edifice reflects very creditably on the efforts of the people in the little congregation." As the *Advocate* observed,

"The zeal of these members who originated the plan to build this beautiful temple can well be imagined, and it needs no encomium from us. It shows what wonderful work can be accomplished when even a comparatively small number of men put their shoulders to the wheel in a good cause."[15]

By 1906 the Blue Hill Avenue–Grove Hall district had become home to the city's middle-class Jewish leadership. Maps 13 and 14, which estimate Jewish population from records of property ownership for 1906–1910 and 1915–1918, respectively, illustrate the growth of the district. "If you want to see life," the *Jewish Advocate* advised in September 1915, "take a walk along Blue Hill Avenue." Adath Jeshurun—in moving to the frame chapel at Lawrence Avenue and then in erecting its imposing synagogue at Brunswick Street—played a crucial role in the growth and consolidation of this Jewish district. For six years, until the organization in 1906 of Congregation Shara Tfilo on Otisfield Street, Adath Jeshurun stood alone as a Jewish outpost in Roxbury and Dorchester. The synagogue and its neighborhood created each other. The small Jewish community already in the Blue Hill Avenue–Grove Hall district in 1900 had attracted the synagogue to the district, and the synagogue subsequently attracted thousands of new Jews, who in turn began establishing an array of new institutions that reinforced the district's appeal to Jewish residents.[16]

Elsewhere in Dorchester and upper Roxbury, as other synagogues and other Jewish neighborhoods began to take root, similar patterns of coordination occurred. By the middle 1910s, as Map 14 shows, substantial Jewish enclaves had emerged in Roxbury's Elm Hill district and in Dorchester's Mount Bowdoin–Franklin Park and Mattapan districts. Early settlers in two of the new districts—Elm Hill and Mount Bowdoin–Franklin Park—erected major suburban temples by the middle 1910s. Mattapan attracted a smaller proportion of middle-class Jews; consequently, neither of Mattapan's early congregations built a synagogue before the 1920s.

Beth Hamidrash Hagadol, Elm Hill's first congregation, was founded in September 1913 by nineteen men. Within two months, the small congregation purchased land and announced plans to construct a synagogue. Elm Hill was still an affluent, predominantly Protestant district; in 1914, trustees of the Roxbury Latin School purchased a large expanse of land on Elm Hill, where they planned to relocate the elite school and its

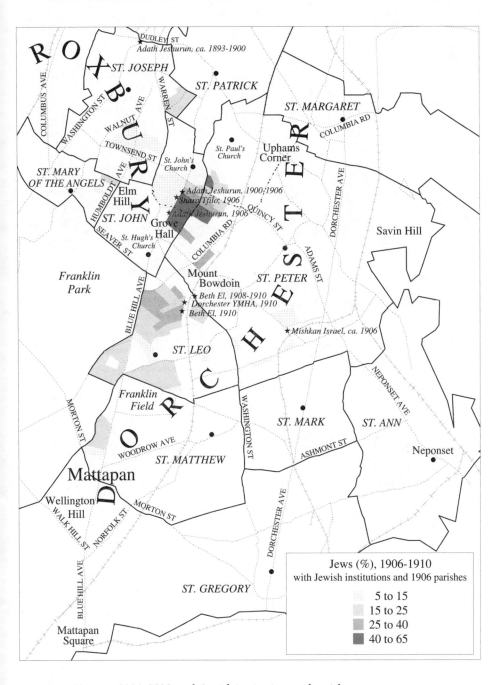

Map 13 Jews, 1906–1910, with Jewish institutions and parishes

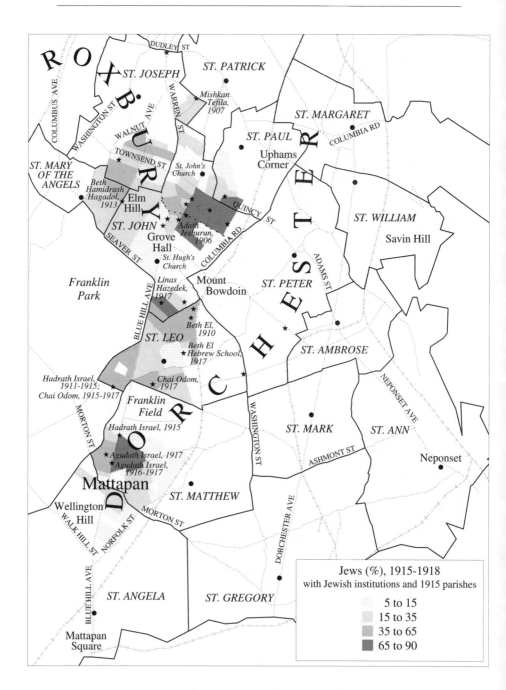

Map 14 Jews, 1915–1918, with Jewish institutions and parishes

playing fields. Four blocks from the Roxbury Latin site, Beth Hamidrash Hagadol completed work on the Crawford Street Synagogue in the summer of 1915. To erect the synagogue, the congregation of approximately fifty families had assumed a mortgage of $75,000. The result was one of the largest and most impressive synagogues in the Boston area.[17]

By the fall of 1922, when Mishkan Tefila broke ground for its new temple on Seaver Street, the Roxbury Latin School had abandoned its plans for the district. The Crawford Street Synagogue boasted a membership of more than four hundred families, and the Elm Hill district had become a major Jewish enclave. Louis M. Epstein, Beth Hamidrash Hagadol's rabbi, writing in 1924, described the audacious decision to erect a modern synagogue on Elm Hill. "Much misgiving was expressed as to the possibilities of success of such an undertaking," according to Epstein's account. "There was no apparent outlook for a real institution. 'Who will come here, save these few?' they asked themselves." But, as Epstein concluded, those pioneer families had built wisely. "The Crawford Street Synagogue is an illustration of the fact that not always is a synagogue built where the Jewish community is, but that sometimes the community is built where the synagogue is," he argued. "Our Synagogue has in a great measure been the making of the Roxbury Jewish community."[18]

Leaders of Beth El made comparable claims for their own temple's role in the history of the Mount Bowdoin–Franklin Park district. Organized in the middle 1900s, the early congregation met and worshiped in a public hall on Washington Street, in the small commercial district that had grown up around Mount Bowdoin Station. By 1910, at least three hundred Jewish families had settled in the district that extended from Mount Bowdoin to Franklin Park. That summer Beth El, with a membership of sixty families, purchased land for a temple on Fowler Street, two blocks from Mount Bowdoin Station. "This new synagogue, when erected, will be the first one in the Dorchester district, where in the past few years hundreds of Jewish families have made their permanent homes," the *Jewish Advocate* stated. Beth El dedicated the Fowler Street Synagogue in September 1912. The structure, with its land, cost $55,000. Capped by a large copper dome, the white stucco building rose high above the houses surrounding it.[19]

By 1920 the Fowler Street Synagogue had grown to four hundred members. Temple Beth El supported a sisterhood, a men's club, a junior council, a free loan society, various adult study groups, a Young Israel congregation, and, in a separate building, a large religious school. "Witness the noble institutions that have grown from this Temple," the congregation's vice-president declared in February 1921, during the installation of new officers. "Right here on this very spot where this beautiful Temple is now located, there was nothing but a solid mountain of rocks but in such a short space of time see what we have accomplished." About 1,300 Jewish families—nearly 6,000 Jews—had made their homes in Dorchester's Mount Bowdoin–Franklin Park district.[20]

The Jewish community of Mattapan grew up around Congregation Hadrath Israel. Founded in 1911, when fewer than two hundred Jewish families lived in Mattapan, Hadrath Israel established its synagogue in an apartment just west of Franklin Field. This location, as Map 13 suggests, was centrally located for a Jewish community that extended from the Franklin Field district—the streets at the northern edge of Franklin Field—south, beyond Franklin Field, to the Mattapan district. In the spring of 1915, Hadrath Israel moved its synagogue into Mattapan, acquiring a large hall on Blue Hill Avenue. That same year, Hadrath Israel purchased land in the center of Mattapan's growing Jewish district and announced plans to erect a permanent synagogue building on the site. But the plans never came to fruition. In 1919, the congregation instead purchased a modest frame church on Woodrow Avenue. By then, about 2,200 Jewish families—10,000 Jews—had already settled in Mattapan.[21]

Alone among Dorchester and Roxbury's four pioneer congregations, Hadrath Israel did not erect a synagogue building during the formative years of its district's Jewish settlement. Adath Jeshurun, Beth Hamidrash Hagadol, and Beth El had all built substantial temple buildings in their first years of existence; these congregations had completed work on their synagogues before any competing congregations had emerged in their districts. But Hadrath Israel faced early competition from other congregations and served a district with few upper-middle-class suburban families. In 1915, when Hadrath Israel relocated to Mattapan, many members from the Franklin Field district had left the congregation and formed Chai Odom. More important competition came from Agudath Israel. Established in Mattapan in 1916, Agudath Israel worshiped in a succession of temporary buildings until 1923, when it dedicated its substantial new temple on Woodrow Avenue, nearly across the street from Hadrath Israel's synagogue. Neither Hadrath Israel nor Agudath Israel supported an English-speaking rabbi in these years, unlike the three other pioneer congregations of Roxbury and Dorchester, whose districts included wealthier, more assimilated families.[22]

While Roxbury and Dorchester's four pioneer synagogues helped define and consolidate patterns of Jewish settlement, they were not crucial to the process. These congregations were as much the products of small, preexisting Jewish communities as they were the causes of subsequent neighborhood expansion. Mattapan Jewry grew quickly in the 1910s and early 1920s, despite the fragmentation of its communal life, the absence of a significant upper-middle-class population, and the failure of any institution to erect a building or organize a program oriented to younger, English-speaking adults. The weakness of Hadrath Israel did not hamper the growth of the Mattapan district. And even the strongest pioneer congregations, like Adath Jeshurun and Beth El, tacitly acknowledged that the Jewish populations in their districts were expanding in areas relatively distant from the early synagogue centers: when the two congregations erected their new school buildings in the 1920s, they located the structures a few blocks away from their landmark temples.[23] The ability of great synagogues to coordinate and concentrate the Jewish demand for housing was limited.

Supply: Catholic Parishes and Jewish Settlement

The Catholic parishes of Dorchester and upper Roxbury were more important than these synagogues in defining the original sites of Jewish suburban growth and in determining the boundaries of Jewish territorial expansion. Organized around powerful institutional cores—in every parish except St. William's, a school and any other parochial structure was built adjacent to the church—and possessing territorial jurisdictions, these parishes created the basic outlines of Jewish settlement. In some instances, Jews purchased or rented existing homes; in others, Jews built new housing on vacant land. But nowhere did Jews easily dislodge Catholic families living near a viable church. Catholic churches proved well equipped to coordinate Catholic neighborhood attachments and, therefore, the supply of housing available to incoming Jews.

Parish Margins

In the fall of 1907, Archbishop William O'Connell initiated a review of parish boundaries in upper Roxbury and Dorchester.[24] The archbishop's principal concern was the situation along Blue Hill Avenue. Elsewhere in Dorchester and Roxbury, parishes had been laid out with the rigorous logic that only a central authority could enforce: each parish maintained one centrally located church, claimed the allegiance of all Catholics inside its boundaries, and could support itself financially. Moreover, most major residential districts in Dorchester and upper Roxbury were served by a strong local church.

But Catholics moving into the growing neighborhoods along Blue Hill Avenue were not well served. As Map 13 illustrates, the first one and one-half miles of Blue Hill Avenue was overbuilt with Catholic institutions. From Dudley Street to Grove Hall, three Catholic churches—St. Patrick's, St. John's, and St. Hugh's—lined Blue Hill Avenue. Past Grove Hall, for three miles south to the city line in Mattapan Square, Blue Hill Avenue presented the opposite problem. Running along the western edge of Dorchester parishes, Blue Hill Avenue lacked any Catholic institutions. Given the existing map, it must have been a straightforward decision that December to establish St. Angela's Parish in Mattapan and to authorize the pastor to begin planning for a church on Blue Hill Avenue.[25]

This decision, however, scarcely addressed Archbishop O'Connell's underlying concern. St. John's Church and St. Hugh's Church, created in the 1890s as mission churches within St. Joseph's Parish, were crowded so close together that his predecessor, Archbishop John J. Williams, had temporarily placed both churches in a single parish when he established St. John's Parish in 1901. Within the parish, a line divided the territory assigned to St. Hugh's Church from that assigned to St. John's. But the two churches were not easily disentangled. Only the basements and exterior structures of both churches had been finished by 1908: St. John's upper church, barely functional, was left "rough and unpainted," and St. Hugh's upper church could not be used at all. Meanwhile, nearby in St. Mary of the Angels' Parish, Catholics were struggling to build even the basement of another church. And two and one-half miles still separated St. Hugh's Church from the site of St. Angela's Church. Blue Hill Avenue passed along the western edge of St. Matthew's and St. Leo's parishes, but both had built their churches elsewhere, closer to their geographical centers.[26]

Serving districts still in early stages of Catholic settlement, the churches of St. Hugh and St. Mary of the Angels were assigned two of the smallest geographical areas in the entire archdiocese. St. John's Church, also assigned little territory, stood in a more densely settled district. In 1908, a year after St. Mary of the Angels' Parish estimated its population at 209 families, St. John's Parish reported that 167 families attended St. Hugh's Church and that 596 families attended St. John's Church. No other Catholic church in all of Dorchester and upper Roxbury was supported by so few people as St. Hugh's and St. Mary of the Angels'. The Catholic population of St. Angela's, the next smallest parish in the Dorchester-Roxbury area, was nearly 50 percent larger than that of St. Mary of the Angels' Parish.[27]

In the summer of 1908, Archbishop O'Connell appointed a special commission to recommend changes in parish boundaries in the Dorchester-Roxbury area. Rev. Francis J. Butler, the pastor of St. Leo's Parish, suggested that some territory from his own parish be taken for the support of St. Hugh's. "St. Hugh's church, being already built and nearly completed," he explained, "must be maintained." Rev. Peter Ronan offered to cede the section of St. Peter's Parish that lay west of Columbia Road and south of the newly formed St. Paul's Parish. On the commission's recommendation, as a comparison of Maps 13 and 14 shows, the archbishop accepted the boundary changes, but he was reluctant to create St. Hugh's Parish immediately. His prudence was justified. Even with the new territory, St. Hugh's Church continued to rely for its support on a small number of Catholics.[28]

Archbishop O'Connell also had to consider the situation at St. John's Church. In addition to their unfinished church, St. John's parishioners supported a school and a convent. Though Father Ronan had agreed to grant territory to St. John's, the commission was not sanguine about the parish's future. Tightly circumscribed by St. Joseph's, St. Patrick's, and St. Paul's parishes, as well as by the territory provisionally assigned to St. Hugh's Church, St. John's faced a difficult future. "Nothing can be done to give St. John's parish the number it should have to support it, unless the present church of St. Paul be closed," the commission concluded in December 1908. "The joining of these two parishes into one would make little over 5000 which ought to be the number of people called upon to support a plant as large as St. John's." The archbishop did not implement this suggestion. St. Paul's Parish, which he had just erected at the start of the year, was a strong and viable parish. It had been established at the initiative of Father Ronan and with territory granted by St. Peter's Parish—perhaps the leading pastor and parish in the archdiocese. St. Paul's was secure, which meant that St. John's and St. Hugh's would continue to struggle together as two ends of a single parish.[29]

Not only had the commission failed to resolve the difficulties of St. John's Parish, but, in removing territory from St. Leo's Parish for the support of St. Hugh's Church, it had aggravated problems farther up Blue Hill Avenue. Father Butler, St. Leo's pastor, had urged the commission to extend his own parish boundaries eastward and southward, with territory taken from St. Peter's and St. Matthew's parishes. "The present location of St. Leo's is not central," he explained. With the new territory, he proposed to construct a mission church in the Mount Bowdoin district— "where one should have been built ten years ago"—and, then, once the Mount Bowdoin church could support its own parish, to "cut off St. Leo's parish at the Railroad." Within these new boundaries, St. Leo's Parish would be centered on Blue Hill Avenue, with territory extending from Grove Hall to Mattapan. The archbishop did not act on this proposal, though it was endorsed by the commission: perhaps the pastors of St. Peter's and St. Matthew's were reluctant to give up the required territory. Ceding territory to St. Hugh's Church and gaining nothing, St. Leo's Parish had been made weaker. There would be no new church in the Mount Bowdoin district and no new provision made for serving Catholics living near Blue Hill Avenue, who remained at the western margin of St. Leo's and St. Matthew's parishes.[30]

The failure of the archdiocese to consolidate a strong institutional presence throughout Dorchester and Roxbury had consequences for Jewish settlement. Where Catholic institutions were weakest, Catholic residents proved most vulnerable to displacement. Thus it was at the margins of parishes—above all, at the margins of parishes already straining to maintain basic services—that Catholics were least likely to resist Jewish in-migration, and it was at the centers of strong parishes that Catholic resistance was strongest. With a broad charge "to redistrict the parishes of Dorchester and Roxbury," the 1908 commission focused almost exclusively on the weakness of Catholic institutions in and near the Blue Hill Avenue corridor.[31] These were the areas—the streets that lay midway between St. John's and St. Hugh's, in the Blue Hill Avenue–Grove Hall district; the section of Elm Hill that lay at the edges of St. Joseph's, St. Mary of the Angels', and St. John's parishes, including marginal streets that the commission had suggested transferring from St. Joseph's Parish to the two weaker parishes; the Mount Bowdoin district, which lacked its own church; and the long stretch of Blue Hill Avenue that extended from Franklin Park to Mattapan, also underserved by Catholic churches—where Jews established their first areas of settlement in Dorchester and upper Roxbury.

The Blue Hill Avenue Synagogue and the Jewish neighborhood that grew around it rose in the center of St. John's Parish, in the corridor between St. John's Church and St. Hugh's Church. By the time the commission was working on its report, as Map 13 shows, Boston's first suburban Jewish enclave had driven a wedge into the crevice that separated the two ends of the parish. The Jewish settlement grew quickly. By the middle 1910s, as Map 14 illustrates, Jews had settled much of the territory assigned to St. John's Church. Catholics who lived on the streets nearest the church and north of the church were not easily dislodged. But Catholics who lived on streets south of the church were leaving in large numbers. While recognizing that "the streets immediately about the church will no doubt be held for many years by faithful families," two settlement-house workers in the 1910s observed that "over 500 souls have moved from the parish in the past year or two on account of the incoming of the Jews." Its parishioners still unable to raise sufficient funds, St. John's Church stood unfinished in June 1917. Speaking to his parishioners in St. Hugh's Church, Monsignor Patrick J. Supple stated the matter simply: "It has been a hard struggle in that end of the parish owing to conditions within the knowledge of all of you."[32]

St. Hugh's Church had been completed in 1913. Its families, fewer in number but wealthier than those at the other end of the parish, had been largely undisturbed at first by the population changes affecting the Blue Hill Avenue district north of Grove Hall. But, as Map 14 suggests, a few Jews had begun to settle in the Elm Hill district, where the corners of three parishes met. In 1913 Beth Hamidrash Hagadol purchased land for its synagogue on the boundary separating St. John's and St. Mary of the Angels' parishes, just two blocks from their border with St. Joseph's Parish. Elm Hill's Jewish community steadily grew. "So many have moved away during the past year—their houses now are occupied by Jews—that three priests here are more than are necessary for the work to be done," Rev. Charles A. Finnigan, the pastor of St. Mary of the Angels' Parish, wrote in 1919.[33]

Pressed by the large Jewish settlements that had emerged not only on

Elm Hill but also in the Blue Hill Avenue–Grove Hall district and the Mount Bowdoin–Franklin Park district, St. Hugh's Catholic population, always small, had almost collapsed by the 1920s. A strong parish densely settled by Catholics determined to support their church would have had great difficulty holding three borders against a new population seeking to expand its area of settlement. For St. Hugh's Church, the task was impossible. "While a few substantial people remain practically all have moved," Rev. John E. O'Connell, the pastor of St. John's Parish, wrote in 1932, assessing the situation at St. Hugh's Church. Both ends of his parish, he concluded, "are undergoing disintegration and there is no other prospect than that of progressing down grade."[34] St. Hugh's Church remained in St. John's Parish.

St. Leo's, the only Catholic institution close to Blue Hill Avenue between Grove Hall and Mattapan Square, proved a formidable hurdle in the path of Jewish settlement. To be sure, large numbers of Jews were settling in the parish in the 1910s, attracted, in part, by the new Temple Beth El, which stood on Mount Bowdoin, at the periphery of the parish. But, as Map 14 shows, nowhere in St. Leo's territory was there a section as thoroughly Jewish as that in the Blue Hill Avenue–Grove Hall district or in Mattapan. Jews lived at the northern and southern edges of St. Leo's Parish. The center of the parish remained predominantly non-Jewish in the late 1910s: the presence of a Catholic church, even a small frame church on a side street, apparently slowed the emergence of a dense Jewish community by holding Catholic families in the neighborhood. "In regard to the influx of Jews, as far as it affects our Catholic population, I should say that our increase is practically untouched by them," the pastor of St. Leo's Parish wrote in late 1915. "Moreover, the Christians are being accustomed to living in the same houses with the Jews and seem to get along peaceably." In 1916, when there were six synagogues in the Blue Hill Avenue–Grove Hall district and three synagogues in the Mattapan district, no Jewish congregation had yet been organized between the Fowler Street Synagogue and either Franklin Park or Franklin Field. It was the Catholics of St. Leo's Parish, not the area's Jews, who were raising money for a proper house of worship that year. Having "gathered a fund of $20,000, and over," Rev. Francis A. Cunningham, the parish's pastor, met with Cardinal O'Connell to discuss plans for the structure, which Cunningham hoped would be "a Roman church on the general lines of St. Clement's in Rome."[35]

But, steadily, Jews consolidated their neighborhoods at the edges of St. Leo's Parish. Jews in the Franklin Field district, who had organized Congregation Chai Odom in 1915, purchased a small synagogue on Nightingale Street in 1917. Also in 1917, Jews in the Franklin Park district organized Linas Hazedek, on Michigan Avenue. Including Temple Beth El, three synagogues now anchored the Jewish enclaves at the northern and southern ends of St. Leo's Parish. Buttressed on one side by Roxbury's Jewish districts and on the other by Mattapan, the Mount Bowdoin–Franklin Park and Franklin Field districts had come to resemble a pincers in the late 1910s: in the grip of the pincers was the core of St. Leo's Parish. By the middle 1920s, Catholics in St. Leo's Parish, even those on the few streets surrounding the church, could no longer resist the Jewish demand for housing. The parish church did not move, but its parishioners eventually did. Laying aside plans for a new church, the modest Catholic population that remained in St. Leo's Parish continued to worship in the frame church now located in a Jewish neighborhood.[36]

As the presence of St. Leo's Church slowed neighborhood change in the Franklin Park and Franklin Field districts, so the absence of such an institution contributed to the rapid growth of a Jewish settlement in Mattapan. The dense Mattapan enclave, as Map 14 shows, was located at the margins of the area's parishes—a half-mile west of St. Matthew's Church and one mile north of St. Angela's Church. Significantly, Mattapan's Jewish neighborhood took root far from Mattapan Square, a small commercial district similar to the Mount Bowdoin and Blue Hill Avenue–Grove Hall districts: St. Angela's Church was located near Mattapan Square. While Mattapan's Jewish settlement expanded deep into St. Matthew's and St. Angela's parishes in the 1920s, three factors—the fact that the Jewish settlement grew from only one side of each parish, the large territory originally assigned to each parish, and the locations of the two churches within the parishes—enabled the parishes to contain the area of Jewish settlement and to maintain the support of large Catholic populations.

In the rest of Dorchester and Roxbury, parishes completed their churches and built thriving schools. But St. Mary of the Angels' Church never rose above its flat-roofed basement, St. Leo's Parish never replaced its early frame chapel with a permanent church, and St. Hugh's Parish never existed. Just four churches in Dorchester and upper Roxbury—these three and St. Paul's—had not organized a parish elementary school by the early 1950s. These were the fingerprints that a burgeoning Jewish community left on Catholic institutions. Yet all three churches persisted, ministering to Catholics who remained within the parish boundaries. These parishes had played leading roles in the struggle that first determined the areas of earliest Jewish settlement and that, by the middle 1920s, shaped the border that divided the great Jewish district from Catholic neighborhoods.

Parish Centers

On every side, that border was defined by Catholic churches. With the exception of St. Leo's and St. Hugh's, the Catholic churches of Dorchester and upper Roxbury successfully staked out and held their parish centers against the expanding Jewish neighborhoods. Some of those churches stood only one or two blocks past the border that separated the two ethnic communities. Catholic residents rallied around those institutions, creating firm buffers that blocked the expansion of Jewish neighborhoods. As Jewish communities had initially formed at the far edges of parishes, where the ties of Catholics to their institutions were tenuous, so Jewish communities discovered their outer geographical limits at the locations where Catholics were most tightly bound to their institutions, at the sites of parish churches.

Jewish institutions themselves provided strong evidence of the strength of Catholic parishes. Almost without exception, as Map 14 shows, synagogues, Hebrew schools, and Jewish community centers were located at the edges of parishes, distant from parish centers. In the middle 1910s, all nine Jewish institutions in the Blue Hill Avenue–Grove Hall district formed a compact cluster in the corridor that separated St. John's from St. Hugh's; none stood near either church. Like buoys moored in the sea, Catholic churches marked out the boundary of Jewish settlement.

"Long before ethnicity became a fashionable political concept, we knew about ethnics, about each group living in its own community," Theodore H. White wrote, describing his childhood as a Jew in Dorchester in the 1920s. "Within the boundaries of our community we were entirely safe and sheltered. But the boundaries were real. We were an enclave surrounded by Irish," he recalled. "Across Franklin Park to the west lay the lands of the lace-curtain Irish, who lived in Jamaica Plain and Roslindale; they were, if not friendly, at least not pugnacious. South of Mattapan Square there were the original settlers, Protestants—and Protestants were not dangerous at all; they did not beat you."[37]

The boundary that mattered most to White was that which followed the railroad tracks running, for most of their length, a few blocks east of Blue Hill Avenue. "Across the railway tracks," White noted, "lived very tough Irish—working-class Irish. The local library lay in such an Irish district, and my first fights happened en route to the library, to get books. Pure hellishness divided us, but after one last bloody-nose battle, I was given safe passage by the Irish boys whenever I went to the library." West of the railroad tracks, as Map 15 shows, was an overwhelmingly Jewish district. Rev. Leo J. Knapp, the pastor of St. Matthew's Parish, noted in November 1925 that few Catholics remained there. The twenty-two Catholic families in St. Matthew's who lived west of Blue Hill Avenue were "practically cut off from contact with our parish church," he wrote. Their approach to the church "is cross-country through winding streets in a Hebrew neighborhood."[38]

Four blocks before Mattapan Square, where the railroad tracks passed beneath Blue Hill Avenue, the band of Jewish settlement found its southern limit. The logic of that terminus is not immediately apparent. Mattapan Square itself, not the short railroad bridge four blocks before it, would have been a more obvious boundary for a community that by the middle 1920s had come to be centered around Blue Hill Avenue. Ben Rosen, who had studied the city's Jewish community in 1920—a time when the boundaries of Jewish life in Roxbury and Dorchester had not yet been settled—had predicted that the Jewish community would continue expanding as far south as Mattapan Square. But Rosen had been wrong. By the middle 1920s, the railroad bridge had become a solid boundary between the quickly growing Jewish district to its north and the predominantly Catholic district to its south. More than forty years later, when African Americans had settled throughout the once-Jewish neighborhoods that lay north of Morton Street, this last boundary between Jews and Catholics still held. "There are definite boundaries in the world of the teens," Mark S. Israel reported in August 1967. "The group I met with are all Jewish and live and roam on Wellington Hill. There is another group, all Catholic, that hangs out in Mattapan Square. The two never meet, because if they did there would be border skirmishes."[39]

To the west, Roxbury and Dorchester's Jewish district was bounded by

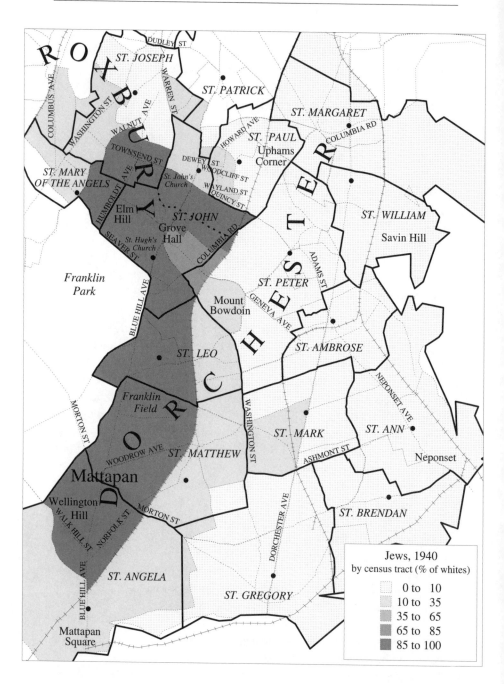

Map 15 Jews, 1940, with parishes

Franklin Park and a set of cemeteries, then, in Roxbury, by Walnut Avenue. Rev. Charles A. Finnigan, the pastor of St. Mary of the Angels' Parish, noted in September 1928 that Walnut Avenue had become the line that separated the Jewish area from the Catholic area of his parish. "In the section of this parish" beyond Walnut Avenue, an area of 740 homes, "we have now only twelve Catholic families, the rest are all Jews."[40]

The northern edge of Jewish settlement lay one or two blocks north of Townsend and Quincy streets. "That part of Roxbury was our world at that time. We remember well the streets and how we walked them to get where we were going and the things that happened on our way to and from school and the people we knew and got to know well," Abraham Weinstein, who lived in Roxbury as a boy in the 1910s and 1920s, later wrote. "The Jewish families stopped at Woodcliff Street and up the hill on Howard Avenue and Dewey Street there were mostly Gentiles, a nice middle class who didn't allow us to forget we were intruders." St. John's Church stood on Blue Hill Avenue at the corner of Woodcliff Street, two blocks north of Quincy Street. At the top of the hill stood St. Paul's Church. While a few Jews lived past Woodcliff Street, "they weren't as numerous as those around Quincy or Wayland Streets." Woodcliff Street was "a sort of dividing line," Weinstein recalled. "There were toughs there, alright! How many times did I run home offended and crying, 'They called me a sheenie!'" Barney Glazer, who grew up in a house that stood on the boundary, remembered the fights that he regularly had as a child, "when one of the Irish lads called me 'that name,' belittling my religion." With amusement, Glazer noted that his "chief opponent," with whom he "fought up and down Woodcliff street on at least 358 occasions," was, between fights, "the angel of St. John's School and Church."[41]

That St. John's Church stood, with its school and convent, at Woodcliff Street was no mere coincidence: throughout Dorchester and upper Roxbury, Catholic churches set the boundaries that divided Jewish and Catholic neighborhoods. Aside from its association with St. John's Church, Woodcliff Street was an insignificant side street. Yet the Jewish district extended past Quincy and Townsend, both more important streets, and reached Woodcliff Street, where the area of Jewish settlement decisively ended. Walnut Avenue, in Roxbury, and the railroad bridge near Mattapan Square were also, at first glance, curious boundaries.

Washington Street, a major street running from Boston through Roxbury, lay just four blocks west of Walnut Avenue, while Columbus Avenue, another major street, lay just west of Washington Street. But it was Walnut Avenue, rather than either of the major streets, that became the boundary between Jews and Catholics. And, stopping just four blocks before Mattapan Square, the Jewish district seemed oddly truncated at its southern end as well.

What caused the Jewish neighborhoods to hug Franklin Park and Blue Hill Avenue so closely—what in the end gave that set of neighborhoods its elongated, rigidly bounded shape—were, it seems, the Catholic churches that had been planted in Dorchester and upper Roxbury before Jews had begun to arrive. St. Mary of the Angels' Church at Walnut Avenue, St. John's Church at the corner of Blue Hill Avenue and Woodcliff Street, St. Matthew's Church just two blocks east of the railroad tracks, and St. Angela's Church near the railroad bridge on Blue Hill Avenue: these four churches, identified in Map 15, defined the western, northern, eastern, and southern limits of the great expanse of Jewish settlement. Reinforcing those limits, standing just a few blocks beyond the ethnic boundary, were the churches of St. Peter, St. Paul, and St. Joseph. Two churches, one at Woodcliff Street and the other at the railroad bridge near Mattapan Square, on sites separated by three miles and more than fifty blocks, bracketed the entire Jewish district on Blue Hill Avenue.

The experience of the four churches that stood like sentries at the border indicates that the institutions themselves were central to maintaining each boundary, that each structure provided a reference point and a community center for its parish, that Catholics were more easily displaced at the margins of a parish and much more difficult to displace at the very core of the parish. By protecting the institutional core, which was generally located at the geographical center of the parish, Catholic residents held as Catholic neighborhoods the whole section of the parish that lay beyond the church. The church's commitment to its geographical area was nearly absolute. Of sixteen Catholic churches in Dorchester and upper Roxbury in the 1930s, just two stood inside Jewish neighborhoods: St. Hugh's, which, as the mission chapel of a divided parish, had been the weakest of the area's churches; and St. Leo's, many of whose Catholic families had resisted moving until the 1920s, long after adjacent areas had been heavily settled by Jews.

Supply: Catholic Parishes and Black Settlement

Parish churches and boundaries have continued their work in the post-war era. As African Americans began settling in Roxbury and Dorchester, some Catholic districts resisted ethnic change more successfully than others. Racial change has progressed one parish at a time; changes in one parish have crossed boundaries into adjacent parishes slowly. Resistance to ethnic change has remained greatest at the institutional cores, as churches have continued to provide a coordinating mechanism for residents attempting to remain in their neighborhoods. At times, especially in the early stages of neighborhood change, Catholic resistance has been violent and viciously racist. That resistance has also meant that Catholics, in general, have proven less likely than Jews to suburbanize and more likely to remain in their old districts, even in those that have become racially integrated. But not all Catholics have resisted. Some, like those in St. Leo's, have simply left.

Parish Margins

In Roxbury and Dorchester's Jewish neighborhoods, racial change proceeded steadily up Blue Hill Avenue. From the areas of early black settlement in the Elm Hill district, blacks moved first into the Blue Hill Avenue–Grove Hall district, then into the Mount Bowdoin–Franklin Park district, then, finally, into Mattapan. By 1960, as Map 8 (p. 38) indicates, African Americans were rapidly consolidating their neighborhoods in Roxbury and beginning to settle in Dorchester. The process of change was relentless. Block by block, blacks by 1970 had displaced Jews from Roxbury to Mattapan. In Roxbury and in adjacent sections of Dorchester, ethnic turnover was complete by 1970, as Map 16 shows. Farther south, racial transition was still in progress, but by the middle 1970s it had ended: the integrated status of Wellington Hill in 1970 was an artifact of the process of neighborhood change.

Racial change in Catholic districts has not followed a comparable block-by-block pattern. Parish boundaries have often coincided with ethnic boundaries. In 1960, as Map 8 shows, St. Margaret's, St. Kevin's, and St. Peter's remained all-white parishes, as their western boundaries held firm against racial change; St. Peter's parish boundary sustained white neighborhoods immediately adjacent to black neighborhoods.

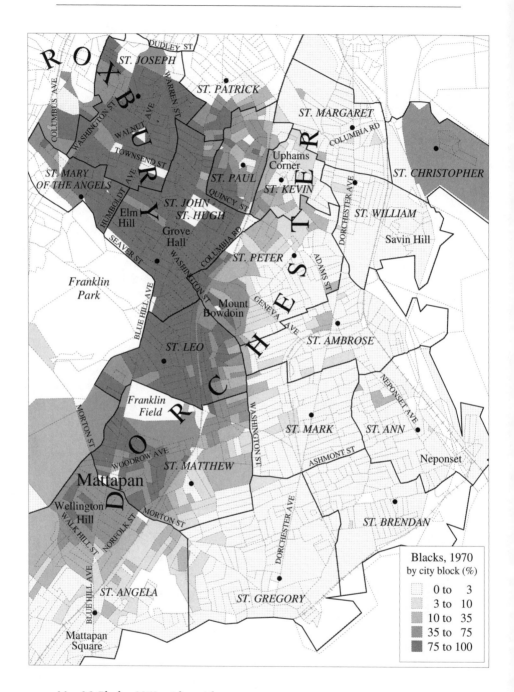

Map 16 Blacks, 1970, with parishes

it's this language—only a white guy could write this book?

Though racial succession transformed many Dorchester neighborhoods in succeeding decades, parish boundaries have continued to define ethnic borders. In 1970, as Map 16 illustrates, the western boundaries of St. Ambrose', St. Mark's, and St. Gregory's parishes separated areas of racial change from predominantly white neighborhoods. In 1980 and 1990, as Maps 17 and 18 show, these same three boundaries separated all-black neighborhoods from racially integrated neighborhoods. And the western edges of three parishes—St. Margaret in 1960–1990, St. William in 1980–1990, and St. Brendan in 1990—marked the boundary between integrated districts and areas that remained overwhelmingly nonblack.

Many parish boundaries, of course, coincide with major streets or with railway tracks. But this fact is not sufficient to explain the relationship between parochial and racial borders. In 1970–1990, for example, Washington Street was most secure as a racial boundary where it coincided with St. Mark's parish border. North of St. Mark's Parish, large numbers of African Americans had crossed Washington Street and settled in St. Peter's Parish by 1970, when St. Mark's territory remained nearly all-white. In 1980 and 1990, when a substantial section of St. Peter's Parish was predominantly black, blocks in St. Mark's Parish were either racially mixed or still white. Meanwhile, south of St. Mark's, overwhelmingly white blocks persisted in St. Gregory's Parish in the area west of Washington Street.

The border that separated the predominantly white parishes of St. William and St. Margaret from areas of racial change offers additional evidence for the significance of parish boundaries. St. William's entire western boundary—which conformed, with near-exact precision, to the racial border in 1980—is made up entirely of minor streets. Except where they coincided with St. William's boundary, these streets presented no hurdle to black settlement. Similar minor streets made up the southwestern boundary of St. Margaret's Parish, a parish line that in 1970 and 1980 effectively divided the predominantly white blocks of St. Margaret's from adjacent, racially integrated blocks in St. Kevin's Parish. And the railroad tracks that form the western boundary of St. Margaret's Parish also proved, on their own, an ineffectual racial barrier; in every parish south of St. Margaret's, blacks had begun settling east of the railroad line by 1970. Yet, as Maps 16 and 17 demonstrate, St. Margaret maintained a racial border at this parish boundary in 1970 and 1980.

Parish boundaries are more than the rail lines and streets that they

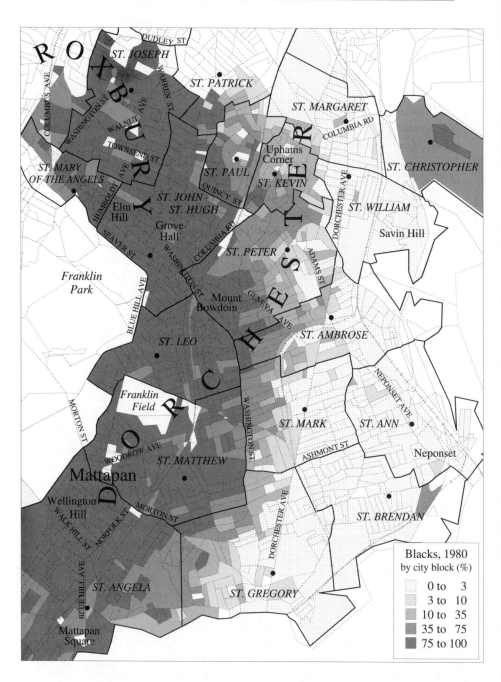

Map 17 Blacks, 1980, with parishes

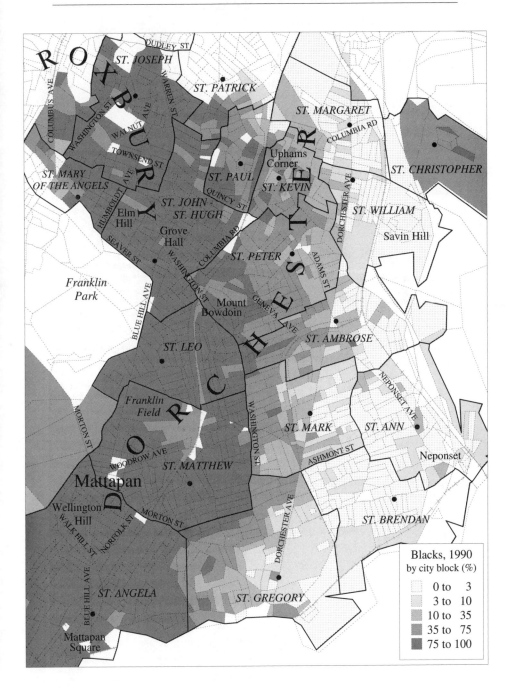

Map 18 Blacks, 1990, with parishes

follow. The trolley tracks that pass through St. Ambrose' and St. Mark's parishes form the western boundary of St. Brendan's. These tracks presented little obstacle to black settlement in St. Ambrose' and St. Mark's parishes in 1980 and 1990, yet they coincided with a sharp racial border along St. Brendan's western boundary. At its northern edge, St. Brendan's Parish also maintained a firm racial boundary: Ashmont Street, a strong barrier to black settlement in St. Brendan's Parish in 1980 and 1990, had been crossed easily by blacks settling in St. Gregory's Parish. Parish boundaries, it appears, independently affect patterns of white resistance and racial change.

Parish Centers

The parish's central structures also help coordinate neighborhood attachments. As the institutional core of the parish, the church (and, often, the school) can anchor white Catholic families in the immediate vicinity, even when whites elsewhere in the parish have moved away. By offering visible and active evidence of its continued commitment to the neighborhood, the church building itself helps solve a coordination problem for white families who might otherwise leave their homes early in the process of ethnic change. Though Catholic families throughout a given parish may be indistinguishable in terms of culture, education, income, and housing stock, clear differences occasionally emerge in their behavior—differences that can be attributed only to their proximity to the parish church. These differences, which helped determine patterns of Jewish settlement in the first half of the century, have helped shape patterns of black settlement in the second half.

In 1960, as Map 8 shows, St. Paul's Church anchored a district of white blocks that was surrounded on all sides by blocks with substantial African-American populations. While a large black community had settled in the southwestern corner of the parish and while blacks were moving onto streets at the northern and eastern edges of the parish, streets nearest the church remained at least 90 percent white. St. John's and St. Joseph's churches, located in parishes where racial change was more advanced, identified the only sections of their respective parishes that remained predominantly white in 1960. And St. Mary of the Angels' Church marked the boundary between three blocks that remained all-white in 1960 and blocks where many black families had already settled.

In 1960, the overwhelmingly black district in Roxbury was centered at the margins of St. Joseph's, St. John's, and St. Mary of the Angels' parishes—and it was bounded by the three parish churches.

Though the area of black settlement in Dorchester and Roxbury had greatly expanded in 1970, St. Paul's Church continued to exert its influence, as Map 16 suggests. Streets in the southwestern section of St. Paul's Parish were almost all-black, but streets elsewhere in the parish—streets near the church and streets beyond the church—held many nonblack residents. That pattern remained substantially intact in 1980 and 1990, as Maps 17 and 18 show. At the parish center in 1970, two blocks, one containing the church and the other immediately adjacent, remained overwhelmingly white. Similarly, in St. Kevin's Parish, streets near the church remained predominantly nonblack in 1970 and 1980, while African Americans settled in the southwestern section of the parish. St. Mary of the Angels' Church also maintained a racial boundary, separating a predominantly African-American district from blocks that were racially mixed.

St. Peter's Church, like St. Paul's, maintained a strong racial border within its parish territory. As blacks settled along the western and northern edges of St. Peter's Parish in 1970, the large section of the parish near the church remained virtually all-white. In 1970 and 1980, few blacks lived on streets near the church and in the section of the parish extending east and south from the church. Though reduced in size in 1990, this predominantly nonblack district remained, still oriented to the church site. Throughout these years, the area of densest black settlement was confined to the western edge of the parish.

St. Matthew's and St. Angela's churches, standing at the boundary between Jewish and Catholic districts since the 1920s, stood in 1970 on the frontier of racial change. As African Americans moved into once-Catholic sections of St. Matthew's and St. Angela's, both church buildings identified streets where white attachments were strongest. The pattern of black settlement, which for three miles had progressed block-by-block up Blue Hill Avenue, had shifted course upon reaching St. Angela's Church. In 1970, as Map 16 shows, white families remained in the district immediately around the church, as blacks moved instead onto side streets to the west and east. "From the information I gathered," Yona Ginsberg wrote in the early 1970s, "it seems that the area around the church remained pretty much white."[42] St. Matthew's Church, too, anchored a distinct cluster of blocks that remained overwhelmingly white in 1970, as large numbers of blacks settled on streets to the west, north, east, and southwest of this white Catholic core.

As St. Angela's Church temporarily blocked the black migration up Blue Hill Avenue in 1970, other Catholic churches have shaped patterns of black settlement in 1980 and 1990. Racial change, which had once followed a steady path through the Jewish neighborhoods along Blue Hill Avenue, has taken a different route through Dorchester's Catholic districts. Columbia Road—running from Franklin Park, along the northern border of St. Peter's Parish, then through the centers of St. Kevin's and St. Margaret's parishes—had become a major corridor for black migration by 1970. But black settlement along Columbia Road came to an abrupt halt at St. Margaret's Parish. The parish border proved an effective barrier in 1970 and 1980. In 1990, St. Margaret's Church, standing at the corner of Columbia Road and Dorchester Avenue, continued to anchor the parish's considerable white population.

Four other Catholic churches stand on Dorchester Avenue. In 1990, when blacks had moved onto many streets east of Dorchester Avenue, these churches marked out the areas where whites demonstrated the strongest attachments to their neighborhoods. Blacks lived along the northern, western, and southern edges of St. William's Parish in 1990, but the parish church itself bordered a set of overwhelmingly nonblack streets. A similar pattern is evident in St. Ambrose' Parish in both 1980 and 1990. In St. Mark's Parish, too, the church in 1990 anchored a central cluster of predominantly white streets east of Dorchester Avenue, even as black families settled to the north and south of that cluster. Even stronger patterns of white resistance are evident in St. Mark's Parish in 1980 and St. Gregory's Parish in 1980 and 1990, where white families remained in large numbers not only on the eastern side of Dorchester Avenue but also on the western side, on streets centered on the parish church. In each parish, the white residents who have been most resistant to displacement have been those who lived near the parish church. The viability and location of the institutional core is at the root of the Catholic attachment to urban neighborhoods.

St. Leo's Parish

In Dorchester there was one large district whose Catholic residents left as quickly as the residents of any Jewish neighborhood. This was the

Catholic section of St. Leo's Parish, which, as Map 15 shows, was located on the eastern side of the parish territory. Relative to other Dorchester Catholics, there was nothing distinctive about St. Leo's parishioners. As Maps 5–7 suggest, on socioeconomic terms St. Leo's Catholic district resembled other Catholic areas. Culturally, nothing set St. Leo's parishioners apart. Their level of homeownership and the nature of their housing stock did not distinguish them. The absence of a parish school surely weakened St. Leo's Parish, but there were other parishes that lacked schools.

Just one fact made St. Leo's Parish unique in 1960: of the seventeen parish churches in Dorchester and upper Roxbury, only St. Leo's Church was surrounded on all sides by Jewish homes.[43] St. Leo's parishioners were physically disconnected from their church. Once African Americans began to settle in the Mount Bowdoin–Franklin Park–Franklin Field district in the late 1950s and 1960s, St. Leo's Church stood in a racially changing neighborhood. For its white parishioners, the church became a reminder of the immediacy of instability and neighborhood change. "The parish geography is predominantly black," Rev. Richard Craig, a curate in St. Leo's Parish, noted in November 1968, "although the major proportion of parishioners is white, approx. 75% white."[44]

By 1970, as Map 16 illustrates, St. Leo's Church was located in an overwhelmingly black district. The great majority of St. Leo's white parishioners, living near Washington Street at the eastern edge of the parish, had severed all their ties to the church. For them, the church had become an alien institution, locked in a hostile and dangerous black ghetto. Most of the "whites on the Washington St. end of the parish," Rev. Joseph A. Gaudet wrote in June 1971, "attend church at other parishes in Dorchester."[45] Unlike Catholics in other parishes, St. Leo's Catholics did not live on streets surrounding an institutional core that could help coordinate their neighborhood attachments. Attending another church was not a permanent solution.

Separated from their church physically and socially, most of St. Leo's parishioners had already moved from the parish by 1970. Since 1962, St. Leo's Catholic population had declined from 5,810 to 1,100.[46] Few whites remained in the eastern section of the parish, once a white Catholic enclave. In Catholic neighborhoods north and south of St. Leo's—in St. Kevin's, St. Peter's, and St. Matthew's parishes—racial change was just beginning in 1970. But in St. Leo's Parish, as Map 16 illustrates, racial succession had already entered its final stages. Of the twenty blocks east of the railroad tracks that were overwhelmingly black in 1970, seventeen were located in St. Leo's Parish. The white Catholics of St. Leo's were leaving as rapidly and with as little violence as the Jews who lived up Blue Hill Avenue. In their flight, the Catholics of St. Leo's Parish demonstrated that a Catholic neighborhood without a central, anchoring institution could neither resist nor adapt to racial change.

Institutions build neighborhoods, and institutions forge paths of neighborhood change. Cultural differences cannot explain the behavior of St. Leo's Catholics. Patterns of Catholic neighborhood attachments—patterns that are evident throughout successive waves of Jewish and black settlement—are directly related to the location and strength of parish institutions. Within a given parish, proximity to the church itself affects residential behavior. And, between one parish and another, parish boundaries shape the decisions of families. While a synagogue or a black church can concentrate Jewish or black demand for housing in a specific neighborhood, neither institution can coordinate housing choices as effectively as a Catholic church.

Evidence from postwar Detroit collected by Thomas J. Sugrue indicates the general relevance of parish boundaries to explaining white resistance. "In Courville, the boundary of Saint Bartholomew's Parish—Seven Mile Road—remained unbreached until the mid-1960s, despite the fact that one of Detroit's oldest enclaves of blacks—Conant Gardens—was less than a mile away. Were you to drive through Conant Gardens, the Courville area, and across Seven Mile you would notice that the housing stock is almost identical. There are no natural or man-made barriers (hills, railroad tracks, etc.). Yet one section remained all white, while the other was increasingly black," Sugrue finds. "Likewise in the Courville area, Dequindre Avenue (a north-south street) remained a fiercely (and successfully) defended boundary through the 1950s and well into the 1960s. Dequindre was the southeastern boundary of Saint Rita's Parish." Sugrue emphasizes the role of neighborhood associations in mobilizing white resistance to racial change in Detroit. But, as he notes, neighborhood associations proved most effective in Catholic neighborhoods, where association boundaries often followed parish lines. In Detroit, in Boston, and in Chicago—where the Hyde Park–Kenwood Community Conference achieved little without the intervention of the University of Chicago—neighborhood associations appear to have successfully mobilized white resistance mainly in areas where parish boundaries and Catholic attachments were already strong.⁴⁷

The source of the Catholic parish's influence is not mystical or mysterious. Catholic churches successfully coordinate residential behavior because they restrict membership to local residents and because the church itself can make a long-term commitment to its neighborhood. As noted, three basic sets of rules sustain this institution: rules defining membership, rules rooting the church and the parish in a fixed location, and rules respecting a hierarchical structure of authority. On each of these dimensions, Catholic parishes differ in fundamental ways from synagogues. The inability of Jewish institutions to define and anchor neighborhoods is based, above all, in the rules that separate synagogue sites from members' homes, rules that make synagogues portable, and rules that locate institutional authority in the congregational membership.

Churches and synagogues alone do not constitute the whole constellation of local institutions. Most parish churches are bound closely to parochial schools and parish halls, and synagogues are part of a network of Jewish institutions that includes religious schools, day schools, and Jewish community centers. Beyond these clusters of ethnic and religious institutions lie social clubs, fraternal organizations, neighborhood bars, settlement houses, local gymnasiums, playgrounds, and, above all, public schools. Jewish children in Dorchester and upper Roxbury were more likely than Catholic children to attend public schools. While concerns with the Boston public schools exacerbated the Jewish exodus after the middle 1960s, I have located no evidence suggesting that Jewish out-migration before that time was related to the quality of schools. On the contrary, through the early 1960s, Jewish parents appear to have been satisfied with the Boston schools; indeed, at least according to anecdotal evidence, many of them moved to the suburbs despite their conviction that the suburban schools were inferior to the Boston schools.

Parochial schools, of course, contributed to the attractiveness of the parish center for Catholic families. Until the 1960s, however, parochial schools were not necessary for coordinating neighborhood loyalties. Even in white Catholic neighborhoods with parochial schools, a majority of elementary school children in 1960 relied on public schools.⁴⁸ Two churches that lacked schools altogether—St. Paul's and St. Mary of the Angels'—proved sturdy enough to help hold the boundary between Jewish and Catholic districts through the 1950s and have been strong enough since then to mark the outer bounds of Roxbury's over-whelmingly black neighborhoods. St. Leo's parishioners, whose parish also lacked a school, maintained a sufficiently strong Catholic presence around their church to shape early patterns of Jewish settlement in Dor-chester. Since the 1960s, the decline of Boston's public schools—a de-cline aggravated by the court-ordered dissolution of neighborhood school districts and by white resistance to racial desegregation—has in-creased the importance of parochial schools in sustaining a white Catho-lic population in Dorchester. But the church remains the central institu-tion in the parish. In districts whose residual white populations have been made up overwhelmingly of the elderly and whose schools have been predominantly nonwhite, Catholics have been much more likely than Jews to remain.

In characterizing the rules that define Catholic and Jewish institu-tions, I draw on evidence from schools and community centers as well as from churches and synagogues. But the territorial parish and the syna-gogue are the preeminent institutions in their respective communities. Though a parish may take pride in its school, no parish exists without a church. And the rules that define schools, community centers, and par-ish halls are derived from the rules that define churches and synagogues.

The synagogue is a product of exile. In the Diaspora, Jewish commu-nal authorities established synagogues as meeting-places and as houses of study and prayer. Synagogues in medieval and early modern Europe possessed no power to compel membership, and rabbis played no neces-sary role in Jewish worship. Communities supported rabbis as religious teachers and scholars, not as clergy. Transplanted to the United States in the eighteenth and nineteenth centuries, synagogues flourished in the absence of communal supervision, becoming themselves the locus of modern Jewish community life. "We have no ecclesiastical authorities in America, other than the congregations themselves," Isaac Leeser, a Phila-delphia rabbi, wrote in 1844. "Each congregation makes its own rules for its government, and elects its own minister, who is appointed without any ordination."[49] A Jewish congregation exists whenever ten men gather with a Torah to worship: there is no need for a rabbi, no permission to seek from a hierarchy.[50] The rule is as old as the synagogue itself. Because of this rule, which is deeply embedded in Jewish legal tradition, congre-gations have assumed the authority to take actions that are otherwise not sanctioned in Talmud or halacha. Since the nineteenth century, this con-

gregational autonomy has been fully realized in a coherent, though un-
stated, set of rules and customs.

Catholicism does not recognize congregational autonomy. Though lay
Catholics helped organize and govern early American churches, bishops
and priests rejected this lay-trustee system. By the end of the nineteenth
century, according to Jay P. Dolan, "the Irish tradition of an authoritarian
clergy and a deferential laity had become the normative model in the
United States."[51] As the halachic rule recognizing the authority of Jewish
congregations facilitated the development of a body of rules that bear
little relation to traditional teachings, so the hierarchical structure of the
Catholic Church has buttressed the authority of canon law. Catholic
churches do not emerge whenever a group of Catholics worship together,
and no group of Catholics can consecrate the Blessed Sacrament without
the agency of an ordained priest. The territorial parish, the basic unit of
the Catholic Church since the fifth century, assumed its current form
with the Council of Trent in the sixteenth century and was the foundation of Catholic organization in colonial America. The proliferation of
national (or ethnic) parishes in the United States overlaid but did not
supplant the system of territorial parishes. As John T. McGreevy argues,
even national parishes have tended to serve distinct territorial enclaves.[52]

Many of the rules that effectively bind Jewish and Catholic institutions
do not appear in books. This is especially true of Jewish rules. Codes of
Jewish law offer little insight into actual practice. "It is a known fact that
these laws were not all strictly observed, even in the earliest synagogues
on record," William G. Tachau argued in the 1920s, "and in more recent
times, especially since the early part of the nineteenth century, they have
been more honored in the breach than in the observance." Given the
circumstances of Jewish life in the Diaspora, where Jews have often been
confined to ghettos and have always lived in predominantly non-Jewish
lands, the halachic mandate that synagogues be the most prominent
structures in a city or town has rarely been followed. And Jewish law
never anticipated the possibility that Jews might voluntarily move away
from a synagogue building. The rules that matter are those that actually
constrain institutional behavior. Consequently, the fullest rendering of
these rules appears not in canon law and halacha but in the histories of
the institutions themselves.[53]

II

Parish and Congregation

At St. Peter's first "lawn party," Rev. Peter Ronan presides from the back porch of his rectory. Founded in 1872, the Dorchester parish had become one of the largest and most prosperous in the archdiocese by the turn of the century. Parishioners, led by Father Ronan, had built a rectory, a convent, a school, and a monumental pudding-stone church. By 1910, five full parishes and portions of two others covered the area that had originally been granted to St. Peter's. *(Photograph courtesy of St. Peter's Parish.)*

4

Jubilee Celebrations, 1910

For two of Boston's most substantial religious institutions, 1910 was a year for celebration. Each remembered its past, each was proud of its present, and each looked forward expectantly to the years to come. The jubilee histories that they published coincided in time, as their origins had coincided in time in 1858, decades before. Yet neither institution in 1910 was recalling a founding in 1858. St. Peter's Parish published its history to honor its pastor on the fortieth anniversary of his ordination as a Catholic priest. And the Jewish congregation Mishkan Tefila was celebrating the fiftieth anniversary of its founding, remembered as 1860.[1] Looking back to the days of their grandfathers and mothers and their own younger selves, the generation celebrating in 1910 still possessed their history in living memory. They recalled two different pasts, emblematic of their different ways of organizing and building institutions.

Mishkan Israel and Shaaray Tefila

Mishkan Tefila had, in truth, three beginnings. Its history began as that of two separate congregations. The older of the original groups, Mishkan Israel, was the third Jewish congregation established in Boston. The other original congregation, Shaaray Tefila, was the city's sixth Jewish congregation.[2] In 1895 the two merged, becoming Mishkan Tefila.

Mishkan Israel was founded in 1858 by a small group of immigrant families. The only other congregations in the city at the time were Ohabei Shalom and Adath Israel. Of the three groups, Mishkan Israel was, for many years, the smallest and least active. Until the early 1870s, Mishkan

Israel worshiped in a series of makeshift halls in the lower South End, a tenement district that was the center of Boston's small Central European Jewish community. "Trains passed our windows to and fro continually," one member wrote, recalling an early hall, "and on *Rosh Hashona,* while the venerable Joseph Barin sounded the *Tekio Gedolu* on the Shofer, it was usually re-echoed by the shrill blast of the engine from without."[3]

In August 1871 the congregation dedicated a synagogue on Ash Street. Members of Mishkan Israel marched in a procession through the streets of the neighborhood, "the elders reverently carrying the sacred scrolls, and the members and pupils of the Sabbath School following in line." The men bearing the Torah scrolls walked "under a red velvet canopy." When the procession arrived at the Ash Street location, the chairman of the building committee "presented the keys of the building" to the president of the congregation. Then "the sacred scrolls were borne in." The congregation's leaders brought the scrolls in front of the ark, where the rabbi offered a prayer dedicating the new synagogue, "after which a circuit of the tabernacle was made seven times, different prominent members of the congregation being honored at bearing the law at each circuit." Once the procession had ended, the congregants listened to speeches in English and German.[4]

In the early 1870s, each of Boston's Jewish congregations worshiped in similar fashion, following traditional customs and rituals, and their synagogues were located within two or three blocks of one another in the lower South End. Not until 1874, when Solomon Schindler was chosen rabbi of Adath Israel by a membership committed to change, did Reform Judaism arrive in Boston. In introducing reforms to Adath Israel, Schindler encountered some resistance: fifteen of the congregation's forty members left in protest. "Step by step, however, he worked his way into the confidence of his parishioners," and, by 1875, Adath Israel's reforms were being imitated by the larger congregation of Ohabei Shalom. As testament to its growing strength, Adath Israel moved in 1885 out of its Pleasant Street building and into a new, much larger temple at the corner of Columbus Avenue and Northampton Street—one mile away from Pleasant Street, at the opposite edge of the South End and near the growing suburban district of Roxbury. In moving, Adath Israel became the first Jewish congregation in the city to relocate its house of worship from one neighborhood to another. Two years later, Ohabei Shalom also moved from the lower South End to the upper South End, dedicating a church on Union Park Street as its new temple in 1887.[5]

In the middle 1870s, as the city's two oldest congregations began adopting religious reforms, Shaaray Tefila, a new Orthodox congregation, was established in the lower South End. Like Mishkan Israel, it resisted the reforms that were transforming Adath Israel and Ohabei Shalom. After worshiping in a series of temporary halls, Shaaray Tefila acquired its own synagogue in 1885. The structure was "the synagogue on Pleasant street lately occupied by the congregation Adath Israel."[6]

Shaaray Tefila dedicated the Pleasant Street Synagogue in February 1885. At the dedication, "the officers and others appointed by the congregation entered with the holy scrolls of the law and advanced toward the holy ark." A prayer was offered in front of the ark, then "the procession moved seven times around the synagogue, while the chanter recited verses from the Psalms." The building sat two hundred persons, with women "seated in a gallery surrounding three sides of the church, being scrupulously separated from the males."[7]

St. Peter's Parish

Just one year earlier, in February 1884, a much different house of worship was dedicated in another part of Boston. St. Peter's Church was erected on Meeting House Hill, at the historic center of Dorchester. The parish included the entire northern half of Dorchester, a growing suburban district into which large numbers of Irish Catholics were moving in the late nineteenth century. Meeting House Hill was aptly named. The white clapboard church of the First Parish in Dorchester, meeting-house of the oldest church in present-day Boston, stood at its peak. Organized in 1630, the First Parish was the only church in the town of Dorchester until the early nineteenth century. "For nearly two hundred years," members of the church recalled in the 1890s, "the First Parish was the town of Dorchester, and within the recollection of many of us the clock on Meeting House Hill was called the town clock." In 1870, when Dorchester was annexed by Boston, Meeting House Hill was still a center of town life: next to the church on Dorchester Common stood the Mather Elementary School, descendant of the oldest public school in the nation, and Lyceum Hall, built for public forums and community gatherings.[8]

The area's Catholic community traced its origins to 1858, when three women organized a Sunday school for Catholic children. There was no Catholic church in Dorchester that year; all of the town was included in the parish of Sts. Peter and Paul, whose church was located in South

Boston.[9] Most of Dorchester's Catholics traveled the substantial distance to the church in South Boston, though a few occasionally attended Mass at St. Joseph's, which stood nearby in upper Roxbury.[10]

In December 1862 the parish of Sts. Peter and Paul was divided, and a new parish, St. Gregory, was created. St. Gregory's Parish included the towns of Dorchester and Milton and part of Quincy. Its church was built in Lower Mills, the southernmost section of Dorchester. Soon after the creation of St. Gregory's, its pastor, Father Thomas R. McNulty, began to travel regularly to the Meeting House Hill section of Dorchester to serve the Catholic families living in the northern section of his parish. On Saturdays McNulty came to hear confessions in a room at Glover's Corner used for Sunday school classes. By 1869 he had established an informal mission on Meeting House Hill. McNulty "began to say Mass on Sundays in Lyceum Hall," and Sunday school classes were transferred to the hall.[11]

But Lyceum Hall could not serve indefinitely as a church and schoolhouse, and the growing Catholic population of northern Dorchester demanded more constant attention than a priest based in Lower Mills could offer. In 1872 McNulty agreed to cede a large portion of his territory for the creation of a new parish in northern Dorchester. John J. Williams, the bishop of Boston, established St. Peter's Parish that fall, appointing Peter Ronan, at the age of twenty-eight, as St. Peter's first pastor. In October, in Lyceum Hall, Father Ronan celebrated the parish's first Mass. Nearby, on Bowdoin Street, on land that Bishop Williams had purchased a year earlier, "the work of excavation had been begun" for a proper church. McNulty had already approved plans for a brick church, comparable in size to his own church in Lower Mills. The building, designed to seat seven hundred people, reflected the modest hopes of a young parish.[12]

Ronan, though, was not one who hoped or planned modestly. Setting aside McNulty's plans, he decided to build a church on a grand scale. The church, he resolved, would be built of stone and would be designed by Patrick Charles Keely, one of the leading church architects of the era. As Susan L. Emery wrote, "These proposals seemed to the prudent Bishop, and to the parishioners as well, very audacious on the part of so young a priest." Reluctantly, the bishop gave his consent, in part because of Ronan's willingness to supervise personally the construction of the church, "at a much less cost and in a better manner than if built by a contractor," and in part because of the small miracle of the land itself. It was not earth alone that the earlier excavation had uncovered. "The new pastor was quick to realize the value of the quarry of Roxbury pudding stone, which ran in a massive ledge along the edge of his property," according to Emery, "and he determined that it should furnish the material of which the structure was to be built."[13]

Ronan's project was startling in its boldness. There were only two other Catholic churches in Dorchester and upper Roxbury in 1872: both St. Gregory's Church and St. Joseph's Church were built of brick, modest in size, and simple and plain in design. What Ronan proposed to erect on Meeting House Hill was a majestic structure. St. Peter's Church declared that the Irish had arrived in Dorchester, indeed that they had arrived in Boston and in America and that they had come to stay. The stone church spoke with authority to the white clapboard First Parish Church, its ancient neighbor on Meeting House Hill. It spoke with a confidence and self-assurance that the two older brick churches could not muster.

Two thousand people gathered on Meeting House Hill in August 1873 to lay St. Peter's cornerstone. The first Mass was celebrated in the lower church on Easter Sunday 1875; that autumn, Ronan was assigned his first curate. The main body of the upper church was finished nine years later, and, in February 1884, St. Peter's Church was dedicated. Archbishop Williams officiated at the ceremonies. "The church was crowded to repletion, the people having begun to assemble as early as nine o'clock" for ceremonies that began that morning at 10:30. At that hour, "the procession of acolytes, priests, and the Archbishop entered the Sanctuary and proceeded around the exterior and interior of the edifice, the priests chanting the psalms and prayers of the ritual, His Grace meanwhile sprinkling the walls with holy water," the *Pilot* reported. Archbishop Williams, assisted by several other clergymen, then celebrated the Solemn Pontifical Mass, accompanied by a hundred-voice choir and a forty-piece orchestra.[14]

In 1891 construction of the church came to an end. A delicate turret was added to the right side of the church that year, and, at the left side, topped by finials, "the grand square tower of St. Peter's Church, visible for many miles around, was completed." Next to the church, a brick rectory of twenty-four rooms had been built in the 1880s. The dream of Father Ronan was realized. A survey of Catholic churches in New England, published in the 1890s, paid tribute to the church on Meeting

House Hill. "No technical description can do more than faintly suggest the grandeur of St. Peter's church, which is a poem of architectural beauty," the book stated. "On the bleak heights a massive temple rose like a dream—rose, as it were, out of the earth like a prayer taking shape and carved in stone, a perfect majesty of noiseless power."[15]

Mishkan Tefila

Miles away from suburban Dorchester, in the tenement district of Boston's lower South End, the Jewish congregations of Mishkan Israel and Shaaray Tefila were worshiping in their two modest buildings in 1891. Twenty years had passed since Mishkan Israel had dedicated its wooden structure on Ash Street, and the congregation remained small. Shaaray Tefila, which had dedicated its Pleasant Street Synagogue in 1885, was "in a flourishing condition," Solomon Schindler wrote in the late 1880s, "counting about eighty members, who are already looking for more appropriate quarters." For a brief period, Shaaray Tefila had been served by two rabbis. Marcus Klatschken, who had served the congregation since 1885, was joined in 1889 by Hyman S. Shoher. In 1890 both men left the congregation; a new rabbi was hired. Rabbi Shoher did not move far, though. He left Shaaray Tefila for a position a few blocks away at Mishkan Israel.[16]

At Mishkan Israel, Shoher could encourage efforts to merge the two institutions. The *Boston Jewish Chronicle* reported in the summer of 1891 that leaders of the two congregations had met and "discussed the feasibility of consolidating the two societies, and forming one of sufficient strength to enable them to procure a suitable building for a place of worship." Eventually, "after a number of conferences," according to Abraham G. Daniels, "a plan for amalgamation was proposed which met with the mutual approval of the members of both congregations." The Commonwealth of Massachusetts granted the new charter in 1895. The name chosen for the reorganized congregation, "Mishkan Tefila," reflected its dual origins.[17]

The Shawmut Avenue Synagogue

After two years without a satisfactory home, Mishkan Tefila purchased a brick church, the former South End Tabernacle, in October 1897.[18] The structure, at the corner of Shawmut Avenue and Madison Street, was located only a few blocks from the temple dedicated by Adath Israel in 1885. As Adath Israel had done twelve years earlier, Mishkan Tefila in 1897 broke decisively out of its original neighborhood when it acquired the Shawmut Avenue structure—moving from the congested lower South End to the district straddling the upper South End and lower Roxbury. Bowfront homes, built in the 1850s and 1860s by middle-class Protestants, lined the district's streets and elegant parks. Writing in 1898, a settlement-house worker observed that "several of the squares here— though almost entirely deserted by their old residents—are still out-wardly as pleasant places of abode as can be found within the main city."[19]

The congregation remodeled the building in the summer of 1898 and dedicated it in September. At the start of the dedication ceremony, the president entered the synagogue and received keys from the chairman of the congregation's building committee. "A procession of the members, bearing the holy scrolls, and the officers of the congregation" followed the president into the building, the *Globe* reported. "When the proces-sion arrived at the ark the scrolls were presented to the oldest members, who made a circuit of the center seats of the synagogue while a well-known Hebrew prayer was chanted." The scrolls were placed in the ark at the conclusion of the procession, and the eternal light was kindled. Rabbi Shoher offered some remarks in German; additional speeches were made by the rabbis of Ohabei Shalom and Adath Israel.[20]

Changing Neighborhoods

Mishkan Tefila flourished and grew in the Shawmut Avenue Synagogue, but many members soon came to regard the location of the building as unsatisfactory. The district that in 1897 promised to attract large num-bers of Jews was instead becoming the center of a growing African-American community. In the spring of 1903, Adath Israel sold its own temple to a black church and set up temporary quarters in a hall in another part of Boston. By then, some of Mishkan Tefila's members had begun to consider moving their synagogue as well. But they had first to contend with the strong opposition of their rabbi. As the *Jewish Advocate* later noted, "It was the work of Rabbi Shoher that prevented for a time the radical members of the congregation from selling the Synagogue to colored Baptists for a church." By 1904 the battle over the location of the synagogue had been joined.[21]

The growing sentiment to sell the Shawmut Avenue Synagogue represented a profound challenge to Orthodoxy. Converting a synagogue into a Christian church is forbidden by Jewish law.[22] But Rabbi Shoher's power to prevent the sale of the synagogue was severely circumscribed. Like all rabbis, he had been hired by his congregation as a teacher, as one trained to provide spiritual guidance. Though he could argue with his congregation's leaders, he could not stop them from going forward with their plans. Early in 1905, it became clear to Shoher that the leaders of Mishkan Tefila intended to act against his judgment. His congregation, having demonstrated the irrelevance of his authority, accepted his resignation. "Spiritual leadership of my former congregation was made impossible," he explained, "when they departed from the footsteps of the righteous."[23]

By February 1905, leaders of Mishkan Tefila had begun discussing the sale of their synagogue building with leaders of the Twelfth Baptist Church, an African-American congregation. The two sides reached agreement in the spring of 1906, and Mishkan Tefila vacated the structure in October. After just a few years in its Shawmut Avenue Synagogue, the congregation "had outgrown its outer shell," Abraham G. Daniels recalled. "With the extension of the city southward the members had drifted thither and a new Temple was sought that would meet the growing requirements."[24]

But not all members had drifted southward: some opposed the congregation's move, and not just for religious reasons. Many of the Jews who still resided in the upper South End and lower Roxbury had hoped to retain the Shawmut Avenue building as a synagogue for their neighborhood. When it became clear that Mishkan Tefila intended to sell the structure to the Twelfth Baptist Church, "intense discussion as to the proper accommodations for the Jewish residents in that district was aroused." In September 1906 Jews remaining in the upper South End and lower Roxbury founded a new congregation, Atereth Israel, and rented a room on Northampton Street.[25]

The Moreland Street Temple

In March 1907, after worshiping for several months in a rented hall near Dudley Street, Mishkan Tefila acquired its new temple. Formerly the Immanuel Congregational Church, the structure was located "in a refined residential location," at the corner of Moreland and Copeland streets, in the Dudley Street district of upper Roxbury. Few Jews lived in the immediate area. The site was located midway along a two-mile route that ran from the congregation's old synagogue, in the upper South End, to the handsome new synagogue dedicated the preceding fall by Congregation Adath Jeshurun, in the suburban Blue Hill Avenue–Grove Hall district. The granite structure featured a steeple and high, peaked roofs and gables, with stained-glass windows facing both Moreland and Copeland streets. The main sanctuary contained an organ, room for a choir, and cushioned pews divided by two aisles. For the second time in ten years and over considerable opposition, the congregation had relocated into a new neighborhood.[26]

Mishkan Tefila dedicated the Moreland Street Temple in May 1907. The congregation had prospered and "grown prodigiously," Solomon Schindler wrote in the dedication booklet—recalling his visit to the little Orthodox synagogue on Ash Street thirty-three years before, when he first arrived in Boston—"and will now assemble in a magnificent stone structure ornamented with a high steeple, and situated in a neighborhood which at that time would have been called 'out of town.'" Boston Mayor John F. Fitzgerald joined a congressman and two Protestant ministers at the dedication ceremonies. As a children's band played, the procession marched through the main doors of the temple, led by "the 100 or more Sabbath school children" of the congregation. "The children were followed by the cantor, Rev. Wolf Magid, officers of the congregation and other Jewish divines bearing the scrolls," the *Globe* reported. Those carrying the scrolls gathered in front of the ark as the chairman of the building committee presented "the keys of the building" to the president of the congregation. Then the scrolls were placed in the ark and "the eternal light was lit." Several prominent guests delivered addresses. The exercises concluded with the entire assembly rising to sing "America."[27]

From 1905 until 1910, Congregation Mishkan Tefila conducted its affairs without a permanent rabbi. Setting their own direction, the congregation began to introduce changes to traditional Orthodox practice, in the process constructing what became Conservative Judaism. With its move into the Moreland Street Temple, Mishkan Tefila immediately introduced "family pews," ending the traditional practice of seating men and women in separate sections of the sanctuary. The congregation decided "to discontinue the German language in its pulpit" and adopted "the Confirmation Rite for boys and girls." Even the congregation's decision to call its house of worship a "temple" rather than a "synagogue" reflected its drift from traditional Orthodoxy. The *Boston Advocate,* the city's weekly Jewish newspaper, recognized "the birth of a new movement in our midst" with the dedication of the Moreland Street Temple. "Though the tendency seems towards Reform of which Adath Israel is the exemplar, we do not believe that the future of Judaism lies that way," the editors of the *Advocate* wrote in May 1907. "Rather the path is being bent like a bow, and that strength is being massed around a new form of conservatism new to Boston, but not new to the great Jewish centres of the Eastern seaboard. The changes in the Mishkan Tefila ritual and usages suggest this."[28]

In August 1910 Mishkan Tefila placed an advertisement in the *Jewish Advocate,* announcing that it was seeking a rabbi—a "young man, modern orthodox, good speaker"—for the High Holy Days; in the advertisement, the congregation indicated that it would consider an "acceptable candidate" for a permanent position. The congregation invited Herman H. Rubenovitz to lead its holiday services that fall. "We are a conservative orthodox Congregation with one of the finest synagogs east of New York," the chairman of the temple's search committee wrote Rubenovitz that September, in extending the invitation. "We are splendidly located in a beautiful residential part of the city, in Roxbury, in the midst of a nice class of Yehudim [Jews]. There is an unusual opportunity for the right man in our Congregation." Rubenovitz, according to the *Advocate,* "made an excellent impression on the members of Mishkan Tefila." In October the congregation voted to offer him a three-year contract at an annual salary of $2,000. At the age of twenty-seven, Rubenovitz agreed to assume Mishkan Tefila's pulpit.[29]

Rubenovitz, a graduate of the Jewish Theological Seminary, promised to promote the cause of Conservative Judaism in his new congregation. In 1910, "outside of New York and Philadelphia, Jewish life was divided between the Orthodox and Reform groups and these were separated by a chasm that seemed unbridgeable," he later wrote. "On the one side was immobility and stagnation, on the other assimilation running riot." If traditional Judaism was to persist in the United States, he believed, it must accept the necessity of change. "A more aesthetic and dignified setting had to be given to the traditional synagogue service if the loyalty and support of our young people were to be won for it," he argued. As an American-trained rabbi two years out of the seminary, Herman H. Rubenovitz accepted the challenge of bringing the message of Conservative Judaism to New England. In November he was installed in the Moreland Street Temple.[30]

Double Jubilee

The next month Mishkan Tefila celebrated the fiftieth anniversary of its founding. Tracing its origins to 15 men who had established Mishkan Israel, the congregation in December 1910 boasted a membership of 171 families. Over the course of its history, Mishkan Tefila had demonstrated the ability to grow and move and prosper. An institution founded in an inner-city neighborhood now worshiped in a respectable suburb. An institution established in a small room in a tenement house now owned an impressive stone temple. And an institution that had followed the traditional customs of an immigrant generation had now embraced progressive reforms. "Glancing backward, once more, to the very humble beginning of the congregation, figuratively speaking, in the Ghetto quarter of Boston, and with the vision of the beautiful Temple now before me," Abraham G. Daniels wrote in the jubilee history, "it is evident that the hand of God had guided the builders, or they would have built in vain."[31]

The jubilee history written that year was not a full history of the congregation. It was, rather, only a history of what Daniels and others in the congregation wished to remember. Infused with the idea that progress was constant and inevitable, it celebrated the dedication of each of the congregation's new buildings but said little about decisions to abandon old buildings and old neighborhoods. There was no mention at all of the traumatic events that had decisively shaped the congregation in the years immediately preceding 1910—no mention of the profound disappointment that the congregation must have felt soon after dedicating its Shawmut Avenue Synagogue, as its members began to realize that African Americans, not Jews, were moving into the neighborhood in which the new synagogue was located; no mention of the extended negotiations that led to the sale of the synagogue to the Twelfth Baptist Church; no mention of the sale itself; no mention of the many Jews who opposed the sale of the synagogue and, seceding from Mishkan Tefila, formed their own congregation; no mention of the several months that passed in 1906 and 1907 when Mishkan Tefila lacked a permanent home; no mention of the battle between the congregation and Rabbi Shoher, which led finally to the rabbi's resignation. Concerning all of these events, the jubilee history was silent. Though the congregation gladly recalled its moves from old neighborhoods and old synagogues, it passed over the painful side of its mobility. There were some matters that were best left unremembered, some truths that one did not speak.

The congregation devoted a full week to its Golden Jubilee celebration, decorating the sanctuary for the occasion. "The altar was covered with American flags and ornamented with bouquets of flowers," the *Jewish Advocate* reported. "Before the Ark was an electric sign, 'Welcome To Our Golden Jubilee.'" The ark itself held the congregation's greatest treasure, the Torah scrolls that gave sustenance and permanence to the Roxbury temple. This was the Law that God had entrusted to Moses on Mount Sinai. Reflecting on a half-century of progress, members of the congregation recalled their small synagogues on Ash Street and Pleasant Street and the larger synagogue that they had recently maintained on Shawmut Avenue. They remembered the joy they had felt when they dedicated each building, the elation when they arrived at Moreland Street three years before. They remembered the excitement when they entered a new synagogue, walking in procession, carrying the Torah scrolls through the doors, and placing the scrolls in the ark. Now, in 1910, as they committed themselves to religious reform, they still looked to the Torah for continuity. "From out of the great store house of Jewish tradition and Jewish literature," Rabbi Rubenovitz declared in his jubilee address, "we must draw material for the construction of the new Ark, within which we are to find our spiritual refuge."[32]

Rubenovitz paid tribute to the founders of the congregation. "There were a mere handful of them cut off from the great body of Israel, poor in worldly goods, driven here by dire necessity, yet notwithstanding all these handicaps, they set to work building Jewish institutions," he observed. "Without weighing chances for success, they banded together and established the nucleus of this congregation. That from such small and humble beginnings, with so many hostile forces arrayed against them, there should have developed this Mishkan Tefila of today, is indeed nothing short of [a] miracle." The title chosen by Daniels for his jubilee history, "From Ghetto to Temple," summarized in four words that miracle of Mishkan Tefila.[33]

The miracle of St. Peter's Parish was progress of a wholly different sort. Its jubilee history, written in 1910 by Susan L. Emery, was entitled *A Catholic Stronghold and Its Making*. There was nothing itinerant about St. Peter's Church. The parish had not traveled from an inner-city tenement district to a developing suburb. It had not dedicated a succession of church buildings or adopted a more liberal interpretation of its religion than that envisioned by its founders or supported by its religious leadership. St. Peter's Parish flourished on Meeting House Hill in 1910 as a stronghold of the faith. From its founding, it had been rooted and permanent. "Troops of sterling Catholic families" had moved into St. Peter's Parish after its formation, according to one of Father Ronan's assistant priests. "The parish, once small in numbers, but mighty in faith and works, has expanded and grown, and taken into its life all this new blood, until to-day it may be said to be one of the surest strongholds of Catholic Faith to be found in all this broad land."[34]

As the parish grew in population and strength, various sections of its territory had been taken for the establishment of new parishes. In 1910, five full parishes and portions of two others covered the area that had originally been granted to St. Peter's Parish. "Seventeen priests," as Emery noted, "now labor in the wide field where once Father Ronan toiled alone." Within the vastly reduced territory of St. Peter's Parish there were, in 1911, 11,500 parishioners and more than 2,300 children in the parish schools; in that year, 410 infants were baptized, 155 persons died, and 111 marriages were celebrated.[35]

Father Ronan had built well. Standing on Meeting House Hill was one of the most imposing sets of parochial buildings in the archdiocese. A four-story convent, completed in 1906, stood next to the church and rectory, and a large school building had been erected opposite them on Bowdoin Street in 1898. "Great emperors have preserved their memory by colossal tombs," Henry C. Towle, a parishioner, declared under an evening sky in June 1908, as the parish celebrated Ronan's Ruby Jubilee. "A great priest has chosen better in leaving as his monument buildings which, by perpetuating his memory as long as they stand, shall be used for the eternal salvation of all succeeding generations."[36]

In their jubilee celebrations, members of Mishkan Tefila and St. Peter's Parish drew strength from traditions that gave each institution permanence as well as promise for the days to come. It was their good fortune, they knew, to be living in an age of progress. What they shared in memory were modest, even obscure, beginnings. But while one institution had grown on a fixed spot of land, the other had grown by moving from place to place. While one had been guided by the long administration of the religious leader the members had come to honor, the other had been led by its own elected officers. For both institutions, the end was the same: progress. Yet the fact that progress was achieved along two separate paths would echo in their neighborhoods in the years to follow.

5
_____

Membership

Two hundred families belonged to Mishkan Tefila in the spring of 1913. Gathered in the vestry of the Moreland Street Temple on a Sunday afternoon, members of the congregation voted to reelect Rabbi Rubenovitz to a new five-year term. The contract increased his salary, which had been set at $2,000 in 1910, to $2,500 in 1913 and $2,750 in 1916. Since its jubilee celebration, the *Jewish Advocate* noted, the congregation had "made phenomenal progress." When the meeting ended, members returned to their homes. While some lived near the Moreland Street Temple, most lived elsewhere. More than one hundred families—a majority of the temple's membership—lived in either the Blue Hill Avenue–Grove Hall district or the Elm Hill district. Thirty families lived in Dorchester, and twenty-three families lived outside of Boston. Mishkan Tefila's membership was widely scattered, and its temple was not centrally located. All but a small minority of the congregation lived south of the temple. As they traveled home up Blue Hill Avenue or Warren Street, many of the temple's members passed the new synagogues of other congregations.[1]

St. Peter's Parish was supported by about three thousand families in 1913. The parish was defined by strict territorial boundaries. When they walked from their homes to their church, none of St. Peter's families passed another Catholic church. The church itself stood at the center of the parish. Since the early 1890s, Father Ronan had ceded outlying sections of his original parish territory for the formation and strengthening of various new parishes. "There is no better evidence of the great material success of your mission," one parishioner observed at the 1908 celebration for Ronan, "than that we, living on the eastern side of Dorchester Avenue, once the main land of your parish, are now merely the beach fringing one side of it." St. Peter's, which had originally included half of Dorchester, now served the dense Catholic population that had settled on and around Meeting House Hill.[2]

For generations, Catholics have recognized the relevance of parish boundaries for defining their communities. Even in the 1990s, boundaries can still matter. The line separating St. William's from St. Margaret's Parish was established by Father Ronan in 1893, when he created St. Margaret's Parish. The boundary runs down the middle of Mayfield and Romsey streets, two small streets lined with well-maintained modest homes. Recently, when Rev. Joseph Hennessey took me for a walk around St. Margaret's Parish, he showed me the house of a man who lives on Mayfield Street. The house stands across the street from this parishioner's boyhood home, where his mother still lives. The two homes are in separate parishes: he and his family attend St. Margaret's Church, while his mother still attends St. William's Church. In a traditional Catholic world, moving across the street could mean leaving your parents and your old community behind.

On the day that Father Hennessey showed me that home on Mayfield Street, he and I spent almost two hours walking around St. Margaret's Parish. He showed me grocery stores and bars and pointed out many homes, including the house where John McCormack, a former Speaker of the House of Representatives, used to live. We walked at a leisurely pace, for he frequently stopped to say hello to parishioners who were out for a walk or sitting on their front porches. After an hour of this, I grew concerned that I was taking up too much of Hennessey's time. When I asked him if he wanted to return to the rectory so he could get back to his work, he just smiled and told me that *this* was his work. Knowing his parish's streets and the people who lived on them was part of his responsibility as a priest in St. Margaret's Parish.

Few rabbis would assume such responsibility. Judaism is the religion of a specific ethnic group. Its places of worship and learning are essentially private institutions, and the leaders of these institutions do not walk the sidewalks of a neighborhood. Christianity exists in the public sphere. According to a 1950s textbook on canon law, "the Church is a society established by Jesus Christ with divine authority for all mankind."[3] Though the typical American urban priest does not aggressively seek converts, Catholic priests are inheritors of a tradition that obliges its

Membership 115

faithful to share the gospel with all people—with Gentile and Jew alike, as Paul taught two thousand years ago. Judaism, of course, depends on Jews alone for its survival.

Rules of membership distinguish Jewish from Catholic institutions in two basic ways. First, a parish boundary excludes Catholics who live beyond it; unlike a Jewish congregation, whose members can live miles from the synagogue, a Catholic parish is tightly bounded. Second, local institutional jurisdictions differ. Within its boundaries, the territorial parish possesses exclusive responsibility for all Catholics who do not identify with a national church. Synagogues enjoy no monopolies. Many Jewish congregations in Dorchester and Roxbury drew members from the same streets and the same districts.

There are exceptions to rules, and American Catholics in the 1990s understand that parish boundaries have become permeable. Until the 1960s, the Catholic Church regarded its territorial parishes as indistinguishable communities, subdivisions of the universal Church that existed because the Eucharist must be celebrated as a local event. It was that doctrine that undergirded territorial boundaries. If the only distinguishing feature of a parish was its place in a local community of Catholics, no reason existed for allowing people to join churches outside their parish. Since the Second Vatican Council, however, the Church hierarchy has recognized distinctions among parishes. One example of a reform that recognizes those differences is the vernacular Mass; another is the frequency with which Catholics now identify with churches not in their own parish.

The rules that governed Catholic life into the 1960s constrained Catholic decisions during the whole period of Jewish settlement in Roxbury and Dorchester and through the formative years of black settlement. Even today, canon law states that "as a general rule a parish is to be territorial."[4] Parish boundaries are still respected by most of Dorchester's Catholics, and Catholics everywhere often still seek permission from their own territorial parish before they receive the sacraments of record in another church.

Boundaries

Mishkan Tefila's membership, already dispersed in 1913, continued scattering in the 1910s and early 1920s. When the congregation assembled in the fall of 1925 to dedicate its new temple on Seaver Street, many members drove into Roxbury from the suburban town of Brookline. Their loyalty to the congregation was not based on the proximity of the synagogue to their homes. Of the forty-two men who sat on the congregation's board of directors, seventeen lived in Roxbury and seventeen lived in the Brookline area. Moses Mishel, the president of Mishkan Tefila in 1925, was himself a resident of Brookline. The temple building stood on Roxbury's Elm Hill, but this was not a Roxbury congregation. "Boston is indebted to you—Boston Jewry is indebted to you," Mishel stated in his address to the congregation at the dedication ceremony. "You have erected a great monument to the Jews of Boston and New England." Each week that fall, Mishkan Tefila sent a bus out to Brookline to pick up members' children for Hebrew school classes.[5]

Jewish institutions do not set territorial boundaries to their members' homes. An 1898 observer noted that the South End's Ohabei Shalom "draws its large and well-to-do congregation almost wholly from other sections of the city." The Hecht Neighborhood House, a Jewish community center and settlement house that had stood in the West End since the early 1890s, observed the same membership rules as the city's synagogues. Though it described itself in 1927 as "all that its name implies, a house which exists for the neighborhood in which it stands," the Hecht Neighborhood House reported that sixty-seven of its members commuted to the West End from Roxbury and Dorchester in the 1928–1929 year.[6]

Even Orthodox synagogues—whose members respect traditional prohibitions against driving on the Sabbath and holidays—do not restrict membership to local residents. Atereth Israel, the Orthodox congregation established in 1906 by former members of Mishkan Tefila, was characterized by a settlement-house worker in the early 1910s as a congregation that was "not wholly local." Agudath Achim, a group that described itself as strictly Orthodox, reported that it had moved its synagogue out of the West End in the 1910s because "most of its members had already gone to live" in Roxbury. And the membership of Beth Hamidrash Hagadol—which built Elm Hill's imposing Crawford Street Synagogue—included several Brookline residents in the middle 1920s.[7]

Jews knew that their ability to remain active in an institution was not conditioned on their residence. In the spring of 1938, Mishkan Tefila mounted an aggressive campaign to persuade former members to reinstate their membership. According to Abraham A. Bloom, the chairman of the congregation's board of directors, even Jews who had left Roxbury and Dorchester for the suburbs had an obligation to support the Seaver Street Temple. "Mr. Bloom stated that those who have helped erect a community building can never sever the ties of their responsibility toward its constant upkeep and maintenance," the *Jewish Advocate* reported. "'Though some may move out of the community in which the Temple was erected,' he said, 'the Temple is fixed and must retain the support of all who helped bring it into existence.'"[8] For Jews, institutional loyalty knows no boundaries.

Territorial constraints on Catholic membership, in contrast, were well defined and unforgiving. In 1953, when Rev. Ralph W. Farrell, the pastor of St. Margaret's Parish, began raising funds to build an addition to the parish high school, he was reminded by the archdiocesan chancellor that he could not solicit contributions "in any other parish"—even from alumnae.[9] The Catholic territorial parish is bounded in every direction. Men and women who lived beyond those bounds could not join the parish's social groups or send their children to the parish school. While there was no bar to an outsider's occasionally attending Mass, canon law forbade someone who lived beyond the parish boundaries to receive sacraments of record in the parish. Baptisms, first communions, confirmations, marriages, funerals: the defining events of Catholic life were restricted to parish residents.

In 1908 several residents of the town of Milton petitioned Archbishop William O'Connell, fearing that they would be left out of the new parish of St. Angela, which had just been established to serve residents of the Mattapan district. Their homes, they explained, stood not in Dorchester but on the Milton side of Mattapan Square, and they argued that the parish territory should be extended across the city line. Their section of Milton "has always been identified with the interests both spiritual and material of that of Mattapan, Boston, Mass.," they argued, "and to be included in any other parish would be a great inconvenience as well as being deprived of a great benefit."[10] They did not want to find themselves beyond the boundary.

There have always been Catholics who resisted the jurisdiction of the territorial parish, who wished to escape the rules governing boundaries. One woman wrote to the chancellor of the archdiocese in the spring of 1953 seeking permission to attend St. Gregory's Church. "My husband

and I, as our families before us, have always been members of St. Gregory's Parish in Dorchester," she wrote. "We both were baptized, received our First Holy Communion and were married in that Church. We were graduated from the Parish School." Recently, she explained, "due to the housing situation we were forced to move two streets beyond the boundary of the Parish into St. Angela's Parish." But she and her husband hoped that their difficulty in finding housing would soon end. "We feel the situation is temporary as we shall move back into St. Gregory's Parish as soon as circumstances permit," she concluded her letter. "May we have your permission to be members of St. Gregory's Parish?"[11]

The answer came quickly. "Although you and your family are free to attend whatever Church is more convenient to you, except for the sacraments of record, I regret that it is impossible to transfer you from one parish to another as long as your home remains in the territory of the former parish," the vice chancellor responded. "Canon Law determines that individuals are members of the parish in whose territory their home is located and excludes the possibility of any Bishop making an exception to this law."[12]

This rule is deeply embedded in Catholic life. In April 1972, Christopher Flynn resigned from the parish council of St. Mark's Parish. An advisory board made up of clergy, religious, and parishioners, the parish council had been created in the late 1960s. Flynn was elected to the council in November 1970; one year later, he was elected the council's chairman. He resigned from the parish council, according to a history of St. Mark's Parish, "because he had moved from the parish."[13] In leaving the neighborhood, Flynn had forfeited his right to participate in St. Mark's affairs. Flynn and his family, like others in the parish, knew this rule.

Until recent decades, Catholics understood almost instinctually that their housing decisions determined their parochial loyalties. "Ugly rumor has it that St. Peter's Parish in Dorchester is to be divided and since I now reside in one of the outlying sections I am rather upset," a Dakota Street resident wrote in a March 1959 letter to Cardinal Richard J. Cushing. "I know that if one moves changes are made but all that is taken into consideration before the move is made."[14] Rules governing boundaries were deeply embedded in the most ordinary decisions, respected as part of the landscape.

In 1959 the Dorchester landscape shifted, momentarily revealing these rules in their uncompromising starkness. The archdiocese redrew boundaries that spring, in an effort to reduce the disparity in size between St. Peter's and the parishes that surrounded it. Though she was moving nowhere, the Dakota Street resident understood that the impending changes threatened to separate her from her old parish. Families whose loyalties to St. Peter's extended back years and generations found themselves on the wrong side of an impenetrable wall. For those who discovered the rule that boundaries exclude, it was a wrenching time. Parishes in Catholic life were areas that families moved into, well-defined districts in which people found homes. But, as Dorchester residents sat down to write to Cardinal Cushing in 1959, they were learning that parishes were equally areas from which outsiders were excluded—and the definition of an outsider paid no regard to affection or loyalty.

In May, after the boundary changes had been announced, a long-time resident of Bloomfield Street wrote to the chancellor of the archdiocese. She and her two sisters were almost "all that is left of a large family who for over eighty years have lived in St. Peter's Parish," she stated. "My Father was the first Superintendent of the Sunday School—before the Church was built. He also sang in the early choir." Suddenly, with the adjustment of parish boundaries, everything was changed. "We are told that we do not belong," she wrote. "We have never belonged to another Parish, I graduated from the Parish school. May we not continue to belong to St. Peter's?"[15]

In responding to the letter, Monsignor Francis J. Sexton, vice chancellor of the archdiocese, affirmed that "Bloomfield Street has recently been transferred from St. Peter's Parish to St. Ambrose Parish." He explained to the three sisters that they could continue to attend Mass at St. Peter's but that they could receive sacraments of record only in St. Ambrose', now their assigned parish church. The implication was clear: these women, who had lived in St. Peter's their entire lives, could not be buried from St. Peter's Church. "It is impossible for you to be considered as members of Saint Peter's Parish," Sexton explained, "while your residence is actually within the boundary of St. Ambrose Parish."[16]

"I am one of the many who will be heart-broken if we are severed from the parish that we, as children, have grown up in," another woman wrote in the spring of 1959, after learning that her street was being transferred to St. Ambrose' Parish. "My mother and father bought their home in St Peter's over 35 years ago for their seven children. All my family has grown up in the parish, have received their sacraments here and were married from St Peter's," she explained to Cardinal Cushing in a hand-written five-page letter. "Since we've been married, my husband and I have always lived in the parish, and we bought our home in the parish, specifically, so that our seven children could also be a part of the parish we love," she wrote. "Because God saw fit, in the past four years we have buried two of our dear sons from St. Peter's." She and her children had never known any grammar school teachers except the sisters of St. Peter's School, and her entire family participated actively in parish organiza-tions. "We have never gone to another church, except on special occa-sions, and we faithfully contribute to the support of our parish as my husband's pay will allow," she added. "To sever my ties with St. Peter's after all these years would indeed be a heartache. If we were forced to leave the parish and travel elsewhere it would not be nearly as sad as to have my relatives and friends over in one yard and the high fence around forbidding me to hurdle it."[17]

Local Jurisdiction

According to a 1950s textbook on canon law, "the territory of every diocese is to be divided into distinct territorial parts; to each part is to be assigned its own church with a definite part of the population, and its own rector as the proper pastor of that territory is to be put in charge for the necessary care of souls." A logical corollary to this rule, enacted in 1952 at Boston's seventh synod, specified that "each of the faithful should be interested in his own parish, and support it in accordance with his means." Parish boundaries existed not merely to exclude others but to maintain within the boundaries a close-knit, locally grounded community. Describing the decision to adjust St. Peter's boundaries, the vice chancellor explained to a parishioner in the spring of 1959 that "a change such as this is bound to be difficult in individual cases such as yours but it is for the greater good."[18]

The territorial parish, led by one pastor, has traditionally exercised exclusive jurisdiction over all Catholics living within its boundaries, except those attending a national church. Indeed, according to canon law, the pastor is also responsible for the souls of non-Catholics in his parish, and interfaith marriages, like Catholic marriages, were always to be held in the bride's parish, "even if the bride be the non-Catholic party." The pastor and his assistants were required to live in the parish—"in the parish residence, which must be near the church"—and to remain confined to the parish territory during their assignment. Except for routine business and scheduled absences, statutes of the Boston archdiocese mandated that priests traveling beyond the parish boundaries receive prior permission from the archbishop. "By constant, active and priestly ministry," the pastor was obligated to make his presence felt throughout the parish and to know each of his parishioners, conducting a regular census. Boston statutes specified that "each parish priest shall make a systematic visitation of all the homes in his parish, so that each home is visited at least once a year, or, in the largest parishes, every two or three years."[19]

Since all Catholics in a territorial parish support a single church, the parish exerts a powerful unifying force on neighborhood life. Within the parish boundaries, all parish activity is centered on a central cluster of buildings: a church and a rectory, and often a school, a convent, and a parish hall. In May 1926, Rt. Rev. Edward F. Hurley, the pastor of St. Matthew's Parish, sought permission from the cardinal to close the parish's secondary chapel; even after St. Matthew's permanent church had been built, two Masses each Sunday continued to be held in the original frame mission church, which stood a few blocks from the new brick church. "I do not see the need of the Chapel. There is no one in the Parish who lives at a distance of twenty minutes walk from St. Matthew Church and St. Matthew Church can easily accommodate the entire Parish," Monsignor Hurley wrote. "Moreover the use of the Chapel for Masses on Sundays is harmful to the parishioners of the Parish inasmuch as it disunites them." Cardinal O'Connell approved the request to close the chapel and to convert the structure into a temporary parish school. A few weeks later, Monsignor Hurley observed that "the closing of the Chapel has not displeased the people and we can take better care of them by having them come to ONE CHURCH." St. Matthew's Parish developed a strong parish center on Stanton Street, where, by the 1940s, a rectory, a convent, and a school flanked the parish church.[20]

This institutional core had its parallel in each of the parishes in Dorchester and upper Roxbury. With the exception of St. John's Parish—which, from its founding, maintained St. Hugh's as well as St. John's Church—each parish has possessed a single cluster of buildings, generally located on a prominent site, and each parish gathers around the altar of a single church. "When, most every morning of the week, I drive from my home on Jones Hill to the subway station at Fields Corner, I do so, in part at least, in order to see Saint Peter's Church," Douglas Shand Tucci wrote in 1972, "the whole great mass that rises up so audaciously before me, and often in sun-drenched splendor, as the streetscape falls quietly away and I emerge into the square." St. Peter's church, rectory, convent, and both school buildings stand together on Bowdoin Street, on Meeting House Hill. The church and rectory of St. Angela's Parish stand on Blue Hill Avenue, three blocks from Mattapan Square, and the parish's school and convent stand just behind the church. The "splendid location" of St. Angela's Church, the *Pilot* noted in 1919, on the occasion of the church's dedication, "will make it an imposing sight to the increasing number of tourists and travellers who pass over the boulevard daily."[21]

Centered on its church, the parish assumes a public character. Rectories are homes as well as offices. They do not close at the end of the day. Children and adults engage in activities in churches, schools, and rectories afternoons and evenings. I watched children come to St. Matthew's rectory after school, staying until their parents picked them up after work. In St. Ann's Parish, Rev. Stephen Madden talks with children and teenagers late into the evening, sharing jokes with them and playing basketball. Sometimes the police call St. Ann's rectory when a young person in the parish gets into trouble, and St. Ann's priests have joined parents at the local police station to bail young parishioners out of jail. "The Christians of a parish are in a true sense neighbors," the *New Catholic Encyclopedia* notes. "In the parish as in no other religious community, locality is the exclusive principle of association."[22]

Within its boundaries, each territorial parish enjoys a monopoly, laying full claim to the loyalties of its Catholic residents. In the 1990s, according to a local priest, there are still parishioners in St. William's whose "view of the world goes from Romsey Street to Freeport Street," from boundary to boundary. No parish finds itself in direct competition with another. Rather, territorial parishes exist in a state of mutual cooperation. New parishes are created with the consent and assistance of existing parishes. Father Ronan built St. Paul's original church in 1896 as a mission church to serve parishioners living in the northwestern corner of St. Peter's Parish. "On New Year's Day, 1908, St. Paul's mission became a separate parish, and was handed over to its new pastor," Susan L. Emery wrote, "not only free from debt, but particularly well equipped."

Almost four decades later, in September 1945, St. Paul's Parish was itself called on to relinquish territory for the organization of a "New Parish at Uphams Corner." In addition to the territory, St. Paul's donated $10,000 to St. Kevin's Parish.[23]

If the guarantee of exclusive jurisdiction explains this cooperative network of territorial monopolies, then the absence of comparable jurisdiction in Jewish rules contributes to the fierce competitiveness among Jewish institutions. "Our sister congregations were annoyed by our boasts, and the fault was not theirs but ours," Rabbi Louis M. Epstein wrote in 1924, reflecting on the early years of Beth Hamidrash Hagadol's Crawford Street Synagogue. "We gave offense, we stirred up a sense of competition between congregations, we were childishly 'chesty.'" To exist, Jewish institutions have traditionally competed for members, for funds, and for prestige. "Look at the budget of any Synagogue, and you will see that from the largest to the smallest they are all struggling," Sumner S. Shore, the president of Beth Hamidrash Hagadol's men's club, wrote in the early 1920s. "Why should as many as seventy-two Synagogues exist in Boston when the number of worshippers could be amply accommodated in, say forty. Why should these Synagogues live and struggle, and compete with each other? Why should the financial burden fall on the shoulders of such a small number of godly men?"[24]

In the early 1920s, Beth Hamidrash Hagadol was planning to construct a large school building adjacent to its synagogue. "We cannot be dormant and succeed," Louis H. Steinberg, the congregation's president, declared. "If we stand still, we lose our place, for other Congregations are working and forging ahead, and unless we keep pace with progress, we will be left behind the working organizations." The *Jewish Advocate,* observing that Adath Jeshurun had just completed a substantial schoolhouse three blocks away, encouraged the two congregations to "share to mutual advantage" the existing structure. The proposed Crawford Street school "will be a duplication of effort and, consequently, a waste at this time," the *Advocate* argued in a May 1923 editorial. "Every attempt should be made to get together, and thus get the most out of one institution before beginning on another. Not to do so is impractical and unfair to the generous givers and to other useful institutions." In a second editorial, printed one week after the first, the *Advocate* repeated its advice, concluding, "Let no pride, of one side or the other, stand in the way of common sense and good judgment."[25]

But the *Advocate*'s counsel went unheeded: the proud and committed leaders of Beth Hamidrash Hagadol were not so easily dissuaded. The proposed addition to the synagogue promised to create an elaborate community facility on the Crawford Street site. Plans presented to the congregation in the early 1920s envisioned a three-story structure with classrooms, offices, assembly halls, a large meeting room, a library, a dance hall, a banquet room, "a gymnasium and indoor play room, a swimming tank and showers, game rooms, club rooms, kitchen, cloak room and dressing rooms." Surely with such an addition the Crawford Street Synagogue would possess a facility that would surpass the efforts of any competitor. In fact, the proposal surpassed the means even of Elm Hill's pioneer synagogue. By June 1925 the congregation no longer spoke of a swimming tank, a gymnasium, or a banquet hall. Unable to raise the necessary funds, the congregation abandoned the project altogether by the end of the year.[26]

In aspiring to build a new Hebrew school and community center, the Crawford Street Synagogue did not demonstrate an unusual ambition. In the 1920s every major synagogue in Roxbury and Dorchester announced plans for a new school building: it was in this decade that Mishkan Tefila erected its temple and schoolhouse, Adath Jeshurun built the Menorah Institute, Shara Tfilo built the Roxbury Hebrew School, Beth El built the Beth El Hebrew School, and leaders of Mattapan's synagogues broke ground for the Dorchester-Mattapan Hebrew School. Several smaller congregations in Dorchester and Roxbury erected new synagogues in the 1920s, others began campaigns for synagogues that were never built, and community centers constructed additions to their existing buildings. In Brookline, Ohabei Shalom and Kehillath Israel built new temples and schoolhouses—while nearby, in Boston's Fenway district, Adath Israel erected its new meeting-house and school building, the first steps in its plan to build a three-million-dollar center around a new temple, and Beth Israel Hospital dedicated its new facility.[27]

Because no Jewish institution enjoys a territorial monopoly and because each seeks to distinguish itself from other institutions, the resources of the Jewish community have often been strained by competing demands for support. The "small number of godly men" described by Sumner Shore, "the generous givers" cited in the *Jewish Advocate*'s 1923 editorial, were men who belonged to many congregations and who supported efforts to construct various synagogues, schoolhouses, and community structures throughout not just Roxbury and Dorchester but the entire Boston area. "After all, the financial burden is generally carried by the same group," the *Advocate* noted in its attempt to dissuade the Crawford Street Synagogue from erecting its own school building. "Wrong it is, therefore, to call upon them unless the need is clear."[28] Ironically, institutions enjoying the most radical autonomy were—because of that very autonomy—bound together by fate and by the need to compete in the same pool for members and funds.

In May 1911, when the Boston Young Men's Hebrew Association (YMHA) announced plans to relocate from the South End into Roxbury, David L. Mekler, a Dorchester resident, protested to no avail that the proposal threatened to undermine an existing institution. The new community center would be "a rival organization" to the more modest YMHA that had already been formed in Dorchester. In the end, he feared, both organizations might fail where one could have succeeded. "If the gentlemen who are behind the organization mean well, why did not they come and say, 'Gentlemen, we heard what you have done so far. We are interested in the work of such an organization, and our wish is to assist you'? Would not that be fair?" Mekler asked. "But the trouble with us Jews, is that we do everything except helping each other, we like to break not to build, and before one society is able to stand on its feet, we plan to organize another society."[29]

Jewish institutions do not lead insulated, bounded lives; they are enmeshed and entangled in a dense web. "Among Jewry," Marshall Sklare has argued, "every congregation must appeal for community support and is entirely on its own resources."[30] In the 1930s and 1940s, forty synagogues stood in upper Roxbury and Dorchester in an area the size of four Catholic parishes. As autonomous and private institutions, congregations worshiped in synagogues that stood just around the corner from— sometimes immediately adjacent to—the synagogues of other congregations. None of them possessed exclusive jurisdiction over their local areas. In the middle 1910s, as Map 14 shows, Adath Jeshurun's Blue Hill Avenue Synagogue was located in the midst of a densely packed set of institutions: seven synagogues, one Hebrew school, and the Boston YMHA all stood in the Blue Hill Avenue–Grove Hall district. In Mattapan, five synagogues and a Hebrew school shared three blocks of Woodrow Avenue in the late 1920s.[31] Given the density of synagogues in Dorchester and Roxbury, Jews often walked past two, three, sometimes a dozen other synagogues on the way to their own house of worship. Some Jews joined no congregation—perhaps they would just purchase seats in a synagogue or a rented hall for High Holy Day services—while other Jews supported several congregations.

Unlike the Catholic church, the American synagogue is an essentially private institution organized for dues-paying members. It is not a public facility serving a distinct local area. "There can be no question that a synagogue is the private property of a congregation," the *Advocate* noted in 1908. Still, it is usually only on the High Holy Days, when the demand for seats exceeds a synagogue's capacity, that a congregation explicitly asserts its private nature, excluding nonmembers without tickets. "The statement has frequently been made that Jewish houses of worship fail to impress the stranger with a spirit of hospitality and welcome," the *Advocate* observed in an August 1906 editorial. "Complaints have often been voiced that the visitor entering a Jewish Temple is coldly received by the sexton, allowed to take a seat near the door and given no prayer book. During the high holidays the unfortunate stranger who is not in possession of a ticket usually fails to receive even these scant courtesies and is rudely denied admission." While the *Advocate* suggested that such complaints might be exaggerated, it nevertheless admitted that synagogues "fail to attract the strangers with that indefinable air of welcome which, it must be admitted, is characteristic of most Christian churches."[32]

Jewish congregations depend heavily on the revenue that they raise from the sale of seats for High Holy Day services. Many Jews in Dorchester and Roxbury, rather than support a congregation throughout the year, only bought tickets to High Holy Day services. Not only established congregations but "so-called 'mushroom' synagogues," temporary houses of worship created by private individuals, competed against one another in the same neighborhoods. Noting that "the business of creating houses of worship for individual profit goes on merrily year after year," the *Jewish Advocate* criticized the practice. "Basements, vacant stores, abandoned theatres, places which all year round are used as dance halls and public meeting halls, are rented by private individuals for the purpose of holding services on the most sacred holidays of the year." Many Jews supported the temporary services because they "cannot afford the admission price demanded by some of our synagogues," the *Advocate* observed in 1929. "Thus, they are forced to seek the lower-priced 'mushroom' synagogues, and by their action detract from the legitimate income of the established synagogues."[33]

To attract members and to sell seats for High Holy Day services, congregations have used several strategies. One, of course, has been to erect an impressive new building. But a more blatant strategy has been employed in the weeks preceding the High Holy Days each fall, when—especially in the first decades of this century—congregations promoted the advantages of their religious services with advertising, handbills, placards, and press releases. "Rev. Julius Karlsberg, the well-known Cantor, formerly with Temple Mishkan Tefila, will render the musical part of the Services, assisted by a large choir of trained singers," the Crawford Street Synagogue announced in 1915. In the fall of 1923, Mishkan Tefila announced that its new cantor, "formerly chief cantor of Budapest," would be officiating at all services and that "a limited number of choice seats will be sold to the public." And Adath Jeshurun, in a front-page advertisement in the *Jewish Advocate* in 1930, assured Boston's Jews that "although the Congregation has elected the service of a Cantor of the first rank the prices of seats are moderate."[34]

Despite the prevalence of this competition to sell seats and attract members, Boston Jewry was shocked when the city's newspapers reported in September 1908 that E. R. Williams, a sailor in the United States Navy stationed in Boston, had been refused admission to the Blue Hill Avenue Synagogue on Rosh Hashana. According to the lead story in a Monday edition of the *Boston Journal,* the vice-president of Adath Jeshurun said that "any man ought to be ashamed to attend divine worship in a United States marines uniform." The story, it was soon discovered, was groundless. When Williams arrived at the synagogue, the rabbi was delivering his sermon: Williams, like others who came at the same time, was told only that no one could be seated until the conclusion of the sermon. But, before the true version of events was known, the original story, impugning the patriotism of the congregation, had already been "flashed by the Associated Press" and brought to the attention of the secretary of the navy and President Theodore Roosevelt.[35]

Only when Boston's Jews realized that "the story was a mere sensational newspaper man's manufacture" did they learn that "spite or congregational rivalry carried the original story to the newspaper men." In retrospect, it was curious that the source of the story had emphasized that Williams, upon leaving Adath Jeshurun, "afterwards visited Temple Mishkan Tefilla and was immediately shown every possible courtesy." Williams himself swore in an affidavit that he had not brought the matter to the attention of any newspaper. After being told by an usher that he could not enter the Blue Hill Avenue Synagogue, he had "quietly left there" and walked over to the Moreland Street Temple. "There I told one of the men about my rejection, and he told me that I ought to put the matter in the papers so as to fix the other party," Williams recalled. "I then told him that that was no concern of his and he answered that if I did not do so he would." Clearly, competition between these two congregations was not always a dignified affair.[36]

6

Rootedness

A parish is more than its buildings. But in 1910 St. Peter's Church testified powerfully to the permanence of a Catholic presence on Meeting
House Hill. As Susan L. Emery observed, "This church is founded literally upon a rock, and is, singularly enough, built of the rock from which
its strong foundations were quarried." That image of the church built by
Rev. Peter Ronan was the central image of the parish history and of the
jubilee celebration held two years earlier. In his jubilee address, Rev.
Florence J. Halloran spoke reverently of "this enduring sermon in stone,
this glorious temple to the all-holy God." It was a church that could no
more be uprooted than the pudding-stone ledge of which it was built.
"Our minds go in triumph to-day from our pastor, Peter, who has literally built this church upon a rock, back through the ages of uninter-
rupted Apostolic Succession, until we come to him whom Christ has
made the Great Pastor, Saint Peter, the spiritual rock on whom, after our
Lord, is built for all time the Universal Church," Halloran said. "When
you and all who now worship here have gone to your reward, and when
your bodies shall have returned to their parent-dust, generations yet
unborn will throng through the doors of St. Peter's."[1]

Inside the church, to one side of the main altar, was a large painting
that depicted Christ giving Peter the keys to the kingdom of heaven. The
image had special resonance in this parish, and Christ's words came
easily to the lips of parishioners: "Thou art Peter; and upon this rock I
will build My Church, and the gates of hell shall not prevail against it."
As a church built from solid rock, Emery observed, St. Peter's "is a living
image of the Apostle Saint Peter, whose name it bears, and it preaches

129

daily Christ's promise to that great Apostle." The keys were a testament to that promise and to the deep foundations of the Dorchester church, which Archbishop Williams had consecrated in 1884 by sprinkling holy water on its walls, making the physical "home of Our Eucharistic Lord" an inalienable part of the parish. The stone church was a tangible symbol of the universal Church.[2]

But if keys represented rootedness to the men and women of St. Peter's Parish, they possessed a very different meaning for the Jews of Mishkan Tefila. Transferring keys was a part of the ceremonies whenever a new synagogue was dedicated, and the group had moved often. Indeed, it was by its moves that the congregation measured its progress. Yet even as it relocated from structure to structure, Mishkan Tefila remained firmly rooted. Linked through Torah with the timeless traditions of Judaism, the congregation persisted apart from any building. Wherever they worshiped, whether in a tenement house in the South End or in a handsome stone edifice in suburban Roxbury, the members of Mishkan Tefila held fast, spiritually and physically, to the Torah. Each time they gathered to dedicate a new synagogue, they marched with the scrolls through the streets of Boston, carried them in procession around the new sanctuary, then deposited them in the ark. Carried under velvet canopies by the congregation's most distinguished members, the scrolls were honored and revered. It was not the building, not the speakers, not even the members themselves, who were central to the dedication ceremony; it was the Torah, the treasure God entrusted to Israel.

The experiences that Mishkan Tefila and St. Peter's Parish celebrated in 1910 were shaped by two sets of rules regarding rootedness. St. Peter's, measuring progress through the growth of its territorial stronghold, knew that both the church and the parish were immobile. Mishkan Tefila, in contrast, measured progress by its ability to move with its membership. Discovering its rules of rootedness in its Torah scrolls, Mishkan Tefila adhered to the unwritten rule that bound the congregation's survival to its portability. When written codes conflicted with this rule, Mishkan Tefila ignored them: Rabbi Shoher was correct in 1905 in arguing that the sale of the Shawmut Avenue Synagogue violated Talmudic law. Members of Mishkan Tefila were not alone in following these unwritten rules. Each of Boston's original Jewish congregations and every congregation in Roxbury and Dorchester—large and small, Reform, Conservative, and Orthodox—has abandoned a synagogue structure and a neighborhood in the last century.

Structural Rootedness

In Catholic theology, the church structure serves as both the house of God and the house of the living Church. It exists as a house of God, as "a true image of the Mystical Body of Christ"—as "an embodiment, a visible manifestation, of what the Church is and believes." The structure also stands as the house in which the living Church itself is gathered. In this capacity, the structure exists "to house a congregation gathered round an altar." The living Church is itself made real in the celebration of the Eucharist, which occurs at the altar of the church building. "Just as the eucharist is the center of Christian worship, so the altar is the ideal center of the ecclesial edifice: all leads to and all leads from the altar," Ignazio M. Calabuig writes. In Catholic theology, Christ Himself is regarded as "the living altar of the heavenly temple." The altar, as Calabuig argues, is "the natural symbol of Christ."[3]

For a church to be consecrated, both the altar and the building must be symbolically rooted and physically immovable. No church without an "*immovable* or *fixed* altar" can be consecrated, according to a 1957 textbook on canon law. Stone is the only material permitted for the table and base of an immovable altar, and the entire table of the altar "must consist of a single natural stone." The church, too, if it is to be consecrated, must be built of either brick or stone; a church constructed of wood or metal may be blessed but not consecrated. Canon law does not permit the celebration of the Mass at an altar that has not been consecrated or in a church that has not been consecrated or blessed, although the diocesan bishop may authorize regular services "in a 'provisional' Church, not blessed, while the permanent church is awaiting construction."[4]

The consecration of a church is a rite reserved to the bishop of the diocese. The ceremony begins outside the locked and empty church. Walking around the church as the Eighty-sixth Psalm is chanted, the bishop sprinkles Gregorian water on the structure's outer walls. When he returns to the front of the church, he requests that the doors be unlocked. He enters the church, accompanied by other clergy and by lay Catholics. Once inside, the bishop resumes the ceremony of lustration, sprinkling water on the church's inner walls and finally on the altar. With the lustration of the altar, the bishop "formally takes possession of the church," having expelled "every evil power from the house of God." The bishop entombs relics in the altar, then, "at 12 places along the walls of the church, which have been marked by consecration crosses, the bishop anoints the walls of the church with sacred chrism," according to the *New Catholic Encyclopedia*. "These crosses symbolize the 12 Apostles, the foundation stones of the heavenly Jerusalem." The bishop concludes the consecration of the church by anointing the door posts at the front of the building. Then he consecrates the immovable altar, anointing it with holy oil and offering "a symbolic sacrifice of incense," in preparation for Mass. The celebration of the Eucharist is "the central fact in the dedication of a church," Calabuig states. "This eucharist is 'situated' or 'placed' in a given context—that is, in a *statio* where all of the local Church is gathered together—bishops, priests, faithful—to express its wish to dedicate . . . a building, open to all the faithful, which will be reserved always and exclusively for the celebration of divine mysteries and other ecclesial activities."[5]

Since canon law discourages the erection of a parish church that cannot be consecrated—and since a preference expressed in canon law has the force of a rule except in cases where the pastor does not regard the execution of the rule as feasible—the typical parish church is built of either stone or brick and houses an immovable altar. Moreover, canon law specifies that "the Most Blessed Sacrament must be kept in an immovable tabernacle set in the middle of the altar." Through the rite of consecration, the church and altar are transformed into "sacred places" devoted to divine worship. Once dedicated, "a church does not lose its consecration or blessing" unless the structure is destroyed or the diocesan bishop converts it to profane uses, which he can do only "if a church can in no way be used for divine worship and if there is no means to restore it." An immovable altar that remains intact cannot lose its consecration, but the altar "loses its consecration if the table or top is separated even for a moment from its base."[6]

Unless it be the specific experience of St. Peter's Parish in Dorchester, which found its quarry beneath its church, nothing is so rooted as a Catholic church. Eighteen Catholic churches, in seventeen parishes, were built in upper Roxbury and Dorchester. Seventeen of them, all except St. Leo's Church, were built of stone or brick—handsome stone churches, like St. Peter and St. Paul; red-brick churches, like St. Ann, St. Gregory, St. Matthew, and St. Margaret; the gray-brick church of St. Brendan; even the unlikely Spanish-mission-style church of St. William, with its pink stucco exterior. And each church had its stone altar. The main altar in St. William's rose eighteen feet and was built entirely of marble.

"Finally, you have received your reward in having the presence of God and your own parish priest," Archbishop William O'Connell declared in July 1910, when he consecrated St. William's Church. "Here you have a house of God and his altar." Another priest who spoke that day praised "this permanent dwelling place for the most high." St. William's Church, he added, "takes its honored place as another fortress of truth along the ramparts of Catholicity."[7]

Describing life in St. Peter's Parish in 1910, Emery emphasized the centrality of the altar and tabernacle. "Rarely during the day is the Eucharistic Lord without the company of some devout worshipper, while troops of children stop for an act of love on their way to and from school, and their elders, in the quiet evening hours, come in numbers to find rest and strength at the feet of Him Who alone can give it," Emery wrote. "One may judge the spiritual condition of a people by asking how many of them receive Holy Communion frequently. What most impresses the observant visitor at St. Peter's is the throng of people who, independently of the Sodalities, approach the Holy Table every Sunday."[8]

Jews are accustomed to a Sabbath procession of quite a different sort, for nothing is so portable as the Torah scroll. Whenever the Torah is read or studied, it is picked up and carried around. Each Sabbath morning the scroll—wrapped in an embroidered cloth covering and crowned with silver ornaments—is removed from the ark with great ceremony, as members of the congregation rise from their seats. Triumphantly, to singing and chanting, the congregation's leaders march with the Torah in a procession through the hall. Congregants reach out, with a book or the fringe of a prayer shawl, ritually to kiss the scroll's cover. When the procession is ended, the Torah is brought to the bimah, where it is opened and read. At the conclusion of the Torah reading, a member of the congregation lifts the open scroll high into the air, so that all might see the holy text, then the scroll is rolled shut and returned to its cloth cover. Congregants carry the Torah in a second procession around the sanctuary, return it to the ark, then close the ark.

In Jewish law, the Torah is valued above all else. The Talmud teaches that a congregation may take a synagogue and turn it into a house of study, but a congregation is forbidden to convert a house of study into a synagogue. Jews who sell a synagogue may use the funds to purchase an ark, a Torah cover, or a Torah, because the synagogue and its furnishings are less holy than the ark, the Torah cover, and the Torah. Jews who sell an ark may use the funds to purchase a Torah covering or a Torah, "but it is forbidden to sell an Ark even in order to build a synagogue because 'one may not descend in matters of holiness,'" according to *Encyclopaedia Judaica*. "The holiness of objects is determined by their proximity, in space and use, to the *Torah* scroll, the most sacred object in the synagogue." Funds raised from the sale of a Torah scroll may only be used to acquire another sacred text or to advance the study of Torah. According to the Talmud, a Jewish community can exist without a synagogue but not without a Torah scroll.[9]

The veneration of the Torah began after the destruction of the Second Temple and its altar. Rabbinic Judaism transformed the Torah into the new "sacred center" of the Jewish people. "The sanctity of scripture outweighed even the Sabbath, and people were expected and permitted to violate Sabbath restrictions to save it and its wrappings from fire—an exemption otherwise applied only to save a human life," William S. Green writes. "Worshippers were expected to rise in the presence of the Torah scroll, and no other type of scroll could be placed on top of it. To touch the parchment of a Torah scroll with bare hands was judged an outrage." When a Torah falls to the ground, Jews fast. When a Torah is torn or burned, Jews tear their clothes in mourning. And when a Torah can no longer be used—when it becomes old or damaged—they gather in a cemetery to bury it.[10]

There is no altar in a synagogue. There are no crosses to anoint, no walls to sprinkle with water, no relics to entomb. In fact, no formal guidelines exist in Jewish law for dedicating a synagogue—the law requires neither specific prayers for a dedication nor the presence of a rabbi.[11] There is not even a requirement that a synagogue be dedicated. Jews may worship in a synagogue that is never dedicated; Jews may worship in a private home. Members of the congregation need only themselves and a Torah scroll to initiate worship in a building. Jews who dedicate a synagogue do not consecrate a structure. Rather, they carry the congregation's Torah scrolls from its old place of worship to the new building and deposit them in the ark. It is an honor, that day's greatest honor, to bear a Torah in the procession.

Mark Mirsky remembers the Torah when he recalls his childhood in the 1940s. As a three-year-old boy, he sat proudly with the synagogue's leaders at the front of Dorchester's Temple Beth El. His grandfather would "raise me up above the congregation," Mirsky writes, "and set me down on blue velvet cushions among silver turrets, peaks of the Torah scrolls." Mirsky was entranced, as men in the Fowler Street Synagogue "clutched and sang to the circular magical books in their arms, chanting Solomon's tongue of the birds, hugging and kissing those metamorphosed princes wrapped in deep piled velvets, azures, crimson, purple, threaded with fat gold braids."[12]

Although several imposing synagogues were built in Dorchester and upper Roxbury, most were modest structures. They were tenement houses, small buildings, and converted churches, like those Mishkan Tefila had known through 1910. Many congregations worshiped in old houses, converting front parlors into sanctuaries and bedrooms into libraries, offices, and rooms for study. There was nothing essential about the synagogue itself. The building—as Abraham G. Daniels indicated in 1910, in his description of the Shawmut Avenue Synagogue—is only an "outer shell," existing as long as a congregation gathers in it with its Torah.[13] Many congregations have moved from structure to structure within a single neighborhood. In its portability, the institution recalls the ancient tabernacle and the Ark of the Covenant.

Although no congregation builds its synagogue as a temporary structure, every congregation is potentially portable. Adath Israel's temple on Columbus Avenue, at the border of lower Roxbury and the upper South End, was the most impressive Jewish structure built in nineteenth-century Boston. Dedicated in February 1885, the Romanesque temple was built of brick, with brownstone and terra cotta trimmings. The Reform congregation of seventy families, described as "the most wealthy and influential in the East," invested $50,000 in the structure. At the dedication ceremony, leaders of the congregation carried the Torah scrolls in procession and placed them in the ark, "made of elaborately carved oak," then a young woman gave the congregation's president the keys to the building. Adath Israel left this temple in 1903, selling the structure for $45,000. "Yesterday the temple Adath Israel, Columbus av and Northampton st, for a long time worshiped in by a Hebrew congregation, ceased to be a synagogue," the *Boston Globe* reported in June 1903, "and became the Columbus-av A. M. E. Zion church, dedicated to 'the glory of God and to the use and service of the African Methodist Episcopal Zion church in America.'"[14]

Only in retrospect can it become clear to a congregation that there is nothing permanent or rooted about a specific synagogue building. At the culmination of a long and expensive campaign to erect a synagogue, no congregation regards its new house of worship as a mere shell. But even in 1885, at the moment that Adath Israel dedicated its new temple, the congregation—like any congregation—understood that institutional survival sometimes meant abandoning one building for another. "Confined as the members had been for a quarter of a century in a small and uncomfortable place of worship," the *Boston Hebrew Observer* noted in 1885, "it was not surprising to mark the words and glances of delight and admiration that followed their entrance into the new sanctuary."[15]

Geographical Rootedness

Not only were there no barriers to abandoning a structure, but there were equally no barriers to abandoning one neighborhood for another. The existence of a Jewish institution does not depend on its continued presence in any neighborhood.[16] When Adath Israel sold its temple in 1903, it was preparing to relocate to an entirely different section of the city. The congregation moved into a temporary hall and, in 1905, broke ground for a monumental white-marble temple on Commonwealth Avenue.[17] The site was located near the Brookline town line, on a handsome residential boulevard in Boston's Fenway district.

Adath Israel had become the first congregation in Boston to relocate from one neighborhood to another when it dedicated the Columbus Avenue Temple in 1885. Ohabei Shalom moved out of the lower South End two years later, and Mishkan Tefila followed in 1897, when it acquired the Shawmut Avenue Synagogue. Within a decade, Mishkan Tefila moved again, dedicating the Moreland Street Temple in May 1907. That September, Adath Israel dedicated its new temple on Commonwealth Avenue. Ohabei Shalom, in 1916, also resolved to move out of the upper South End. Postponing its plans because of the war, the congregation acquired "the site for the new edifice" in 1920. On Beacon Street, in Brookline, Ohabei Shalom dedicated its new temple in 1928, adjacent to a congregational center that it had erected three years before.[18]

In the fall of 1916, Mishkan Tefila announced its own plans to relocate. For the third time in twenty years, the congregation prepared to move to a new section of the city. "The shifting of the Jewish population and the rapid growth of the congregation make this change imperative," the *Jewish Advocate* reported. "No definite steps have been taken as to the site, but two sections are under consideration. They will probably build either near Franklin Park or in the Allston-Brookline section." The Moreland Street Temple had proved little more than a resting place: like the lower South End in 1897, like the upper South End in 1906, the Dudley Street district in 1916 was not a satisfactory location for a major Jewish institution. "Though we have a commodious Temple at the present time," Mishkan Tefila announced in a promotional brochure, "we feel that in line with our history of progress in the past, and in order to render the maximum of service to Judaism and to the community, we ought to be more centrally located."[19]

At their annual congregational meeting in February 1917, the members of Mishkan Tefila voted to move to the Elm Hill district, near Franklin Park and Grove Hall. "The section of Roxbury adjoining Franklin Park has come to be one of the most thickly populated districts of the Jewish community," the congregation explained in its brochure, "and it is there that our institution must be situated." Members of Mishkan Tefila immediately established a committee to search for a site for "a new and larger temple" and a school and community center. The congregation purchased land the next year at the corner of Crawford Street and Elm Hill Avenue, converting the house on the lot into a temporary schoolhouse "until more favorable conditions will permit beginning the constructing of the new house of worship."[20]

But the alternate proposal—to relocate to the Brookline-Allston area—was not easily rejected. In the fall of 1919, almost three years after the matter had first been raised and apparently settled, Mishkan Tefila's members appear to have been engaged in a fierce internal struggle, with a significant minority arguing that the new temple should instead be built in Brookline. At a meeting of the congregation's board of trustees that fall, "it was decided that the work of the congregation be extended to Brookline, and that a branch of the Religious School be opened there," the *Advocate* reported. "This step was taken because of the fact that many members of the congregation have removed to Brookline." In announcing its Brookline school, Mishkan Tefila was careful to reaffirm its commitment to Roxbury; the group was probably allaying a widespread and growing fear that it was on the verge of abandoning the Elm Hill project for Brookline. "The work in Roxbury will be continued as heretofore," the congregation declared. "The plan to erect a larger and more commodious Temple in Roxbury will be adherred to, and a campaign is to be started to bring about the realization."[21]

At a December 1919 banquet, Mishkan Tefila began its formal appeal for funds, and in February 1920 the congregation purchased the majestic Seaver Street site. Mishkan Tefila broke ground for its new temple in October 1922. Noting that Mishkan Tefila expected to spend more than $500,000 on the temple, the *Boston Evening Transcript* observed that "the congregation is planning this building for posterity." By the spring of 1924, the congregation had sold its property on Crawford Street as well as "the old temple" on Moreland Street.[22]

Mishkan Tefila gathered to dedicate the Seaver Street Temple in September 1925. Its president, Moses Mishel, who received "the key to the new edifice" from the chairman of the building committee, walked with other officers in "the procession with the Scroll of the Law." Nine men carried the Torah scrolls down the temple's center aisle, as the congregation stood at their seats and the organist played music arranged to the words of the Twenty-fourth Psalm. "The Jew and the synagogue are inseparable," Mishel stated in his address. "The synagogue follows the Jew and the Jew follows the synagogue." Four years later, in September 1929, Mishkan Tefila dedicated its new community center and schoolhouse on Elm Hill Avenue, on land behind the temple.[23]

Rules linking survival to portability shaped not only Boston's oldest, wealthiest, and most liberal congregations—Ohabei Shalom, Adath Israel, and Mishkan Tefila—but all of the city's Jewish institutions. The Boston YMHA moved from the South End to Roxbury in 1911, and the Hecht House, the other major Jewish community center in the Roxbury-Dorchester area, moved from the West End to Dorchester in 1936. Even the West End YMHA left the West End, relocating to Roxbury in the late 1930s. Beth Israel Hospital, established on Roxbury's Elm Hill in 1916, moved out of Roxbury and into the Fenway district in 1928, dedicating a modern facility four blocks from Harvard Medical School.[24]

Many of Dorchester and upper Roxbury's Orthodox synagogues also traced their origins to other parts of Boston. Agudath Achim, a congregation that limited its membership "to strict observers of the Sabbath," moved to Roxbury from the West End in the 1910s, while Anshe Shepetovka moved in the 1920s. Between 1924 and 1929, four congregations—Atereth Israel, Chevra Mishnaeth Shomreh Shabas, Anshi Volin, and Beth Jacob—each relocated from the South End, with two of them establishing synagogues in upper Roxbury and two in Dorchester's Mattapan district. Nevey Zedek—whose synagogue in lower Roxbury had once attracted a pious congregation on Saturday mornings of "black-bearded elders" and "their ponderous women in shining black silks clutching at cleanly arrayed infants"—moved to Dorchester in 1936. And Boston's preeminent Hasidic congregation, established in the West End by Pinchas Horowitz, relocated to Dorchester in the middle 1940s under the leadership of his son, the new Bostoner Rebbe, Levi Horowitz.[25]

Colloquially, even the most substantial Jewish structures in Boston took their names from their streets: the Blue Hill Avenue Synagogue erected by Adath Jeshurun, the Seaver Street Temple built by Mishkan Tefila. The practice was pervasive. Jews spoke of the Fowler Street Synagogue, not Temple Beth El; they spoke of the Moreland Street Temple, the Crawford Street Synagogue, the Woodrow Avenue Synagogue, the Nightingale Street Synagogue, the Fessenden Street Synagogue. In December 1927, as Ohabei Shalom prepared to lay the cornerstone for its new temple in Brookline, the *Jewish Advocate* noted in an editorial that the structure "will be called 'The Beacon Street Temple.'" The *Advocate* then recalled the previous two temples occupied by Ohabei Shalom, observing that "perhaps, many of the older members of the Congregation, who saw the early beginnings of Warrenton and Union Park Street Synagogues, did not realize that they would also witness the laying of the cornerstone of the new Temple." In borrowing names from streets, Jews understood, if only subconsciously, that it was the street and not a synagogue's presence in the district that was truly lasting.[26]

Catholics live in another world. For them, it is the parish that names the neighborhood and the church that names the street. Finding Dorchester and Roxbury's Catholic churches is not difficult: they stand by St. Brendan Road, St. Gregory Street, St. Margaret Street, St. Marks Road, St. William Street. Named for the second pastor of St. Ann's Parish, McKone Street runs behind St. Ann's Church. Ronan Park, on Meeting House Hill, is, of course, named for the founding pastor of St. Peter's Parish. The Catholic church is a permanent structure, and the parish, rooted in a specific geographical area, is permanently identified with its locality. "It is essential to the Eucharistic celebration as a sacramental rite that it be localized," according to the *New Catholic Encyclopedia.* "The Eucharist must be celebrated by one congregation in one place."[27]

Parishes are places on maps. They are geographical areas, neighborhoods with names like St. Peter's, St. Mark's, and St. Matthew's. "We grew up in Dorchester," Boston City Councillor Lawrence S. DiCara wrote in 1977, "in that very special part of Dorchester we came to call home—St. Gregory's Parish—where the two-decker meets the two-toilet Irish, where the three-decker meets the three-car family, the most middle American of middle-American neighborhoods." Only an outsider would have to be told that St. William's is Savin Hill, that St. Peter's is Meeting House Hill, that DiCara's St. Gregory's Parish is Lower Mills. Through most of this century, newspaper listings of apartments for rent in Dorchester read like a Catholic directory. As the *Globe* noted in 1971, "It is still as common for houses and apartments to be advertised as in St. Gregory's, St. Ann's or St. Brendan's as in Ashmont, Neponset or Codman Hill."[28]

John Cadigan, who was five years old when his family moved to St. Margaret's Parish in the 1890s, looked back on his life and his neighborhood more than eighty years later. "I've always lived in St. Margaret's parish," he stated. "We lived on Edison Green, and then moved and my father bought a house on top of the hill on Buttonwood Street. When I got married, I lived down on Morely Street, for a number of years, then moved to a house on Rosecliff Street and that's about thirty-five years ago. After that I moved to my present abode, down on St. Margaret's Road," Cadigan explained. "I guess the only reason is—what's the use of moving if you like what you have and you're here?"[29]

As he dedicated St. William's Church in 1910, Archbishop O'Connell alluded to the inseparable bond between the parish and its neighborhood. Emphasizing that "day after day till the end of time God himself will come in the mass here to be adored," the archbishop told parishioners to reflect on what this meant for themselves, their families, "and the whole district" of Savin Hill. Seventy years later, when St. William's Church was destroyed in a fire, the identification of the parish with its locality remained fierce. "When you talk about St. William's Church, you're talking about Savin Hill," William O'Shea, one of the church's parishioners, explained to a newspaper reporter in September 1980. "If you don't rebuild St. William's, it'd be like taking Savin Hill off the map."[30]

7

Authority

In 1868, when Rev. Peter Ronan was ordained, the Boston diocese covered a large territory. Ronan received his first assignment, as a curate, in New Bedford, a whaling and fishing city in southeastern Massachusetts. Then, in April 1872, the Boston diocese was divided: the section of the diocese that lay in Rhode Island and southeastern Massachusetts was set off as the new diocese of Providence. After declining an invitation to serve the Providence diocese, Ronan returned to Boston and received a new assignment from Bishop John J. Williams. On the last Sunday in September 1872, Father Ronan "preached his farewell sermon" in New Bedford. "The congregation during the past four and a half years have become much attached to him, and were much affected on the occasion of the parting service," the *New Bedford Mercury* reported. "His late parishioners with one accord join in praise of his character and work, and in regret that he is called to leave them."[1]

Upon arriving in Dorchester, Father Ronan introduced himself to his new parishioners. He was twenty-eight years old. "At once the people's heart was gained to him," Susan L. Emery wrote. "They were ready to follow at his call." St. Peter's Catholics, grateful that Bishop Williams had established the new parish and assigned them a pastor, immediately accepted the authority of the young priest. "In appearance he was youthful, almost boyish," Rev. Florence J. Halloran, a curate, declared in his 1908 jubilee sermon. "But he came to a people as loyal as ever drew breath. They did not question, they obeyed; and soon they learned that their young pastor was worthy of the most implicit obedience and the most devoted and generous loyalty."[2]

Mishkan Tefila, advertising for a new rabbi in August 1910, had prospered for five years without a permanent rabbi. Since 1905—when Hyman S. Shoher had resigned in protest during negotiations to sell the Shawmut Avenue Synagogue—Mishkan Tefila had grown in size, acquired and dedicated the Moreland Street Temple, and adopted religious reforms. To find a rabbi, the congregation's members placed an advertisement in the *Jewish Advocate* and solicited suggestions from other Jewish leaders across the country. "From our advertisement columns," the *Advocate* noted in a front-page story, "it will be seen that Congregation Mishkan Tefila is seeking the services of a rabbi in regular and orderly form." The advertisement was blunt: "Wanted a Rabbi," it read in bold letters. Interested candidates were advised to send their applications to Edward J. Bromberg, the chairman of the temple's search committee, "giving full qualifications, degrees or previous appointments, with copies of testimonials."[3]

That fall, members of Mishkan Tefila elected Herman H. Rubenovitz to a three-year term. A 1908 graduate of the Jewish Theological Seminary, Rubenovitz was serving a small congregation in Louisville, Kentucky, when he learned of the vote. He wrote to Joseph S. Phillips, the congregation's secretary, to discuss the terms of a contract. Responding quickly, Phillips notified Rubenovitz that the board of trustees had met "for the purpose of acting upon the conditions under which you would give the call to fill our pulpit any consideration." At the board's instruction, Phillips enclosed a copy of the temple's by-laws. "Our Rabbi as you will see at a glance," Phillips wrote, "is subject to the control of the Board in all matters." Within two weeks, Rubenovitz had agreed to the contract and been installed in the Moreland Street Temple.[4]

Mishkan Tefila's by-laws, published in 1913, described the rabbi as a "salaried officer," elected "by ballot at the annual meeting of the Congregation." His salary and the length of his term were determined by a vote of the full membership. To be considered for reelection, the rabbi was required to make application to the congregation's board. "The Rabbi shall faithfully and punctually attend every religious service, labor for the spiritual welfare of the Congregation and perform all functions appertaining to his office under the direction of the Board of Trustees," the by-laws stated. "The Rabbi shall not be absent from the religious services at any time or from the City for any extended period without the permission in advance from the President."[5]

A Jewish congregation is controlled entirely by its members. A congregation comes into existence by the mutual decision of any group of ten Jewish men, a minyan.[6] The group controls its own property, judges its internal disputes, and exercises the right to hire or not to hire a rabbi. These rules are themselves rooted in the fundamental rule that empowers any group of Jewish men to worship—indeed, to perform any ritual act, except the ordination of a rabbi[7]—without the permission or assistance of a rabbi or any other external authority. "It was unfortunate . . . that the Jewish Church in this country had no ecclesiastical board to govern the whole body and to decide important questions," an assimilated New York Jew told a newspaper reporter in 1877, as he spoke scornfully of Jewish immigrants from Eastern Europe. "Any one of their people with knowledge enough of Hebrew to recite a few passages of the Talmud is looked up to as a leader who has inherited from the God of Moses the right to interpret the laws."[8] Governed by rules that render the rabbi and any religious hierarchy superfluous, a Jewish congregation enjoys complete autonomy.

A Catholic parish, in contrast, exists within a hierarchical structure. By the last decades of the nineteenth century, American bishops had asserted their authority over every aspect of church life. "The Vatican Council of 1870 decisively pushed the church in this direction when it proclaimed the infallibility of the Pope and encouraged the centralization of the church in Rome," Jay P. Dolan has argued. "Such centralization of authority filtered down throughout the church, enhancing the authority of both bishop and pastor." A 1907 handbook, prepared for parishioners in the Milwaukee archdiocese, firmly articulated the basis of Church authority. "The Church is not a republic or democracy, but a monarchy," the handbook declared. "While the faithful of the laity have divinely given rights to receive all the blessed ministrations of the Church, they have absolutely no right whatever to rule and govern." As a 1957 textbook on canon law explained, "The Church is by divine institution a *hierarchical society.*"[9]

The power to establish or suppress a church rests with the diocesan bishop. Within the parish, the pastor has traditionally had complete authority over funds and over policy questions, though his authority is ultimately circumscribed by that of the bishop. The bishop appoints priests to a parish and supervises them during their tenure; parishioners can neither hire nor dismiss a priest. The sacramental nature of the

Catholic Church helps explain the strength of its hierarchy. Because of the centrality of the sacraments, especially the celebration of the Eucharist, to Catholic worship, and because of the necessary role of the clergy in most sacramental rites, no body of Catholics can gather for community worship without the agency of a priest. The rootedness of the parish and its church structure as well as the system of cooperative territorial monopolies depends, in large part, on the maintenance of these rules of authority. Even after the Second Vatican Council, this hierarchical conception of the Church continues to shape the relationship of the bishop to the pastor and of the pastor to his parishioners.

Creation and Dissolution of the Institution

Each of the seventeen parishes in Dorchester and upper Roxbury was established by the Ordinary (the diocesan bishop), and no church was built without his formal consent. Canon law specifies that only the Ordinary can create a new parish or authorize the building of a new church—and only he can close a church or suppress a parish. Before erecting a new parish, the Ordinary must consult with the pastors of "neighboring churches," a rule that helps ensure that each parish exists in a cooperative relationship with other Catholic parishes. Unlike the city's Protestant churches, H. Paul Douglass observed in his study of Springfield, Massachusetts, the city's Catholic churches "have been deliberately and strategically located in harmony with the development of the city until they completely and adequately cover it."[10]

Even St. Hugh's—a mission church built in anticipation of a parish that would never be organized—was erected wholly on the authority of the Boston archbishop. In November 1913 Cardinal William O'Connell personally dedicated the church. In his honor, its façade and main sanctuary were "tastefully decorated with the coat of arms of His Holiness, the Pope, and of His Eminence, the Cardinal, and a profusion of American flags and Papal and Cardinal colors."[11] Parishioners had funded St. Hugh's Church and their pastor had supervised the completion of the structure, but authority for the enterprise came directly from the cardinal.

Lay Catholics cannot establish a parish. Over the years, a number of Catholics have written to the Boston archbishop, encouraging him to authorize a new church in one neighborhood or another. There were the

Catholics who lived in the Mattapan district of Milton who signed a petition in 1908 asking that their district be included within the limits of St. Angela's Parish. There was the woman who in 1950 suggested the need for a new church in Ashmont, and the woman who in 1960 asked the cardinal to consider establishing a small chapel in Codman Square. Each of these letter-writers emphasized that many families would benefit from the new churches. In recommending that the archbishop authorize a church in Ashmont, the Dorchester resident explained that "many of us in this area, on an inclement day, cannot attend mass as each of the surrounding churches are so far away." She emphasized that hers was "just another suggestion in an avalanche of suggestions" that she knew the archbishop must receive. As a lay Catholic, she could do no more than offer the suggestion. Only the Ordinary could act on it.[12]

No hierarchy authorized the creation of Chevra Shas, a Jewish congregation that was born on a Saturday morning in the spring of 1928.[13] Indeed, when the organizers of the congregation woke up that morning, put on their suits and hats, and left for Sabbath services, none of them knew that they were about to establish a new synagogue. It all seemed an ordinary enough day. They were members of Hadrath Israel. They walked that morning to their synagogue, on Woodrow Avenue in Mattapan, as they walked every Saturday morning. Who could have known what was about to happen? As they arrived at the synagogue, they climbed the stairs to the main hall. Like every Sabbath morning, worship began with preliminary prayers and the morning service, which preceded the Torah service. Altogether, an hour, no more than an hour and a half, passed before the beginning of the Torah service.

As the preliminary prayers and morning services proceeded, the rabbi was becoming increasingly agitated. Four boys planned to become bar mitzvah that morning. Talking to the fathers of those boys, the rabbi insisted that two of the four families—he did not name which ones—should take their sons and their relatives and friends downstairs for the Torah service. How could four families share the limited number of honors available during the reading of the Torah? he asked. Better, the rabbi said, that the families should split up for the Torah service: that way, there would be twice as many honors to go around. But none of the families liked the idea of taking their sons and their guests downstairs into Hadrath Israel's small chapel. None of them supported the rabbi's suggestion. Before long, others in the congregation began to join in the discussion. As one member of the congregation continued chanting the morning service, the shouting grew louder and angrier. The audacity of the rabbi! To suggest that families should worship downstairs! Who does he think he is! Midway through the morning service, the congregation fired the rabbi, asking him to leave Hadrath Israel at once. Having dismissed the rabbi, most members of the congregation returned to their morning prayers and prepared for the Torah service.

Some members, however, were appalled by what had just occurred. Even though they all understood that the rabbi served at the pleasure of the congregation and that worship does not depend on his presence, still—still—who did these people think they were? Treating a rabbi like that, and on the Sabbath yet! As the rabbi left the building, some members of Hadrath Israel followed, apologizing, furious at the members who had humiliated him. Enough people walked out to form a minyan of their own, and one of them, a well-to-do umbrella manufacturer, owned his own Torah scroll. So they walked from the Hadrath Israel synagogue over to Samuel Finkelstein's home, at 11 Wilcock Street, less than three short blocks away.[14] There, in a living room, perhaps a front parlor or a den, the group returned to the Sabbath morning service, resuming their prayer and putting Mr. Finkelstein's Torah to good use.

At that moment, Congregation Chevra Shas was born. None of those men returned to Hadrath Israel. As Jonathan D. Sarna observed in his discussion of the American synagogue, "Tensions, which at the community level must remain forever unresolved, do frequently find resolution at individual synagogues, since those who dissent can legitimately go elsewhere or found new synagogues more to their taste." Congregational revenge can be sweet. Chevra Shas purchased land for its synagogue that June. The lot, on which the congregation planned to build a large brick structure, stood immediately across the narrow street from the frame synagogue of Hadrath Israel. In September 1928, Chevra Shas dedicated a basement synagogue on the site. The upper portion of the structure was never built.[15]

Minus the rancor, this is how every synagogue in Boston was organized: a group of men came together one day to worship. Rabbis were generally absent in a congregation's formative years. Even when a rabbi was present, as at the organization of Chevra Shas, his being there was irrelevant to the process of creating the institution. The American synagogue is "a clear manifestation of the American free enterprise system," according to Daniel J. Elazar. "Any group that wished to do so could create a synagogue entirely on its own initiative, neither seeking the assistance nor requiring the approval of any other body." Thus Boston's original congregations—Ohabei Shalom, Adath Israel, Mishkan Israel— were all organized on the authority of the families who made them up. "The Jewish congregation in Boston, formed recently, will hold its service today in the rooms of the congregation on Oswego Street," the *Boston Evening Transcript* reported in December 1858, describing the organiza- tion of Mishkan Israel. "This congregation, known as the Israelitische Gemeinde Mishkan Israel, is formed of about a dozen families who have recently made America their home."[16]

The dissolution of a congregation, like its establishment, is a simple matter, done entirely on the authority of its members. Although the first decades of the twentieth century saw the creation of many new syna- gogues in Roxbury and Dorchester, there were several instances, even in those years, of congregations that failed. Chevra Mishnaeth Shomreh Shabas, which moved from the South End to Roxbury in the 1920s, dissolved in the 1930s. "As a result of the strict pietistic qualifications for membership, this group became so small that it was unable to main- tain its synagogue," according to a Works Progress Administration re- searcher. "In 1936 a younger group in the congregation paid the debts of the congregation, taking possession of the synagogue and forming a new congregation." Beth Abraham, organized by "Jews of Roxbury" in June 1916, was disbanded within four years. Another congregation, one of the first Jewish institutions established in upper Roxbury, dissolved in 1913, five years after it had been organized, and made arrangements to sell its synagogue. The sale was a private affair: the building was owned not by the congregation but by six of its members.[17]

Control of Funds and Property

A synagogue structure, like all the property and funds of a congregation, belongs to the group's members. While the congregation, as a corporate entity, has usually owned its land and synagogue, in many instances individual members have held property for the group's use. In December 1903, when he and other members of Adath Jeshurun began discussing plans to build a new synagogue, George Wyner purchased land on Blue Hill Avenue for the proposed structure; one year later he "transferred the deed to the Congregation." The Otisfield Street property on which Shara Tfilo constructed its synagogue and religious school was made up of three pieces of land, each purchased originally by Simon Cabelinsky; in 1910, 1915, and 1923, Cabelinsky successively granted each of the deeds to the congregation. Similarly, Chai Odom built the Nightingale Street Synagogue on land that was purchased in 1917 by Louis Wolff, a member of the congregation. In July 1918, at a congregational meeting, the members of Chai Odom voted to purchase the property, including the small building that was serving as the congregation's temporary synagogue, from Wolff.[18]

Members themselves have complete responsibility for decisions regarding their congregation's property and buildings. Thus in the fall of 1923, when members of Atereth Israel, a small Orthodox congregation, hoped to purchase Mishkan Tefila's old temple on Moreland Street, they made an appeal for assistance directly to the full membership of Mishkan Tefila. At High Holy Day services, held in the unfinished basement on the Seaver Street Temple site, two leaders of Atereth Israel came and addressed Mishkan Tefila's members, arguing that the congregation "should not allow the edifice [on Moreland Street] to go out of Jewish possession."[19]

By-laws and congregational constitutions carefully specify the extent of the congregation's authority. For example, the by-laws of Mattapan's Kehillath Jacob, adopted in October 1926, state that the full membership is responsible for setting dues, establishing seating policies and prices, electing officers and setting their salaries, acquiring land and constructing buildings, and approving all expenditures exceeding ten dollars.[20] Nothing limits the authority of a Jewish congregation to raise and spend funds—except, of course, the resources of its members, their willingness to share those resources with the congregation, and the amount of money that the group can borrow on its own credit and on the credit of its members.

Prudence has not always ruled the affairs of Jewish institutions. Free of external constraints, congregations have sometimes overreached, acquiring or building structures that have been justified not by the existing resources of the congregation but by hopes of greater glory. One structure in upper Roxbury, previously the Elm Hill Baptist Church, was acquired in 1908 by members of a newly organized Jewish congregation. Five years later the congregation dissolved, and the building was sold to another congregation, Agudath Achim, which assumed two mortgages totaling $12,200. Agudath Achim, like the congregation before it, proved unable to make regular payments on its mortgage. In 1918 the Wareham Savings Bank foreclosed on the synagogue. For the next two years, until it was purchased for the new Hebrew Teachers College, the structure was left vacant.[21]

While many congregations experienced financial difficulties, the greatest risks were taken by the city's largest and most prominent synagogues. In their ambition to build and to grow, these congregations accumulated massive debt. Beth Hamidrash Hagadol began work on the Crawford Street Synagogue in the summer of 1914 with $5,000 in donations, though the congregation estimated that the cost of the finished structure would be $100,000. To complete the synagogue within a year, the congregation assumed a mortgage of $75,000. Adath Jeshurun, which dedicated the Blue Hill Avenue Synagogue in 1906 and the Menorah Institute in 1923, did not retire the mortgages on its two structures until 1947. Temple Adath Israel assumed a mortgage of $600,000 to finance its new meeting-house and school building in the Fenway, which it completed in 1928 at a cost of $1,200,000. Ohabei Shalom, whose leaders were determined not to "falter in their endeavor to build a temple center and a new synagogue" in Brookline, announced a $100,000 bond issue in 1924, explaining in a public statement that they had "run short of funds." By the end of 1928, when Ohabei Shalom dedicated its new temple, the congregation had spent $850,000 on the two buildings. Between bonds and a mortgage, Ohabei Shalom had probably borrowed $500,000 to finance the construction.[22]

Mishkan Tefila was not alone in assuming debt, but it came closer than any other major congregation to outright bankruptcy. In December 1927, more than two years after Mishkan Tefila had dedicated the Seaver Street Temple, the congregation had not yet laid the temple's cornerstone. "Only when Mishkan Tefila was out of its financial difficulties," the chairman of its board explained, "could this event be celebrated." The cornerstone would never be laid. Mishkan Tefila's battle to remain solvent, which raged relentlessly from the middle 1920s through the late 1930s, almost destroyed the great congregation. Yet neither Boston's Jews nor the congregation's own histories have ever recognized the extent of the crisis, ever realized that the magnificent temple on Seaver Street was a symbol not of wealth and stability but of reckless planning and painful reckoning. The temple and the schoolhouse built in the 1920s together cost $1,100,000. This was money that the congregation of six hundred families did not have. Of the $1,100,000, about $200,000 was raised in donations. The rest of the money, about $900,000, had to come from loans. Although Mishkan Tefila borrowed money from its members and from banks, the congregation came to rely primarily on first-mortgage bonds. Through two bond issues, in 1926 and 1928, the congregation received $750,000, which it used to retire some earlier loans and to pay new bills coming due.[23]

The financial crisis was already acute in the middle 1920s: in 1926, in a congregation that received about $90,000 in annual revenues, "the running expenses exceeded the current income by $17,000." At a congregational meeting held in January 1927, Abraham A. Bloom, the chairman of Mishkan Tefila's board of directors, "spoke to all present, and asked them if they would pay one year's dues in advance, as we are in dire need of money." One week later, at a special board meeting, Bloom stated that "the Congregation must have $25,000.00 at once"; to raise funds, the board began planning an "Emergency Banquet," which was held that June in the temple hall. For the congregation, as the banquet's program book noted, it was "a time of great need." Mishkan Tefila announced a "$75,000 Emergency Campaign" in December 1927, its budget committee explaining that "the Temple will be able to finance itself satisfactorily after this amount has been raised." In January 1929—a few months after the congregation had broken ground for its schoolhouse, obtaining the necessary funds from its second issue of mortgage bonds—"the financial needs of the Congregation were again discussed," according to minutes of the congregational meeting, "and various suggestions were made as to how to increase the revenue."[24]

With the onset of the Depression, Mishkan Tefila's fiscal crisis became a true emergency. In June 1931 the congregation informed its bondholders that it could not pay "the 6% dividend due July 1st"; by the fall, the congregation was having difficulty "meeting current obligations and also salaries." Soon it was clear that the congregation could not repay loans, could not pay salaries on time, and could not honor its original obligations to bondholders. Boston's First National Bank, to which Mishkan Tefila owed $18,000 plus interest, agreed in June 1935 to settle its claim against the congregation for a payment of $2,500. The congregation's board struggled to raise even that small sum, even as it understood the greater difficulty in addressing the demands of bondholders, who had organized into a committee. It was a bleak time: Elihu D. Stone, the president of the congregation, "counselled against a defeatist attitude" in remarks to board members, "and pointed to the 10% settlement with the First National Bank as an index of what is possible in the way of settlement with the bond holders committee." That summer, at another board meeting, "the chairman of the special finance committee reported that the financial condition of the Temple was worse than [at] any time in its history." In May 1936—after the bondholders committee refused the board's offer to redeem the first-mortgage bonds at 20 percent of face value—members of the board debated how Mishkan Tefila "could prevent a foreclosure" and the loss of its temple. "During the past seven years we have been greatly handicapped by financial difficulties and the overwhelming burden of our indebtedness," Rabbi Rubenovitz wrote in December 1936, in a letter to the board. "That the congregation has carried on through this period of hardship is cause for thanks to Almighty God."[25]

In December 1937, Mishkan Tefila finally reached a settlement with its first-mortgage bondholders. Since the early 1930s, the congregation had been unable to make regular dividend payments on the 6 percent bonds or to amortize any of the debt: in 1937, the face value of outstanding first-mortgage bonds was $720,000 (the congregation having redeemed $30,000 in bonds in the late 1920s). With the agreement, the value of the bonds was "written down to $300,000" and the interest rate was more than halved; by the new terms, Mishkan Tefila committed itself to redeeming the bonds over the next fifteen years. The congregation had finally taken its first step "out of the wilderness of Bondholders to the promised land of redemption." In the late 1930s and early 1940s, as Mishkan Tefila began to fulfill the terms of the bondholders agreement, the sense of permanent emergency abated. "It must be remembered that during my term of office as President, Mishkan Tefila experienced a terrible crisis," Elihu D. Stone later noted. "Throughout that period we were confronted with the question, 'To be or not to be.'" Stone had served as president from 1933 through 1944. As Stone indicated in September 1949, referring to one of the men who had served with him, it was their work for Mishkan Tefila in the 1930s "which was so essential to its survival at that time, and made it possible for us to reach this day."[26]

In deciding to spend $1,100,000 on a new temple and school building, Mishkan Tefila demonstrated the risks of unlimited congregational authority. Ironically, in February 1926, when the congregation had announced its first issue of mortgage bonds, the *Jewish Advocate* emphasized that "the direction of the affairs of this important institution is in the hands of a remarkably able Board of Directors." Many of them were "young men who have already made excellent names for themselves in the business world," the *Advocate* noted, men who would continue to manage the congregation's affairs "along the present conservative lines."[27]

But few synagogues in the 1920s followed conservative business principles. Across the country, according to Jack Wertheimer, "congregations embarked on a frenzied building program during the 1920s," aggressively competing against other synagogues for members and stature. Congregations embraced the ideal of a synagogue-center, a grand facility that would serve not only as a house of worship but also as a general communal center. The synagogue-center movement inspired Mishkan Tefila's plans as it inspired the plans of Boston's other leading synagogues in the 1920s: Adath Israel in the Fenway; Ohabei Shalom and Kehillath Israel in Brookline; and Adath Jeshurun, Beth El, and Beth Hamidrash Hagadol in upper Roxbury and Dorchester. "Some of the worst real estate speculations have been in connection with the erection of synagogues," Israel Goldstein, one of the nation's leading Conservative rabbis, declared in the fall of 1929. "Even conservative business men who would not venture such risks in their personal business, have built synagogue edifices with lavish reckless hand, pausing not to consider the aftermath, mortgage interests, amortization, and other maintenance expenses." The burden of indebtedness enervated congregational life. Mishkan Tefila, like many other congregations in the United States, struggled in the late 1920s and 1930s even to maintain existing congregational activities.[28]

Had there been restraints on congregational authority—had members and their boards been restricted in their power to raise and spend funds—the enthusiasm for building would not have resulted in such fiscal irresponsibility. But, as Mishkan Tefila discovered, delightedly at first, then terribly, Jewish rules offered few restraints. "Rabbis are not often consulted by building committees," Goldstein observed. The central problem of the American synagogue, he argued, was "the unwarranted predominance of lay authority" in every aspect of congregational life, nowhere more evident than in "the over ambitious building craze."

This was a peculiarly Jewish problem, established in the rules defining Jewish institutions. "The situation offers a sad contrast to the situation in the church," Goldstein noted. "In the Catholic church the authority has always proceeded from the clergy."[29]

Catholic law forbids lay Catholics to own church property, either as individuals or as a corporate body. Catholic law equally forbids parish priests to own church property. According to canon law, only a "moral person," such as a diocese or a parish, can own property: church property belongs to the moral person, not to the parishioners or clergy who "make up a moral person." To disentangle the moral person recognized by the church from the individual people who compose that moral person, the archdiocese of Boston vests the ownership of all church property—all parish churches, school buildings, parish residences, convents, parish halls—in the "Roman Catholic Archbishop of Boston, a corporation sole." While parish property is acquired and administered by the pastor of each parish, with funds raised within the parish, it is the archbishop of Boston who formally owns the property and who supervises the pastor's actions. Many people "think every church is a distinct entity," Cardinal Cushing observed in 1969, "but every church is a unit of a corporation and Richard J. Cushing is the trustee."[30]

Within the parish, the pastor is responsible for the acquisition and disposal of all church property. For these actions, he requires the permission of the Ordinary but not of any lay parishioners. Statutes that governed the Boston archdiocese in the 1950s state that "priests shall discuss money and the financial support of the parish, its schools and activities, only in passing, rarely, and by way of exception." That policy has changed since the Second Vatican Council. In many parishes in the 1990s, priests work closely with parishioners in setting budgetary priorities and in raising funds. Canon law now encourages pastors to establish finance councils, whose members include lay Catholics in the parish. "As part of its financial advisory role," leaders of the Boston archdiocese state in 1997 guidelines, "the finance council is to help the pastor prepare budgets, develop an annual report to the parish and address the revenue as well as the expense aspects of parish operation."[31]

Despite these reforms, the pastor retains the authority to act without regard for the will of his parishioners. That authority—and the decision of Rev. Francis J. Crowley to exercise it after his church was destroyed in a fire—angered many lay Catholics in St. William's Parish in the early

1980s, who sought an active role in supervising parish finances and planning the new church. "Fr. Crowley had promised the Building Committee that they would be deeply involved in the insurance settlement," members of the parish explained in a public letter. "After committee members had spent countless hours obtaining estimates from the construction business and insurance adjusters to determine the true value of the old church, Fr. Crowley agreed to an insurance settlement without even notifying the Building Committee of the offer. This unilateral and arbitrary action in complete disregard of his promise ended the Building Committee's usefulness." As one parishioner, Bernard Moran, explained in January 1982, "My own concern is that this is a dictatorial situation, that he can say, 'I'm going to do it whether you like it or not.'"[32]

The authority of the pastor within his parish was well established by the late nineteenth century. "The more priests became involved in organizing parish communities and building churches, the more common became the 'brick and mortar' pastor," Dolan argues. "It now was the priest, not the lay people, who organized the parish and built the church, school, rectory, convent, and any other parish buildings."[33] In this regard, there was nothing atypical in Father Ronan's achievement in St. Peter's Parish, in his singleminded determination to build a great pudding-stone church on Meeting House Hill, then a set of other parochial structures. Every one of the eighteen Catholic churches in upper Roxbury and Dorchester was built under the direction of its parish priest, as were each of the schools, convents, and rectories. There is no exception to this rule. At no time did lay Catholics seize the initiative from their clergy.

But the authority of the parish priest is itself strictly limited: no pastor may purchase or sell property, erect new buildings, or repair existing structures without the explicit, written permission of the diocesan bishop. Thus, as parishioners in St. William's Parish argued that their pastor was ignoring their advice as he planned the new church, a bishop explained that Father Crowley was abiding by the rules. "The procedure is to have plans like these passed through the [archdiocesan] building commission and the chancellor, with the final decision resting with the cardinal," Bishop Lawrence J. Riley stated in January 1982. "In the church, the final authority rests with the ordinary." Several months earlier, Cardinal Humberto S. Medeiros had approved plans for a new church, parish hall, and rectory in St. William's Parish.[34]

The diocesan bishop must approve any major expenditure of parish funds and any changes in the parish's properties. In a 1932 letter, Cardinal O'Connell reminded the pastor of St. Matthew's Parish that "my permission must be obtained for any expenditure in excess of $100." Statutes enforced by the Boston archdiocese in the 1950s required that parish priests receive the written permission of the diocesan bishop "for any change in the existing investments and banking of parish funds" or for spending parish funds for any purpose except routine maintenance and administrative expenses. "Without permission of the Ordinary no immovable property shall be bought, sold or mortgaged," the statutes stated. "No parish priest shall hire or lease, sell, assign, transfer, trade or in any way alienate any church property unless with the written consent of the Ordinary." Parish priests were required to submit regular financial reports to the Ordinary, even file "the combinations of all safes which contain church property."[35]

According to canon law, the Ordinary may not grant his consent for the construction of a new church—or any other parish building—unless he "prudently foresees" that the parish can bear the cost of erecting and maintaining the facility. The need to justify an expenditure to a superior has kept pastors relatively conservative, so the pace of construction has depended on the contributions of parishioners. As James W. Sanders has observed, the policy followed in Boston parishes was "one of first designing a monumental church, then building the basement with available funds and roofing it for church services, and then building the upper church as money came in, a process that took ten to twenty years." If funds were not available to complete a church, it was left unfinished. "One such basement church still raises its stunted head barely above ground level," Sanders noted; the church is St. Mary of the Angels', in Roxbury. If funds were not sufficient to begin work on a permanent church, which was rare, the new church was never begun.[36]

In the middle 1910s, the pastor of St. Leo's Parish was planning to replace the parish's original frame church with a more substantial structure. "I am writing to request permission from Your Eminence to provide larger accommodations for our congregation which has outgrown the limits of the present little church on Esmond Street," Rev. Francis A. Cunningham, St. Leo's pastor, wrote in a 1915 letter to Cardinal O'Connell. In his reply, the cardinal authorized Cunningham to continue soliciting donations from parishioners. A year later, having raised a fund of $20,000, Cunningham met with Cardinal O'Connell to discuss the proposed church; Cunningham estimated that the church would cost $40,000. "His Eminence instructed me to raise the sum of $30,000 before beginning the work of our new church," Cunningham wrote after the meeting. "I shall endeavor to reach the required figure, if possible, within a year." But when the year had passed, he instead sought permission from the cardinal to spend $349 to paint the old church. Increasing numbers of Jews were settling within the parish boundaries, and Cunningham laid aside plans for the new church.[37]

Catholic parishes have rarely assumed large debts. The assertion made by leaders of the Crawford Street Synagogue in 1928—that, in retiring their mortgage, they had achieved "an almost impossible task"—would have astonished any Catholic parish in Dorchester or Roxbury. Membership and jurisdictional rules limit competition between parishes, and authority rules guarantee that no parish can erect a building without the consent of the archbishop. St. Matthew's Church was built, one section at a time, over several years. In 1915, five years after the completion of the church basement, Rev. John A. Donnelly, the pastor, received permission from Cardinal O'Connell to borrow $30,000 to construct the outer walls of the upper church. Four years later, after retiring this loan, Donnelly began planning for the completion of St. Matthew's Church. St. Peter's Parish was "entirely free from debt" in the middle 1890s, soon after it had completed work on its church and rectory. Over the next decade the parish built a school building and a convent. "Your parish property at the present time could not, in my judgment, be duplicated for less than $400,000," Father Ronan said in June 1908, addressing St. Peter's parishioners. "I am pleased to tell you that it is free from debt."[38]

Determination of Policy and Doctrine

The authority of the clergy in Catholic institutions extends not only to the creation and dissolution of parishes, the construction of buildings, and the control of funds, but also to all matters of doctrine and policy. "Parish priests shall guard against even the appearance of lay interference in the priestly work of the parish," Boston archdiocesan statutes stated in the 1950s. On their own authority, parishioners could not require a priest to celebrate Mass in the vernacular before the Second Vatican Council or celebrate it in Latin after the council's reforms. And the priest himself owes obedience to the Ordinary. The 1952 synod that promulgated the Boston statutes stated that "in this Synod the Archbishop, and he alone, is the legislator; after the Synod he alone is the authentic interpreter of the Statutes." The Ordinary also reserved the authority, after the conclusion of the synod, to issue "new laws for the clergy and faithful."[39]

There was little room for discretion or innovation in any aspect of Catholic worship, either by parish priests or by lay Catholics. As a textbook on canon law declared in the 1950s, "It pertains exclusively to the Holy See to control the sacred liturgy and to approve liturgical books." Canon law specified the frequency and nature of sermons. Statutes in the Boston archdiocese set strict rules for the celebration of the Mass, specifying that altar boys "shall wear black cassocks (no other color) and surplices" and that "the Mass bell shall not be a gong or tube, but only a small hand bell." Other Boston statutes regulated church music in exquisite detail—forbidding the use of any musical composition not previously approved by the Ordinary, stating that "no musical instrument except the organ" was permitted, and listing fourteen separate rules regarding the recitation of High Mass.[40]

For most parishioners, the authority of the archbishop of Boston extended beyond Sunday Mass. The Ordinary, according to canon law in the 1950s, was responsible for approving books and articles prior to publication, including all writings by clergy, all writings by lay Catholics on religion, and all submissions made by lay Catholics to magazines and newspapers regarded as hostile to Catholicism or to morality. The Ordinary was responsible, too, for condemning books "which might be harmful to faith or morals" and prohibiting Catholics from reading them. Forbidden books included obscene texts, books critical of Catholicism or religion generally, as well as writings favorable to communism, divorce, and the Masons. Priests could deny the sacraments to any Catholics who published or read books in defiance of Church law.[41]

The Boston archdiocese itself published a newspaper. During Mass one Sunday in September 1908, priests throughout Boston read a letter to their parishioners announcing that Archbishop O'Connell had purchased the *Pilot,* a weekly Catholic newspaper, from its private owners. "The message stated that it is not sufficient that a paper, to be called a Catholic paper, should be owned or even published by a Catholic," according to a report in the *Boston Evening Transcript.* "The Church assumes no responsibility for individual action unless it bears the stamp of her recognition or approval." Having purchased the *Pilot,* the archbishop of Boston enlisted parish priests to sell newspaper subscriptions to lay Catholics. "We urge that all Catholics read The Pilot and other approved Catholic papers and magazines," the Boston statutes stated in the 1950s. When the archbishop "decreed" new laws for the archdiocese, the statutes noted, he published them in "The Pilot, the official organ of the Archdiocese."[42]

Lay Catholics, who had no recognized right to change church ritual or to read controversial texts, also possessed little authority over the education of their children. Parish schools in Dorchester and Roxbury were organized by priests, with the permission of the archbishop. "A few years ago you told me to build a school as soon as I thought it well to do so. Hence these plans," Rev. John A. Daly, the pastor of St. Mark's Parish, wrote to Cardinal O'Connell in December 1921. After the cardinal approved Daly's plans, St. Mark's Parish built its school. Monsignor Edward F. Hurley, the pastor of St. Matthew's Parish, argued that a school would stimulate the interest of his own parishioners. "This Parish seems isolated and the people seem to feel that there is no progress in it," he explained to Cardinal O'Connell in May 1926, offering a proposal for a parish school. "I believe that if your Eminence will permit me to go on with the work for which I have asked permission they will be satisfied and they will manifest greater willingness to cooperate for the definite good of the Parish."[43]

The Second Vatican Council challenged, but did not entirely overturn, the hierarchy's traditional authority. Canon law since the 1960s has promoted lay participation in the parish's ritual and administrative life—though the pastor, "under the authority of the diocesan bishop," retains responsibility for the parish and for maintaining the integrity of church ritual, "being vigilant lest any abuses creep in." Many parishes created advisory councils in response to the Second Vatican Council; statutes adopted by the 1988 Boston synod required every parish to establish a pastoral council. Composed of lay Catholics and led by the pastor, pastoral councils work with the pastor in overseeing parish activities, including "evangelization, worship, religious education and service activities." Pastors now consult not only with pastoral councils but also with finance councils and school advisory boards.[44]

But the involvement of lay Catholics in parish affairs has not destroyed

clerical authority. Reforms of the Second Vatican Council were implemented whether or not parishioners welcomed the changes. In the
1960s, when St. Mark's pastor, Monsignor Walter F. Donahue, began
encouraging parishioners to serve as lectors, they were initially reluctant to participate. Large numbers of parishioners—"conservative by nature and not anxious to become involved, as Vatican II says, in associat-
ing themselves with Christ in his saving mission"—also appear to have
resisted Donahue's decision in 1968 to establish a parish council and
to consult with it on a regular basis. Moreover, the authority of any
parish council is limited. Monsignor Donahue himself noted that he was
"the one responsible to God for the parish, and, as such, [had] to have
the power of ultimate decision." Restricted by canon law to "a consul-
tative vote only," parish councils are relatively weak institutions in most
American parishes. Sometimes they do not exist at all.[45]

While Jewish doctrine is grounded in the Talmud and rabbis are traditionally respected as experts in Jewish law, it is the members of the
congregation who possess the actual authority to settle matters of ritual
and policy for their synagogue. As Monsignor Donahue looked to his
parish council for advice, so the membership of a Jewish congregation
often look to a rabbi for advice. But as Donahue reserved to himself "the
power of ultimate decision," so, too, the members of a synagogue retain
ultimate authority. The authority of neither Donahue nor a Jewish congregation depends on the existence of a source of advice: thus pastors
can make decisions without the consent of pastoral councils and Jewish
congregations can settle disputes and change basic rituals without consulting a rabbi.

Ohabei Shalom and Adath Israel, Boston's oldest congregations, embraced Reform Judaism at the initiative of their members. In the middle
1870s, a reform-oriented set of young members gained control of each
congregation, introducing the organ into religious services and establishing mixed-sex, family pews. Members of Adath Israel, who elected
Solomon Schindler as their rabbi in 1874, also adopted a new prayer
book. By the 1890s—encouraged by Rabbi Schindler and his successor,
Charles Fleischer—Adath Israel's members had banned yarmulkes and
hats from their temple, invited Christian ministers to speak from their
pulpit, and shifted Sabbath services from Saturday to Sunday mornings.
Ohabei Shalom, which adopted the Union Prayer Book in 1899, followed
a less radical path of reform. Not until the middle 1910s did Ohabei

Shalom join the Union of American Hebrew Congregations, the national federation of Reform temples. Its members elected their first Reform rabbi, Samuel J. Abrams, in 1920.[46]

Mishkan Tefila began challenging Orthodox doctrine in the first years of the twentieth century. Against the counsel of Rabbi Shoher, who resigned the congregation's pulpit in 1905, its members sold their synagogue on Shawmut Avenue to a Baptist church. In the years between 1905 and 1910, when they supported no permanent rabbi, members of Mishkan Tefila adopted some minor reforms—a confirmation ceremony for boys and girls, English rather than German sermons—and, more significant, they introduced family pews. But members of Mishkan Tefila made no changes to the religious service itself. They continued to use a traditional prayer book, to cover their heads during worship, to say their prayers in Hebrew, to exclude all musical instruments from worship, and to maintain an all-male choir. "Reform will regard this as unprogressive and orthodoxy as heretical," the *Boston Advocate* noted in 1907, "but logic does not control life, and sentiment cannot wholly grip it."[47]

Mishkan Tefila's members were still defining their version of an Americanized Judaism when they elected Rubenovitz as their rabbi in 1910. A graduate of the Jewish Theological Seminary, Rubenovitz identified strongly with the emerging Conservative movement. Convinced that the congregation's traditional style of worship lacked "good taste and proper decorum," he concluded that Mishkan Tefila needed to adopt additional reforms "if our youth were to be won for the traditional service." Rubenovitz could argue the case for those reforms, but he knew that members alone had the authority to effect change. Mishkan Tefila's 1913 by-laws stated that "no important change shall be made in the ritual nor shall any new form of worship be accepted" except upon the recommendation of the board of directors and with the consent of a majority of the congregation's members. "Many were the hours I had to spend in heated discussion with those who opposed any change of method and congregational policy," Rubenovitz recalled. "The younger members were all with me, but the older men, with very few exceptions, saw in my suggestion a move in the direction of Reform. They argued that a modernized religious service would involve the use of the organ and a mixed choir, and that such a change would inevitably lead to the adoption of the 'Union Prayer Book,' and would turn our congregation into a Reform Temple." Frustrated by the opposition, Rabbi Rubenovitz considered leaving the congregation.[48]

In late 1913, after returning from a tour of the synagogues of Paris, Berlin, and Vienna, Rubenovitz wrote again to the congregation's board and "suggested certain modifications in our mode of religious service in line with what I had seen abroad in the great European centers of Jewish life." After a year-long debate, the congregation's members accepted his recommendations. "At a stormy meeting" in the fall of 1914, they voted—"67 in favor and 54 against"—to introduce an organ into their religious services and to include women in the congregation's choir. Nearly ten years after Rabbi Shoher had resigned the congregation's pulpit, Rubenovitz had succeeded in mustering a majority of members behind the standard of Conservative Judaism. Mishkan Tefila's members had made their final break from Orthodoxy. Their cantor, Julius Karlsberg, refusing to implement the changes, "severed his relations with the congregation."[49]

With the springtime festival of Shavuot in 1915, Mishkan Tefila introduced its organ and mixed choir under the direction of a visiting cantor. Leaders of the congregation explained that the changes did not represent a movement toward Reform Judaism. "The ritual and order of prayers are not to be tampered with, and there is to be no change of prayer-book, or shortening of services," the *Jewish Advocate* reported. "In the thickly populated sections of Roxbury and Dorchester the need has long been felt for a service thoroughly Jewish in tone and content which shall appeal to the younger generation by its decorous and beautiful form. It is in the hope of meeting this need, and thus saving our young people for Judaism and the synagogue, that the directors of Temple Mishkan Tefila have decided on the use of the organ." After interviewing several candidates that summer, the congregation's members elected a new cantor, Michael Magidson, who had been trained in Berlin and Munich. "Cantor Magidson comes to the congregation at the beginning of a new era in its history," the *Advocate* observed. "While remaining loyal to the principles and practices of conservative Judaism, Temple Mishkan Tefila is now definitely aligned with the forces making for progress and advancement in Jewish life."[50]

The authority of a congregation's membership is vast, and that authority is not restricted to congregations that have embraced Reform or Conservative Judaism. As Hadrath Israel's rabbi realized on the Sabbath morning that he was escorted out of the building, Orthodox congregations also possess full authority to resolve ritual issues. The pioneer congregations of Roxbury and Dorchester—Adath Jeshurun's Blue Hill Avenue Synagogue, Beth El's Fowler Street Synagogue, and Beth Hamidrash Hagadol's Crawford Street Synagogue—modified Orthodox practices in the 1910s and early 1920s, introducing late Friday night services, English-language hymnals, and, on a limited basis, family pews. In the winter of 1924–1925, the members of Agudath Israel fiercely debated the placement of their bimah, the ceremonial reading table used during the Torah service. The by-laws of Mattapan's Kehillath Jacob, adopted in 1926, reflected the extent of the membership's authority in a typical Orthodox congregation. Kehillath Jacob's members, according to the by-laws, possessed "the entire and exclusive management, direction, supervision and control of the affairs of the Corporation," and the congregation's elected president, not a rabbi, was responsible for "the general executive direction of the operation of the Corporation in its religious and other matters."[51]

The most learned rabbi is powerless against a congregational majority. Acting only on a vote of their members, congregations have changed or abandoned many of Judaism's oldest practices. As Marshall Sklare observes, "The directors of each congregation determine their own ritual; ethnic bonds make it well-nigh impossible to read any group out of the fold regardless of its deviant behavior."[52] The Conservative movement might never have emerged, according to Sklare, if a different set of rules had governed Jewish institutions. Because they possess the power to define ritual and worship, members of a Jewish congregation control all internal policy.

Selection and Dismissal of Clergy

American rabbis are employees, hired and dismissed by congregations. Rabbis are paid salaries, they are responsible to the congregation's membership, and they serve according to terms negotiated between themselves and the congregation. "At any of their meetings, among other things," according to the by-laws of Kehillath Jacob, members "may select a Rabbi, Cantor (Chazan) and Shamos (Beadle) for the Corporation." Kehillath Jacob, organized in 1926, did not hire its first rabbi until 1939, when members elected Samuel I. Korff.[53]

A congregation can summarily dismiss its rabbi, as Hadrath Israel did that Saturday morning in 1928. But this is rare. More often, since contracts usually specify terms of employment between a congregation and

its rabbi, the process of contract renewal is itself sufficient reminder to
the rabbi of his congregation's authority. A 1972 story in the *Boston Globe*
described the case of a rabbi at a Long Island synagogue who discovered
"quite by accident" that his congregation was advertising in a national
journal for a rabbi to replace him. Even under better circumstances,
renewing a contract is a difficult affair for a rabbi. "His contract discussions are not with the president of a congregation or the chairman of a
personnel committee, or with any one or two men who control a decision whether he is in or out," one rabbi explained to the *Globe*. "He is
instead the subject of a personnel committee of monumental proportion." Regarded most of the time as a respected leader, the rabbi is reduced at the time of contract renewal to the place of "a supplicant em-
ployee."[54]

Congregations have refused to renew contracts because of personality
differences, policy disagreements, even changing fiscal priorities. Several
congregations in Roxbury and Dorchester dismissed rabbis or, when a
rabbi left, waited months or years before hiring a new leader so they
could divert money used for the rabbi's salary to other uses. "Boston
abounds in Rabbiless Synagogues," a member of the Crawford Street
Synagogue wrote in May 1927, implicitly criticizing his own congregation. "The common excuse is that these Orthodox houses of worship were so overburdened with debts that the congregations could ill
afford the 'luxuries' of the services of Rabbis." In the middle 1920s, the
three most prominent Orthodox congregations in Roxbury and Dorchester all lacked rabbis—the Blue Hill Avenue Synagogue, from January
1925 through July 1926; the Crawford Street Synagogue, from July 1925
through April 1928; the Fowler Street Synagogue, from November 1925
through September 1929. The *Jewish Advocate*, in an April 1926 editorial, condemned the practice, criticizing "the words of those who
coarsely dare bring business psychology and the trader's logic into God's
House: they don't have to pay the salary to the Rabbi and so they can pay
off a mortgage and perhaps even invest, etc., etc."[55]

Herman H. Rubenovitz understood, as well as any rabbi, a congregation's authority. One of the great pulpit rabbis in the history of Boston
and the Conservative movement, he was revered by his congregation.
"The soul of Mishkan Tefila and the Soul of Rabbi Rubenovitz are one
and inseparable," B. Leonard Kolovson, the vice-president of the congregation, said in 1944, when the congregation elected Rubenovitz "Rabbi

of Congregation Mishkan Tefila for Life," granting him life tenure and a pension in his retirement. When Rubenovitz died, in 1966, his successor, Rabbi Israel J. Kazis, recalled all that had passed since Rubenovitz had accepted the pulpit at the Moreland Street Temple. "For fifty-six years," Kazis declared, "Rabbi Rubenovitz kept and fulfilled his sacred charge and mission at Temple Mishkan Tefila, in our community, in New England and in our country."[56]

The search in 1910 had been a historic success. By 1923 Rubenovitz was receiving a salary of $5,000. At their annual meeting in January 1924, members of Mishkan Tefila unanimously reelected him for an additional ten years. Under the terms of the new contract, his salary increased steadily from $6,500 in 1924 to $10,000 in 1929, then remained at $10,000 until the contract expired. But Rubenovitz never completed this ten-year term. Like Mishkan Tefila's financial crisis, his resignation in 1930—and his anxious effort, two years later, to return to his old job—is an episode that was never recorded in newspapers or recounted in congregational histories. The experience, which starkly reaffirmed the congregation's authority, was more humbling for Rubenovitz than his original application in 1910 or any negotiations to renew his contract.[57]

An ardent Zionist, Rubenovitz notified the congregation's board of directors in the summer of 1929 of his intention to resign his position "in order to be able to assume greater responsibilities in Palestine and serve Judaism at large." The board agreed to accept his resignation, effective in 1930, and to release him from his ten-year contract. In December 1929, at the annual meeting of the congregation, Rubenovitz submitted his formal resignation. "The time has now come for me to relinquish the leadership with which you invested me," he stated in his letter to the membership. "As you know, it is my hope and intention to settle in Palestine." He explained that he planned to leave Boston at the end of the summer. "I consider the cause of Mishkan Tefila and of Palestine equally sacred. I have served the one twenty years; I now want to serve the other," Rubenovitz wrote. "The subtle threads of memory, devotion and love, will always bind me to Mishkan Tefila. Neither space nor time shall sever these bonds while yet my life continues." In the summer of 1930, after a banquet held in his honor, Rabbi Rubenovitz and his wife left for Palestine.[58]

The congregation's board searched for a new permanent rabbi, but progress was slow. One member rose at a board meeting in June 1931 to criticize the search committee, "stating that it had been in existence for over a year and that no suitable candidate has yet been named." For the High Holy Day services in 1930, the congregation had paid $500 for the services of a visiting rabbi. Meanwhile, since there was no rabbi to deliver a sermon or a lecture, the congregation had invited "laymen speakers . . . to occupy the pulpit on Friday nights." Finally, in the fall of 1931, two years after Rubenovitz had announced his resignation and more than one year after he had left, the congregation elected a new rabbi. Perez Halpern was elected for an initial one-year term "at a salary not exceeding $5,000.00."[59]

When his contract expired, a divided board voted not to reelect Rabbi Halpern: Mishkan Tefila's financial condition was worsening in 1932, and the congregation—which worshiped in the monumental Seaver Street Temple—had concluded that it could no longer afford a full-time rabbi. At a congregational meeting held in August 1932, members voted to "engage [a] Rabbi to officiate on High Holidays only" and, after considering another candidate, decided to ask Rabbi Rubenovitz to accept those three days of employment. A few months earlier, Rubenovitz had sent a letter to a member of the board "in which he wrote that he was in financial need." Back from Palestine, Rubenovitz agreed to officiate at the High Holy Day services. Still, he hoped for steadier work. That October, at a meeting of the board of directors, Rubenovitz told members that he knew the congregation's "problems were becoming more complex." But he added, according to the board's minutes, "that he was prepared to work with us, that a simple living must be had, and that further arrangements must be made." The board discussed "Rabbi Rubenovitz's suggestion for further arrangements" and appointed a three-member committee to speak with the rabbi and to determine the feasibility of rehiring him on a permanent basis. It did prove feasible: Rubenovitz agreed to accept an annual salary of $4,160, less than half of his former salary. In the fall of 1932, Rubenovitz returned to Mishkan Tefila as its full-time rabbi.[60]

The uncomfortable three-year episode was soon forgotten. Presumably no irony was intended when Elihu D. Stone, the congregation's president, declared in May 1933, "Mishkan Tefila is personified by our Rabbi and the Temple under his leadership could be an example for other congregations."[61] Stone's statement was accurate, and not only because of the high regard in which Rubenovitz was held by the temple's members. In impelling Rabbi Shoher's resignation in 1905 and in refusing to reelect

Rabbi Halpern in 1932, the congregation demonstrated two ways in which a Jewish institution can dismiss its rabbi. In supervising the activities of its rabbi, in requiring him to seek permission from the membership before he could miss a Sabbath service or leave for a vacation, the congregation maintained its authority throughout its rabbi's tenure. And in hiring a rabbi—advertising, interviewing, creating a search committee, and approving contracts in open votes—the congregation asserted its own autonomy and authority. In every instance, Mishkan Tefila gave witness to the rules that define Jewish institutions.

There is no want ad in St. Peter's past. The laypersons of St. Peter's Parish have never advertised for a priest or set up a search committee. They have never negotiated a contract with a priest, never hired a priest or dismissed a priest. None of this is their business. St. Peter's parishioners do not discuss salary with a priest; indeed, it has been the parish priest himself who has controlled and dispensed the parish's funds. Describing the faith of the parish's founding families, Rev. Florence J. Halloran later recalled, "They petitioned the Bishop, and they prayed to God, to send them a pastor, and their prayer was heard." In the first hundred years since St. Peter's was established in 1872, the parish knew only four pastors, and it was served well by them. Each of those four— Peter Ronan, 1872–1917; Joseph G. Anderson, 1917–1927; Richard J. Haberlin, 1927–1959; and James H. Doyle, 1959–1975—was assigned to the parish by the bishop of Boston and was accountable, throughout his pastorate, to the bishop.[62]

According to canon law, "all clerics, but especially priests, are bound by a special obligation to show reverence and obedience each to his own Ordinary." Canon law grants the Ordinary full responsibility for appointing and reassigning parish priests. The priest derives his authority "not from the local community but from the authority passed down to him from the papacy itself through the diocese bishop," W. Lloyd Warner and Leo Srole argued. "He is an officer in the Roman Catholic government and is responsible to it alone." Boston statutes in the 1950s stated that pastors could not be absent from their parishes for a vacation or on any Sunday or holy day without first receiving the archbishop's written permission.[63]

In the nineteenth and through most of the twentieth century, the bishop of Boston personally selected and appointed each pastor in his diocese. Richard J. Cushing, who served as archbishop from 1944 until his death in 1970, maintained two folders that he consulted whenever a vacancy occurred. He determined whether a "first assignment or second assignment" was appropriate for the parish, then instructed his chancellor to bring the proper folder to their meeting. Monsignor Thomas J. Finnegan, Jr., who served as Cardinal Cushing's last chancellor, recalls these meetings. For vacancies in smaller parishes, Finnegan referred to the folder that contained the names of curates, reading names to the cardinal in order of seniority. For vacancies in large parishes, Finnegan referred to the other folder, which contained the names of priests who were already pastors, and read, one by one, the names of pastors serving "in the boondocks." Finnegan paused after reading each name, as Cardinal Cushing thought about the priest, thought about the parish, and considered the match. "Hmmm," the cardinal might say after the first name was read. "No," he might say after the second name. "Hmmm," after the third name. Then, finally, at the first or fourth or tenth name that he heard, the cardinal would smile and say, "Call him." On the instruction of the cardinal, the chancellor then contacted the priest to find out if he was interested in the appointment. If the priest expressed interest, Cushing made the appointment.[64]

After the Second Vatican Council, the archbishop of Boston reformed the process of clergy assignment. Although he maintains his authority over appointments, the archbishop now acts, in most cases, with the assistance of a diocesan board and with the advice of parishioners. Cardinal Cushing established the Office of Clergy Personnel in the 1960s to oversee the assignment of curates, a function which, at various times, had been supervised by the secretary, the chancellor, or the Ordinary himself. In the 1970s, Archbishop Humberto S. Medeiros expanded the office's responsibilities. The Clergy Personnel Board now offers recommendations for the assignment of pastors, submitting the names of at least three candidates to the archbishop for his decision. In making its recommendations, the board considers the views of parishioners expressed at a parish consultation meeting, where parishioners are encouraged to describe the needs of their parish and outline the general qualities that they desire in a pastor. The archbishop, consulting the board's list as well as any additional comments from the regional bishop, reaches his decision. If the priest he selects does not object to the assignment, then the archbishop makes the appointment.[65]

Traditionally, the appointment was for life. "Once appointed," the

Globe reported in 1972, "a Catholic pastor has been able to count on remaining a pastor until death or retirement, except in rare cases." The pastor not only enjoyed life tenure but, controlling parish funds, could set his own salary and the salaries of his curates. In 1972 Archbishop Medeiros ended the old system of life tenure and variable salaries. Beginning that July, all pastors in the Boston archdiocese have served for six-year terms and, with curates, have received salaries according to a diocesan schedule. Although pastors are appointed, reappointed, and reassigned by the archbishop, the archbishop may not, without just cause, dismiss a pastor before the end of his term. For the term of his assignment, according to canon law, "a pastor has a parish in his own right." Parishioners, who since the 1970s have been consulted on an initial assignment to the parish, are not consulted before a pastor is reappointed or transferred. They cannot keep a well-regarded priest from leaving or fire an unpopular priest.[66]

Rev. Charles A. Finnigan, who became pastor of St. Mary of the Angels' Parish in 1916, was frequently criticized by his parishioners. "His vagaries, his impertinence, rudeness—and indeed insults are known and generally discussed when Church affairs are mentioned; his treatment of his curates—faithful and lovable young Priests—have almost resulted in open rebellion to his course," one man wrote in 1928, in a letter to the cardinal. "The writer feels obliged to say it is the general consensus of opinion of the parishioners, that for his own good, for the good of the Church, the pastor ought to be changed elsewhere." Several parishioners, and even Father Finnigan's own curates, expressed serious concern in the 1920s and 1930s, explaining to Cardinal O'Connell that Finnigan refused to spend funds to heat the church or to provide sufficient food for his curates and staff. The whole parish, a layperson wrote in 1937, was "under the jurisdiction of one who acts mentally afflicted." But, because they enjoyed no authority over Father Finnigan, the men and women of St. Mary of the Angels' Parish were powerless to dismiss him. The situation, one person noted in the late 1920s, forced "the great majority of parishioners to endure him because they could do nothing else." Finnigan remained pastor until his death in 1953.[67]

Even after the Second Vatican Council, parishioners can do nothing but endure an objectionable pastor: this was the lesson learned in the 1980s by the men and women of St. William's Parish. Widespread opposition to Rev. Francis J. Crowley emerged in the spring of 1981, a few months after St. William's Church was destroyed by fire. Disappointed by the response of Cardinal Medeiros and chancery officials, who refused several requests to meet with them, St. William's parishioners formed a committee and made their concerns public in January 1982. They argued that Father Crowley had shown "disinterest, disdain and overall disregard of his pastoral responsibilities." In an open letter the committee stated that Crowley had undermined youth activities, neglected parishioners and curates, harmed the parish school, mismanaged parish funds, and planned for the new church without regard for parishioners' opinions. Through "his intransigence, indecision, duplicity and dishonesty," parishioners wrote, "he has created an atmosphere of distrust to the degree that few, if any, members have faith in his word."[68]

That January John Madden, a member of the committee, explained to the *Boston Globe* that St. William's parishioners were "just asking for a hearing." Bishop Thomas V. Daily, the chancellor of the archdiocese, finally agreed to meet with the committee, which was made up of some of the parish's most active lay leaders. Members of the committee, sitting around a long conference table in the chancery building, waited forty-five minutes before Bishop Daily entered the room. Wearing a long purple robe, Daily said nothing until he took his seat at the head of the table. He sat down, folded his arms across his chest, then spoke. He offered no welcome. "Frank Crowley's my guy," Daily bluntly stated, as he looked at the parishioners. "What else do you have to say?" For the next fifteen minutes, parishioners quickly reviewed their many concerns about Crowley's performance. Daily remained silent. "He never said a word. He never questioned us," Joe Burnieika, one of the parishioners, later recalled. "He just stared at each speaker as we spoke." When the parishioners finished outlining their concerns, Bishop Daily declared, "As I said at the beginning, Frank Crowley's my guy," then he stood up and left the room. In 1984, when his six-year term ended, Crowley was reappointed by the archbishop to another term as St. William's pastor.[69]

Parishioners lack authority not only to dismiss unpopular pastors but also to keep effective and successful pastors. In the fall of 1995, St. Ann's parishioners learned that Cardinal Bernard Law had reassigned their pastor, Rev. Thomas Walsh, to a parish in the suburban town of Franklin. Walsh enjoyed great popularity in St. Ann's Parish. A Dorchester native, he had led the parish's campaign to renovate the church, had reached out to children at the parish school and attended their softball games, and had regularly shown up at neighborhood get-togethers. The cardinal's decision frustrated and saddened parishioners. "I'm very angry. We battle and we battle to keep this parish alive," one St. Ann's parishioner told the *Boston Globe* in October 1995. "Then you're given someone like Tom Walsh who has put the parish back on its feet, and he's taken away from you." An archdiocesan spokesperson, asserting that the archdiocese remained committed to urban parishes like St. Ann's, explained that the cardinal had to consider the needs of the whole archdiocese when he reviewed the assignment of priests. "Emotionally, it's kind of difficult leaving," Father Walsh admitted. "But I know it's what God wants me to do."[70]

Congregational Worship

The strength of this hierarchical authority rests on the centrality of the Eucharist and other sacraments to Catholic worship. "The celebration of the Eucharist is the source of all parish ministries," St. Matthew's Parish declared in a 1990 report prepared for the regional bishop's visitation. "We celebrate the Mass daily with special formalities on Sundays." In its own visitation report one year later, St. Mark's Parish placed similar emphasis on the Eucharist. "Without the Mass," St. Mark's committee wrote, "there is no parish." The Eucharistic celebration, an occasional event in nineteenth-century churches, emerged in the twentieth century as the defining event of regular parish life. "The pastor is to see to it that the Most Holy Eucharist is the center of the parish assembly of the faithful," canon law states. "He is to work to see to it that the Christian faithful are nourished through a devout celebration of the sacraments."[71]

Only an ordained priest can celebrate the Eucharist, administer the other sacraments, and preside over divine services. In the second half of the nineteenth century, as clergy and lay Catholics embraced an increasingly elaborate set of devotions and religious services, "the priest, more than ever before, became the central figure in the parish," Jay P. Dolan writes. "Without him a public devotional life was not able to exist." No group of Catholics, however large or devout or learned, can celebrate Mass without an ordained priest. A priest alone possesses the authority to baptize a child, hear confession, conduct a wedding, anoint the sick, or perform a funeral.[72]

Because the parish can survive only with the participation of an ordained priest, lay Catholics must submit to the authority of their priest and to the hierarchy that assigns him. The authority of the clergy—the

this does not sound like the 19e

authority to establish parishes, control property, make policy, and appoint pastors—and the continued relevance of canon law are due to the nature of Catholic ritual and worship. "The priest is the key person in any Catholic parish, and his role in the functioning of the parochial system is so important that without him the parish would cease to exist," Joseph H. Fichter has written. "The concept of a 'religion without a priesthood,' or of a religion in which the ministers of God are merely employees, directors, or supervisors of congregations, is completely alien to the religious institution of Catholicism. All parochial activities . . . depend upon the priest."[73]

Jewish religious services and ritual events derive no special legitimacy from a rabbi's presence. "Talmudic Judaism rejected the distinction between laity and clergy. A rabbi could do nothing prohibited to a layman," Emanuel Rackman wrote. "Daily and Sabbath services were led by laymen—cantors or readers. Very often the rabbi did not even attend the synagogue." Circumcision, bar mitzvah, marriage, funeral: for none of these events does Jewish law require or assume the presence of a rabbi. "To be a rabbi," Rackman observed, "meant nothing—or nothing else—than to be a pious Jew learned in the Law." There are no sacraments in Judaism. From its origins, the synagogue service has consisted entirely of prayer and Bible reading.[74]

A Jewish congregation exists whenever ten Jewish men worship together. "Ten male adults constitute a quorum in any place," according to *Encyclopaedia Judaica,* "and there is no need for a synagogue building or an officiating rabbi to hold divine services." Removed from the traditional communal controls that characterized European Jewry, the American synagogue in the nineteenth century became both the central institution in Jewish life and an institution enjoying complete autonomy. "Here each congregation is a law unto itself," the *Jewish Encyclopedia* asserted at the turn of the century. "It may elect its own ministers and arrange its services at will." A synagogue can exist without a rabbi, and it flourishes without the permission or assistance of any hierarchy. This authority structure requires members themselves to assume full responsibility for preserving the congregation. An institution that depends on its members for survival eschews geographical limits on its members, competes for members against other institutions, and recognizes the urgency of relocating when members themselves move.[75]

III

Neighborhood

In the late 1960s, local residents walk past the G&G delicatessen or linger at the corner. For decades, the G&G was a central gathering spot for Dorchester and Roxbury's Jews. Men kibitzing over coffee before they went off to work, teenagers on a date, ward heelers and politicians (like Julius Ansel, a local political figure)—all of them passed their time at a booth or at one of the delicatessen's small tables. They also came on crisp fall nights during election season, crowding the streets as presidents, senators, and city councillors asked for votes. (*Photograph courtesy of the* Boston Globe.)

8
_____

Towns, Suburbs, and Neighborhoods

Far from the dust and noise and congestion of the city, Dorchester and upper Roxbury emerged in the late nineteenth century as attractive suburban communities. With the development of efficient streetcar lines, a husband and wife could raise their family in a quiet residential neighborhood yet commute to work in downtown Boston. "Dorchester is a wholesome community, with a neighborly spirit," the Dorchester Board of Trade wrote in 1916, "the home of 161,000 people, the best housed, the happiest, the healthiest and the most successful and progressive."[1] From the 1870s through the first years of the twentieth century, Dorchester was the very model of a suburban district. In a time now forgotten—in the age of the horsecar, the trolley, the subway, the elevated, the streetcar—it was in districts like Dorchester and upper Roxbury that middle-class families realized the suburban ideal.

Roxbury and Dorchester traced their histories to 1630, when English settlers founded the two towns. Roxbury's village center emerged near Dudley Street, where the various roads skirting the hills of upper Roxbury met the road that passed through lower Roxbury and into Boston. There, on the town green, early settlers organized the First Church of Roxbury and, nearby, the Roxbury Latin School. Dorchester's residents set aside Dorchester Common, their town green, at the crest of Meeting House Hill, where they built Dorchester's grammar school and First Parish Church. Through the eighteenth century, Dorchester and Roxbury remained quiet farming communities. Not until the nineteenth century did the character of the towns begin to change.[2]

Homes, businesses, and small factories began crowding into lower

Roxbury in the 1830s and 1840s. This district, which extended from Boston's South End to Roxbury's town green, became an appendage of Boston. From lower Roxbury it was barely two miles to Boston's wharves, and less than that to City Hall, the State House, or Boston Common. "During the years 1830–1860 large numbers of mill workers' row houses were constructed near the factories," Sam Bass Warner, Jr., wrote. By 1870, lower Roxbury had become a "working class area," according to Warner, "a small drab section of little two- and three-story wooden houses and barracks such as could be found in any New England mill town."[3]

As the great city swallowed lower Roxbury whole, it merely peopled upper Roxbury and Dorchester. At Dudley Street, where Roxbury began to rise up on its steep hills, lower Roxbury came to an abrupt end: at the hills, at the historic town center near Dudley Street, upper Roxbury began. Geographically and socially, the highlands of upper Roxbury dominated the entire district. For many years after Roxbury was annexed by Boston in 1868, all Roxbury was frequently referred to as "Boston Highlands." Dorchester, annexed in 1870, extended southward and eastward, meeting upper Roxbury along a high plateau. From that plateau, the wide expanse of Dorchester "sloped off eastward to the sea, its more or less gentle slopes interrupted here and there" by a series of hills.[4]

"Until well along in the present century," according to an 1895 account, upper Roxbury continued to be "occupied by farms." But the farms were disappearing. "Beginning in the late eighteenth century men of wealth and fashion built large houses about the hills of Roxbury," Warner wrote. "The steepness of much of its land kept out industry while the same topography made the highlands land suitable for summer houses and gentlemen's estates." By the middle of the nineteenth century, the estates and summer homes had supplanted most of the old farms in upper Roxbury. Although increasing numbers of middle-class families were settling in upper Roxbury, "the big suburban rush" did not begin until the 1870s, after Roxbury had been annexed by Boston. "Here in 1870 were the substantial middle class houses of Boston businessmen and the handsome estates of an earlier era," Warner wrote. "These families enjoyed small community life and actively participated in it."[5]

Dorchester attracted few country estates. It was less hilly than upper Roxbury, more distant from Boston, and covered a much larger territory: through the middle of the nineteenth century, most of Dorchester's land was still devoted to farming. In 1806, with the growth of the town's population, the Second Church had been established "in the south part of the town," in what became Codman Square. Two villages, one at Meeting House Hill and the other at Codman Square, served the inner and outer farming districts of the town. At the southernmost rim of Dorchester, on the Neponset River, three other settlements formed around mills at Neponset, Lower Mills, and Mattapan. An observer described Dorchester in the 1830s as "an agricultural and manufactory town of over 3500 inhabitants, large farms covering broad acres, and factories." In the 1850s and 1860s, when "main streets and some rear blocks were peppered with commuters' houses" in the vicinity of Meeting House Hill, a modest suburban district emerged in Dorchester. But this was a small area, close to Boston. Dorchester's plateaus and hills were "ideally suited to inexpensive residential construction," Warner argued, "but in 1870 they were too far for mass commuting to Boston and most of their surface was taken up by truck gardens and other small farms."[6]

In the 1870s and 1880s, with the extension and improvement of horsecar service, Dorchester and upper Roxbury became middle-class suburbs of Boston. "What a few years ago was a rural town, is now a part of the growing metropolis," the pastor of Dorchester's Second Church declared with some prescience in 1873. "And these fields where cattle grazed, are soon to be occupied by a compact population." Across upper Roxbury and Dorchester, on the urban periphery, new neighborhoods appeared and old communities seemed to disappear as tens of thousands of commuting residents overwhelmed the past. "Houses are now springing up on hill and plain," an account published in 1881 stated. "A few of the old farms are left, but the majority have been cut up by streets and divided into building lots." In the late 1880s and 1890s, with the electrification and further extension of streetcar routes, suburbanization "attained the proportions of a mass movement," Warner wrote. "The rate of building and settlement in this period became so rapid that the whole scale and plan of Greater Boston was entirely made over."[7]

By 1900 the total population of upper Roxbury and Dorchester exceeded 100,000; in the three decades since 1870, the population of Dorchester alone had increased from 12,000 to 80,000. Suburbanization was the achievement of Boston's middle class. "The new suburbs were a society of tradesmen, salesmen, small manufacturers, professionals, and artisans, men working hard to make a good living and to get ahead,"

Warner argued. The houses that were built across Dorchester and upper Roxbury in these years reflected a new, common understanding of middle-class life. These suburban neighborhoods were entirely residential, attracting people whose jobs were elsewhere. "The architecture was also novel. The detached wooden house, especially the single-family house, predominated," Warner wrote. "They were building a wholly new environment, but the omnipresence of vacant land lulled builders into having no thought of the future. Each homeowner wanted to believe that his new house was in the country, or at least near it, though in fact in ten to fifteen years his house and land would be lost in a great plain of new streets and new houses."[8]

As large numbers of lower-middle-class families began moving to the first areas of suburban settlement, the band of central-middle-class construction shifted outward. Dorchester's inner neighborhoods—described in the early 1910s as "still clinging to a faint suggestion of eighteenth century village life, and having a strong substance of nineteenth century suburbanism"—were changing by the turn of the century, with the village and middle-class suburb "encroached upon and retreating before the twentieth century three-decker." There were, of course, as Warner observed, several "eddies in the general flow," small areas that resisted the general tendency toward socioeconomic succession. Neighborhoods like Savin Hill, in northern Dorchester, and Elm Hill, in upper Roxbury, persisted as upper-middle-class suburbs into the twentieth century, long after lower-middle-class families had settled in adjacent neighborhoods. But these were exceptions. By the 1910s, the wooden three-decker was becoming ubiquitous in most parts of upper Roxbury and Dorchester. "Such a home . . . is well calculated to appeal to the ambitious clerk, mechanic and the like," two settlement-house workers wrote in the 1910s. "Admittedly the houses are cheaply constructed of medium grade material and with hurried workmanship. But they do offer and establish a standard of living which is well above what most of their occupants were accustomed to in the more crowded parts of the city."[9]

Suburban development, in knitting Dorchester and upper Roxbury into the metropolis, brought an entirely new population into the old towns. As immigrants and their children arrived in Boston and rose into the middle class, they joined American-born families in the movement out to the suburbs. The predominantly Yankee towns that were annexed by Boston became the suburban neighborhoods of a middle class that was becoming increasingly heterogeneous. Many of those settling in Dorchester and upper Roxbury in the last decades of the nineteenth century were Irish Catholics. By the turn of the century, Jews were also beginning to settle in these suburbs.

Between 1900 and 1920, the total population of Dorchester and upper Roxbury doubled in size, to more than 200,000 persons.[10] A substantial minority of that population was Jewish: about 44,000 Jews lived in the two districts in 1920, and the Jewish population was growing rapidly.[11] Another large minority was composed of Yankees. But, as Marion Booth and Ordway Tead noted in the 1910s, "the preponderant element here is, of course, of Irish descent."[12] In 1920 upper Roxbury and Dorchester were home to many tens of thousands of Irish Catholics: upper and central middle class, lower middle class, and working class. The suburban character of northern Dorchester "stands as both a cause and an effect of the incoming of a decidedly worthy and progressive type of Irish family," Booth and Tead observed. "The whole life of the district noticeably retains much of its tone and quality because those of this better class have made comfortable homes here and have had some interest in preserving and cultivating the green and fertile areas which they found."[13]

Through the first suburban wave, in the 1870s and 1880s, three Catholic parishes served all of Dorchester and upper Roxbury. These three were the founding parishes: with one exception, every other parish in modern-day Dorchester and upper Roxbury grew directly out of St. Joseph's, St. Gregory's, or St. Peter's.[14] As the pace of suburbanization increased, territory from these three parishes was taken for the establishment of new parishes. Between 1889 and 1914, in a span of twenty-five years, twelve new churches and eleven new parishes were erected to serve the Catholics of upper Roxbury and Dorchester. As Booth and Tead noted, "The newcomers have in short order established the foundations of a local life quite as refined and substantial as that which the Yankees had left."[15]

St. Margaret's Parish was established in the summer of 1893 to serve families living in the northeastern corner of St. Peter's Parish. Parishioners began worshiping in their new wooden church on Boston Street that November. It was a temporary facility. In March 1895 Rev. William A. Ryan, St. Margaret's pastor, purchased a large estate at the corner of Columbia Road and Dorchester Avenue, a prominent site in the very center of the parish's population. There he planned to build a permanent church, rectory, and school. Mass was first celebrated in St. Margaret's Church, in the basement, on Christmas Day 1900. Four years later, in November 1904, the completed church was dedicated. In his dedication sermon, Rev. Peter Ronan "described North Dorchester as he knew it, thirty-two years ago,—a section beautiful with gardens and orchards, but whose total Catholic population was not more than one hundred and fifty," the *Pilot* reported. "The natural beauties have in large part disappeared, he said, to make way for the far greater spiritual beauties embodied in the temples of God."[16]

With a small and compact territory, St. Margaret's Parish was supported by large numbers of faithful parishioners. Writing in the early 1910s, Booth and Tead noted that "the expansion of St. Margaret's offers a typical example of a parish among a thriving body of Irish Americans." Organized in 1893 with 1,500 persons, the parish "today counts 6,000 souls as under its ministrations," they wrote. St. Margaret's School, which opened in 1910, just two or three years later "already contains four hundred children in the first few grades." This was a stable suburban community. "Some of the families that settled here have by this time moved farther out," Booth and Tead observed, "but most of them remain and constitute a fairly successful class whose children can start life on a normal, hopeful basis."[17]

In another part of Dorchester, in the district along Blue Hill Avenue where Dorchester met upper Roxbury, a large Jewish community had formed by the 1910s. This community, which emerged in the 1900s around the Blue Hill Avenue Synagogue, was Boston's first suburban Jewish settlement. In 1907, one year after Adath Jeshurun dedicated the synagogue, a leader of the congregation referred with pride to "the present standing of their members . . . Jewish immigrants who by faithful industry had risen so as to be able to move out into better and more healthful quarters where they now possess an excellent place of worship."[18] The Jewish community in the Blue Hill Avenue–Grove Hall district, though still small in the middle 1900s, included much of Boston's middle-class Jewish leadership.

But by the middle 1910s, as thousands of lower-middle-class and working-class Jews settled in the Blue Hill Avenue–Grove Hall district, more prosperous Jews were moving to other parts of Roxbury and Dorchester. The Blue Hill Avenue–Grove Hall district declined in socioeconomic status as it became more densely Jewish. "To be lived well life cannot always be passed in crowds," Booth and Tead observed. "If the streets are to be kept clean, the houses repaired and the general air of orderliness maintained, the traditions which have made for such conditions must not be swamped by an inrush of those who still conform to West and North End or even Russian standards." While the district's original Jewish residents had purchased single-family homes, which were well maintained and "kept up with attractive gardens and good lawns," an increasing number of Jews moving into the area were building multifamily structures or converting old houses into tenements. "It is here that the danger lies," Booth and Tead argued. "The Jewish property holders do not hesitate to build cheap brick blocks or poorly constructed three-deckers, and in the event of this a type of family lower in the economic scale is attracted and the richer families go farther out." Mordecai M. Kaplan, visiting the Blue Hill Avenue–Grove Hall district in the spring of 1915, observed that the area had become "to all practical purposes a Ghetto."[19]

In the late 1900s and early 1910s, three new, middle-class Jewish neighborhoods began forming in Mount Bowdoin, Mattapan, and Elm Hill. In the summer of 1910, when Mount Bowdoin's Jews announced plans to erect a temple on Fowler Street, the *Jewish Advocate* observed that "the undertaking points directly to the spread of the community into the suburban parts of Boston."[20] Five imposing synagogues stood in suburban Boston by 1915. Four of them, all except Adath Israel's Reform temple, were located in upper Roxbury and Dorchester: Adath Jeshurun's Blue Hill Avenue Synagogue, Mishkan Tefila's Moreland Street Temple, Beth El's Fowler Street Synagogue, and Beth Hamidrash Hagadol's Crawford Street Synagogue. Each of these structures had been built—or, in the case of the Moreland Street Temple, acquired—in the decade since 1905. But these synagogues, the oldest and most prestigious in their respective neighborhoods, were owed no special allegiance by Jews in these districts. Already by 1915 a total of fifteen synagogues had been organized in upper Roxbury and Dorchester. In the middle 1920s there were about thirty synagogues in the area, as well as several Hebrew schools and community centers.

Dorchester and upper Roxbury were a quilt of residential neighborhoods by the 1920s. Catholics lived throughout much of the area, but many Yankee families were still living in outer Dorchester, and there was a large swath of Jewish neighborhoods along Blue Hill Avenue. Though most areas were lower middle class and central middle class, there were growing sections of working-class families and there remained pockets of wealth. In Dorchester, Irish and Yankee families maintained upper-middle-class neighborhoods in Savin Hill, Ashmont, and the Melville Avenue–Wellesley Park district. Roxbury's Elm Hill had become by the early 1920s the seat of the area's upper-middle-class Jewish community.

Rising above Franklin Park, the Elm Hill district was one of Boston's most desirable neighborhoods. Several handsome mansions stood on Elm Hill, but most residents lived in single-family homes, apartment hotels, and large two- and three-family structures "which in their exteriors conformed to the shingle style houses of the neighborhood."[21] It was in the Elm Hill district that Mishkan Tefila dedicated its new temple in 1925. While some middle-class Jews had begun to move entirely out of the area in the late 1910s and early 1920s, settling in the town of Brookline, and while a few others were scattered across other parts of Roxbury and Dorchester, most lived on Elm Hill.

Elm Hill's original Jewish congregation, the Crawford Street Synagogue, celebrated its "Tenth Anniversary Jubilee" in May 1924. In the brief span of a decade, Beth Hamidrash Hagadol had grown into "the largest and most noteworthy Orthodox Congregation in Boston, honored and respected by all." Committed to a modern, liberal Orthodoxy, it was an active member of the United Synagogue of America, the federation identified with Conservative Judaism. The congregation's rabbi, Louis M. Epstein, was a renowned scholar and president of the Rabbinical Assembly, the national body of rabbis aligned with the Conservative movement. Under Rabbi Epstein's leadership, the Crawford Street Synagogue was flourishing. The congregation maintained a men's club, a sisterhood, a junior council, and a Hebrew school. "Late Friday Evening Services, Sabbath Afternoon Study Hour, Public Forums, Jewish History classes, Hebrew Classes, lectures, congregational welfare or general community welfare activities keep our young people bound to our institution and to Orthodox Judaism by a thousand threads of loyalty," Epstein noted in 1924. For older members, Beth Hamidrash Hagadol supported traditional groups studying the Talmud.[22]

The Crawford Street Synagogue, built of red brick trimmed with stone, was an impressive structure.[23] Set back from the street behind a circular driveway and an elegant, wrought-iron gate, the synagogue extended nearly to the rear of its large property. The main sanctuary rose three stories and sat twelve hundred people. The congregation "owns the most attractive house of worship in Roxbury, situated on a magnificent stretch of natural green, ornamented by the delightful fragrance and joyful color of the early spring blossom," Rabbi Epstein wrote in 1924. "It owns a school building adjacent to it and a parsonage on Ruthven Street. In all, two hundred thousand dollars cannot buy it today." There was a mortgage debt outstanding on the property, but, as the congregation's president, Louis H. Steinberg, and its rabbi observed during the tenth jubilee celebration that spring, so prosperous a congregation—the pride of suburban Elm Hill Jewry—could easily retire its debt. Indeed, leaders of the congregation were already planning to purchase land for a cemetery and to replace the existing school building with a large, modern structure.[24]

9

Membership and Mobility

Even as Roxbury and Dorchester's Jewish neighborhoods emerged and grew, they began to unravel. Ben Rosen, writing in 1920, observed that the communities were already "losing part of their Jewish population: the well-to-do class, who are moving to districts outside of Boston City, to Brookline, Allston, the Newtons, etc."[1] By the middle 1920s, central- and upper-middle-class Jews were leaving in large numbers, attracted especially to the new suburban enclave in Brookline. Their time in Dorchester and upper Roxbury had been eventful but short. Their legacy was tangible. To the increasingly dense lower-middle-class and working-class Jewish neighborhoods that lay along Blue Hill Avenue, "the well-to-do class" left a network of institutions. The most substantial synagogues, schoolhouses, and community halls that would ever be built in Dorchester and Roxbury were all products of the period 1905–1925. Living memorials to a suburban past, these buildings of brick and limestone continued, for decades more, to serve the tens of thousands of Jews who crowded into these neighborhoods.

But those who moved away did not abruptly leave their institutions behind. Rules of membership allowed Jews who relocated to the suburbs to continue to participate in, even lead, institutions in Roxbury and Dorchester. At least in their first years in suburbs like Brookline and Newton, many middle-class Jews continued to support the old institutions they had helped establish and finance. They continued to celebrate weddings in those institutions, to send their children to school in those institutions, and to participate in the social and communal life that centered on those institutions.

In contrast to this Jewish understanding of membership, Catholic rules limited membership to families who lived within the parish. For Catholic families, moving from a neighborhood meant cutting all ties with their church, their children's school, and their parish's social life. Barriers to exit were low for Jews and high for Catholics. Membership rules, which facilitated the rapid suburbanization of Boston's middle-class Jews, retarded the suburbanization of the city's middle-class Catholics.

By themselves, of course, synagogues did not cause suburbanization. The temptations of the suburbs were great. Outside the city, where open land abounded, middle-class families could build large homes on large lots, recreating the rural ideal that had brought an earlier generation of suburbanites to upper Roxbury and Dorchester. Suburban homes were a refuge from the busyness and hustle of urban life, from the European immigrants and black migrants who huddled in urban neighborhoods. Beginning in the 1930s, federal housing programs and banks started actively to steer middle-class homeowners away from urban housing and toward new, single-family suburban homes.

But it was the sudden ubiquity of the automobile in the early 1920s—and the decision of federal, state, and local governments to dedicate public resources to building roads and highways for the new mode of transportation—that created the modern suburb. The automobile allowed residents to commute into the central city from distant residential areas. "American automobile registrations climbed from one million in 1913 to ten million in 1923, when Kansas alone had more cars than France or Germany," Kenneth T. Jackson wrote. "By 1927 when the American total had risen to twenty-six million, the United States was building about 85 percent of the world's automobiles, and there was one motor vehicle for every five people in the country." Between 1920 and 1930, when the total population of Dorchester and upper Roxbury increased 16 percent, the populations of Brookline and Newton increased 26 and 42 percent, respectively. Like the streetcar before it, but on a more massive scale and in more lasting fashion, the automobile reconfigured the geography of urban America.[2]

The reconfiguration was total. It was in the 1920s, as many scholars have shown convincingly, that the modern suburb was born. But the transformation of urban neighborhoods in the 1920s was an equally profound event. The suburban settlement in Dorchester and upper Roxbury, which began in the late nineteenth century and persisted into the late 1910s, ended decisively in the early 1920s—except among Catholics. "Storekeepers had transformed Erie Street from the quiet residential neighborhood my grandparents had sought as Jewish pioneers in the district into a semipermanent bazaar," Theodore H. White wrote, recalling his childhood in Dorchester's Mount Bowdoin–Franklin Park district. "Herrings were stacked in barrels outside the fish stores, and flies buzzed over the herrings . . . There were four grocery stores, several dry-goods stores, fruit and vegetable specialists, hardware stores, mama-papa variety stores, penny candy stores."[3]

The great body of middle-class Jews, who had established the Jewish enclaves of Roxbury and Dorchester and built the area's leading institutions, moved away, following middle-class Protestants to the suburbs. Once begun, the Jewish exodus did not slow. As the neighborhoods of Dorchester and Roxbury grew poorer and more densely populated, suburban life receded into memory. Even memory was obliterated as three-deckers filled parks and open fields, as old single-family houses were converted into multifamily dwellings, as suburban temples became urban synagogues. Many Jews were entering the middle class, and rules of membership in their institutions minimized the social cost of suburbanization. Middle-class Catholics, anchored by rules that required members to live within parish boundaries, were much less likely to relocate to the suburbs.

These stark differences in Jewish and Catholic attachments to the old neighborhoods were fully apparent by the early 1920s, and race was irrelevant to them: by the 1950s, when African Americans began rapidly settling in formerly Jewish and Catholic sections of Dorchester and Roxbury, the basic outline of the urban exodus was three decades old. Not only were the different neighborhood attachments apparent by the 1920s, but the process of out-migration itself brought consequences. Any Catholics who left for the suburbs were immediately shut off from their old institutions. Thus few middle-class Catholics left, the few who left were quickly forgotten, and the many who stayed continued to support their churches and schools.

For Jews, none of this was true. Many Jews who moved out to the suburbs continued to play prominent roles in the synagogues and schools and community centers of Dorchester and Roxbury. Suburban Jews were role models for Jews in these urban neighborhoods, continuing reminders that attaining middle-class social status meant moving to a new home in a distant place. But another consequence of the Jewish exodus threatened to undermine the entire institutional base of Roxbury and Dorchester Jewry. Though memberships in old synagogues and social clubs eased the passage to life outside the city, suburban Jewish families, once settled in their new homes, began establishing new institutions in more convenient locations. Suburban ties to urban institutions in Roxbury and Dorchester began to wither.

The total number of Jews in upper Roxbury and Dorchester almost doubled in the 1920s and remained relatively stable until the early 1950s, but the number of middle-class Jews supporting the area's institutions diminished year by year. From the middle 1920s onward, these institutions reckoned with financial crisis. Reinventing themselves to appeal to the working-class and lower-middle-class residents of their immediate neighborhoods, they also worked frantically to retain the loyalty of their suburban members. Unlike the Catholic neighborhoods and institutions that still flourished into the 1940s and 1950s, the teeming Jewish neighborhoods of Roxbury and Dorchester rested on a precarious foundation. Now all but forgotten, the massive exodus of the 1920s had transformed the American city.

Miketz, 1924

In 1924 December came a short while after May. As he had done since assuming the congregation's presidency in January, Louis H. Steinberg spent the last Sabbath service of the year in his seat next to the ark, looking out at the congregation in their pews. He had been engaged in a difficult reelection contest with another member of the Crawford Street Synagogue, and congregants were due to vote the next day. Steinberg listened to the day's designated Torah portion, to *Miketz*, and he was galvanized, discovering a lesson not just for him and the Crawford Street Synagogue but for all Boston Jewry. "I stood at my place on the Altar," he later recalled. "The Holy Scroll had just been taken from the Ark by the Cantor, the reader had just unrolled it to the proper portion for the week, and commenced reading *Micketz*":[4]

> Then Pharaoh said to Joseph, "In my dream, I was standing on the bank of the Nile, when out of the Nile came up seven sturdy and well-formed cows and grazed in the reed grass.[5] Presently there followed them seven other cows, scrawny, ill-formed, and emaciated—never had I seen their

likes for ugliness in all the land of Egypt! And the seven lean and ugly cows ate up the first seven cows, the sturdy ones; but when they had consumed them, one could not tell that they had consumed them, for they looked just as bad as before. And I awoke. In my other dream, I saw seven ears of grain, full and healthy, growing on a single stalk; but right behind them sprouted seven ears, shriveled, thin, and scorched by the east wind. And the thin ears swallowed the seven healthy ears. I have told my magicians, but none has an explanation for me."

And Joseph said to Pharaoh, "Pharaoh's dreams are one and the same: God has told Pharaoh what He is about to do . . . Immediately ahead are seven years of great abundance in all the land of Egypt. After them will come seven years of famine, and all the abundance in the land of Egypt will be forgotten. As the land is ravaged by famine, no trace of the abundance will be left in the land because of the famine thereafter, for it will be very severe. As for Pharaoh having had the same dream twice, it means that the matter has been determined by God, and that God will soon carry it out."

Steinberg listened to Joseph's words and thought of men like Benjamin Snider and Harris Swartz. Early leaders of the congregation, both men now lived in Brookline. Snider—one of the congregation's founders, a major donor to its building fund, and still a member of its board of directors—sat on the board of trustees of Ohabei Shalom, which was completing work on its new temple center just four blocks from his Brookline home. Swartz, a former vice-president of the congregation, had relinquished his seat on the board of the Crawford Street Synagogue in 1923. Swartz had joined in the movement to build a modern Orthodox synagogue in Brookline, contributing generously to Kehillath Israel's building fund and sitting on its building committee. That very weekend the *Jewish Advocate* devoted its lead story to the imminent dedication of Kehillath Israel's synagogue, "Brookline's first temple" and the central institution of Boston's newest suburban Jewish community. Louis Steinberg surely noticed the news story and understood the excitement. Perhaps he was even planning to attend the ceremony in Brookline.[6]

But as Steinberg listened to Pharaoh's two dreams, his mind fastened most of all on what events in Brookline portended for the future of Elm Hill Jewry. Over and over, his thoughts returned to men like Swartz and Snider. Although both remained members of the Crawford Street Synagogue, their time of active service to the Roxbury congregation was ending. Looking out at the faces of his congregation, Steinberg listened as the reader chanted *Miketz.* "I then realized that this Biblical story applied to existing conditions in our Congregation, and I then determined that advantage must be taken of the few years of plenty that our parishioners were enjoying and to endeavor to relieve our institution of all burdens, of debts and mortgages, ere the lean time should arrive," Steinberg wrote soon afterward. "I realized that a large number of the money element of our community were moving away; that they were being replaced by people of moderate means who would be unable to carry the tremendous burdens of a large institution."[7]

Steinberg accurately understood the changes that were transforming Elm Hill Jewry. By the middle 1920s, upper- and central-middle-class Jewish families were leaving for Brookline in large numbers. Minna B. Wolff, the president of the Crawford Street Synagogue's sisterhood, "continued the work under the most trying conditions" in the years after 1924; it was during her administration, according to a 1928 account, that "a great many active members had left the district."[8] Like the other Jewish neighborhoods across Roxbury and Dorchester, the Elm Hill Jewish community was still new: it had existed for little more than a decade. In 1924 the Crawford Street Synagogue celebrated its tenth anniversary, and in the same year Mishkan Tefila relocated to the site of its unfinished Seaver Street Temple. But the socioeconomic status of Elm Hill Jewry was eroding with unexpected swiftness. Although for decades more Elm Hill would be preeminent among the Jewish neighborhoods of Roxbury and Dorchester, its real glory would reside in the past. It would no longer be home to Boston's most prosperous Jews. On the last Saturday in 1924, on *Shabbat Miketz*—when Kehillath Israel prepared to dedicate its new synagogue in Brookline, when Ohabei Shalom worked to complete its temple center, and when Steinberg mused over the significance of Pharaoh's dreams—the future of Boston Jewry shifted to Brookline.

That morning Steinberg reflected on Joseph's interpretation of the two dreams and his instruction to Pharaoh:

> "Accordingly, let Pharaoh find a man of discernment and wisdom, and set him over the land of Egypt. And let Pharaoh take steps to appoint overseers over the land, and organize the land of Egypt in the seven years of plenty. Let all the food of these good years that are coming be gathered, and let the grain be collected under Pharaoh's authority as food to be stored in the cities. Let that food be a reserve for the land for the seven years of famine which will come upon the land of Egypt, so that the land may not perish in the famine."

The plan pleased Pharaoh and all his courtiers. And Pharaoh said to his courtiers, "Could we find another like him, a man in whom is the spirit of God?" So Pharaoh said to Joseph, "Since God has made all this known to you, there is none so discerning and wise as you. You shall be in charge of my court, and by your command shall all my people be directed."

Listening to Joseph's plan for Egypt, Steinberg determined to pursue his own plan for Beth Hamidrash Hagadol. Since his election twelve months earlier, he had been engaged in an acrimonious struggle with other leaders of the congregation, and his ideas for the administration of the synagogue had been honed in the struggle. Now the prophecy of impending famine strengthened his resolve. "I saw that we were greatly burdened with debts," he wrote, "and realized that if we were to survive, we must clear our Congregation of all encumbrances." In Steinberg's judgment, the Crawford Street Synagogue had no priority more urgent than the redemption of its mortgage debt.[9]

There were many who disagreed with Steinberg. "I placed my plans before my Board of Directors and some of the pioneers of our Congregation," he recalled, "and found considerable obstruction in some quarters." Executing his plan required reducing other congregational expenses and dismantling many of the synagogue's programs. Since 1918, when Rabbi Epstein had been elected and installed by the Crawford Street Synagogue, the Elm Hill congregation had supported an array of activities that attracted not only traditional Orthodox Jews but younger, American-born men and women. In insisting on the primacy of retiring the congregation's debt, Steinberg was arguing that the Crawford Street Synagogue could not continue to afford these various programs. Perhaps, too, Steinberg sympathized with those who feared that Rabbi Epstein, in advocating a modern approach to Orthodoxy, was transforming Beth Hamidrash Hagadol into a Conservative congregation. Steinberg apparently did nothing to dispel the belief that, should he win reelection as president, he would subject the rabbi and the rabbi's salary to close scrutiny.[10]

The congregation met the next day—Sunday, December 28—to elect its president. "The election was a spirited one," according to the *Jewish Advocate,* and "there was intense rivalry between Mr. Steinberg and his opponent, Victor Kaufman." Kaufman was a founding member of the congregation and a former president. It was during his presidency that the congregation had hired Epstein, and Kaufman remained a strong ally of the rabbi. In the end, Steinberg won reelection, defeating Kaufman. In his remarks to the congregation's members, Steinberg promised to conduct the Crawford Street Synagogue's "affairs in an efficient and business-like manner," and he pledged "to make an impartial and serious study of all differences that have cropped up in the past, with a view to removing any cause for factionalism, and ill feeling, which have no place in a synagogue." Steinberg remained the congregation's president for the rest of the decade. Redeeming the mortgage debt had become the congregation's principal objective: though the Crawford Street Synagogue soon purchased land for a cemetery, it abandoned its project to build a large Hebrew school and community building.[11]

The import of Steinberg's victory was clear at once. Within days of the election, Rabbi Epstein "formally tendered his resignation" from the congregation and announced that he would leave that summer. Noting that "he has no definite plans for himself as yet," Epstein explained that his resignation was prompted not by the promise of another job but by the politics of the Crawford Street Synagogue. "The rabbi has not been receiving the proper co-operation of his congregation," the *Advocate* stated, "and he assigns the consequent lack of harmony as the reason for the step taken." Three years passed before the congregation elected a new rabbi. Not until the spring of 1928, when the congregation was on the verge of burning its mortgage, did it again assume the expense of a rabbi—and the new rabbi, unlike Epstein, had no connection to the Conservative movement. Victor Kaufman could not have felt great joy at the mortgage-burning celebration. Although he still sat on the congregation's board, he made no public contribution toward the mortgage; nor did he help organize the celebration.[12]

Epstein, who had been the first rabbi of Elm Hill's leading synagogue, in the summer of 1925 became the first rabbi of Brookline's Kehillath Israel. In Brookline Epstein could serve many of the middle-class families who had brought him to Roxbury just a few years earlier. He remained at Kehillath Israel for the rest of his career. Under his leadership, the Brookline congregation in the middle and late 1920s began "to lead the way in conducting strictly orthodox services along the most modern lines" and in making "Orthodox Judaism attractive to the rising generation." His achievement at Kehillath Israel would be paralleled in Boston only by Rubenovitz's achievement at Mishkan Tefila. As the *Jewish Advocate* observed decades later, Epstein was a "rabbi of towering public importance," establishing in Kehillath Israel a major synagogue-center and a stronghold of Conservative Judaism.[13]

On a Tuesday evening in June 1925, as Epstein prepared to leave Roxbury, members of the Crawford Street Synagogue gathered in a Brookline hall to honor him. They presented him with "a beautiful automobile as a gift from his numerous devoted friends." The congregation's four former presidents, including Kaufman, served on the reception committee and helped to organize the banquet. One person—Steinberg, the congregation's current president—was conspicuous in his absence. Speakers praised Epstein's commitment to the "young people," describing the activities that he had organized at the Crawford Street Synagogue to make traditional Judaism attractive to American-born Jews. David M. Shohet, who was pursuing similar goals from his pulpit at Dorchester's Temple Beth El, rose to pay homage to Epstein. "In no uncertain terms he lauded the character and scholastic attainments of Rabbi Epstein and pointed out the force that he has been in the Roxbury district," the *Advocate* reported. "While Roxbury should lament his leaving," Shohet declared with a smile, "it should rejoice over the fact that he is only going over to Brookline 'as all progressive Jews seem to be doing.'" Had he been in attendance, Steinberg might have thought of Pharaoh's dreams and derived smug satisfaction from the chuckles and guffaws.[14]

Brookline and Newton

A few affluent Jewish families had begun to settle in Brookline and the adjacent Boston districts of Allston and Brighton at the turn of the century. Many of the first Jews moving to Brookline were of Central European descent. As one of Boston's most prestigious suburbs, the community was, according to a 1907 story in the *Boston Evening Transcript,* "the richest town in the entire world."[15] The magnificent Temple Adath Israel, dedicated that year on Commonwealth Avenue, was located between Boston's upper-class Back Bay and the town of Brookline. Built by the wealthiest Reform congregation in New England, Temple Israel—a name used with increasing frequency—served many of the prominent, assimilated Jews who had settled in Brookline. But Temple Israel was not a Brookline institution, and its ritual had never been acceptable to observant Jews: it was a congregation that attracted members from all over the Boston area; its temple, located physically in Boston, stood one and one-half miles from the section of Brookline where most Jews, including growing numbers of Eastern European Jews, were settling; and its ritual was Reform.

In the spring of 1911, a group of ten Jews formed a small Orthodox congregation in Brookline, using their own homes for religious services. For most Jews, the organization of this congregation, which became Kehillath Israel, marked the true beginning of the Brookline Jewish community. In 1917 Kehillath Israel received a charter from the state and acquired a modest structure on Harvard Street, in the midst of Brookline's growing Jewish district. As Kehillath Israel prepared to erect a modern synagogue, Ohabei Shalom and Mishkan Tefila both made plans to relocate their temples. Ohabei Shalom moved from the South End to Brookline in the 1920s. Mishkan Tefila, which in the late 1910s had considered building its new temple in Brookline, decided instead to relocate to the Elm Hill district. In the winter of 1919–1920, when Mishkan Tefila purchased the Seaver Street site, it organized a branch religious school in Brookline. The branch school existed only intermittently in subsequent years, using rented space. On a more regular basis, the congregation hired a bus to transport members' children from Brookline to the Elm Hill school.[16]

By the fall of 1929, when Mishkan Tefila dedicated its new schoolhouse in Roxbury, three imposing synagogue-centers stood in or near Brookline. On Harvard Street, four blocks from Coolidge Corner, Kehillath Israel maintained its new temple and schoolhouse. Ohabei Shalom worshiped nearby, in its new buildings on Beacon Street. And a few blocks away, on Boston's Riverway, stood the monumental school and meeting-house of Temple Israel, whose members continued to worship in their white-marble temple on Commonwealth Avenue. With the sole exception of Adath Israel's temple, all of these structures had been completed in the period 1925–1929. In 1930 about 8,000 Jews lived in Brookline: Jews, who had constituted less than 3 percent of Brookline's population in 1920, now represented 17 percent of the town's residents. Another 4,000 Jews lived in the Allston and Brighton districts of Boston, adjacent to Brookline.[17]

Even as Brookline's Jewish community continued to grow, another suburban Jewish community began forming in the nearby city of Newton. No more than a few hundred Jews had lived in Newton in 1920: organized around a small Orthodox synagogue, this immigrant settlement had existed in Newton's Nonantum district since the late nineteenth century. By 1930 the Jewish population of Newton had increased to about 1,400, and most of the new residents had no connection to the older community in Nonantum. These new families formed the nucleus of an upper-middle-class suburban Jewish community. "There can be no doubt that the trend of the Jewish population has definitely set in toward Newton," Rabbi Rubenovitz wrote in 1932, "just as fifteen years ago it was in the direction of Brookline."[18]

That November, Rubenovitz raised the possibility of creating a branch religious school in Newton, "with the idea of winning friends for Mishkan Tefila in Newton, as well as holding those of our members who have moved out there." What concerned Mishkan Tefila's leaders—who insisted that the school must not become "a nucleus for a new shul [synagogue]"—was the prospect that Newton's Jews would establish an independent, competing institution. But Mishkan Tefila took no action on the proposal to create the school. In 1935 a group of Newton Jews began considering plans to erect their own synagogue and religious school. "If that were done it would mean that Mishkan Tefila, as well as other Boston Congregations, would ultimately lose many members now residing in Newton," Myer H. Slobodkin, the chairman of Mishkan Tefila's executive board, argued in October 1935. He recommended that Mishkan Tefila convene a mass meeting "of the other Boston Synagogues affected with the view to provide adequate school facilities for the residents of Newton, and in this way prevent the possibility of losing members." But Slobodkin received little support for his suggestion, and it was not pursued.[19]

The Jewish families who gathered in Newton for High Holy Day services in 1935 proceeded with their plans to establish a congregation and organize a religious school. Temple Emanuel, a Conservative congregation, quickly prospered. In December its members purchased land in Newton Centre "for the erection of a Temple, Educational and Community Centre." The structure was built in 1937; in the early 1950s, the congregation built an auditorium and new classrooms. "We have a congregation which has grown from 26 families to 738 families in 15 years," Albert I. Gordon, Temple Emanuel's rabbi, stated in 1950. "Our classrooms are filled to overflowing with children. Those who come to worship in the synagogue or in the chapel are crowded into areas built for far fewer numbers than we try to accommodate." By 1950 about 8,000 Jews lived in Newton. That spring, a group of Newton Jews formed Temple Shalom, a Reform congregation. Another group established Temple Reyim in West Newton in 1952; originally organized as the Newton Jewish Community Center, Temple Reyim became Newton's second Conservative congregation.[20]

But Brookline remained the preeminent center of suburban Jewish life. About 19,000 Jews lived in Brookline in 1950—fully one-third of the town's population—and another 13,000 Jews lived in the adjacent districts of Allston and Brighton.[21] In South Brookline, an area detached from the main section of Brookline but close to Newton, Jews had organized Temple Emeth, a Conservative congregation. Elsewhere in Brookline and the Allston-Brighton area, the Jewish community in 1950 supported three Reform congregations (Temple Israel and Ohabei Shalom, as well as Temple Sinai, which had been founded by former members of Temple Israel), three Conservative congregations (Kehillath Israel, Beth Zion, and B'nai Moshe), and two Orthodox congregations (Young Israel of Brookline and, in Brighton, Kadimah). At the intersection of Harvard and Beacon streets, Coolidge Corner was the heart of Brookline Jewry. In 1946 Boston's Associated Jewish Philanthropies (AJP) rented space near Coolidge Corner for "a temporary recreational center to serve the Brighton-Brookline-Newton areas." Two years later the AJP purchased land near Cleveland Circle—on Beacon Street, at the border of Brookline, Brighton, and Newton—and announced plans one day to build a permanent community center on the site.[22]

Jewish Neighborhoods, 1924–1951

After studying the needs of Jewish communities throughout the Boston area, the Associated Jewish Philanthropies had concluded in the middle 1940s that both of the area's great Jewish concentrations—the suburban cluster of Brookline, Brighton, and Newton, and the urban neighborhoods of Roxbury and Dorchester—required the services of new community centers. Roxbury and Dorchester were served by the Boston YMHA and the Hecht House, the two leading community centers in the Boston area. Because no comparable institution existed in the Brookline area, the AJP had set up its temporary facility in Coolidge Corner. But despite the dramatic growth of suburban Jewry and the lack of any permanent community structure serving the Brookline-Brighton-Newton area, the Associated Jewish Philanthropies argued in 1946 "that the new building in Dorchester-Mattapan should come first."[23]

In the late 1940s and early 1950s, the Jewish community in Roxbury and Dorchester was still the largest in New England. About 70,000 Jews lived in the area in 1950, almost twice the number that lived in Brookline, Brighton, and Newton. From the late 1920s through the early 1950s, the number of Jews living in Roxbury and Dorchester had barely fallen. At its peak, in the late 1920s and early 1930s, the Jewish community of Roxbury and Dorchester had numbered 77,000.[24] Over more than two decades it had declined only slightly in size, to 74,000 in 1940 and to 70,000 in 1950.[25] Most of the decline was concentrated in the Jewish neighborhoods of upper Roxbury, but even in Roxbury, the Jewish community remained large and substantially intact: Roxbury Jewry, which had numbered 30,000 persons in the late 1920s and early 1930s, had fallen to 28,000 in 1940 and 24,500 in 1950.[26] "The stability of this population over the past sixteen years is especially noteworthy," Saul Bernstein observed in his 1946 report for the Associated Jewish Philanthropies. "While it is recognized that there are many and varied factors which may affect population movement during the post war and later periods, it seems reasonably certain that the Jewish population of Roxbury-Dorchester-Mattapan will be substantial enough to justify expanded Center facilities and services for many years."[27]

A substantial African-American community had existed in upper Roxbury since the 1920s. Socially and physically, the black community on Elm Hill was removed from Boston's principal black settlement, which was located in the South End and lower Roxbury. Although it was an unfair prejudice, Judge Harry J. Elam emphasizes, "there was a feeling that those of us who lived on the Hill were better" than those who lived in lower Roxbury and the South End.[28] From 1920, when there were fewer than 1,000 blacks in upper Roxbury, the Hill's community had grown steadily—to 3,200 in 1930, to 5,700 in 1940, and to 11,100 in 1950.[29] According to the *Guardian*, the first black-owned store in the district had been a "little grocery store." Since that grocery store had opened, the *Guardian* observed in 1939, "other colored business enterprises" had been established, "until we now have beauty parlors, real estate offices, tailoring establishments, barber shops, restaurants, tav-

erns, billiard parlors, funeral directors, launderies, dry goods empori-
ums, umbrella and sport clothing outlet, colored clerks in drug stores
and a colored managed and staffed First National Store, colored help in
M. Winer Stores, the Economy Stores and Tom's Spa all on Humboldt
Ave."[30]

Elm Hill's black community was nearly as old as its Jewish community.
Though a source of occasional neighborhood tension, the growth of this
African-American district in the 1940s continued a longstanding pattern
of gradual expansion. It caused little excitement or comment among
Jews. "My street, Howland Street, was not entirely Jewish," Nat Hentoff
wrote. At the far end of Howland Street lived many black families, and
each day several blacks walked past Hentoff's house on their way to the
streetcar. "We saw the same travelers every day, every month. But we
never nodded or spoke to them, nor they to us," Hentoff noted. "On
our part of the street, they were referred to, not unkindly, as schwartzes.
Not unkindly, because these schwartzes were clean, neat, and properly
purposeful. But they *were* colored." St. Mark Congregational Church
still defined the district's center. The church had moved from the South
End to upper Roxbury in the fall of 1926—just one year after the dedication of Mishkan Tefila's Seaver Street Temple. By 1950, black families on
Elm Hill had settled on streets extending from Catholic sections of St.
Joseph's Parish to Jewish neighborhoods on Elm Hill and in Grove Hall.
But this African-American district remained at the margins of Roxbury's
Jewish and Catholic neighborhoods.[31]

Jewish life in upper Roxbury continued to thrive in the late 1940s and
early 1950s. To demonstrate that the Jews of Dorchester and Roxbury
required additional community facilities, Benjamin Lambert described
the situation faced by the Boston Young Men's Hebrew Association in
the winter of 1947–1948. Located in the Elm Hill district, at the corner
of Seaver Street and Humboldt Avenue—one long block from Temple
Mishkan Tefila and four or five short blocks from upper Roxbury's black
community—the Boston YMHA had served Roxbury Jewry since the
early 1910s. According to the minutes of a December 1947 meeting, "Mr.
Lambert stated that the Boston Y.M.H.A. now has 2281 members and
106 organized activities which meet weekly. This is the largest number in
the Boston Y.M.H.A.'s history and represents a limit of what the building
can service. For the past few weeks there has had to be a restriction on
the entrance of new clubs into the Y.M.H.A., necessitated by the over-

crowding that now takes place." A June 1950 report on Roxbury Jewry, prepared for the Associated Jewish Philanthropies, noted "that the Negro population is moving closer to the Jewish area but there is some opinion that there will be no noticeable increase in their number for another 15 years." Thus, as a report the previous year had stated, the Boston YMHA was expected to "fill an important community need in the Roxbury area for years to come."[32]

The Jewish neighborhoods in Dorchester were large and still distant from the racial frontier. "While there has been evidence of Jewish families moving out of the area to Brookline, Newton, Hyde Park and Milton, it is the opinion of local residents that other Jewish families have been moving in from other parts of Boston," stated a June 1950 report prepared for the AJP. "In any case, it is quite apparent that Dorchester-Mattapan includes the largest Jewish clustering in Boston." The Hecht House, which in 1936 had relocated into Dorchester from the West End, was the major Jewish community center in the area. Leading synagogues in Dorchester included not only Agudath Israel's Woodrow Avenue Synagogue and Beth El's Fowler Street Synagogue, worshiping in their suburban-era structures, but also Chai Odom's Nightingale Street Synagogue and Kehillath Jacob's Fessenden Street Synagogue. Temple Beth Hillel, established in 1944 by members of the Dorchester-Mattapan Hebrew School on Morton Street, was the only Conservative congregation in Dorchester—and, with Mishkan Tefila, one of the two non-Orthodox congregations among Dorchester and Roxbury's forty synagogues. "Hebrews have between $\frac{1}{3}$ & $\frac{1}{2}$ of all the parish area," Rev. Waldo C. Hasenfus, the pastor of St. Matthew's Parish, noted in a 1946 letter. "The Hebrews threaten the life of the parish."[33]

Bakeries and grocery stores and fruit shops lined Blue Hill Avenue for three miles in the early 1950s, the small shops hugging the mighty river as it rushed through its floodplain, as it passed through the Jewish neighborhoods of Roxbury and Dorchester. More than sixty kosher butchers, fresh sawdust covering their floors and fresh chickens hanging by their feet in the windows, contributed to the sights and smells of the area. But it was delicatessens, one in particular, that gave the district its special character. "Of all the fortresses only one reached the proportions, could claim palatial amenities that testify to a high culture, that immense landmark which any traveller who has passed down Blue Hill avenue will smile in recognition of, the G&G," Mark Mirsky remembered. "On the tables of the cafeteria talmudic jurisprudence sorted out racing results, politics, the stock market, and the student could look up from his 'desk' to leer at the young girls sipping cream soda under the immense wings of their mothers; watch the whole world of Blue Hill avenue revolve through the G&G's glass gate."[34] Each election year a large wooden platform was erected outside the G&G. That platform was the routine campaign stop and election-eve gathering place of state representatives, city councillors, mayors, candidates for state and national offices, presidents and vice-presidents of the United States. From across Dorchester and Roxbury, Jews and Catholics alike would come to the G&G. They would come on crisp fall nights to the delicatessen at the corner of Blue Hill Avenue and Woodrow Avenue, part of the crowd gathered at this unlikely citadel of American democracy.

From the 1920s into the 1950s, Dorchester and Roxbury's working-class and lower-middle-class Jewish neighborhoods teemed with life. It is easy to recall this world with fondness. "As I passed one brick two-family house with little cement lions on either side of the walk, several younger couples were sitting on the steps with drinks in their hands," Francis Russell wrote, remembering a walk that he took on Wellington Hill in the late 1940s. "One woman half-smiled at me as I passed, and I found myself wishing they had asked me to stop and share a drink with them. A placid, timeless moment, before the first stars came out."[35] But these years were not timeless. The ascendancy of the ethnic neighborhood was brief. The ethnic era was bracketed on one side by socioeconomic succession, on the other by racial succession.

Changing Neighborhoods, Changing Memberships

Gathering in December 1919 for the congregation's sixtieth-anniversary banquet, members of Mishkan Tefila formally inaugurated their drive for a new temple. By then the main issue was settled: after three years of discussion, the congregation had reiterated its commitment to building the temple and schoolhouse in upper Roxbury. Later that winter, Mishkan Tefila announced that it had purchased a large estate at the corner of Seaver Street and Elm Hill Avenue. Those who argued that Mishkan Tefila should build in Roxbury rather than in Brookline had decisively won the battle.[36] But a decision that seemed sensible and prudent in 1919 must have seemed cruelly short-sighted in 1925: in the six years that passed between Mishkan Tefila's decision to build in Roxbury and the dedication of its temple on Seaver Street, half of the congregation's leaders had moved from the Roxbury-Dorchester district to the Brookline-Brighton-Allston district. Louis Steinberg, listening to the biblical account of Pharaoh's dreams in December 1924, was not crafting fiction when he thought of the socioeconomic transformation of Elm Hill. The exodus to Brookline was real, affecting even the leadership of a congregation investing in a grand new temple in Roxbury—and that exodus had gained sudden force in the early 1920s.

As Map 19 shows, nearly every member of Mishkan Tefila's board of directors lived in Roxbury or Dorchester in 1919.[37] Only one of the congregation's twenty directors lived in Brookline. Although the *Jewish Advocate* stated that fall that "many members of the congregation have removed to Brookline," those members were not representative.[38] Given the high status of the men sitting on Mishkan Tefila's board, it appears that Boston's central- and upper-middle-class Jewish leaders were still heavily concentrated in Roxbury and Dorchester as late as 1919. Nothing but speculation about future shifts in population patterns could have justified serious discussion of building the new temple in Brookline. The middle-class attachment to Roxbury and Dorchester had not yet been disrupted.

In a matter of two or three years, that attachment had ended. For Boston Jewry and for the old streetcar suburbs of Dorchester and Roxbury, a great watershed was reached. By 1925, as Map 20 shows, seventeen members of Mishkan Tefila's board of directors resided in or near Brookline, while seventeen lived in Roxbury and five lived in Dorchester.[39] This dramatic change in the residences of board members was not an artifact of membership turnover on the temple's board. Of the twenty men who had sat on the board in 1919, only seven remained in the Roxbury-Dorchester district in 1925; eleven had settled in the Brookline-Brighton-Newton area. Given that the six years between 1919 and 1925 exactly corresponded with the project of erecting the Seaver Street Temple, probably no segment of Boston Jewry's central- and upper-middle class should have been so firmly rooted in Roxbury during those years as Mishkan Tefila's board of directors. That so large a proportion of the board moved in the early 1920s suggests the scale of the general exodus.

Not only had Brookline eclipsed the various sections of Roxbury and Dorchester as a middle-class stronghold but Elm Hill had consolidated

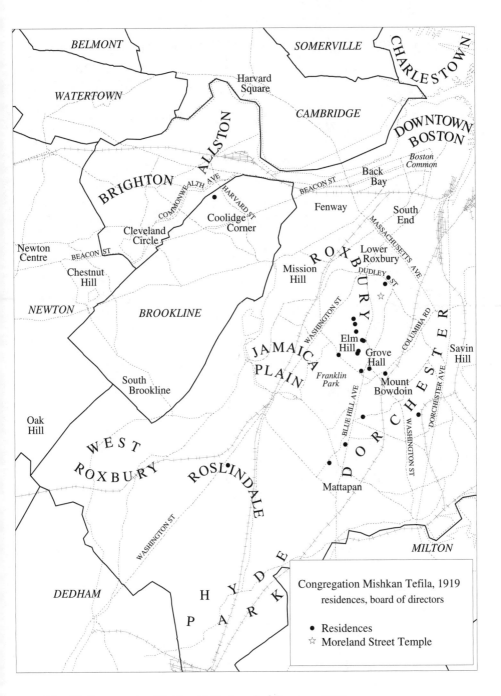

Map 19 Congregation Mishkan Tefila, board of directors, 1919

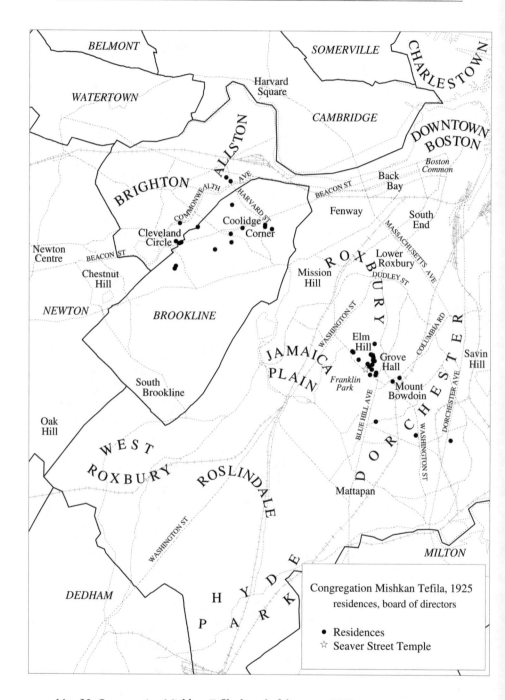

Map 20 Congregation Mishkan Tefila, board of directors, 1925

its status as the preeminent Jewish neighborhood within Roxbury and Dorchester. While in 1919 members of Mishkan Tefila's board were scattered across Roxbury and Dorchester, in 1925 those who had not moved to Brookline lived tightly clustered on Elm Hill. At a time when the neighborhoods of Roxbury and Dorchester generally had declined in their attraction to central- and upper-middle-class Jews, Elm Hill retained a residual appeal. With just 6 percent of the renter-occupied and 3 percent of the owner-occupied homes in upper Roxbury and Dorchester, Elm Hill in 1930 included more than half of the homes in the area renting for at least $75 and 22 percent of the homes valued at more than $20,000. The average home in the Elm Hill district rented for $65—in the next most expensive census tract in Dorchester and Roxbury, the average home rented for $52—and about three hundred of Elm Hill's households maintained quarters for domestic servants. "The goodly part of the congregation" at St. Hugh's Church, Rev. John E. O'Connell noted in 1932, consisted of "Irish maids in Jewish families."[40]

Yet it was only in relation to the rest of Dorchester and Roxbury that Elm Hill remained a desirable neighborhood for middle-class Jewish residences; relative to Brookline, Elm Hill had deteriorated sharply. Its decline was apparent to Louis Steinberg, whose Crawford Street Synagogue was one of Elm Hill's leading institutions. Its decline was equally apparent to Rabbi Rubenovitz, who expressed alarm at the changes that had occurred in the neighborhood by the middle 1920s. "Owing to our present location we do attract to our Services many people who are unacquainted with the standards and methods of Mishkan Tefila," he wrote in February 1926, less than six months after the dedication of the Seaver Street Temple. "If left to themselves, they disturb other worshippers, possibly without intending to do so. They simply do not know any better." As Simon Finberg, the chairman of Mishkan Tefila's school committee, explained that December, a basic problem confronting the congregation was "the continued shifting of our membership from Roxbury to Brookline and Newton."[41]

Once begun in the early 1920s, that shift was never arrested. "The general economic situation of the country has greatly deteriorated," Rubenovitz wrote in December 1932, "but this does not seem to have stopped the tendency of our people to migrate from one part of the city to another."[42] As Jewish families in Roxbury and Dorchester attained middle-class status in the 1930s and 1940s, they moved to one of the growing suburbs. Many of Mishkan Tefila's board members still lived in Roxbury or Dorchester in 1950, as Map 21 shows, but most resided in Brookline or Newton. Within Roxbury and Dorchester, Elm Hill's relatively high status had declined by 1950; the old cluster on Elm Hill had dissipated somewhat, as several board members chose instead to live in Dorchester. And the pattern of suburban residences had also changed. While most families in 1950 continued to live near Beacon Street in Brookline, Brighton and Allston had lost their appeal for upper-middle-class families, and new suburban settlements had emerged in South Brookline and Newton. But these were small changes compared with the transformation that had occurred between 1919 and 1925. The basic residential map established in the early 1920s was still intact in the early 1950s.

What had changed in this time was the total number of middle-class Jewish families in the Boston area. Though no complete list of Mishkan Tefila's membership survives from the period 1914–1949, it is likely that a substantial majority of members remained in Roxbury and Dorchester in the 1920s and 1930s, even after most board members had settled in Brookline.[43] This discrepancy between the congregation's leaders and the rest of its members was probably diminishing by the 1940s, however, as an increased proportion of Jews moved into the middle class. In 1950—when forty-two board members lived in the Newton-Brookline area, twenty-one lived in the Roxbury-Dorchester area, and six lived elsewhere[44]—39 percent of the congregation's total membership lived in Brookline, Brighton, or Newton, while an additional 5 percent lived in other areas outside Roxbury and Dorchester.[45] "It is noteworthy," Rabbi Israel J. Kazis remarked in 1952, "that the lay leaders of Congregation Mishkan Tefila, though living in other parts of the Greater Boston community, have remained loyal and are active as ever in the Temple."[46] Although the congregation's governing board was more heavily suburbanized than the general membership, Mishkan Tefila by 1950 had come to depend on a large and growing suburban base. Even Rabbi Kazis lived in Brookline: his home stood five blocks from Coolidge Corner. Sharp changes in residential patterns in the early 1920s had inexorably altered the institution's membership.

Leaders of Dorchester's Temple Beth El, preparing in 1935 to celebrate their own institution's twenty-fifth anniversary, reflected on the transformation of Roxbury and Dorchester. They recalled the men and women

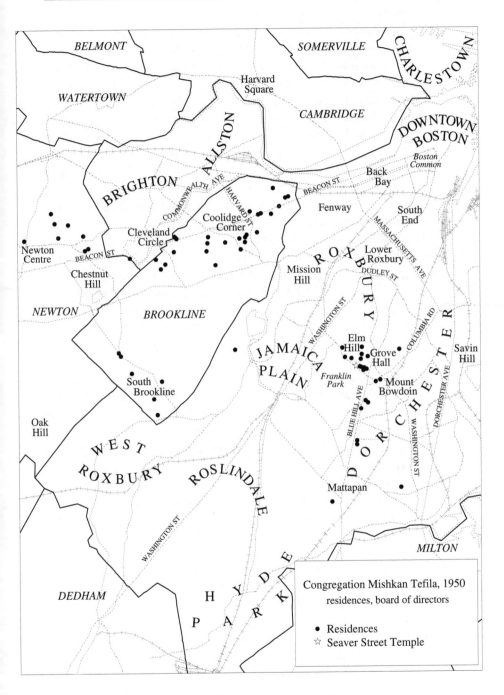

Map 21 Congregation Mishkan Tefila, board of directors, 1950

who had organized Beth El when Dorchester's Mount Bowdoin district had been a middle-class suburb. "The Dorchester community traces its organized existence since that time," the congregation reported. "Many families have moved to other districts, but most of these early groups will be represented at the Beth El's 25th anniversary banquet." In an editorial, the *Jewish Advocate* congratulated Beth El on its anniversary. The congregation maintained the flourishing Fowler Street Synagogue as well as the Beth El Hebrew School, the leading religious school in Dorchester. As the *Advocate* noted that December, "The present leaders of the synagogue and the Hebrew School have worked indefatigably and faithfully for many years to maintain and support these institutions, despite the migratory tide towards Brookline and Newton."[47]

The suburban exodus affected not only synagogues like Beth El, Beth Hamidrash Hagadol, and Mishkan Tefila, but also the two major community centers in Roxbury and Dorchester. Records from the Hecht House and the Boston Young Men's Hebrew Association offer further evidence of the out-migration of the area's central- and upper-middle-class Jews. These records also demonstrate the ease with which those Jews could move out to Brookline or Newton without disrupting their ties to institutions in Dorchester and Roxbury.

The Hecht House opened in Dorchester in 1936 with little tradition of a locally based leadership. Indeed, it was because residents of the West End had not controlled the institution that the Hecht House had been able to move from the West End to Dorchester. Of the twenty-nine men and women who sat on its governing board in 1940, only six lived in Roxbury or Dorchester. "There are few families of wealth" in Dorchester, a Hecht House report stated in 1937. The district "is a stopping place for the Jews, who as soon as they are financially able, move on to Brookline and Newton." In the late 1940s the Hecht House changed its by-laws, replacing its self-perpetuating board of trustees with a board elected by the full membership. The board of directors in 1951 included twenty-eight members from the Roxbury-Dorchester area and fourteen from Brookline and Newton. While local residents had achieved majority representation on the board, the Hecht House continued to attract the support of many suburban residents.[48]

The Boston YMHA, unlike the Hecht House, had been established in Roxbury by residents of the district, who in 1911 had gained control of the YMHA's charter and transplanted the institution from the South End.

"They developed an *esprit de corps* which made the Boston Young Men's Hebrew Association a local center," Barbara Miller Solomon wrote. "But as more prosperous members increasingly moved out of the district to Brookline, Brighton and Newton, the spirit which the original group had imparted also vanished in the mid-1920's. No longer in sound financial condition the 'Y' turned to the Federated for help and direction." In 1928 the Federated Jewish Charities undertook support of the Boston YMHA, accepting it as a constituent agency. But the Boston YMHA maintained its independent governance structure. Of the thirty members on the board of directors in 1940, fourteen lived in the Roxbury-Dorchester area, while the other sixteen lived in the Brookline-Brighton-Newton area. The suburban members of the board, according to a 1940 study, "originally resided in the Dorchester and Roxbury section and have moved in recent years."[49]

Changing Institutions

In the short term, the Jewish institutions of Dorchester and Roxbury benefited from the continued support of their suburban members. But over the long term many of these people organized and supported new suburban synagogues, community centers, and schools. Participation in older institutions often proved to be a temporary phenomenon, continuing only until a family's integration into a new community and a new set of institutions. Mishkan Tefila's occasional efforts to organize a branch Hebrew school in Brookline or Newton reflected this underlying anxiety about members' long-term loyalties. Leaders of the congregation recognized that keeping the support of suburban members required that the benefits of remaining active in the Seaver Street Temple were greater than the cost of commuting into Roxbury. As alternatives developed—as temples and religious schools emerged in Brookline and Newton—the relative benefit of membership in Mishkan Tefila was greatly diminished, and suburban members were less likely to continue paying dues to the Seaver Street Temple. Branch religious schools, Mishkan Tefila's leaders hoped, would not only eliminate the inconvenience of a long commute but also frustrate the development of competing institutions.

The urban exodus forced Roxbury and Dorchester's institutions to pursue a dual strategy: on the one hand, they strove to maintain the support of suburban members, but, on the other, they sought to serve their immediate neighborhoods. Given the difficulty of sustaining the loyalties of members who were moving to Brookline and Newton, these institutions adapted to the needs of residents in Roxbury and Dorchester. In their programming and practices, they were transformed along with their neighborhoods. At the same time, with their increasing dependence on a poorer membership, these institutions began to confront financial problems. Ultimately, those financial concerns came to threaten the viability of Jewish institutions in Roxbury and Dorchester, requiring them to consider new strategies in order to survive.

Programming and Religious Practices

Through its first years in Roxbury, the Boston YMHA had stressed the importance of clubs, classes, speakers' forums, cultural events, social gatherings, and athletics. But these programs reflected the interests of the district's original Jewish leaders. As the composition of Roxbury and Dorchester's Jewish population changed, so too did the demands on the Boston YMHA. "It is a known fact that the Jewish people of Roxbury and Dorchester have been moving out quite rapidly to Brighton, Brookline, and Newton. A glance at our own Board of Directors personnel shows this trend," a March 1941 report stated. "It is important to recognize that the caliber of person who has moved into the community does not measure up to the quality of person that has left; by this is meant the kind of activity that the average member of this community now participates in. Very often, motion pictures and dances are the total activities of many members of this community."[50]

The dominance of this "caliber of person" had dramatic consequences for Roxbury and Dorchester's leading synagogues. Until the middle 1920s, the Roxbury-Dorchester area had been the center of the Conservative movement in Boston. "At one time," as Rabbi Kazis later recalled, "there were four Conservative rabbis within [a] $\frac{1}{2}$ mile of each other in Roxbury [and Dorchester]."[51] Mishkan Tefila, Boston's oldest Conservative congregation, was located in Roxbury. Also located in upper Roxbury and Dorchester were three other congregations that had embraced much of the Conservative program—Beth Hamidrash Hagadol's Crawford Street Synagogue, Adath Jeshurun's Blue Hill Avenue Synagogue, and Beth El's Fowler Street Synagogue. Unlike Mishkan Tefila, these three congregations described themselves as modern Orthodox. The line that eventually distinguished Orthodox from Conservative congregations had not yet been settled: thus Kehillath Israel, in Brookline, which would later become one of New England's leading Conservative congregations, also regarded itself as a modern Orthodox congregation in the 1920s. Significantly, Louis Epstein, who in 1925 became the first rabbi of Kehillath Israel, came to the congregation directly from Roxbury's Beth Hamidrash Hagadol.

Adath Jeshurun, the oldest of Roxbury and Dorchester's congregations, had begun forging "a new form of conservatism" by the middle 1900s, according to the *Boston Advocate*. In the 1910s and early 1920s, Adath Jeshurun, Beth El, and Beth Hamidrash Hagadol supported late Friday night services, published English-language hymnals, and invited guest speakers to lecture during services. They even introduced family pews and mixed choirs into their Friday night services. Mordecai Kaplan, visiting the Blue Hill Avenue Synagogue in December 1914, noted that on Friday night "the main auditorium of the synagogue was filled with young and middle aged people, men and women sitting together." All three congregations embarked on ambitious building programs in the early 1920s, and all three stressed the importance of organizing activities and adapting religious practices to make Judaism attractive to a younger generation. These congregations were active members of the United Synagogue of America, and they were served by English-speaking rabbis educated at the Jewish Theological Seminary. Rabbi Epstein, as the president of the Rabbinical Assembly in the 1920s, led the third major arm of the national Conservative movement.[52]

Some members of these congregations, however, had little sympathy for the Conservative program. Adath Jeshurun "seems to be a house divided against itself," the *Jewish Advocate* observed in 1911. "At one moment it is more than abreast of modern orthodoxy, at another its influence is used to promote a standpattism, which can be of little use." Mordecai Kaplan noted in his journal that Adath Jeshurun's rabbi was engaged in a struggle with "the old timers who constantly interfere with his work." When he attended a children's service in December 1916, Kaplan learned immediately of the disdain felt by some members of the Blue Hill Avenue Synagogue for their rabbi's innovations. "I found seated at the back of the room where the childrens services were going on a number of old fogies who kept on conversing among themselves," Kaplan wrote, "and about whom I was told that they strenuously objected to these childrens services."[53]

Although advocates of a more liberal approach succeeded through the early 1920s in overcoming the resistance, their success did not survive the decade. By the late 1920s, the Conservative movement had disintegrated in the pioneer congregations of Roxbury and Dorchester. "It was only through the influence of the modern orthodox rabbis of the synagogues in our community, that organizations of young folks were able to function within the temple," Samuel A. Margolis, the former president of the Crawford Street Synagogue's junior council, stated in September 1925. "At present we have a sad situation in three of the synagogues in Roxbury and Dorchester, in each of which the rabbis have left and the governing boards of which congregations have apparently no intention whatsoever to fill the vacancies with other rabbis of modern thought and tendencies." The lower-middle-class and working-class Jews who now dominated Jewish life in Roxbury and Dorchester decisively rooted out Conservative influences and restored traditional Orthodoxy. "During the last few years thousands of Jewish families have moved into this section," Rabbi Rubenovitz wrote in January 1927. "By far the greater number of these new comers to Roxbury, Dorchester, and Mattapan have little knowledge or understanding of conservative Judaism." The three congregations abandoned late Friday night services, hymnals, mixed choirs, special youth programs, and family pews. They severed their relations with the United Synagogue and ceased hiring Conservative rabbis.[54]

Conservative Judaism was the suburban expression of middle-class, Americanized Jews. In Boston, it was born in Roxbury and Dorchester. Only with the exodus of middle-class Jews in the 1920s did the impetus for Conservatism pass from the Roxbury-Dorchester area to Brookline and Newton. Though Marshall Sklare set out "to write a sociology of Conservative Judaism rather than a history," his contention that Conservative Judaism emerged in areas of third settlement—in areas like Newton and Brookline, rather than in second-settlement areas like Roxbury and Dorchester—has long been the standard account of Conservatism's geographical origins. Jack Wertheimer, however, examining a few congregational and local Jewish histories, has suggested "that the first generation of Conservative synagogues was founded in areas of *second* rather than third settlement." The evidence from Boston supports Wertheimer's argument. David Kaufman's description of Adath Jeshurun as a transitional institution—as a congregation that broke with traditional forms but did not fully embrace the synagogue-center ideal—is an incomplete characterization, since it implies that Adath Jeshurun, even in the

1910s and early 1920s, was qualitatively different from Brookline's Kehillath Israel. In fact, the modern Orthodox congregations of Roxbury and Dorchester were indistinguishable from the early Brookline congregation. Not until the urban exodus of the middle 1920s did their paths of congregational development diverge. Kehillath Israel consolidated its commitment to Conservative reforms, while the age when the Blue Hill Avenue Synagogue, Fowler Street Synagogue, and Crawford Street Synagogue had also stood in the ranks of nascent Conservatism was soon forgotten.[55]

Mishkan Tefila, alone among Roxbury and Dorchester's congregations, remained loyal to the Conservative movement—though not without some difficulty. "Owing to the shifting of the Jewish population," Rubenovitz observed in the early 1930s, "a great many new people have come into the Roxbury-Dorchester district who know but little of the aims and ideals of Mishkan Tefila." The congregation, he insisted, had to be vigilant. "I hardly think it necessary to dwell on the importance of decorum," Rubenovitz wrote to his board of directors in February 1926. Since "the men on the pulpit cannot enforce order from where they are," he asked members of the congregation's board to assist the sexton "on the floor of the Temple" each Saturday morning. "Surely the men who have made such sacrifices for Mishkan Tefila in the past, will not shrink from rendering this additional service," Rubenovitz argued that February. "To allow things to drift as they have during the past few months, would mean that the character of our Service would steadily deteriorate, and finally descend to the level of the old type Orthodox Synagogue."[56]

Mishkan Tefila's survival as a Conservative congregation was due largely to three factors: first, it had openly embraced the Conservative cause by the 1910s and thereafter did not regard itself as Orthodox in any sense; second, it had introduced family pews, a mixed choir, and an organ into all its major religious services, ensuring that these liberal reforms became the general rule rather than exceptional practices; and third, unlike Roxbury and Dorchester's modern Orthodox congregations but like Brookline's Kehillath Israel, it continued to enjoy the support and leadership of large numbers of central- and upper-middle-class members who had moved to Brookline and Newton. All three factors ensured that Conservative Judaism persisted in the Seaver Street Temple. In the end, that persistence was not due to the leadership of Rabbi Rubenovitz. While Mishkan Tefila and Kehillath Israel were well served by their rabbis, it was only because majorities in both congregations continued to support Conservative reforms that they continued to support the two rabbis. The presence of Rabbi Rubenovitz in the Seaver Street Temple and of Rabbi Epstein in the Brookline temple were consequences—not causes—of their congregations' commitment to a Conservative program. As Epstein had learned at the Crawford Street Synagogue and as other Seminary rabbis had learned at Beth El and Adath Jeshurun, congregations and rabbis parted ways when they disagreed over fundamental issues.

Finances

Rabbi Epstein had left Beth Hamidrash Hagadol immediately after the congregation had reelected Louis Steinberg as its president. Steinberg's ostensible goal, though, had been not to eliminate modern Orthodoxy but to retire the congregation's debt. Similarly, it was for financial as much as for theological reasons that all three congregations dismissed their rabbis in the middle 1920s and did not act quickly to hire new ones. The ascendancy of working-class and lower-middle-class Jews in the affairs of Roxbury and Dorchester not only transformed the character of the district's institutions but also undermined the financial health of those institutions.

Structures themselves reflected the changed socioeconomic status of Dorchester and Roxbury. Most of the district's major buildings—its leading synagogues, religious schools, and community centers—had been built and dedicated by 1925. After the middle 1920s, Jews in Roxbury and Dorchester broke ground for just two significant buildings. One was the Mishkan Tefila schoolhouse, on Elm Hill, which the congregation dedicated in 1929. The other structure was Kehillath Jacob's Fessenden Street Synagogue, in Mattapan. Dedicated in the spring of 1939, the synagogue was a modest brick building, erected by a generation that lacked the wealth of the district's suburban founders.[57]

Through the remaining decades of Jewish life in Roxbury and Dorchester, the structures built in 1905–1925 formed the area's institutional backbone. Roxbury's Elm Hill and Blue Hill Avenue–Grove Hall districts, which had attracted large middle-class suburban settlements in the 1900s and 1910s, contained many substantial community buildings. Dorchester's Mattapan district, which had never attracted many upper-middle-class Jews, contained few major structures. "Sad to relate," the *Jewish Advocate* observed in May 1926, one month before ground was broken in Mattapan for the district's only religious school, "there is no other Jewish community which is so barren, so devoid, of an institution for the proper training and development of our younger generation as is Mattapan." More than a year later, Rubenovitz noted that "in this entire district there isn't one Jewish school-house properly equipped to do its work in a modern and efficient manner." A foundation and "part of the ground floor" were all that stood of the projected schoolhouse; work had been "discontinued because of the lack of support and the indifference of the community." A June 1930 study, which noted that the schoolhouse was still "unfinished for lack of funds," found a "total absence of any provision of social, cultural and recreational activities of an organized character" in the Mattapan district. Although the Dorchester-Mattapan Hebrew School was finally dedicated on Morton Street that fall, Mattapan Jewry continued to depend on an underdeveloped infrastructure. The great ethnic neighborhoods that lay along Blue Hill Avenue in the 1930s, 1940s, and 1950s inherited an institutional network that reflected the geographical biases of an earlier time.[58]

Moreover, that institutional network had depended on the generosity of middle-class supporters for its financial viability. Given the competition inherent in Jewish institutional life, Roxbury and Dorchester's early Jewish residents had established various new institutions in areas already well served by existing synagogues and Hebrew schools. A set of institutions that depended on the overstretched resources of a middle-class neighborhood was not easily supported by a working-class neighborhood. "The Roxbury district in which this congregation is located has undergone considerable change during recent years," Rabbi Rubenovitz told a visitor to Temple Mishkan Tefila in 1940. "The wealthy Jewish families who lived in this area and helped build this large and costly temple and center have moved out of the district and have been replaced by persons of lower economic levels, making more difficult the support of this synagogue and other local community institutions under Jewish auspices."[59]

After the middle 1920s, congregations often lacked the funds to subsidize religious schools, and many parents could not afford to pay tuition. Like the Boston YMHA, which in 1928 turned to the Federated Jewish Charities for financial support, several Hebrew schools began to require outside aid, appealing to community agencies and suburban Jewry. "A group of about 100 prominent men have organized into a Brotherhood of the Beth El Hebrew School," the *Advocate* reported in October 1928. "It is hoped that this Brotherhood will be of great assistance in solving financial problems during the ensuing year." Adath Jeshurun's Menorah Institute raised funds by sponsoring an annual concert. "In addition to deriving an evening's pleasure," the Menorah Institute stated in its February 1929 announcement, "the audience will also help an institution which most assuredly must receive support, if it is to continue to exist."[60]

The four major Hebrew schools in Dorchester and Roxbury were insolvent by the late 1940s. Although the area's Jewish community was nearly as large as it had been one or two decades earlier, the generation-long exodus of affluent Jews had taken its toll. "Sociological processes, especially the process of the shifting of population, have been going on, changing profoundly the face of formerly densely populated Jewish localities, depleting them of well-to-do and higher middle class families on the one hand, and infiltrating them with lower middle class and poor families on the other hand," a June 1950 report stated. "Gradually, the schools in those localities found themselves unable to secure from local sources the financial means to cover their skyrocketing expenditures. After a valiant struggle for several years during the post-bellum period (1945–47), they finally decided to turn to the Associated Jewish Philanthropies for financial assistance."[61]

In 1948–1949, the four Hebrew schools in Greater Boston that were running the largest deficits were Dorchester and Roxbury's four leading schools. The AJP made "emergency loans to the Beth El Hebrew School and to the Menorah Institute in the amounts of $5000 and $4000 respectively." The Mishkan Tefila School and Beth Hillel's Dorchester-Mattapan Hebrew School, which received no assistance from the AJP that year, ran deficits of $9,000 and $7,000 respectively. In 1949–1950, the AJP repeated its emergency appropriations to the Beth El Hebrew School and the Menorah Institute, concluding that "they will not continue to exist without such assistance." The Dorchester-Mattapan Hebrew School also appealed to the AJP for aid. Of the congregations supporting Dorchester and Roxbury's principal religious schools, only Mishkan Tefila, with its large suburban membership, could still cover its school's deficit by the early 1950s. The other three schools required community subsidies. In 1950–1951, the AJP appropriated $3,500 to the Dorchester-Mattapan

Hebrew School, $4,000 to the Menorah Institute, and $5,300 to the Beth El Hebrew School. Enrollments in these schools were large and relatively stable. "In localities where the synagogues themselves lead a pitiable existence," the June 1950 report argued, religious schools deserved to be regarded as a community responsibility.[62]

Synagogues, however, even those leading "a pitiable existence," could expect no funding from the Associated Jewish Philanthropies. In agreeing to support the three religious schools in Roxbury and Dorchester, the AJP argued that the schools were communal as well as congregational institutions. Since synagogues by definition were congregational, their welfare was regarded as a private matter. After the middle 1920s, Dorchester and Roxbury's congregations struggled to pay their expenses. Without a substantial base of middle-class members, they encountered difficulties in raising funds for operating expenses and for mortgage payments. The decisions of the area's leading congregations in the middle 1920s to reduce costs by temporarily eliminating the position of rabbi proved a harbinger of things to come. In the 1930s, with the onset of the Depression, some of the major congregations in Dorchester and Roxbury functioned for years without a permanent rabbi: the Blue Hill Avenue Synagogue, 1929–1939; the Fowler Street Synagogue, 1933–1942; the Nightingale Street Synagogue, until 1944; the Fessenden Street Synagogue, until 1939.[63]

According to the congregation's one surviving financial report, Adath Jeshurun spent $17,100 in 1938.[64] Of that amount, the congregation paid visiting rabbis a total of $250, its cantor $3,000, its choir $1,800, its sexton $1,300, and its janitor $1,100; spent $1,700 for electricity and heat; and paid $4,300 toward the mortgages on the Blue Hill Avenue Synagogue and the Menorah Institute. Because it was able to raise only $15,700 in dues, donations, and High Holy Day tickets in 1938, Adath Jeshurun spent a $400 balance in its bank account and took $1,000 from its cemetery. The congregation ended the year with a final balance of $12.77 in the bank.

The Crawford Street Synagogue also faced financial problems. Louis Steinberg had been right: the years of plenty ended in the middle 1920s. Two decades into its lean years, Beth Hamidrash Hagadol had become a poor, struggling congregation. Between 1945 and 1951, the congregation's annual budget was about $21,000; in 1924, it had exceeded $28,000. Although inflation had increased costs by the early 1950s, congregational receipts had declined in every area. Membership dues, which had totaled $6,600 in 1924, averaged about $5,000 in the period 1945–1951. Donations, which had yielded $7,400 in 1924, accounted for about $4,800 in annual revenues in 1945–1951. And ticket sales for High Holy Day seats, which had raised $12,300 in 1924, raised about $8,400 annually in 1945–1951. To balance its budget each year in the postwar era, the Crawford Street Synagogue depended on a transfer of $2,000–4,000 from its cemetery account. Sumner Greenberg—who sat on the congregation's board and whose father-in-law, from the late 1930s into the 1960s, helped lead the congregation—later recalled matter-of-factly, "The only thing that kept us alive was the cemetery."[65]

Catholic Neighborhoods, 1924–1951

[handwritten margin note: I'm thinking it's the parish that's much as Church]

Whereas the continuing bustle of activity on Blue Hill Avenue in the 1930s and 1940s masked profound changes in the area's Jewish community, life for Dorchester and Roxbury's Catholics was not similarly transformed. Since the turn of the century, middle-class Catholics had been moving out of the area to Boston's suburbs, but there is evidence neither of an abrupt acceleration of this pattern in the 1920s nor of a drastic decline in the area's socioeconomic status by the early 1950s. The difference between Jewish and Catholic residential mobility was due, in part, to different rates of socioeconomic mobility—Boston's Jews, in general, moved more quickly than Catholics into the middle class, and Catholic neighborhoods had already been predominantly working class and lower middle class in character by the 1920s.[66] But the difference was also due to different sets of institutional rules. Catholics moving outside their parish boundaries paid higher costs than Jews moving from their neighborhoods. And because Catholics who did move to the suburbs could not participate in the activities of their old parish, suburban Catholics did not serve as leaders and role models for Dorchester and Roxbury's Catholics. Rules, therefore, frustrated the mass exodus of middle-class Catholics and limited the influence of those who left. As a consequence, most Catholic institutions and neighborhoods remained stable and strong through the early 1950s.

Dorchester's total Catholic population in the early 1950s was as high as it had ever been. About 118,000 white Catholics lived in Dorchester in 1950, as many as had lived there in 1940 and a few thousand more than had lived there in 1930.[67] Nearby in upper Roxbury, the white Catholic population, which had remained stable at 22,000 since the late 1920s, had begun slowly to decline in the 1940s as African Americans settled on once-Catholic streets in St. Joseph's Parish. But the decline was slight through the early 1950s; indeed, it is invisible in St. Joseph's annual records of infant baptisms, marriages, deaths, and school attendance.[68] In 1950 about 19,000 white Catholics still lived in upper Roxbury.

The 137,000 Catholics of Dorchester and upper Roxbury were served by sixteen territorial parishes. Monsignor Thomas J. Finnegan, Jr., who would become the chancellor of the Boston archdiocese, recalled that Dorchester and upper Roxbury's Catholic population was "enormous" in the early 1950s. The area, he noted, was "almost a diocese unto itself." Though the three parishes of upper Roxbury "suffered in varying degrees from the exodus of Catholics to the outlying districts," according to the 1944 archdiocesan history, there was little evidence of socioeconomic decline in the thirteen Dorchester parishes. In 1940, when St. Mark's pastor ended his parish's monthly collection, "the parish was not only out of debt, but had a bank account approaching $200,000," the parish history states. Through the 1940s and early 1950s, St. Mark's Parish prospered spiritually and financially. Each week more than 8,000 people attended one of the parish's eight Sunday Masses, and the parish invested heavily and constantly in improvements to its church and other parochial buildings.[69]

The continued vitality of Catholic institutional life was reflected in the many new parochial structures that were built between the middle 1920s and early 1950s. When St. Mark's Parish opened its new convent in January 1926, it became only the fifth parish in Dorchester and upper Roxbury to complete a full set of parish buildings (church, rectory, convent, and school).[70] Over the next several years, other parishes did the same. St. Ann's Parish finished its last major building in 1927. St. William's and St. Angela's parishes each completed their physical plants during the Depression, in the middle 1930s. And St. Ambrose' and St. Matthew's completed their last important structures in the early 1940s. Rules of membership, in frustrating the out-migration of middle-class Catholics, had maintained the financial stability of Catholic institutions in an era when Jewish institutions were undermined by the unrelenting exodus of their leading members. While Jews built few significant structures after the middle 1920s, Catholics continued to build.

New Catholic structures strengthened the area's dense network of parishes during the very time that the geographical biases of the Jewish community's founding generation were frozen into place. Established according to hierarchical rules of authority, Catholic parishes had been neatly laid out across Dorchester and upper Roxbury. This logical design required central authority and central planning, both absent in the rules of Jewish institutions. And the construction of new Catholic buildings after the middle 1920s reinforced the relative equality of the various parishes in Dorchester and upper Roxbury. Early advantages enjoyed by the area's five largest parishes were steadily diminished as other parishes completed their own parochial structures. The even geographical distribution of Catholic institutions, buttressed by rules of membership and authority, contrasted sharply with the uneven distribution of Jewish institutions.

Recognizing the abundance of support for existing parishes, Boston's archbishops established two new Dorchester parishes. Cardinal William O'Connell organized St. Brendan's Parish in the fall of 1929 to serve Catholics in Cedar Grove, taking territory for the new parish from St. Ann's and St. Gregory's parishes. In November 1933, once its outer shell and basement church were completed, St. Brendan's Church was blessed. Twelve years later, in the fall of 1945, Archbishop Richard J. Cushing erected a "New Parish at Uphams Corner." St. Kevin's Parish immediately purchased a telephone building on Columbia Road, converting it into a makeshift church. In rooms above the church, the parish established a school. Cushing came to St. Kevin's Parish in April 1947 to bless the parish "centre," a former parking garage that the parish intended to use for social facilities and additional classroom space. "When materials and funds are available," the *Boston Post* reported, "a new and larger St. Kevin's Church will rise on the grounds that now separate the church proper from the centre." In the late 1940s, as established Jewish synagogues and Hebrew schools struggled to remain solvent, this new parish—located in one of the oldest and densest sections of northern Dorchester—brimmed with confidence. In his April 1947 visit to St. Kevin's Parish, Archbishop Cushing declared that the parish "is the fastest growing one in the archdiocese."[71]

The Catholic parishes of Dorchester and upper Roxbury remained financially secure in the late 1940s and early 1950s. Among Catholic institutions, there was little evidence of the financial deterioration that had transformed most of the area's Jewish institutions since the 1920s. Because they consistently raised more funds each year than they spent, Dorchester and Roxbury's parishes accumulated substantial surpluses. Even small parishes maintained balances that exceeded $40,000. The largest and strongest parishes, St. Peter's and St. Mark's, reported surpluses of $170,000 and $230,000 in 1947 in their respective accounts with the chancery. According to its parish history, St. Mark's Parish was "the leading financial bulwark of the Archdiocese." Parishioners donated liberally not only to their own parish but to various archdiocesan collections. "I must take this opportunity to pay tribute to the members of this parish," Cushing told St. Mark's parishioners in 1945. "You are the most generous in the whole Archdiocese of Boston."[72]

Suburban Connections

It was from the flush parishes of Dorchester that the archdiocese borrowed funds in the 1940s and 1950s to subsidize new suburban parishes. Dorchester and Roxbury's parishes kept their surpluses on deposit at the archdiocesan chancery. With the permission of the pastor, the archbishop drew on those deposits to extend low-interest loans to young, struggling parishes in Boston's suburbs. This "revolving fund" emerged in the postwar era as a central financial institution of the Boston archdiocese. In 1953, for example, St. Matthew's Parish lent $50,000 to the archdiocese. In the next year, the archbishop wrote to the pastor of St. Mark's Parish, seeking "to borrow $75,000 of St. Mark's funds to put stagnant parish funds to work for other parishes." Through the revolving loan fund, Rev. James McCarthy later observed, St. Peter's and other Dorchester parishes "helped suburban parishes get off the ground."[73]

There was irony in this redistribution of wealth from the city to the suburbs, and no one would have been more sensitive to it than the leaders of Dorchester and Roxbury's Jewish institutions. After a generation-long exodus of middle-class Jews, the Jewish neighborhoods of Dorchester and upper Roxbury had become incapable of supporting their large and maldistributed network of synagogues, community centers, and religious schools. Dorchester, including Mattapan, was in "decline as a Jewish center," Sidney Steiman, Beth Hillel's rabbi, observed in the early 1950s. "The population has been pushing into Brookline, Newton, South Brookline and Milton. Many of Beth Hillel's supporters and leaders have taken positions of leadership in their new communities."[74] Rules of institutional membership, by facilitating the Jewish exodus, had indirectly sapped the strength of the area's institutions. Although the area's Jewish population was nearly as large in 1950 as it had been in preceding years, it was skimmed of much of its local leadership. The institutional crisis was rooted neither in racial change nor in a reduction in the size of the area's Jewish population. Rather, it was caused by the ongoing socioeconomic transformation of the community.

There were no boundaries to the crisis. From Elm Hill to Mattapan, every major Hebrew school was insolvent and depended on a large annual subsidy. Synagogues—large and small, Orthodox and Conservative—no longer received sufficient regular income to pay their bills. Even Mishkan Tefila, which had regained fiscal stability after reaching its 1937 bond agreement, confronted mounting financial problems by the early 1950s. It is clear "that our income is falling and that expenses are rising," Mishkan Tefila's executive committee reported in April 1951. "The rise in expenses will be due to increase in teachers salaries, necessary higher costs of everything including costs of needed repairs and conversely our income will be less due to the fact that some members are moving away from the Roxbury community and are being replaced by new members enrolling in the lower membership classifications."[75] Like each of the other Jewish institutions in Dorchester and upper Roxbury, Mishkan Tefila struggled with growing annual deficits. These institutions could and did adapt their policies to changing neighborhood constituencies, but they could not adapt to bankruptcy nor to the accelerating loss of their most active members.

In the early 1950s, as increasing numbers of long-time members moved to the suburbs, several of Roxbury and Dorchester's Jewish institutions began to consider new programs to nurture suburban loyalties. Maimonides School, Boston's preeminent Jewish day school, announced plans in June 1951 "to establish a branch" in Brighton. Maimonides' board of directors decided to create the branch school "in response to numerous requests by parents living in the Brookline, Brighton, Allston and Newton area." Also in 1951, Beth Pinchas—like Maimonides, a Dorchester institution—organized a "Brookline-Newton Auxiliary," encouraging suburban residents to support the work of Boston's largest Hasidic congregation. And Mishkan Tefila, which had been making sporadic attempts since the late 1910s to organize a branch Hebrew school in

Brookline or Newton, resolved again to establish a suburban branch. At their annual congregational meeting in May 1950, members of Mishkan Tefila voted to create "a branch Center and Schoolhouse somewhere in Newton or Brookline."[76]

Institutional rules, especially rules of membership, had done their work with unforgiving logic. High barriers to exit helped maintain the strength of Dorchester's Catholic parishes. Jewish institutions, in contrast, reeled under the strain of a middle-class exodus that had begun in the 1920s and continued through the 1930s and 1940s. Moving out to the suburbs without immediately severing their ties to Dorchester and Roxbury's institutions, middle-class Jews ultimately created a competing network of suburban institutions and drifted away from synagogues and schools that they had left behind. While institutions in Dorchester and Roxbury initially responded by appealing to local residents, by the early 1950s many Jewish institutions began to recognize that their long-term survival depended on sustained suburban support. Branch facilities and auxiliaries promised to strengthen their parent institutions.

At the conclusion of Mishkan Tefila's annual meeting in May 1950, Rabbi Kazis rose to congratulate the congregation on its vision. The decision to establish branch facilities in the Brookline-Newton area, he declared, "marked a famous landmark, an historic turning point" in the congregation's history. Invigorated by the support it would receive from its suburban branch, the congregation could now look to its future with confidence. "When we gather here together" in 1958 to celebrate Mishkan Tefila's centennial, Kazis predicted, the newly fortified congregation will have fulfilled "the dream and hope of many generations of Mishkan Tefila folk." On that day the Seaver Street Temple would surely be the scene of much rejoicing.[77]

10

The Uprooted and the Rooted

For St. Peter's Parish, 1958 was a year like any other. One hundred years had passed since the "little Sunday-school" had opened near Meeting House Hill, and two-thirds of a century had passed since the parish had completed work on its pudding-stone church. As Douglass Shand Tucci observed, St. Peter's Church had become "the pre-eminent landmark of Modern Dorchester." Each Sunday, when about one hundred people attended services at the white-clapboard First Parish Church, St. Peter's Parish conducted ten separate Masses for 8,300 active parishioners.[1]

Flanked by its thriving daughter parishes, St. Peter's was the largest parish in the archdiocese. In 1958, 145 couples were married in St. Peter's Church, 490 infants were baptized there, and more than 2,200 children were enrolled in the parish's parochial and Sunday school classes. St. Peter's prosperity was easily measured: by the end of 1958, the parish surplus on deposit at the archdiocesan chancery had grown to $426,000. Functioning on the scale of a large New England town, St. Peter's suffered from an embarrassment of strengths. Having most recently relinquished territory in the 1940s for the establishment of St. Kevin's Parish, St. Peter's in the spring of 1959 again reduced the size of its territory, transferring some outlying streets to neighboring parishes. The Catholic stronghold on Meeting House Hill had never seemed so secure.[2]

For Mishkan Tefila, 1958 seemed a special year. In December, members gathered in their temple for a three-day centennial celebration. But Rabbi Kazis's prophecy of a few years earlier had been proved only partially true. Mishkan Tefila remained strong on the occasion of its centennial, but it had not stayed in Roxbury. The congregation now worshiped in Newton. It had sold the temple and schoolhouse on Seaver Street, for just $109,000, to the Lubavitz Yeshiva, a Jewish day school.[3]

At the dedication of the Newton temple, on a Friday evening in May 1958, Mishkan Tefila's leaders "walked down the center aisle of the Sanctuary, each one with a Torah in his arms and with his son by his side," Kazis wrote. "As they ascended the pulpit they turned the Torahs over to their sons who in turn placed them in the newly dedicated Ark." With the procession, members of the congregation recalled the promise that attended Mishkan Tefila each time it dedicated a new house of worship; they recalled the institutional continuity guaranteed by institutional mobility. "Temple Mishkan Tefila has ofttimes been characterized as a 'stadt shul,' a great central synagogue which serves as a place of assembly for the entire community. No designation could be more apt," the *Jewish Advocate* stated. "It has proved itself a congregation with roots and loyalties, one which moves with its membership."[4]

Mobility guaranteed the congregation's survival. If Mishkan Tefila was to remain in Roxbury, its leaders had concluded in the middle 1950s, "in not more than ten years the Temple would be compelled to close its doors and cease to function, and the great traditions forgotten." Although scholars have subsequently criticized the decision of the congregation to relocate to Newton, they have failed to identify any other action by which the institution could have been perpetuated. Given Jewish rules and the urban exodus, a decision to stay indefinitely in Roxbury was a prescription for institutional suicide. Certainly Mishkan Tefila's leaders believed that the choice they confronted was stark and urgent. "With us," Rabbi Kazis argued in December 1953, "it is a matter of life or death."[5]

While Catholic institutions had no alternative but to stay put, Jewish institutions survived and prospered because they were portable. Membership rules, which since the 1920s had facilitated the exodus of middle-class Jews and frustrated the Catholic exodus, still affected these neighborhoods. But in the 1950s and 1960s, rules of rootedness assumed greater prominence. In these years neither the archdiocese nor the Jewish community federation supported special programs to assist Roxbury and Dorchester's institutions. Without central guidance, synagogues, parishes, and religious schools groped to respond to the erosion of their memberships and financial bases, and these institutional actions had consequences for local residents. Catholic parishes—which could not move and which received routine, if piecemeal, support from the arch-diocese—reinforced residents' neighborhood attachments. Jewish insti-tutions unwittingly exacerbated the concern that the future of Boston Jewry lay elsewhere than along Blue Hill Avenue. Responsible for their own survival, synagogues either moved or collapsed. In a 1966 editorial prompted by the death of Rabbi Rubenovitz, the *Jewish Advocate* recalled the rabbi's outstanding institutional achievement. Since assuming the congregation's pulpit, the *Advocate* noted, Rubenovitz had built Mishkan Tefila "into a spiritual brotherhood with strength to construct two of the great sanctuaries in this area and to move geographically."[6] No pastor of St. Peter's ever received such a eulogy.

Neighborhood Change, 1951–1958

In the early 1950s, ethnic boundaries that had endured for three decades started to shift and disintegrate. A group of Jewish leaders met in Decem-ber 1951 to discuss the growing tension between upper Roxbury's blacks and Jews. Though fights between Jewish and white Catholic teenagers had been common for years throughout Dorchester and Roxbury, the emerging concern with Jewish-black relations reflected the quickening pace of racial change. Simon Rosen, the president of the Boston YMHA, the Jewish community center located on Seaver Street, stated that "in his opinion the neighborhood is not changing." That Rosen felt compelled to address the issue, however, suggests that other Jews were reaching a different conclusion. Henry C. Berlin, representing the citywide Jewish Community Council (JCC), argued at the same meeting that "Negroes in the Roxbury neighborhood are here to stay." A few days later, Robert E. Segal, who also sat on the Jewish Community Council, suggested that neighborhood tensions between blacks and Jews were due in part to "the fact that Negroes are moving into the Roxbury area and the Jews are inclined to resist this 'invasion.'"[7]

Residential Change

African Americans had lived on Elm Hill since the 1920s. Not until the 1950s, though, was the growth of upper Roxbury's black community accompanied by a significant decline in the size of nearby Jewish and

Catholic communities. Postwar prosperity, federal mortgage guarantees, and suburban housing development were accelerating the white exodus. "The town's building boom has not abated," Sylvia Rothchild wrote in 1956, describing the suburb of Sharon. "Streets stretching like tentacles from the main thoroughfares meet each other in the woods and fields." As Catholics and Jews left for the suburbs, African Americans settled in Dorchester and upper Roxbury in ever-increasing numbers. Many of these black families came from the South End and lower Roxbury, where they had been displaced by urban renewal. Many others were newcomers to Boston. African Americans settled in Roxbury's Catholic districts and in parts of Dorchester, but racial succession in the early and middle 1950s progressed most rapidly in the once-Jewish enclaves of Roxbury. The entire Jewish population of Roxbury and Dorchester—which had fallen only slowly between 1930 and 1950, from 77,000 to 70,000—fell to 58,500 by the middle 1950s. In Roxbury alone, the Jewish population fell from 24,500 to 15,500 between 1950 and 1955.[8]

Mark Mirsky—recalling a day in the early 1950s when he had been campaigning in Grove Hall for his father, a state representative—described his encounter with one of the first black families in the area. "They greeted me with incredible politeness, invited me in for tea, signed the papers and encouraged me to deliver the little talk I had prepared on Wilfred S. Mirsky and virtue in politics. Soft Southern accents and courtesy, a South Carolina manse on Blue Hill avenue," Mirsky noted. "Later in the day, an old lady clung on that street to my father's coat, begging him, find me a nice Jewish tenant for downstairs, Mr. Mirsky, please. Please? I'll rent it cheap, Mr. Mirsky, please, please . . ." The Grove Hall–Blue Hill Avenue district "is a changing neighborhood, with poor, older housing which has been neglected for years," a 1956 study of Boston's Jewish community found. "The indications are for a continuing rapid decrease of Jewish population," the study added. "The non-white people will continue to come into this area and in larger numbers as housing further deteriorates."[9]

Elm Hill was also changing fast. The neighborhood "is one of the few mixed areas [in Boston] not yet predominantly black," the *Christian Science Monitor* observed in the spring of 1954, "although the trend is toward another all-Negro district." Leaders of Freedom House, an Elm Hill community organization, "say that fear of property devaluation is the basis of most resentment to incoming Negro residents in any area," the *Monitor* reported. "But they say upper and middle income Negroes make good property owners. In the Upper Roxbury area they have not only kept up, but in many cases improved, the condition of their residences." Jews, however, continued to leave the district. By 1956, Albert I. Gordon argued, the "decline" in the Jewish population on Elm Hill was reaching the point where it could "best be described as a flight."[10]

Through the middle 1950s, Dorchester's Jewish population fell only slightly in size, but the exodus to the suburbs was threatening the area's stability. While the 1956 community study predicted that the area "will probably remain substantially Jewish for the foreseeable future," Gordon disagreed. According to him, the Jewish neighborhoods of Dorchester were "rapidly deteriorating." North of Franklin Field, in the Franklin Park–Mount Bowdoin and Franklin Field districts, the Jewish population fell from 17,000 to 14,500 between 1950 and 1955. South of Franklin Field, in the Mattapan district, the number of Jews remained steady. Though the Jewish population was declining in most parts of Mattapan, hundreds of Jewish families were purchasing single-family homes in new subdivisions near Mattapan Square. But the consequences of decades of out-migration were clear. "The action was no longer in Dorchester but out in Newton, Brookline, Sharon, where the girls were wealthy, their ranch houses dazzling brick after the brown wooden bunkers on the avenue," Mark Mirsky recalled. "Eisenhower came by the G&G for a sandwich but there was no rally. The crowd that assembled there on Sunday mornings and autumn nights before election was imperceptibly shrinking."[11]

For Mirsky, the G&G delicatessen—on Blue Hill Avenue in the midst of the Mattapan district—symbolized all that had changed by the middle 1950s. "Jack and Marion's in Brookline was the place to take a girl, not the G&G, their sandwiches were bigger, the decor 'fabulous.' The G&G by comparison looked sad, old-fashioned," he wrote. "Anyone who could afford it was taking his date to the movies in Newton. A young man caught home in Dorchester on Friday or Saturday night looked like a reject, cut-rate goods." Jack and Marion's stood in Brookline's Coolidge Corner, which, by the middle 1950s, was supplanting Blue Hill Avenue as the center of Jewish life in Boston. More Jews now lived in Brookline, Newton, and Brighton than in the Roxbury-Dorchester area. And new suburban Jewish communities were growing fast: between 1945 and 1957, when Sharon's total population grew from 4,000 to 8,000, its Jewish population grew from 300 to 4,000. "The ranks in the G&G were not yet thinned noticeably but the seed crop was gone," Mirsky stated. "The loins of Israel sat in Jack & Marion's."[12]

Violence

Until the early 1950s, tension between Roxbury's Jews and African Americans had been minimal. Of much greater concern were the frequent fights between white Catholics and Jews. This problem was as old as the Jewish presence in Dorchester and upper Roxbury. Jews spending a quiet Saturday in Franklin Park in the fall of 1911 were "compelled to leave the park," according to the *Jewish Advocate,* when "gangs of young roughs" molested them. "Several Jews were mauled," the *Advocate* reported, "and gangs yelled, 'Kill the Jews.'" By the middle 1940s, assaults on Jews and confrontations between Jews and Catholics had become routine. *Newsweek* devoted a story in November 1943 to the anti-Semitic violence in Dorchester. And Wallace Stegner, in a lengthy article that appeared in the *Atlantic Monthly* in July 1944, argued that Boston's Catholic leaders should actively repudiate the attacks on Dorchester and Roxbury's Jews. The violence was often planned, "preceded by the question, 'Are you a Jew?'" Stegner found. "Gangs laid for Jewish boys coming out of Hecht Neighborhood House, roamed Franklin Field and Franklin Park in search of cross-lot walkers. Sometimes they appeared in cars, which pulled up beside Jewish youths to disgorge half a dozen attackers." The anti-Semitic violence of Catholic gangs remained a major concern of Jews throughout Dorchester and Roxbury in the early 1950s. "The condition is serious," Daniel Rudsten wrote in July 1951, "has always been serious—and is definitely of explosive nature."[13]

At times, Jews and blacks formed informal alliances to defend themselves from attacks by white Catholics. In October 1951, one Jewish mother reported that "Negro students" at Roxbury Memorial High School "have been asking the Jewish students to help 'fight off the Irish.'" But by the late 1940s, the citywide Jewish Community Council had also begun receiving reports of assaults by African-American teenagers on Roxbury's Jews. As racial succession proceeded in the 1950s, residents of the Elm Hill and Grove Hall districts became increasingly concerned with the rising level of violence by blacks settling in the area. Otto and Muriel Snowden worked with other African-American leaders and with

Jews to address the problem. Prominent members of Elm Hill's black community, the Snowdens were committed to maintaining a racially integrated, lower-middle-class neighborhood on Elm Hill. Through Freedom House, which they organized in 1949, they encouraged cooperation between the district's African-American and Jewish residents. But violence, social segregation, and the rapid Jewish exodus undermined Freedom House's efforts.[14]

A single event on the last night of 1952 proved a watershed. On New Year's Eve, Jacob Zuber was brutally beaten and kicked to death in an Elm Hill park. "The slaying netted his assailants just $7, plus some change that may have been in a small purse he carried," the *Boston Globe* reported. "The purse is still missing. His empty wallet was found beside him."[15] Quiet and unassuming, Rabbi Zuber had emigrated from Europe at the end of the war; in Roxbury, he made a modest living as the assistant rabbi at the Crawford Street Synagogue. For the first nine days of January 1953, accounts of his murder and related stories were featured on the front pages of Boston's major newspapers. The murder fulfilled the worst fears of Roxbury Jewry. In private meetings as well as in public statements, Jews regarded the crime as the outgrowth of years of anti-Semitic assaults and delinquent behavior in Dorchester and Roxbury.

Jewish leaders apparently regarded as equally plausible the chances that the assailants were white Catholic or black.[16] But since Zuber was killed in Roxbury—in a neighborhood that was changing racially and where the victims of recent muggings stated that their assailants had been black—his murder fed the concerns and prejudices of Jews unsettled by the progress of racial succession. Roxbury residents already lived in fear. Rabbi Zuber himself had just installed new locks on the windows of his family's first-floor apartment, after burglars had "attempted on four separate occasions this year" to break into the home. Other residents in the area refused to open their doors to strangers or to allow their children to play outside after dusk. "It's terrible," one resident told the *Globe*. "We're afraid to go out alone and I'm even nervous when I'm alone here at night." With Zuber's murder, these concerns assumed new urgency. More than three years later, in June 1956, the rabbi of a small Orthodox congregation in Roxbury—reporting that "colored boys" had been regularly "breaking windows in the synagogue" and that some of those youths had stoned and "spit upon" elderly Jewish men walking to evening services—would observe "that Rabbi Zuber's tragic death is much in the minds of his congregants."[17]

African-American and Jewish leaders expressed their outrage at the murder and pledged to stop the growing violence. "No modern dramatist, seeking to pen a heart-rending epic of human tragedy," the *Jewish Advocate* declared in its lead editorial, "could possibly have created a more convincing story about Boston's troubled Roxbury area than a hoodlum's fists have now written by the slaying of Rabbi Jacob I. Zuber." One week after Zuber's murder, a group of black and Jewish leaders joined city officials at Freedom House to establish the Roxbury Citizens Committee. "Never in my twenty years of living and working in Roxbury," Otto Snowden declared, "have I seen all segments of the community so unanimous in their feeling that this type of thing must be prevented." Bound together by tragedy, upper Roxbury's blacks and Jews hoped in January 1953 for "the development of the true spirit of neighborliness in a changing neighborhood." But in matter-of-factly describing Roxbury as "a changing neighborhood," community organizers acknowledged the frustrating fact that racial succession was already under way. A year or two before Rabbi Zuber's murder, for reasons unrelated to the upsurge in violence, Roxbury Jewry—and, with it, the dream of a stable, integrated community in Elm Hill—had begun to collapse.[18]

The Uprooted: Jewish Institutions, 1951–1958

In the early and middle 1950s, at a time when the area's Jewish population was just starting to fall in a substantial way, several Jewish institutions in Dorchester and upper Roxbury concluded that there was no future for them in their old neighborhoods. While the decision to move to the suburbs reflected the growth of Roxbury's black population and the decline of its Jewish population, the decision was ultimately grounded in the generation-long exodus of middle-class Jews. Synagogues were depleting their cemetery funds to maintain operations, and the area's largest religious schools depended on annual subsidies to stay open. Maimonides School and Mishkan Tefila, which had each announced plans to establish branch facilities, abandoned the plans, convinced that full relocation was necessary to sustain the loyalties of suburban members.

Only portability, embedded in Jewish rules of rootedness, could ensure the survival of Jewish institutions; no hierarchy guaranteed their existence. But relocating meant abandoning neighborhoods that were still home to tens of thousands of Jews. Each institution that moved increased the pressures that were not only pushing Jews out of these neighborhoods but also pulling them to the suburbs. Institutions that did not move—some because they were committed to staying in Roxbury and Dorchester, but most simply because they lacked the leadership or resources to move—instead dissolved. Whatever their fate, all these institutions contributed to the exodus of Jewish families.

Five Jewish institutions in Roxbury and Dorchester decisively cast their lots with the suburbs in the early and middle 1950s. They were Hebrew Teachers College, Boston's principal Hebrew high school and Hebrew teachers' training school; Beth El and Atereth Israel, both Orthodox congregations; Maimonides School, a Jewish day school; and Mishkan Tefila, a Conservative temple. Three of the institutions had been located in Roxbury and two had been located in Dorchester. Two of the institutions were Hebrew schools and three were synagogues; of the synagogues, two were Orthodox and one was Conservative. These institutions were diverse, yet all of them were united in the belief that their very survival depended on relocation.

Hebrew Teachers College—which, since its founding in the early 1920s, had been located on Roxbury's Crawford Street—announced in November 1951 that it had purchased a structure in Brookline. "Our decision to acquire the new building was motivated by the inadequacy of the old Crawford Street building, the change in the character of its neighborhood, in the residences of our students and prospective students and the general population trends in the City of Boston," Lewis H. Weinstein, the president of the college's board of trustees, explained. "Moreover, many of us have felt for a long time that a more central and suitable location would attract new students who are unwilling or unable to commute to Roxbury." Hebrew Teachers College moved to Brookline the following summer, selling its Roxbury structure to Freedom House. Many Jewish leaders "believed that we would hurt the Jewish community in Roxbury by moving, and that there was really no necessity for the move," Eisig Silberschlag, the dean of the college, later recalled. "Weinstein and I were threatened with excommunication for breaking up a well-established Jewish community in a suburban environment. We survived the threats, we were vindicated by subsequent developments: the deterioration of Roxbury, the growth of Brookline." In its first school year in Brookline, Hebrew Teachers College reported "a record enrollment of 308 students." As the college's bulletin observed in January 1953, "Our faith in the new location and in the new building was vindicated at the very outset."[19]

Temple Beth El, unlike Hebrew Teachers College, stood in an over-whelmingly white and Jewish district in the early 1950s. But the con-tinuing exodus of middle-class Jews threatened the Fowler Street Syn-agogue's survival. "Beth El with its rich history as a religious and educational center in the Dorchester area was faced with the steady movement of families to the newer parts of the city and the suburbs," the *Jewish Advocate* later explained. "This shifting of population was threat-ening to overwhelm the Congregation and reduce it to a shell." The congregation formally separated itself from the Beth El Hebrew School, which was running massive deficits, and began sponsoring an annual reunion to raise funds. Rabbi Abraham Koolyk soon concluded, though, that only by creating a suburban congregation could Beth El guarantee its continued existence. At Koolyk's initiative, a group of Newton resi-dents organized a new Beth El congregation in June 1955. Koolyk, whose salary was paid entirely by the Dorchester congregation, received permis-sion from his board of directors to spend one Sabbath each month in Newton. "We realized that we were not long for this world. He was right to go somewhere else," George Halzel, a board member, recalled. As Murray Block stated, "There was some ill feeling, some resentment, but we had to be logical. We saw the handwriting on the wall." With the support of Koolyk and other leaders of the Fowler Street Synagogue, the Newton congregation grew quickly. It purchased a building in the spring of 1956. A year later—when Atereth Israel, whose Roxbury syna-gogue had been destroyed in a fire, accepted an invitation to relocate and merge with the Newton congregation—it assumed the new name Beth El–Atereth Israel.[20]

In the early 1950s, Maimonides School was located in a historic clap-board mansion in Dorchester, five blocks from the Fowler Street Syna-gogue. Established in the 1930s by Rabbi Joseph B. Soloveitchik, the Jewish day school had outgrown the building. In 1948 Maimonides' leaders had leased additional space in a Roxbury Hebrew school and announced plans "to erect a modern school building" in Dorchester. But they were now considering plans to build the structure in the suburbs instead. The school's president and three of its four vice-presidents lived in Brookline or Newton. "I didn't think Maimonides' place was in Rox-bury. The trend was elsewhere," Rabbi Moses J. Cohn, the school's prin-cipal, said, as he recalled the board's decision in the early 1950s not to acquire the building that had once housed Hebrew Teachers College. "The only solution was to move to where the Jewish population was moving, to the Brighton-Brookline area." Maimonides School purchased the Menorah Institute building, in Roxbury, in the middle 1950s, after attempting unsuccessfully to rent the Mishkan Tefila schoolhouse. But this was an interim solution. The Roxbury structure was only "a temporary facility," Maimonides' leaders stated in December 1955. "Within the next year a modern building will be erected." The school purchased land in Brookline in the spring of 1956, then announced plans to erect "a new and modern building" on the site. Two years later, the school launched a campaign to raise $500,000 for the project.[21]

Mishkan Tefila, working in the early 1950s to retire the debt on the Seaver Street Temple and schoolhouse, had postponed its plans to establish a suburban branch. When the mortgage was finally redeemed, in the fall of 1952, almost half of the congregation's members lived outside of Dorchester and Roxbury. The congregation, which was declining in size, depended on large loans and cemetery funds to pay its operating expenses. Concerned for the temple's future, twenty-seven members—most of them board members and nearly all of them residents of Newton or Brookline—met with Rabbi Kazis in April 1953. "We cannot possibly keep Temple Mishkan Tefila in Roxbury alive as we know it today," Abraham A. Bloom, a long-time leader of the congregation, argued that evening. "We must set up a meeting house and schoolhouse in the suburban area," Kazis contended, "and use our present Temple for the High Holiday Services." A year later, without convening a meeting of the full congregation, the board of directors purchased land in Newton not for a suburban branch but for a large new temple. Many members living in Roxbury and Dorchester were angered by the decision, arguing that "they were being abandoned" and that "'outsiders' were kidnapping the Temple to Newton." The congregation broke ground in the fall of 1955, soon after opening a temporary schoolhouse and office in Newton. Struggling to raise sufficient funds, Mishkan Tefila completed the Newton temple in 1958, at a cost of $1,500,000. The congregation then sold the Roxbury buildings. The move "vastly improved" the congregation's fiscal health. Five years after the dedication, Mishkan Tefila burned the mortgage on the Newton property. With a membership of 824 families, the largest in its history, the congregation announced that it could accept new members "only as vacancies occur."[22]

Moving an institution is a difficult task. "When the idea of a Temple in Newton started taking shape," Nathan Yamins, Mishkan Tefila's president, wrote in 1958, "so many almost insuperable obstacles were en-countered that its construction and completion can truly be said to be a miracle." To relocate successfully, institutions must act early and deci-sively; delaying the move is risky and usually fatal. First, relocation requires substantial financial resources and the support of a large mem-bership. Even two prominent institutions like Maimonides and Mishkan Tefila encountered problems raising funds in the 1950s, while Newton's Beth El depended in its early years on Rabbi Koolyk, whose salary was paid by members of Dorchester's Fowler Street Synagogue. Second, relo-cation requires the support of members living in the new location, and only a serious commitment to move can maintain their loyalty. If the congregation did not act soon, Rabbi Kazis warned in April 1953, "we chance the possibility of losing our younger men to reform temples"—or, left unmentioned, to suburban Conservative temples. Third, reloca-tion requires a suitable site, a location not already saturated by exist-ing institutions. Koolyk showed foresight when he helped organize Beth El of Newton, the first Orthodox congregation convenient to Newton's growing suburban neighborhoods. Had he waited and been forced to compete with an established Orthodox congregation, he—and Beth El—might have failed. When Mishkan Tefila announced its intention in 1953 to establish a center in Newton, the four principal Conservative temples in Newton and Brookline joined in protest. They argued, to no avail, that the area's Jewish population could not support another Conservative congregation.[23]

Because institutions could move from Dorchester and Roxbury only when they were still viable, most left neighborhoods that were predomi-nantly Jewish. These institutions relocated once their leaders had be-come convinced that the urban exodus posed threats to institutional survival, but before those threats were fully manifest. About 58,500 Jews still lived in Dorchester and Roxbury—15,500 of them in Roxbury—when Beth El was organized in Newton, when Maimonides purchased land in Brookline, when Mishkan Tefila broke ground on Newton's Ham-mond Pond Parkway, and when Hebrew Teachers College graduated the first high school class that had never sat in a Crawford Street classroom.

In the 1950s, only the Jewish institutions south of Franklin Field, in Dorchester's Mattapan district, remained relatively robust. Supported by a large Jewish community and distant from neighborhoods undergoing racial change, Mattapan's leading institutions expanded their facilities and programs. In 1956 Kehillath Jacob dedicated a new school and community building next to its synagogue on Fessenden Street. Two years later, Agudath Israel dedicated its own modest school building, attached to the rear of the Woodrow Avenue Synagogue. This addition, though, dwarfed by the massive synagogue, reflected how dramatically the working-class congregation and its neighborhood differed from the suburban community that had erected the Woodrow Avenue Synagogue in the 1920s. The ongoing financial problems of the Dorchester-Mattapan Hebrew School also served as a reminder that Mattapan's Jewish institutions were buffeted by the same forces at work in the rest of Dorchester and Roxbury.[24]

In Roxbury and in nearby sections of Dorchester—from Franklin Park and Mount Bowdoin to Franklin Field—institutional disintegration was palpable by the middle 1950s. It was in Roxbury that Jewish depopulation and African-American settlement began, so it was there that the consequences of institutional inaction were starkest. School enrollments and congregational memberships were declining in the middle 1950s, and financial problems worsening. In the 1954–1955 school year, when the Menorah Institute ran an operating deficit of $8,000, only eighty-two students attended the school; enrollment had fallen by half over the preceding four years, while the deficit had doubled. The Crawford Street Synagogue, which had collected $13,000 in membership dues and seat sales in 1951, collected just $8,000 in 1956. To cover its deficit in 1956, Beth Hamidrash Hagadol relied on $7,000 in donations as well as $6,000 from its cemetery, charity, and Hebrew school funds.[25]

In the spring of 1955, the three major Roxbury congregations, including Mishkan Tefila, simultaneously "discontinued their respective Hebrew schools." Adath Jeshurun and Beth Hamidrash Hagadol had both concluded that they could no longer afford to maintain their schools, even with subsidies from the Associated Jewish Philanthropies. The Mishkan Tefila School, meanwhile, ran a deficit of $28,000 in 1954–1955; the congregation funded the deficit, but only 37 of the school's 251 students were children of temple members. Rabbi Kazis, noting that "Temple Mishkan Tefila is continuing its obligation for Hebrew education by developing a new Hebrew education program in the Newton area," announced that the congregation had decided to close the Roxbury school. Responding to the imminent school closings, the Associated Jewish Philanthropies helped organize and sponsor a community

Hebrew school. The Combined Roxbury Hebrew School, created in 1955 by the merger of Roxbury's three major religious schools and funded in part by the three congregations, met for two years in the Mishkan Tefila schoolhouse. But with enrollment declining and expenses rising, the Combined Roxbury Hebrew School closed in 1957. Roxbury's three outstanding Hebrew schools—Adath Jeshurun's Menorah Institute, Beth Hamidrash Hagadol's Yavneh Hebrew School, and the Mishkan Tefila School—had ceased to exist.[26]

Congregations, too, were dissolving. The Boston YMHA, which had hosted High Holy Day services since the 1920s, announced in the summer of 1956 that it was discontinuing the practice because of "the continuous exodus from the Roxbury neighborhood to the suburbs." With its decision, the YMHA sought "to help maintain and strengthen the existing religious institutions in Roxbury, which have been experiencing a loss of membership and income." Sons of Abraham—which had dedicated its brick synagogue on Wayland Street in 1925, on the same fall day that Mishkan Tefila had dedicated the Seaver Street Temple—went out of existence early in 1958. Anshe Shepetovka, on Lawrence Avenue, and Young Israel of Greater Boston, on Ruthven Street, also dissolved their synagogues in 1958. And Agudath Achim, which had moved into Roxbury from the West End in 1913, was closed by the spring of 1959. Once abandoned, Agudath Achim's former synagogue on Intervale Street was vandalized. Intruders threw books on the floor, smashed windows, and attempted to set fire to the structure. "Pews were broken into kindling wood. Cast iron pipes had been ripped and removed," the *Boston Globe* reported in April 1960. "A memorial tablet, bearing the names of members and relatives, was found destroyed."[27]

Roxbury's foremost congregations persisted, but in agony. For Beth Hamidrash Hagadol and Adath Jeshurun, normal congregational life ended in 1956, when financial problems forced both institutions to dismiss their rabbis.[28] Each synagogue faced the future on its own: no hierarchy could provide a rabbi or pay a heating bill. Submitting his resignation to Adath Jeshurun, Rabbi Eliezer Berkovits "expressed his deep regret that circumstances beyond his and the congregation's control compelled him to sever a relationship that was so harmoniously and mutually rewarding."[29] The Crawford Street Synagogue and the Blue Hill Avenue Synagogue—with Mishkan Tefila, the preeminent congregations of Roxbury since the earliest days of Jewish settlement—could not afford rabbis at the moment when their need for leadership was greatest. Huddled together, looking to suburban supporters for aid, proud congregants in Roxbury worked to sustain their dying institutions. The fate of these institutions could not have reassured the thousands of Jewish residents who still lived in these neighborhoods. Withering away, institutions that stayed in Roxbury helped to push increasing numbers of Jews out of the area.

Other Jewish institutions, in moving or signaling their intent to move, exacerbated the Jewish flight even more. For institutions dependent on their own resources, this consequence of relocation was an externality: the first priority of any institution is to secure its own survival. So externalities abounded. The orientation between residences and institutions was thrown on its head. From the early 1920s until the early 1950s, rules of membership had eased the movement of middle-class Jews from the Dorchester-Roxbury area to Brookline, Brighton, and Newton. As long as institutions themselves remained viable and did not move, though, rules alone provided no positive reasons for residents to leave urban neighborhoods. But this changed in the 1950s. Institutions like Maimonides or Mishkan Tefila that made investments in suburban sites were responding to the fact that their constituencies had become heavily suburbanized during an era when the institution itself had remained in the city. The institutional commitment to move, while a reaction to past population movements, triggered new waves of out-migration.

"We lived on Vesta Road, in Dorchester. It was a *very* nice area," Frieda Cooper recalled. In the middle 1950s, Cooper moved to Brookline with her husband and their daughters. "We had two girls going to school, one attending Maimonides and the other taking classes at Hebrew College. Hebrew College had moved to Brookline, and Maimonides said that by September they would have their school in Brookline, too," Cooper remembered. "We had had no intention of moving, but it made sense to be closer to the schools. Why stay behind in Dorchester? It would be hard commuting to Brookline." But Maimonides, as the Coopers soon learned, would not relocate to Brookline that September—or, for that matter, for a few more promised Septembers to come. "We moved just on *stories* that Maimonides would move," Cooper concluded. "We should have stayed."[30]

For institutions, though, staying was not a long-term option. In disintegrating in Dorchester and Roxbury or, more dramatically, in relocating to the suburbs, Jewish institutions proved incapable of making credible commitments to their local neighborhoods. Autonomous and portable, they fed the exodus of Jewish residents. First in Roxbury, then neighborhood by neighborhood in Dorchester, the evisceration of institutional life proceeded more suddenly and more decisively than contemporary population movements. Jewish life continued in Roxbury and Dorchester in the 1950s. At least in Dorchester's Mattapan district, Jewish life continued to thrive and bustle. Indeed, it was just because tens of thousands of Jews still delighted in their community life that the difficulties of the area's schools and synagogues would prove so portentous.

The Rooted: Catholic Institutions, 1951–1958

[handwritten marginalia: is it partly the #s or just the ambition?]

Catholic institutions were different. When residential change began affecting Catholic churches in Dorchester and upper Roxbury, Catholics knew that institutional survival was tied to the neighborhood defined by the parish territory. A church could not move. Rules dictated that a territorial parish could not relinquish responsibility for its geographical area, and no church could close except on the authority of the Ordinary. Each parish depended on its own parishioners for financial support. To the extent that the Boston archdiocese engaged in redistributive policy in the 1950s, redistribution still meant the transfer of funds from parishes in Dorchester to new suburban parishes. But in the assignment of priests, the archdiocese regularly redistributed another, valuable resource. Because they guaranteed each parish a pastor, Catholic rules maintained leadership not only in prosperous districts but in neighborhoods struggling with the urban exodus.

Change came slowly to Roxbury and Dorchester's Catholic neighborhoods. Except in four parishes in and around upper Roxbury, the area's white Catholic population remained stable through the middle 1950s. Nearly every Dorchester parish was flourishing. St. Brendan's Parish opened its school in the fall of 1952 and its new convent in the following year. St. Mark's Parish completed an eight-room addition to its already large school in 1954. St. Gregory's Parish built a new rectory, an eighteen-room addition to its convent, and an eight-room addition to its grammar school. And, in the spring of 1957, Archbishop Cushing established St. Christopher's Parish. Created out of territory that had previously been assigned to St. Margaret's Parish, St. Christopher's was organized to serve the large public housing project that had recently opened on Columbia Point. From the new parish on Columbia Point to the older parishes that were building new structures and new classrooms, Dorchester's Catholic institutions stayed strong.[31]

Even parishes on the racial frontier—parishes whose boundaries extended deep into changing Jewish neighborhoods—reported brief increases in their Catholic populations. In the early and middle 1950s, St. Leo's Catholic population grew rapidly. Rev. John J. Watson, St. Leo's pastor, began planning to replace the parish's small frame church with a new structure. He searched for an appropriate site and, noting that "St. Leo's is a growing parish," also proposed organizing a grammar school. The influx of Catholics into the parish was due both to a new housing project and to the exodus of Jews. Rev. Francis X. Turke, who served as a curate in the 1950s, recalled that "the Jewish people were starting to move out at that time and some Italians and Irish Catholics were coming in." But St. Leo's Indian summer was brief. In 1957, as Father Watson looked forward to "ever better times in the years ahead," others began to recognize that the sudden strengthening of parishes like St. Leo's was a transitory phenomenon. Although in the early stages of the Jewish exodus white Catholics moved into neighborhoods being vacated by Jews, this period ended quickly. Over the long term, it was African Americans and not white Catholics who settled in these districts. And, as African-American neighborhoods expanded, they began to grow into areas that had once been heavily Catholic.[32]

Racial succession transformed St. Joseph's Parish in the 1950s. Encompassing much of upper Roxbury, St. Joseph's was located between the growing black neighborhood in the Elm Hill district and the large, poor black neighborhoods in lower Roxbury and the South End. As blacks settled in the parish territory that bridged these districts, St. Joseph's white parishioners began to leave en masse. The number of infant baptisms in the parish declined sharply, from 281 in 1950, to 174 in 1955, to 130 in 1957.[33] Between 1950 and 1957, the number of marriages in St. Joseph's Parish declined from 80 to 33, the number of deaths recorded by the parish fell almost in half, and enrollment in St. Joseph's School declined 40 percent. By the middle 1950s, white Catholics were leaving parishes on St. Joseph's periphery. The Catholic exodus was already under way in St. John–St. Hugh's Parish, a few blocks north of Grove Hall, and it was beginning in St. Mary of the Angels' and St. Paul's parishes.

Anchored in its neighborhood, assigned a well-defined territory, and possessing little appeal for most blacks, the Catholic parish became the institutional nexus for white resistance. Membership rules exacted a high cost from exiting families, and rules of rootedness kept the parish oriented to its immediate neighborhood. Parishioners who moved to the suburbs were lost to the parish, so the parish actively encouraged parishioners to stay. The parish was a fortress for old-time residents, stoutly maintaining familiar rituals, social events, and the neighborhood's disappearing ethnic character. Its pastor and curates continued to provide vigorous leadership, reinforcing for white Catholics the permanence of the parish's commitment to the neighborhood. In a time of change, the parish offered stability.

But rules alone do not fully explain the endurance of the parish as a white institution in a racially changing neighborhood. Conscious policies of racial discrimination helped restrict entrance into the parish's institutions at a time when the area's population had begun to change. When a large white Catholic population still lived in the parish, black Catholics faced hostility in the parish's school and church. David Nelson, a black Catholic who lived in St. Joseph's Parish in the middle 1950s, later recalled that "St. Joseph elementary school was all-white and he was discouraged from attending." Unable to enroll in his parish school, Nelson attended Sunday school classes at a black mission. "At that time it was a mortal sin not to send your children to parochial schools if you were Catholic," Nelson noted, "but this never seemed to apply to black or other minority families."[34]

By the late 1950s, large numbers of black students had begun to attend classes at St. Joseph's School. The parish still contributed to neighborhood stability, but increasingly this stability was grounded not in the district's white past but in its interracial present and black future. The church and school that had long retarded the exodus of white Catholics remained central institutions after the onset of racial succession. Moreover, parish boundaries limited the consequences of the parish's transformation. The changes that came to St. Joseph's in the 1950s and that had begun to affect three neighboring parishes had no impact on the main body of Dorchester parishes. Whereas the fates of Jewish institutions across Dorchester and Roxbury were intertwined, each Catholic parish was self-contained, a bounded population organized around a single cluster of institutions. Just one lesson of St. Joseph's Parish knew no boundaries: despite a radical population upheaval, the parish remained active and deeply rooted in its neighborhood. At a time when its Catholic population and resources were diminishing quickly, its commitment proved credible.

Institutions and Neighborhoods, 1959–1967

Institutional precedents established in the 1950s reverberated into the next decade. Until 1967, metropolitan organizations established no programs to assist the synagogues and parishes of Dorchester and upper Roxbury. Thus Jewish and Catholic institutions confronted dramatic changes within the constraints of long-established rules. These rules provided an underlying logic to the responses of Dorchester and Roxbury's institutions, despite the seeming absence of coordination on a community-wide scale. Catholic parishes faced change with renewed commitments to their neighborhoods. Synagogues, equally bound by rules, survived population change only when they relocated to the suburbs—and the experience of Roxbury's three leading Hebrew schools, all of which had closed in the middle 1950s, had already demonstrated that institutions receiving support from a community federation were no more secure than synagogues. As parishioners rose into the middle class and as they became concerned by racial succession, Catholic institutions provided stability and reassurance in the midst of change. In similar neighborhoods contending with similar forces, Jewish institutions fled or disintegrated, contributing to the increasingly frantic exodus of Jewish residents.

Neighborhood Change

Between 1950 and 1960, the white Catholic population of Dorchester and upper Roxbury declined from 137,000 to 119,000; by 1967, it had declined to 105,000.[35] That decline was concentrated in upper Roxbury and in nearby Dorchester parishes. Large numbers of African Americans and smaller numbers of Hispanics settled in these districts, as thousands of Irish and Italian Catholics left for the suburbs. Parishes elsewhere in Dorchester were still overwhelmingly white and Catholic, though even the sturdiest parishes were losing some young, middle-class families. "St.

Margaret's parish has been vigorous since 1893, and continues to flourish like the green bay tree," the *Boston Traveler* reported in February 1967. As Rev. Richard F. O'Halloran explained, "It's handy to everything—downtown, shops, hospitals, rapid transit. And don't forget Catholic parents with young children like to live close to the church and the school. No matter where you are in St. Margaret's parish, you're not far from the church and school." While increasing numbers of students were attending public rather than parochial school by 1967, the parish's school-age population remained steady. More than six hundred students attended St. Margaret's School, and another four hundred children, enrolled in public schools, attended Sunday school classes in the parish. The school and the church were a steadying presence, counteracting pressures on St. Margaret's parishioners to leave for the suburbs.[36]

Jews, whose institutions aggravated rather than checked the suburban exodus, were in a panicked rout by 1967. The Jewish population of Dorchester and upper Roxbury had fallen sharply in the 1950s: from 70,000 in 1950, to 58,500 in 1955, to 47,000 in 1960.[37] In the early and middle 1960s, the net out-migration became ever faster. By 1967 just 25,000 Jews remained.[38] From Roxbury, block after block for three miles up Blue Hill Avenue to Mattapan, African-American neighborhoods had displaced Jewish neighborhoods. "For a while, as richer Jews moved out, poorer Jews moved in," Rabbi Koolyk observed in February 1967, "but as the community deteriorated the Jews stopped moving in and just moved out."[39] No more than a few hundred Jews remained in Roxbury in 1967. Just 3,000 were left in the section of Dorchester bounded by Franklin Park, Mount Bowdoin, and Franklin Field; this district, once home to 17,500 Jews, was now described as a "Negro ghetto."[40]

Only in the section of Dorchester that extended from Franklin Field to Mattapan Square were there still large numbers of Jews in 1967, but the population was changing swiftly. Morton Street, which for decades had marked the institutional and commercial center of Mattapan, served as a rough dividing line in 1967. To its north, in the district that extended to Franklin Field, lived 6,500 Jews; its population now nearly half black, this area had been home to 13,400 Jews as recently as 1960. To the south of Morton Street, toward Mattapan Square, lay the only neighborhood in the Roxbury-Dorchester area that was still predominantly white and Jewish. About 13,500 Jews lived in this district. But even this community—

the final remnant of a Jewish settlement that, just a decade and a half earlier, had stretched up Blue Hill Avenue through Dorchester and deep into Roxbury—had started to unravel.

Jews in the Morton Street–Mattapan Square district, concerned about the pace of racial succession, had begun to fear by 1965 that "their area will switch from all-white to all-Negro and thus be segregated again." They hoped to "prevent residential panic and departure of greater numbers of white residents as Negroes move into the area." By 1967, though, about 1,500 African Americans had settled in the district and the Jewish exodus was accelerating. "Some persons are optimistic," the *Globe* reported that summer. "The transition period is over, I think," one Jewish resident said. "Most of the homes to be sold are sold. I don't think any more whites will move out. There's a balance now." But few shared his optimism. In October 1967, Kevin H. White and Louise Day Hicks appeared at a breakfast forum at Mattapan's Fessenden Street Synagogue, seeking votes in the upcoming mayoral election. "A number of the questions from the audience to both candidates," the *Globe* reported, "reflected the racial tension and fear that neighborhood changes have brought to the Jewish community in Mattapan." Panic selling was reported on several streets in the district, as Jews rushed to leave the area. The G&G delicatessen, symbol of Mattapan Jewry, was "now enjoying a dinner clientele of middle-income Negroes."[41]

By 1967 Blue Hill Avenue passed through Boston's largest African-American neighborhoods. About 60,000 blacks lived in upper Roxbury and Dorchester.[42] While African-American neighborhoods extended into formerly Catholic sections of St. Joseph's Parish and St. John–St. Hugh's Parish in Roxbury, the greatest centers of black population had developed in the districts that had once been Jewish. From the original black enclave on Elm Hill, African Americans had moved across upper Roxbury and into Dorchester, and many had begun to settle in Mattapan. Most of these residents were poorer than those who had traditionally lived in upper Roxbury. This massive shift in population created tensions not only between blacks and whites but also among blacks. Middle-class blacks still regarded Elm Hill as "*the* prestige area in all Massachusetts," but by the early 1960s large numbers of them were concerned about "the rise in social problems in the area, including a mounting number of unwed teenage mothers and anti-social teenage gangs." Chester Rapkin, summarizing his interviews with these middle-class residents, noted that they were concerned about the decline in city services, the growing "number of 'unstable' families, and the fact that the neighborhood [was] becoming too much of a ghetto."[43]

Catholic Institutions

Parishes responded to population changes with a resolute determination to continue their work in the neighborhood. Having lost many active parishioners and suffering from mounting financial problems, the few parishes deeply affected by change started serving constituencies that were largely nonwhite and non-Catholic. In the school year 1966–1967, St. John's School reported that 257 of its 299 students were black. "It is a complex parish, now mostly black," Rev. Thomas C. Burns, the pastor of St. John–St. Hugh's Parish, had asserted in February 1964. "Conditions in Roxbury are getting worse week by week. Revenue has dropped sharply," he wrote the next winter. Seeking $3,000 from St. John–St. Hugh's deposit at the chancery to pay fuel bills and replace radiators, Burns noted in 1965, "I hope things will improve but feel they will continue to go down."[44]

Centered in St. Joseph's and St. John–St. Hugh's parishes, upper Roxbury's African-American community extended in 1967 across three other parishes. These were St. Leo's and St. Paul's parishes, in Dorchester, and St. Mary of the Angels' Parish, in Roxbury. "St. Paul's, Dorchester is fast becoming a mission territory," Rt. Rev. Francis F. McElroy, its pastor, argued in May 1965. A "solid core of old-time parishioners" continued to live in the parish and to support its traditional activities. But most of the area's population, including "Negroes" and "indigent and uncooperative white Catholics," presented new challenges.[45] Contributing to the vulnerability of these three parishes was the fact that none possessed a parish school. Indeed, with the exception of the recently established St. Christopher's Parish, these were the only three parishes of Dorchester and upper Roxbury's seventeen that did not have schools. With underdeveloped institutions, these three parishes were less effective than other parishes in maintaining the loyalty of their members.

St. Leo's Parish—which a decade earlier, when Jews had begun to leave Dorchester, had discussed building a new church and organizing a parish school—now confronted a growing exodus of its white Catholic parishioners. African Americans, having already settled in the once-Jewish

Franklin Park and Franklin Field districts of the parish, were now rapidly moving into the parish's Catholic districts. "The income of this parish is consistently less each week," Rev. George H. Callahan, St. Leo's pastor, wrote in April 1966. To paint the parish's church and rectory, Callahan withdrew $2,000 from St. Leo's chancery deposit. "It is most welcome," he wrote to the chancellor that June, thanking him for sending the funds. "You must know that this parish is no longer the St. Leo's of old." The church, because of "costly vandalism," was now kept locked except during Masses. Rev. Shawn G. Sheehan, who succeeded Callahan as pastor, explained to the chancellor that he needed two assistant priests. "Despite the over-all decline in the parish the number of young families and so of CCD enrollment has increased," Sheehan wrote in June 1967. "We still have over 800 families. There may be a big reduction in this number within the next few years. If there is, I shall report it. At the same time I hope that parishes such as this will have enough priests to carry on the different types of pastoral and apostolic work that will be called for in the changed circumstances, types of work which in fact we are already undertaking here and which we find quite arduous and time-consuming."[46]

As Sheehan suggested, "parishes such as this" recognized that they had no future apart from their neighborhoods. In four ways, these changing parishes affirmed their commitment to their local districts in the 1960s. First, they organized campaigns to discourage panic selling and to urge long-term residents to stay in the parish. Second, they continued to repair and maintain the parish's buildings. Third, owing to long-established diocesan practices as well as ad hoc aid, they remained staffed and financially viable. And fourth, they sponsored a variety of new parish activities, seeking new ways to maintain the parish's relevance in its changing neighborhood.

Parish priests worked actively to discourage their parishioners from leaving the parish. By the late 1950s, Rev. John J. Watson, the pastor of St. Leo's Parish, had grown concerned about the moving plans of his parish's white Catholic residents. "At one point, the pastor had us make an announcement at Sunday Mass," recalled Rev. Francis X. Turke, who was then a curate in St. Leo's, "telling people to let us know if you know of anyone who wants to move in or if you're thinking of selling." The pastor, according to Father Turke, "wanted to maintain the status quo, wanted to maintain stability in the neighborhood." In the fall of 1962, one parishioner reported, the pastor posted "signs all around that [said] Those who pray together stay together." But by the middle 1960s, large numbers of Catholics had begun to move from the parish. Rev. James Lyons, who served as a curate in St. Leo's at that time, recalled the efforts made by the parish's priests to stop the exodus. The parish held many meetings in the middle 1960s, at which priests attempted to teach racial tolerance and urged white Catholics to stay. At each meeting, Lyons remembered, St. Leo's priests vowed that the parish would continue its work. Priests exhorted white Catholics not to abandon St. Leo's, arguing that the parish would survive.[47]

As evidence of the parish's long-term commitment to its district in the face of population changes, priests continued to maintain the parish's property, sometimes at substantial expense. Father Callahan received permission from the chancellor in June 1966 to paint St. Leo's Church and its rectory and to lay vinyl floor-covering in the aisles of the church. At a time when St. Leo's revenues were rapidly falling, Callahan spent more than $8,000 on the two projects. St. John–St. Hugh's Parish, too, continued to invest in its two churches and other parish buildings in the early and middle 1960s. In 1961 its pastor, Rev. Thomas C. Burns, withdrew $18,000 from the parish's chancery deposit in order to replace a large church window and to point the façade of St. John's Church. He also decided to have the large cross at the apex of the church façade "gold-leafed at a cost of $500.00." Between 1963 and 1966, St. John–St. Hugh's pastor withdrew several thousand dollars from the parish's dwindling chancery deposit to install a new boiler and new radiators in St. John's Church, to do "some electrical work in the School Hall," to pay fuel bills, and to make some emergency repairs to parish buildings. St. Paul's Parish also invested heavily in its church in these years, despite the decline of its white Catholic population. When he had become St. Paul's pastor, Rt. Rev. Francis F. McElroy had inherited "a project for the reconstruction of the Church, both inside and out." By the end of 1960, St. Paul's Parish had spent $161,120 for the project, depleting the parish's entire chancery deposit of $136,511 and requiring the parish to borrow $24,609 from the archdiocese. In the summer of 1961, McElroy received permission to spend $1,350 to finish painting St. Paul's rectory. "Because of the lack of funds," he explained to the chancellor, he had painted only half of the rectory the preceding summer.[48]

The archdiocese pursued no formal policy of assistance to parishes like St. Paul's. At least until the middle 1960s, it was sufficient for the parishes of Dorchester and upper Roxbury that the archdiocese existed, assigned clergy, and had an interest in the survival of its parishes. These facts were not inconsequential. That St. Paul's Parish could borrow funds from the chancery—and that it was led by a priest, let alone by a distinguished pastor assisted by two curates—suggests how struggling parishes in Dorchester and Roxbury survived at a time when the archdiocese restricted its formal subsidies to churches in the city's oldest and poorest districts. Each parish in the early and middle 1960s was served by a pastor as well as by two or three curates, and the archbishop paid attention to specific parochial needs when he made assignments. In 1962, Cardinal Cushing assigned Rev. Harold A. Furblur, an African-American priest, to St. John–St. Hugh's Parish. Two years later, Father Burns described the importance of two other curates to the life of the parish. "I would appreciate it greatly if the curates here could stay. It is a complex parish, now mostly black. The result then is that the 'School and Youth Problem' is some what difficult," Burns wrote in a letter to the chancellor. "Fr Publicover did an excellent piece of work with the school. Fr Foley has the best youth program I know of. For these reasons, I make this request." The cardinal agreed to keep three curates in St. John–St. Hugh's Parish.[49]

As most of their long-time white Catholic families left, these parishes developed new ways of serving their neighborhoods. McElroy, in St. Paul's Parish, argued in 1965 that his two curates were "among the hardest-working priests in the Archdiocese." They, of course, performed "the usual work" of any parish, "e.g. Caring for the 125 sick at home or convalescent homes, C.Y.O., Sodality, etc.—Programs for all age groups." But St. Paul's curates also assumed additional responsibilities because of the nature of the parish's residents, working diligently to persuade reluctant families to send their children to religious classes. Despite great changes, these parishes continued to view their worlds and their duties in geographical terms. "From Blue Hill av. to Washington st. and south to Mattapan, the racial issue is going to be very crucial here," Father Sheehan, St. Leo's pastor, argued in August 1967. "It is already." While some urban congregations were waiting in 1967 for their middle-class congregants to return from the suburbs, the *Boston Globe* observed that Sheehan had other concerns. Sheehan "believes in a more dynamic ministry among the people at hand . . . 'out, out on the street, out where the action is,'" the *Globe* reported in February. "Curates at St. Leo's work with youth groups, senior citizens and alcoholics." Even a staff member for a Jewish agency, sent to Dorchester to identify ways to assist its Jewish population, commented on Sheehan's commitment to the area. "Father Sheehan, Pastor, St. Leo's," the February 1967 note reads. "He was a seminary professor, who took a church, and believes in being involved in community, and really is."[50]

Most of Dorchester's parishes remained relatively secure through the middle 1960s. But the responses of the few parishes confronted by crisis in those years demonstrated the credibility of a parish's commitment to its neighborhood and the relevance of rules in understanding institutional behavior. These parishes still nurtured their long-time white parishioners, reinforcing white resistance to change, but they also began to develop new programs to serve the poor, nonwhite, and non-Catholic residents settling within the parish's boundaries. To survive, parishes pursued similar strategies despite the lack of coordination at the archdiocesan level. In neighborhoods that white Catholics were leaving in large numbers, the parish offered continuity and stability. Rules constrained the parish, and the parish's commitment helped contain the exodus.

Jewish Institutions

Jewish institutions in Dorchester and upper Roxbury continued to follow the relentless logic of their own rules, contributing—through action and through inaction—to the undoing of their local communities. Discussing why "Jewish people no longer aspire to live" in the Dorchester-Roxbury area, staff members at the Boston YMHA–Hecht House noted in January 1960 that "fine institutions (educational and religious) have moved to the suburbs."[51] Once begun, institutional collapse and abandonment continued without pause. Institutions like Maimonides and Beth El, which in the middle 1950s had committed themselves to suburban locations, finally moved out in the 1960s. Institutions like Adath Jeshurun and Beth Hamidrash Hagadol, which in the middle 1950s had begun to confront severe financial crises, finally dissolved in the 1960s. Many more institutions relocated or closed. By the end of 1967, Jewish institutional life was effectively dead both in Roxbury and in the district of Dorchester bounded by Franklin Park, Franklin Field, and Mount Bowdoin. All that remained in that vast area—in its heyday home to

47,000 Jews, several congregational Hebrew schools, two Jewish day schools, a Hebrew high school and college, a community center, function halls, and more than twenty synagogues—was a single synagogue and a Lubavitcher day school.[52] Only in the section of Dorchester that extended from Franklin Field south to Mattapan did a significant institutional presence remain in the middle 1960s.

Early in 1960 the Boston YMHA closed its home on Seaver Street and merged with Dorchester's Hecht House. With the support of the Associated Jewish Philanthropies, the newly named Boston YMHA–Hecht House had just built a large new gymnasium at a cost of $450,000. Since the 1940s, the AJP had discussed erecting "a modern and large Center building" to serve the Roxbury-Dorchester district. Plans for the new building were continually postponed, as the AJP's energies were diverted to the campaign to erect "the Jewish Community Center serving the Brookline-Brighton-Newton area." Still, the AJP and the Hecht House had continued to discuss a new Dorchester structure, and in 1956 leaders of the YMHA began participating in these discussions. While arguing that "it is too early to speculate as to the future of the 'Y,'" George J. Arafe, the YMHA's president, recognized that "the movement of the Jewish population out of Roxbury" threatened the YMHA's future on Seaver Street. In the spring of 1959, as construction began on the new gymnasium, the YMHA's board authorized the AJP to sell the YMHA building on Seaver Street and to apply funds from the sale to the new structure in Dorchester. The Robert Gould Shaw House, a settlement house that served African Americans in Roxbury and the South End, considered acquiring the building. But in April 1960, after the Shaw House declined to purchase the building, the AJP sold the Seaver Street structure to Seventh-Day Adventists for $50,000. Nearly half a century after the Boston YMHA had moved from the South End, its Roxbury years were ended.[53]

Beth Pinchas, Boston's leading Hasidic congregation, relocated from Dorchester to Brookline in August 1961. Having moved in the 1940s from the West End to Dorchester, the congregation was again responding to population trends. When Rabbi Levi I. Horowitz, the Bostoner Rebbe, had learned that a suitable property in Brookline had become available, he had called on a few Jewish leaders for advice. As the *Jewish Advocate's* Bernie Hyatt recalled, the Rebbe argued that the time had come to leave Dorchester, but he was concerned that he did not yet have enough supporters in Brookline to establish a minyan. "We all said: You have to move," Hyatt remembered. "You have no alternative." In November 1961 Beth Pinchas formally dedicated its new synagogue. On its front page, the *Advocate* described the "parade of Sefer Torahs" down Beacon Street in Brookline. Twelve convertibles, with a passenger in each car carrying a Torah scroll, drove slowly behind Beth Pinchas's oldest congregant, who walked with his Torah scroll under a canopy. Once they arrived at the new Brookline synagogue, members of Beth Pinchas placed the Torah scrolls in the ark. The ark itself had been removed from the congregation's old synagogue in Dorchester and installed in the Brookline structure.[54]

Mogain Emoshia L'Beth David, a smaller Hasidic congregation, had also relocated to the Brookline area in 1961. The congregation had been organized in Roxbury in the middle 1920s by followers of the Talner Rebbe, Grand Rabbi Meshulem Z. Twersky. An intimate, private congregation, Mogain Emoshia L'Beth David had met in the Rebbe's Intervale Street home. Beth David sold its Roxbury structure to Community Gospel Center in the winter of 1960–1961 and, by February 1961, the Talner Rebbe and his congregation had reestablished Beth David on a quiet residential street on the Brighton-Brookline line.[55]

Maimonides School dedicated its new facility in Brookline in September 1962, after a decade of discussion and planning. In 1956 Maimonides had purchased land in Brookline for a new structure, then began raising funds in 1958. But many of the school's supporters were dissatisfied with the proposed location for the new school. So in May 1959 Maimonides acquired a new site in Brookline. At its annual dinner in January 1960, Maimonides initiated a campaign to raise $1,000,000. Moving the school from Roxbury to Brookline would not only benefit the present student body, Morris Borkum, the co-chairman of the campaign, argued, "but will make it attractive to potential students, also." Lawrence Laskey, another leader of the campaign, declared that "the future of the school rests upon the construction of new facilities." Maimonides broke ground for the Brookline school in June 1960. In the fall of 1962, its high school and administration buildings completed, Maimonides dedicated the structure. The dedication exercises began with "a solemn processional of honored guests, school leaders and the entire student body and faculty," the *Advocate* reported. "Heading the procession were school founders and benefactors carrying the Torah scrolls beneath a canopy for the sacred ceremony of transferring the Torah from the school's former Roxbury site to the Ark of the new Chapel." High school and kindergarten classes immediately began meeting in the Brookline facility. Elementary school classes remained in Roxbury's Menorah Institute until the completion, in the fall of 1965, of an additional structure on the Brookline campus.[56]

Toras Moshe, an Orthodox synagogue, relocated from Roxbury to Brighton in 1964. Organized in Roxbury in the early 1920s, the congregation had been considering plans to relocate since the 1950s. When it mailed out High Holy Day tickets in 1961 to "every past and present member," it stated that the willingness of Toras Moshe's supporters to pay for the tickets "will be the deciding factor relative to our continuing our beloved Synagogue." Mickey Lazrus, the president of Toras Moshe's brotherhood, declared in May 1962 that "relocation is certainly imminent." He observed that "it is truly remarkable that we have continued to function in view of the trying conditions that exist in our synagogue's location." Toras Moshe sold its Roxbury structure to Holy Mt. Zion Church in the spring of 1964. It then voted to relocate to Brighton and merge with Congregation Kadimah. "Our synagogue has been reborn," Israel Lichtman, Toras Moshe's president, wrote on the occasion of the merger. That November, Kadimah–Toras Moshe "embarked upon a $100,000 Development Program for renovation and expansion" of the Brighton synagogue.[57]

The Lubavitz Yeshiva, the Jewish day school located in Mishkan Tefila's former buildings in Roxbury, announced in June 1965 that it was organizing kindergarten classes in Brighton. For this suburban branch, the Lubavitz Yeshiva—which had taken the name New England Hebrew Academy—used classrooms in Kadimah–Toras Moshe's "newly renovated building." The school's leaders soon resolved to relocate the entire school out of Roxbury, purchasing land in Brookline in the fall of 1967.[58]

While institutions that relocated to the Brookline-Brighton-Newton area maintained their membership and financial bases as well as their stature in the Jewish community, institutions that remained in Dorchester and Roxbury were steadily marginalized—losing their prominence even as they were losing their battles to survive. The dissolution of Jewish congregations continued in the early and middle 1960s. Shara Tfilo's Otisfield Street Synagogue, one of Roxbury's oldest synagogues and once one of the leading Orthodox congregations in Boston, closed in the fall of 1961. The congregation sold its synagogue and school building to the Mount Calvary Holy Church, a black Pentecostal church. Nusach Sfard closed its synagogue on Lawrence Avenue in the winter of 1962–1963, selling the structure to Rehoboth Church of God. Young Israel of Dorchester dissolved by late 1964. Nusach Hoari Anshei Lubavitz, a Lubavitcher congregation that had been worshiping in Dorchester since the 1920s, sold its modest Glenway Street Synagogue to Church of Christ in 1966 for $15,000. That spring, at its "final meeting," the congregation voted to affiliate itself with the New England Hebrew Academy, which maintained a small congregation at its Roxbury school. A few months later, in January 1967, Linas Hazedek dissolved and agreed to sell its Michigan Avenue Synagogue, also in Dorchester, to Rehoboth Bethel Church Apostolic for $13,200.[59]

The Crawford Street Synagogue closed in 1964. Louis H. Steinberg, who forty years earlier had prepared the congregation for the lean years to come, was still active in Beth Hamidrash Hagadol when the congregation disbanded. He was now seventy-five years old. The congregation's revenues had nearly evaporated by the early 1960s, and its leaders regularly drew on the cemetery fund to pay congregational expenses. In December 1963, the board of directors set up a committee "to look into the matter of a possible site for the re-location of our Synagogue." By then, the Boston Redevelopment Authority had decided to erect, on the synagogue site, "a central activity center" to serve upper Roxbury, which had been designated an urban renewal area. Disingenuously insisting that the city's decision to "take over the Synagogue" had forced a reluctant and vibrant congregation to vacate its old neighborhood, the congregation's leaders sought substantial compensation from the government. The Crawford Street Synagogue estimated that it needed "approximately $600,000 to $750,000 in order to re-locate" to Brookline or Newton. The city took the Crawford Street property in the summer of 1964, then razed the synagogue. It paid the congregation more than $300,000. "To sell to the government was a good decision. Otherwise, we would've had to walk away from the building and get nothing," Sumner Greenberg, a board member, recalled. "We saw a good chance, and we took it." For the next year or two, leaders of Beth Hamidrash Hagadol sporadically discussed plans for reestablishing the congregation near Coolidge Corner, but the plans were not realized. There were already several synagogues in Brookline, and "we didn't want to step on anyone's toes," Greenberg explained. "We were older, we didn't have the energy, and we were not that wealthy." The Crawford Street Synagogue was dead, its assets transferred to the congregation's cemetery fund.[60]

In 1963, the Blue Hill Avenue Synagogue announced that it was "considering the establishment of a branch in another part of the Boston area." However, for the Blue Hill Avenue Synagogue, as for the Crawford Street Synagogue, relocation was no longer a viable option. Adath Jeshurun had waited too long. The oldest synagogue in Roxbury and Dorchester, for decades one of New England's great congregations, the Blue Hill Avenue Synagogue was reduced to a pitiable state. Each entrance to the building, except the main door, was boarded up, and a spiked metal fence guarded the main entrance. "Adath Jeshurun is dying an almost blasphemous death," the *Boston Sunday Globe* reported in May 1966. "Her congregants, save the faithful 'minyon' few, have fled from Roxbury blight to more pleasant surroundings. And she is being stoned in her abandonment to humiliating proportions by an army of vandals. They know not what they do." Most of the synagogue's "inspiring stained glass windows" had been destroyed, replaced by plywood. Teenagers disrupted services, stole valuable religious items, desecrated prayer books and Torah scrolls, and attacked the few, elderly congregants. "If these people are not stopped," George Frank, the congregation's president, feared, "the synagogue will be stripped of all its religious objects including the torahs and it will be impossible to conduct services." Several black ministers met with Frank to discuss ways to end the violence against the synagogue and its congregants, but the attacks continued. In August 1966, Frank notified the local office of the Anti-Defamation League that vandals had dismantled and stolen parts of the synagogue's front steps. "They've cleaned out the inside, now they're starting on the outside," he stated. "When is someone going to help us?"[61]

Jewish agencies, supported by long-time suburban members of the Blue Hill Avenue Synagogue, responded to the crisis by considering ways to "dispose of the building" and to relocate congregants out of Roxbury. But the congregation's leaders refused to let outside agencies determine their synagogue's fate. "With regard to the sale of the property of Congregation Adath Jeshurun," Frank reminded the Jewish Community Council in December 1966, "just let me say that all decisions in this matter are exclusively in the control of the Board of Directors of the Congregation, since the Congregation owns the property." In August 1967, Adath

Jeshurun finally sold the synagogue building to Ecclesia Apostolic, a Spanish-speaking congregation, for $25,000 in cash. The First Haitian Baptist Church acquired the structure a decade later, subsequently repairing and restoring it at substantial expense. The magnificent shell of the Blue Hill Avenue Synagogue still houses a devoted Roxbury congregation, but by the summer of 1967 the synagogue itself was defunct. Adath Jeshurun donated its Torah scrolls to suburban Boston's two flourishing Orthodox congregations, Young Israel of Brookline and Newton's Beth El–Atereth Israel.[62]

Rabbi Abraham Koolyk must have accepted the Torah scrolls for Beth El–Atereth Israel with some sadness. When he had arrived at the Fowler Street Synagogue in 1950, his congregation in Dorchester and the congregation at the Blue Hill Avenue Synagogue had both been large and vital. Though their financial problems were steadily growing, the two working-class congregations had remained centers of Jewish life. Now, events had swiftly and decisively vindicated Rabbi Koolyk's urgent work in planting Beth El in Newton. Even if briefly, he must have paused—sighing, remembering—as he accepted these last treasures of a dead synagogue. A few months earlier, he had spoken ruefully of the synagogues in Dorchester and Roxbury that had "declined to non-existent levels, just shadows of their former selves."[63]

Newton's Beth El–Atereth Israel had thrived in the middle and late 1950s, while Dorchester's Beth El had declined. Rabbi Koolyk, who had continued to receive his entire salary from the Fowler Street Synagogue, requested permission from the Dorchester board to spend two Sabbaths every month in Newton. "I objected. I said, 'Make a decision—one way or the other,'" George Halzel, a board member, recalled. "I said that if I were him I would go with Newton. That's up and coming. We're dying." In the summer of 1960, Koolyk moved to Newton Centre and became the full-time rabbi of Beth El–Atereth Israel. Two years later Abraham Shonfeld, the Fowler Street Synagogue's cantor, joined Koolyk in Newton. The Dorchester congregation continued to function, but its future in Newton had been secured. "There was no bitterness when Rabbi Koolyk left," Halzel later explained. "There was a feeling of well-wishing for him." In December 1964, Beth El–Atereth Israel broke ground in Newton for a modern brick synagogue and school building. "Beth El–Atereth Israel represents continuity in two important dimensions," the *Jewish Advocate* observed in its editorial. "Being Orthodox, it follows the age-old traditions of Jewry. Stemming from Beth El of Dorchester, it brings the original dedicated spirit of one of Boston's early Congregations into the suburbs." The Newton congregation dedicated its new structure in May 1966; the previous fall, the Beth El Hebrew School had relocated from Dorchester to Newton. In the spring of 1967, the Fowler Street Synagogue voted to sell its historic structure to Church of God and Saints of Christ, and Dorchester's Beth El formally merged with Newton's Beth El–Atereth Israel.[64]

The *Boston Globe* published a photograph in 1967 that showed Rabbi Koolyk adjusting small lights on Beth El–Atereth Israel's memorial plaques. "Many of the plaques were moved from the original Dorchester temple," the *Globe* noted, "so they would not be forgotten."[65] Beth El survived only because it had moved. In an earlier age, Beth El, Adath Jeshurun, and Beth Hamidrash Hagadol had all been landmark suburban congregations. They had stood together in the late 1910s and early 1920s as modern Orthodox congregations, supporting rabbis from the Jewish Theological Seminary who promoted liberal reforms. Through the middle of the century, they had been three of New England's most prominent Orthodox synagogues. But by 1967, all three congregations had closed their synagogues in Dorchester and Roxbury. Adath Jeshurun and Beth Hamidrash Hagadol were dissolved: the Blue Hill Avenue Synagogue and the Crawford Street Synagogue live on only in the mist of memory. Of the three institutions, only Beth El persisted. Custodian of Adath Jeshurun's most precious relics, Beth El–Atereth Israel became custodian of memory. In Newton as it had in Dorchester, the congregation continues to meet for worship, to study Torah, and to educate its children.

Mattapan

"In little over a decade, 15 congregations have either dissolved or left Boston, and the Jewish community which once numbered 70,000 families [sic] in a bustling Roxbury-Dorchester triangle is now a bare trickle," the *Boston Globe* noted in February 1967. "All that remains of the once flourishing Jewish community is the overflow Morton-Mattapan section."[66] About 20,000 Jews still lived in the area that extended from Franklin Field south to Mattapan Square. But Mattapan's Jewish community was a rump. From its inception, Mattapan Jewry had been bound up with the rest of Dorchester and Roxbury's Jewish community. Most of the

area's major institutions—its great temples and synagogues, its community centers, and its Hebrew schools—had been built not in Mattapan
but in other sections of Dorchester and Roxbury. Consequently, Mattapan's Jews relied on many institutions that, by 1967, had already closed
or moved.

Lacking strong suburban memberships, synagogues and schools in
Mattapan had not yet committed themselves to relocating. And they
remained open: Mattapan stood at the far end of the historic band of
Jewish settlement, so its institutions were the last to be affected by racial
succession. Still, Mattapan's institutions were in decline, weakened by
the same exodus that had transformed all of Dorchester and Roxbury's
Jewish institutions since the 1920s. The Dorchester-Mattapan Hebrew
School depended on an annual subsidy from the Associated Jewish Philanthropies and, beginning in the middle 1950s, the school's enrollment
had steadily fallen. Between 1955–1956 and 1960–1961, the number of
students enrolled in the school fell from 560 to 370, while the AJP's
subsidy increased from $4,500 to $12,500.[67] In 1965–1966, 324 students
were enrolled in the school. A growing proportion of Jews remaining in
Mattapan were elderly and poor in the middle 1960s, and they struggled
to maintain the institutions in their district.

In stark geographical terms, Mattapan's institutions were precariously
positioned. The center of Mattapan's Jewish community since the 1920s
had been the intersection of Morton Street with Blue Hill Avenue. Not
only had the district's institutions been established near Morton Street,
but, as Map 22 shows, most of them were located in the first few blocks
that extended from Morton Street north toward Franklin Field. In that
area stood the large cluster of synagogues on Woodrow Avenue—Hadrath Israel, Chevra Shas, Anshi Volin, Ohel Torah, and Agudath Israel's
suburban-era Woodrow Avenue Synagogue—as well as Temple Beth
Hillel and the Dorchester-Mattapan Hebrew School, Beth Jacob, Young
Israel of Mattapan, and even the G&G delicatessen. Just one significant
institution, Kehillath Jacob's Fessenden Street Synagogue, stood in the
area that extended south from Morton Street.

But with the steady advance of population change up Blue Hill Avenue, Morton Street in 1967 was becoming a boundary. "North of Morton
St., between there and Columbia Road, is a neighborhood already beset
with deterioration, blight, crime, and general slum conditions," a Jewish
observer wrote in November 1967. "Most of the Jews who could have

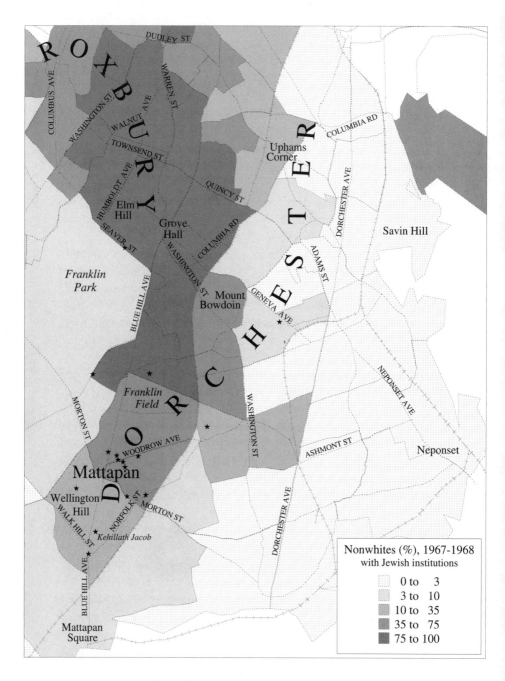

Map 22 Nonwhites, 1967–1968, with Jewish institutions

already moved out of this section." In 1967, as Map 22 illustrates, almost half the residents in the area that extended north from Morton Street to Franklin Field were black. The district that extended south from Morton Street to Mattapan Square, in contrast, was still heavily white and Jewish. It was the last predominantly Jewish enclave in the Dorchester-Roxbury district. "History, tradition and neighborhood sentiment makes Morton St. a pretty absolute boundary," this observer wrote in his report for the Jewish Community Council. Given the demographic situation in 1967, the references to "history" and "tradition," though entirely baseless, can be understood as the creation of "neighborhood sentiment." Because of the progress of racial succession, many Bostonians in the middle 1960s were coming to view Mattapan—bounded at its northern edge by Morton Street—as a neighborhood that was distinct from the rest of Dorchester. For Jews as well as for the white Catholics of St. Angela's Parish, Mattapan had assumed a fiercely separate identity.[68]

This separate identity was untenable. The effort to define Morton Street as "a pretty absolute boundary" was an effort to stop the very changes that had temporarily made the street an attractive barrier. Even in the middle 1960s, when Morton Street was emerging as a racial frontier, Jews had already begun to flee streets south of Morton; about 1,500 African Americans had settled in the area by 1967. And, ominously for the area's Jewish community, cutting Mattapan off at Morton Street meant cutting Mattapan Jewry off from nearly the whole of its institutional base. The Jewish neighborhood in Mattapan was quickly coming apart by 1967. That no Jewish institution could commit credibly to a permanent presence in the neighborhood contributed to the flight, as it had contributed to the flight of Jews from the rest of Dorchester and Roxbury. But in Mattapan, where nearly every remaining institution but the Fessenden Street Synagogue stood beyond the Morton Street boundary, the flight of Jewish residents in 1967 verged on panic.

St. Peter's Church and the Seaver Street Temple, 1967

Parishioners who lived along St. Peter's northwestern boundary lived at the very edge of racial change by the early 1950s. Through the end of the decade, though, the parish boundary held firm as a racial border. The all-white blocks along St. Peter's boundary in 1960 abutted blocks that were virtually all-black: St. Peter's white parishioners lived literally across the street from whole blocks of houses that over the past decade had shifted from white to black occupancy, and those parishioners had not moved.[69]

In 1960, as Map 8 (page 38) shows, more than two miles had separated Morton Street from the closest all-black blocks. But racial change came more quickly and more thoroughly to Mattapan than to St. Peter's Parish. In 1967, when Jews were fleeing even distant districts of Mattapan, only those white Catholics living near St. Peter's border had begun to move out in large numbers. The steadying presence of the parish institutions helped buttress white resistance to racial change—resistance that was sometimes violent and always ugly—and helped reassure old-time as well as new residents of the parish's continuous commitment to the district.

Although St. Peter's Parish was significantly reduced in size by 1967, it remained by far the largest parish in Dorchester and upper Roxbury. Monsignor James H. Doyle, St. Peter's pastor, reminded a newspaper reporter of "a symbol of the stability of the parish" when he referred to the parish by "its popular nickname, 'The Rock.'" More than two thousand children were enrolled in the parish's parochial and Sunday schools, and four hundred boys participated in the parish's baseball league. In the early and middle 1960s, the parish spent $50,000 for a new elevator in the convent and $20,000 for repairs to the church tower. And in the 1967 Cardinal's Jubilee Campaign, an unprecedented effort to solicit funds directly for archdiocesan needs, St. Peter's parishioners were expected to raise $250,000. Still, as Cardinal Cushing observed, the "parish is changing very rapidly from what it was in the past." The Catholic stronghold was being shaken to its roots. Reflecting on his church and on the "prevailing winds of change," Monsignor Doyle was succinct. "It's a beautiful old altar, and I won't change it!"[70]

Jewish and Catholic institutions were largely on their own through the middle 1960s. Not until 1967 did leaders of the archdiocese and leaders of Boston's Jewish community begin to take coordinated and conscious action to assist residents and institutions in upper Roxbury and Dorchester. To be sure, the Associated Jewish Philanthropies—and its successor, the Combined Jewish Philanthropies (CJP)—had provided subsidies to Hebrew schools, and the archdiocese had provided clergy and occasional loans to parishes. But these actions were either entirely unrelated to the emerging crisis in Dorchester and Roxbury, like the assignment of priests, or ad hoc measures limited to emergency situations. The cardinal still relied on St. Peter's prosperity. And the archdiocese offered only piecemeal support to the few parishes, like St. John–St. Hugh's, that were near collapse.

The African Americans settling in Roxbury and Dorchester were overwhelmingly non-Jewish and non-Catholic. For Catholic and Jewish institutions alike, the influx of blacks and the out-migration of whites threatened institutional viability. "Area now consists of a few Italian families—perhaps 12—small remnant of Irish—the rest colored people. Those who are Christians—mostly Southern Baptists or Methodists—estimated 3% Catholics now in Roxbury," Rev. John J. Philbin wrote early in 1968, describing the population of St. John–St. Hugh's Parish. "Impossible for existing families to continue to maintain an institutional set up that was flourishing 25 years ago."[71] St. John–St. Hugh's Parish continued to operate through the middle 1960s because rules kept it open, kept it staffed, kept it concerned solely with its local population, and, finally, kept it rooted. These rules guaranteed that churches, once established, could continue to preach good news in the face of adversity. While the presence of Philbin and other clergy had helped sustain St. John–St. Hugh's Parish through the preceding decade's changes, by the middle 1960s it was becoming clear that the parish could not remain viable without the active assistance of the archdiocese.

Since they were not tethered to their neighborhoods, Jewish institutions could ensure their futures by aggressively pursuing new locations. "Had we not moved the congregation," Rabbi Kazis stated in the middle 1960s, recalling Mishkan Tefila's decade-old decision to relocate, "the oldest Conservative Jewish congregation in America would have disappeared." A walk down Seaver Street in 1967 demonstrated the cost of Jewish portability. The New England Hebrew Academy, which a decade earlier had purchased the property from Mishkan Tefila, utilized the schoolhouse but lacked the resources to maintain the temple. "Today the temple is empty; its congregation is located in Newton," the *Globe* observed in February 1967. "The formerly pruned grounds collect paper scraps and childish scrawls; its hedges bear rotted leaves. The temple's white exterior is marred by rusty drippings." The school's janitor said, "It would make a wonderful police station. It's a shame. Nothing's any good when it isn't being used." A few panes of the temple's stained-glass windows were shattered. "Somebody been throwing rocks at them windows," one boy explained.[72]

More than the windows were broken. Institutional decay contributed to the exodus of Roxbury and Dorchester's remaining Jewish residents. Alone and palpably abandoned, Jews left in ever larger numbers, running not only from racial and socioeconomic changes but from the boarded-up Hebrew schools and the alien synagogues dedicated to Christ. They moved to suburbs along a path beaten both by an earlier generation of Jews and by their institutions.

Population change came more slowly to Catholic neighborhoods and, when it arrived, came parish by parish. Many parishes continued to flourish, protected and insulated by parish boundaries. And other parishes, like St. Peter's, confronted growing challenges. But only the willingness of the archdiocese to establish radical new programs could ensure the survival of those few parishes that were already crippled by the exodus of white Catholic residents and the in-migration of African Americans. For these parishes in the middle 1960s—for parishes like St. John–St. Hugh's—long-established rules of Catholic membership and rootedness no longer sufficed.

11

Authority in an Age of Crisis

Rev. John J. Philbin had purchased a bucket of red paint and arrived on time at the front entrance of his church.[1] Now, on this Saturday morning in January 1968, he stood with the bucket and a few brushes, and he waited. He was cold and he was alone. At Mass the previous weekend, Philbin had told his parishioners that the front doors of St. Hugh's needed painting and that he—Father Philbin—intended to paint them. He had announced the day and the time that he planned to paint the massive doors, and he had asked for some help. Anyone was welcome, he said, to join him. He privately regarded the project, including the choice of bright red paint, as an act of defiance, a public statement that the parish would survive. "No one in his right mind would paint metal doors in the middle of winter," he remembered thinking. Residents of Grove Hall might think that the priest was crazy, but they would know that he had no plans to abandon the district.

Monsignor Thomas J. Finnegan, Jr., the vice chancellor of the archdiocese, had worked with the cardinal to assign Philbin to the parish and to find archdiocesan funds to ensure the parish's survival. Barely two months had passed since Philbin had arrived in St. John–St. Hugh's Parish, and already Philbin was exasperated. "There was a rumor going around that we were leaving," he later recalled. Philbin hated the rumor, but even he had to wonder if it might not be true. If any parish in Dorchester and upper Roxbury was to become the first to close, his would be an outstanding candidate. Just 125 Catholic families, many desperately poor, now lived in the parish, one-tenth the population of a decade earlier; many Catholics had left in the months since the riot in

June, which had started near St. Hugh's Church and ripped through the blocks of Blue Hill Avenue that lay within the parish boundaries.[2] Indeed, Philbin's own appointment contributed to fears that the archdiocese was coming close to abandoning the parish. In announcing the appointment, Cardinal Cushing had specified that Philbin was to be the "administrator" of St. John–St. Hugh's Parish. Though he was given responsibility for the parish, Father Philbin had not been named pastor. The parish had no pastor.

Rita and Robin White, returning home from an errand, noticed Philbin standing in front of St. Hugh's Church. Rita was ten years old, and her sister Robin was six. Both girls stopped and realized that no one had shown up to help Father Philbin paint the doors. The two girls said that they wanted to help. Philbin hesitated, explaining that he did not think Mrs. White would appreciate her daughters' getting red paint on their dresses. As Robin waited with her priest, Rita ran home, received permission from their mother, and returned. Side by side, the priest and the two young girls painted the doors. "Well, I guess I'm a failure. I'm not much of a pastor," Philbin said, as he watched Rita carefully paint her small section of the door and as Robin did her best to assist. "I couldn't get anyone to help me." Rita's response was swift: "But you kept your word, Father." Three decades have passed since that exchange, and St. Hugh's doors are still bright red.

Beginning in 1967, the archdiocese and Boston's central Jewish agencies took direct action in Dorchester and upper Roxbury. For Catholics, ad hoc policies implemented in the late 1960s and 1970s evolved into a new archdiocesan commitment to maintain the financial and spiritual viability of inner-city parishes. For Jews, the actions of central agencies were guided by the fact that local institutions were autonomous organizations; Jewish agencies assisted Jewish residents in these neighborhoods, but Jewish rules of authority constrained the ability of any citywide agency to intervene on behalf of a specific institution. Consequently, during an intense neighborhood crisis that lasted through the middle 1970s, the last of the Jewish institutions in Dorchester and Roxbury closed, while archdiocesan policy guaranteed the permanence of Catholic institutions. The endurance of Dorchester and Roxbury's parishes through the 1980s and 1990s—and the continued presence of Catholic residents in these districts—has rested, ultimately, on a system of hierarchical authority.

Authority and Institutions

The Grove Hall–Blue Hill Avenue district anchored Boston's largest black community in the spring of 1967. A few shopkeepers, some elderly residents, and the ghostly shell of the Blue Hill Avenue Synagogue were the only vestiges of the district's Jewish past. African-American families had even settled on the once-Catholic streets near St. John's Church. Rev. Thomas A. Dwyer, the pastor of St. John–St. Hugh's Parish and Father Philbin's predecessor, watched helplessly as his parishioners deserted the parish. Long-time patterns of residential segregation constrained housing choices for blacks and caused whites in Mattapan and in St. Peter's Parish to view racial integration with alarm.

Boston in the 1960s was spared summers as long and hot as those in many other cities, but its June 1967 riot was nevertheless an abrupt reminder of how swiftly and thoroughly the city was changing. No one was killed, and the flames and violence were confined to the city's African-American districts. But the riot echoed down Blue Hill Avenue and throughout the predominantly white neighborhoods of Dorchester. Even before the riot, Boston's Jews and Catholics had begun to recognize the dimensions of the urban crisis and to see that this crisis was engulfing neighborhoods they thought they knew well. They seemed almost shocked at the discovery, and the riot amplified the shock.

Authority and Catholic Institutions

In the spring of 1967, Philbin was a curate in West Roxbury's Holy Name Parish, one of the largest and most prosperous parishes in the archdiocese. He knew that Cardinal Cushing was searching for priests who could provide fresh leadership in Roxbury and Dorchester. That fall, Rt. Rev. Francis J. Sexton, the chancellor of the archdiocese, called Philbin and asked him if he would be willing to assume responsibility for St. John–St. Hugh's Parish. Philbin traveled to Grove Hall and walked down Blue Hill Avenue, past the boarded-up stores and vacant lots, considering the chancellor's request. "It was soon after the riot," he recalled. "This was a neighborhood very different from what I was used to." He accepted the assignment.[3]

The Association of Boston Urban Priests (ABUP), which had been organized that summer, met with Philbin and endorsed his appointment.

The cardinal and much of the chancery regarded ABUP with suspicion. Established by about twenty priests in response to the riot, ABUP challenged the church hierarchy to assume a new, more active role in dealing with the problems of poverty and racism. In September, when Thomas Atkins, an African-American civil rights activist, announced his candidacy for city council, members of ABUP offered their public endorsement. "The age and style of ABUP members have not impressed people with power in the archdiocese," one Roxbury priest wrote in 1970. "The Cardinal himself has remained aloof. He has met with ABUP on occasion and told them to do what they want, but not to involve him or expect financial aid from the allegedly impoverished archdiocese."[4]

Cardinal Cushing pursued a different strategy to assist the parishes of Dorchester and upper Roxbury. At the cardinal's request, Rt. Rev. Thomas J. Finnegan, Jr., the vice chancellor of the archdiocese, conducted a comprehensive study of these parishes in the summer and fall of 1967. "The cardinal was concerned with Dorchester, with what was happening there," Finnegan recalled. "These parishes were all interrelated. This was a solid, vast, interconnected Irish enclave. Then, all of a sudden, we were hearing these rumbles. We had to help people adjust. We had to reassure people." Finnegan identified two sets of parishes that required urgent assistance. One set—St. John–St. Hugh's, St. Mary of the Angels', and St. Joseph's—was in upper Roxbury, where black neighborhoods were already well established and where traditional Catholic institutions served few people and struggled to remain viable. The other set of parishes—St. Matthew's and St. Angela's—still contained large districts of white Catholics in 1967, but these districts lay adjacent to Dorchester's former Jewish neighborhoods, which were undergoing rapid racial change. Between the fall of 1967 and the fall of 1968, Cushing assigned a new pastor (or, in the cases of the three Roxbury parishes, an "administrator") to each of the five parishes.[5]

In assigning these priests, Cushing was following Finnegan's strategy. "We wanted to put strong priests in these parishes as pastors. We wanted men with good, solid parish experience, with sound judgment, with strong spiritual values," Finnegan remembered. "We wanted these priests to go out into the field, to attend neighborhood meetings, to show the concern of the Church, to witness the presence of the Lord. We told them to be *in persona Christi.*" Finnegan was conservative, and he did not conceal his disdain for radical politics. He probably felt some antagonism toward ABUP's agenda, but he shared the group's commitment to addressing urban problems. "My advice to these new priests was simple," he later said. "Walk around your parish. Tell people, 'I'm here—to learn, to listen, to help.'" And Finnegan promised to find the funds to help these priests in their work. "I couldn't say to John Philbin, 'Go down to Roxbury and serve the people,' without my being able to say to him that I would support him and help out where necessary," Finnegan stated. "The pastor was out in the field, and we would support them. We didn't expect them to sit in the cold or to raise $35,000. We assured them that we would keep the buildings open, dry, and heated."[6]

In the late 1960s and early 1970s, Finnegan—who became chancellor in January 1968—assumed personal responsibility for finding funds to support the work of Dorchester and Roxbury's priests. "Monsignor Finnegan had the sense that something important was happening," Philbin recalled. "He would do anything to help us." Philbin, for example, inherited a large and decaying set of structures when he began serving in St. John–St. Hugh's Parish. Since its inception, the parish had supported two separate churches. In the spring of 1968, Philbin recommended maintaining St. Hugh's Church, but he sought permission to close St. John's and to transfer its Sunday Masses into the basement of the parish school. The cardinal granted permission. But even these reduced facilities required immediate repairs. Finnegan persuaded the archdiocese's finance department in 1968 to allocate $15,000 for work on St. John's School and $22,500 for work on St. Hugh's Church, with the money being assembled and budgeted in ad hoc fashion.[7]

Philbin, like other priests in Roxbury and in a few Dorchester parishes, lacked the money to pay even small bills or to cover basic operating costs. Consequently, he worked aggressively to locate funds to sustain the parish, including appeals to his former parishioners in West Roxbury. "I am doing the best I can to keep all requests for money from the Diocese at a minimum," Philbin wrote to Finnegan in July 1968. "Many of my friends have been most helpful—without them, and *you*, we would have phased right out of existence by now." The parish's difficulties continued, though, even with the ad hoc assistance. "Financially, each week is a crisis. Last year many friends from West Roxbury sent us money, but this has practically ceased now," Philbin wrote in 1969, in a letter to the cardinal. "Without the aid from your Parish Sharing Plan we could not even hold this beachhead." But the archdiocese continued to support the parish. In the fall of 1970, in a letter to Philbin, Finnegan expressed the hope that "we may somehow continue to show the visible presence of Christ in the midst of the tension and turmoil which so often engulf us."[8]

Humberto Medeiros, who became the archbishop of Boston that fall, firmly supported this policy. He recognized the financial crisis that was menacing several parishes and threatening the viability of many parish schools. Schools were undermined not only by the continuing exodus of Catholics to the suburbs but also by the decline in the number of women entering religious orders. Until the 1960s, parishes had depended on a cheap supply of teachers, nuns who lived in the parish convent at minimal expense. Now, even as the fiscal bases of parishes eroded, the costs of hiring teachers were rising. In July 1972, St. Kevin's Parish announced that it was seeking volunteer teachers "to keep its inner-city parochial school going." St. Ambrose' parishioners, concerned in 1973 that their pastor was preparing to close their school because of budget constraints, protested vigorously until the pastor relented.[9]

Inheriting a preexisting system of churches and schools, reluctant to close any institutions, and conscious of a responsibility to serve the poor, Medeiros articulated a vision for the Boston archdiocese in a 1972 pastoral letter. His missive, entitled "Man's Cities and God's Poor," argued that Catholics could not evade their responsibility for responding to the urban crisis. He contended that the problems of poverty and racial discrimination required immediate action. "Otherwise," he wrote, "ours will be a country drowning in passion and blood." He quoted the teachings of the Second Vatican Council to remind his parishioners that "the joys and hopes, the griefs and the anxieties of the men of this age, especially those who are poor or in any way afflicted, these too are the joys and hopes, the griefs and anxieties of the followers of Christ." In the letter, Medeiros committed the archdiocese to a program of continued aid for urban parishes, and he urged affluent parishes to both participate in and raise money for the work of poorer parishes.[10]

By the middle 1970s, the archdiocese was subsidizing the work of several parishes in Dorchester and Roxbury. Year by year, this program of ad hoc assistance—financed initially by an archdiocese that had never conducted a professional fundraising campaign and did not directly tax any of its parishes—developed into a systematic program of subsidy. Three principles, inchoate in the middle 1960s, were firmly established by the middle 1970s. First, except under extraordinary circumstances, the archbishop would not close churches, schools, or rectories. Second, the archbishop would locate funds for the maintenance of these institutions, especially inner-city schools, when the pastor could demonstrate the necessity of that assistance. And third, the archbishop would assign his strongest and most effective priests to parishes experiencing the most difficult problems.

While all three principles were rooted in the plan first devised by Monsignor Finnegan in 1967, only by the late 1970s did Roxbury and Dorchester's Catholics come to recognize that the immediate crisis had passed. St. Mary of the Angels' parishioners, who had lacked a resident priest for several months, expressed relief in the winter of 1976–1977, when the archbishop assigned two priests to the parish. "At least now we know the church will be staying around," one parishioner told a reporter. By the following winter, Rev. Eugene Sullivan, the superintendent of the archdiocesan schools, observed, "That panic isn't there any more—the fear of parents putting their children into parochial schools that they will end up closing." Though funding remained a constant problem, inner-city pastors now could depend on a regular system of financial support from the archdiocese. They and their parishioners welcomed the end of an era of uncertainty. The credibility of this archdiocesan commitment was demonstrated in the 1980s, when arsonists destroyed St. William's and St. Ambrose' churches in Dorchester. Both parishes built new churches, with the archbishop's consent and support.[11]

Of the sixteen parishes in Dorchester and upper Roxbury, six received financial support from the archdiocese in the 1995 fiscal year, with parish subsidies ranging from $50,254 to $228,334. At least three or four additional parishes have required subsidies in past years. According to Rev. William Schmidt, the archdiocesan secretary for pastoral services in the early 1990s, parishes are not expected to receive subsidies on a permanent basis, except to support a school; subsidies not intended for parish schools are meant only to assist parishes through periods of crisis and transition. "Our subsidy is about $50,000, which goes entirely to the school," Rev. John L. Doyle, St. Peter's pastor, stated in the fall of 1996. "The Archdiocese regularly sends a consultant to look at our books and decide what we need." More than money, the shrinking supply of priests is forcing the archdiocese to begin planning for the eventual consolidation of some parishes. To facilitate that process, the cardinal grouped parishes throughout the archdiocese into geographic clusters in the middle 1990s, encouraging neighboring parishes to work together, share resources, and plan for their collective future.[12]

Authority and Jewish Institutions

In the winter of 1966–1967, Robert E. Segal, the executive director of the Jewish Community Council, asked Mark S. Israel to establish "a program of neighborhood improvement and stabilization in the area from Franklin Park to Mattapan Square." Until that winter, no Jewish agency had taken action—in part because no agency possessed obvious authority to deal with the problems of the exodus, and in part because the suburban leadership of these agencies was indifferent to the growing crisis. The Jewish Community Council had traditionally restricted its attention to anti-Semitism and ethnic relations. As late as the spring of 1966, in fact, the JCC regarded antiblack discrimination as the Jewish community's primary concern in Roxbury and Dorchester. But by the end of the year Segal was convinced that the growing panic of Mattapan Jewry deserved urgent attention, and he persuaded a reluctant Combined Jewish Philanthropies to fund Mark Israel's position.[13]

Israel met with community leaders, Dorchester residents, and local business owners in the winter and spring of 1967. He recognized the need to bring stability to the Jewish districts of Mattapan, which had begun to undergo racial change. To reassure Jewish residents—and to establish a sense of community among the Jews, Catholics, and African Americans who now lived between Morton Street and Mattapan Square—Israel decided to organize a neighborhood association. In April he met with about ten people in Gloria Werman's home, on Wellington Hill. "This was the best group I have met, intelligent, committed to Mattapan, want to stay," Israel noted. "They got a real gleam in their eye about the idea of a community organization."[14]

That June, when about two hundred Mattapan residents, nearly all of them white and Jewish, gathered in the auditorium of the Solomon Lewenberg School, the Mattapan Organization (TMO) was formally created. But the timing was not auspicious: within days of the meeting, the Roxbury riot and the Six-Day War both began. "Does the last named crisis, absorbing this Jewish community's energies and resources, mean that this worthwhile attempt to stabilize a community worth stabilizing will be shunted aside? Does the wave of violence and destruction in the Grove Hall area mean that White and Jewish families will flee Mattapan in increasing numbers? Will the 'hidden agenda' of racial antipathy emerge to be frankly faced?" the *Jewish Advocate* asked in an editorial. "And, finally, is the Jewish Community Council at least twenty years too late in its laudable attempt to preserve this neighborhood as the last and perhaps only vibrant, healthy, interracial community in this city?"[15]

While many contemporary observers understood that the crisis of Mattapan Jewry was simply the latest stage in an ongoing Jewish exodus from Dorchester and Roxbury, none recognized the fundamental contradiction built into the JCC program. On the one hand, Israel helped establish a neighborhood association and a business association, and he worked closely with both groups—and with local religious leaders—to stop panic selling, arrest growing problems in the local public schools, encourage cooperation among business leaders, and provide security to local synagogues. All this activity buttressed a program to slow the Jewish exodus from Mattapan. On the other hand, Israel worked to relocate Jewish residents and businesses from Roxbury and from predominantly black districts in Dorchester. He also assisted Jewish congregations in selling their abandoned synagogues. Especially after the riot, Israel could not ignore these requests for assistance. But each time he helped an elderly Jew move from Elm Hill to Mattapan—each time he helped sell an old synagogue—he demonstrated the weakness of a Jewish commitment to a specific neighborhood. Mattapan residents surely noticed.[16]

To the extent that Israel received support from religious leaders in his work to stabilize Mattapan, the support came largely from Catholic priests. He met a few times with Rev. Shawn G. Sheehan, St. Leo's pastor, and he received constant help from St. Angela's Parish. "After the Jewish Community Council, the most significant institutional support comes from St. Angela's Parish. One of the priests of the parish is on the Executive Board and is one of the most active members," Israel wrote in May 1968. "The rabbis have participated very little." When Rev. Paul J. McManus became St. Angela's new pastor that month, he immediately contacted Israel. He hosted a meeting of the Mattapan Organization's executive board in June. According to the minutes of the meeting, at the end of the evening, McManus "addressed the group and expressed his pleasure at being part of TMO. Rev. McManus had been active in Cambridge in fighting the Inner Belt."[17]

Dorchester's rabbis rarely became active in neighborhood affairs. Synagogues were not territorial institutions. Moreover, since no central agency distributed rabbis, few of Dorchester's working-class synagogues could compete for the region's strongest and most talented rabbis. Herbert I. Simckes, Hadrath Israel's long-time rabbi, "agrees with everything everyone says, when they say it," Israel commented in 1967. "He adds little. He has old fashioned ideas about morality, in a modern time. He says, if only parents took better care of their kids." Mildred Kaufman, a branch librarian at the Mattapan Public Library, criticized Rabbi Samuel I. Korff, who served Kehillath Jacob, the only major synagogue between Morton Street and Mattapan Square. "Rabbi Korff does nothing for TMO, either does not or will not allow use of Temple facilities for the old or the teenagers. When a boy scout troop wanted use of the temple hall once a month, Rabbi Korff said it would have to be paid for," Kaufman stated in 1968. "It grieves us to report that in all of this," Robert E. Segal wrote in the summer of 1969, "we have had scant cooperation from the synagogues in the changing area."[18]

Even when they were on the verge of dissolution, synagogues continued to insist on their autonomy. "It seemed very clear that even though two synagogues were opposite each other on the same block, neither would entertain the notion of merging with the other," a group of Jewish leaders concluded in January 1970, after meeting with representatives of Agudath Israel and Hadrath Israel, both on Woodrow Avenue. "At the present time, they seem to be in the mood to go their separate ways even at the cost of both facing failure, rather than trying to become more viable by joining forces." Hadrath Israel, relocating to Hyde Park, sold its synagogue that spring to the Faithful Church of Christ.[19]

Moreover, the Combined Jewish Philanthropies and the Jewish Community Council, which by the late 1960s recognized the need for a "multi-service center" in Mattapan, rejected suggestions that the center be established in a synagogue. "At a meeting of the local rabbis which convened at my study at *the request of Mark Israel when he first arrived in Boston*," Rabbi Samuel Korff wrote in August 1969, "it was emphasized to him that the deteriorating situation in the Dorchester and Mattapan area could be ameliorated considerably by strengthening each individual synagogue as a local community center serving the needs of the immediate area." But, as Korff noted, "our voices were unheeded." In 1969, when Korff's synagogue was the most substantial Jewish institution left in Mattapan, the JCC rebuffed his recommendation that it use his facilities for the proposed community center. Stephen R. Morse, the assistant director of the JCC, explained to Korff that locating the center at Kehillath Jacob would "directly help" the Orthodox synagogue, "and if that should be the case then C.J.P. should also try to re-establish a conservative congregation in the area." Instead of consolidating a Jewish presence at Kehillath Jacob, the JCC rented space for its community center in a former dentist's office.[20]

As Mattapan's Jews contended with the collapse of their institutions in the late 1960s and early 1970s, they remembered the old Mishkan Tefila buildings and felt betrayed. In April 1968 the CJP had purchased the Seaver Street structures from the New England Hebrew Academy— which then relocated to Brookline—and gave the two buildings, for one dollar, to the Elma Lewis School of Fine Arts. The CJP did not use any community funds to acquire the buildings, but rather depended on special private donations to raise the necessary $200,000. Boston's leading newspapers and political leaders hailed the gift as a magnanimous symbol of black-Jewish cooperation. But the temple had already fallen into disrepair, and Elma Lewis and her school lacked funds to maintain the structure. Many Jews regarded the transfer with bitterness, as proof that the city's Jewish leaders had abandoned Dorchester Jewry. "If you can give away $200,000, how much have you done for the Jewish businesses in the Negro areas who have been burned or looted out of business?" one person asked that April, in a letter to the CJP. "Also what are you doing for those who escaped the senseless attacks and are now being harassed and/or being threatened with violence if they don't agree to sell their holdings for a token payment?"[21]

In the first week of September 1969, a small group of Jewish leaders gathered in downtown Boston to discuss the crisis confronting Mattapan's Jewish community. Two months earlier, Rabbi Gerald B. Zelermyer had been attacked with an acid bomb on the threshold of his Mattapan home. Zelermyer's temple, Beth Hillel—and its religious school, the Dorchester-Mattapan Hebrew School—had stood prominently on Morton Street for decades. But by late July, just three weeks after the attack on Zelermyer, the JCC was hearing "insistent rumors that the edifices are to be sold." Although leaders of Boston Jewry and the congregation's own rabbi opposed the sale, the rules of Jewish institutions dictated their own inexorable logic to the leaders of the congregation. "Needless to say,"

Robert M. Segal wrote that summer, "the effect of the sale of the physical assets of Beth Hillel on that community would be catastrophic."[22]

Beth Hillel's leaders sold the two buildings in August. "They are possibly the most important structures left," Stephen R. Morse argued in an internal JCC memorandum. "It is apparent that the situation is changing rapidly with buildings being transferred for use other than that which is beneficial to the Jewish Community. The effect of the wholesale transfer of these edifices is demoralizing the remaining Community. It is doubtful that even those who want to move, can move as fast as necessary religious and other services are being withdrawn." A few months later, the congregation merged with a synagogue in West Roxbury, four miles away from Mattapan. "The selling of Temple Beth Hillel was a shock!" Janice Bernstein, an active member of the Mattapan Organization, declared at the September meeting. "The residents were misled—why so much mistrust?" she asked. "Sold down the river," she said. The sale was not easily forgotten. "We used to go to Beith Hillel on Morton Street," another Dorchester resident later recalled. "When they closed two or three years ago I knew that was it. If they close it's a sign that Jews don't live here any more."[23]

At the September 1969 meeting, Janice Bernstein's concern over institutional abandonment extended to the YMHA–Hecht House, Dorchester's large Jewish community center. When she and others had helped to establish the Mattapan Organization, they had been "assured" that the YMHA–Hecht House would not be sold or moved. But, as Bernstein knew, plans were now being made by the city's Jewish leaders to sell the structure. In the summer of 1970, the CJP announced the sale of the YMHA–Hecht House to the Lena Park Housing Development Corporation. Rev. Shawn G. Sheehan, St. Leo's pastor, was a founder and the chairman of the nonprofit organization that purchased the building.[24]

The infrastructure of Mattapan Jewry was crumbling quickly. In the early 1970s, the last of Dorchester's synagogues closed or relocated. The exodus was now a rush. A series of fires, set at three synagogues in the spring of 1970, exacerbated the sense of panic. Chai Odom, selling the Nightingale Street Synagogue, followed its rabbi to Brighton. Agudath Israel announced after the fires that it would make repairs to the Woodrow Avenue Synagogue and "stay behind" in Dorchester. And Chevra Shas, which had been attempting to relocate since the summer of 1969, pleaded with suburban Jews to contribute funds. "Our Torah has been *desecrated!* Our Sanctuary has been *vandalized!* Our People have been *dispersed!*" the congregation stated in its November 1970 appeal. "If we do not relocate at once, we must close the doors of this sacred house of worship forever." All three synagogues testified to institutional portability—one in moving, one in its choice to "stay behind," and one in its advertised assertion that survival required relocation. These congregations knew that no hierarchy could guarantee their existence.[25]

Chevra Shas closed its synagogue in the fall of 1971, then relocated to Newton. Agudath Israel was dissolved the following summer. And Kehillath Jacob, which had established a branch in Newton in 1971, closed the Fessenden Street Synagogue in the winter of 1973–1974. The *Boston Herald,* describing the last services in Agudath Israel's Woodrow Avenue Synagogue, observed that the sale of the synagogue to the Salem Seventh-Day Adventist Church was "the inevitable result of the area's Jewish to black transition." A few men, elderly and poor, attended services that day, as they always had. "The elders look at the empty pews and the cartons packed with prayer books and they see their lives pass before them," the *Herald* stated. At the conclusion of the service, "the last of the 23 sacred scrolls were carefully carried from the big red brick building," the *Globe* reported, "and the 10 old men went home again."[26]

Jewish Exodus

The Jewish exodus was already nearing its end by 1967. Of the 25,000 Jews who still lived in Roxbury and Dorchester, about 13,500 lived in the section of Mattapan that lay south of Morton Street. And this area, the last Jewish district in the Dorchester-Roxbury area, was changing quickly. Between 1960 and 1967, its black population had grown from 48 to 1,500. The Jewish migration from Mattapan, as from all of Dorchester and Roxbury, was continuing without respite. "Some of our streets," one Jewish resident wrote in May 1968, "already have as many as fifteen Negro families all bunched together." That fall, another resident expressed the fear that "the transition is happening so fast that within a year Mattapan will be a ghetto."[27]

Fewer than 16,000 Jews remained in Dorchester and Roxbury in 1970; 10,000 Jews and 5,000 blacks lived in the district extending from Morton Street to Mattapan Square. As Map 16 (page 84) shows, the Morton Street boundary had thoroughly disintegrated. Blacks made up half of

Wellington Hill's population by 1970, and Jews even at the most distant edges of Mattapan were frantically trying to sell their homes. "There is a deep sense of abandonment by the institutions that support community life, i.e. synagogues, professionals, stores, etc. They now feel trapped even though a significant percentage live on good streets, relatively safe in comfortable, modest, single-family homes, etc. They talk about wanting to leave," a September 1972 report concluded, summarizing interviews with Jewish residents of Mattapan. "They are basically frightened by what has happened in the neighborhoods immediately north of theirs and they see the beginnings of similar disruptions in their own neighborhoods."[28] Perhaps three thousand Jews remained in Mattapan in the middle 1970s, and this remnant population dwindled down to several hundred by the end of the decade.

The swift collapse of Mattapan Jewry was the final stage of the long Jewish exodus from Dorchester and Roxbury. Mattapan's Jews knew from hard experience that they could not depend on their institutions to rally their community, and a growing concern with street crime, arson, burglaries, and changes in the public schools aggravated the sense of crisis. The Solomon Lewenberg Junior High School, which had stood on the crest of Mattapan's Wellington Hill since 1930, testified to the area's transformation. Serving a district that included all of Mattapan—from Franklin Field to Mattapan Square—the school for decades had educated a student population that was overwhelmingly Jewish, lower middle class, and college-oriented. Jews, who in 1963 had made up 80 percent of the student body, composed just half of the student body by 1965; one-quarter of the students in 1965 were African American, many of them very poor. The chairman of the Boston School Committee noted matter-of-factly in June 1966 that the Lewenberg School was "approaching an imbalanced state." In an editorial in June 1967, the *Jewish Advocate* argued that the school was "the focal point for racial antipathies . . . which imminently threaten to thwart all attempts to stabilize the area. There are rumors, not substantiated, of beatings and knifings on school premises." The school committee's policy of open enrollment—which permitted black students from outside the district to attend the school and white students in the district to attend other schools—hastened the school's resegregation. By the fall of 1968, two-thirds of the students in the Lewenberg School were black. One year later, more than 90 percent of the school's students were black.[29]

The early 1970s was a time for eulogy and requiems. "There are still a few left, cowering behind police locks, burglar alarms, heavy steel grilles, pretending to do business," Mark Mirsky wrote in 1972, describing Jewish shopowners on Blue Hill Avenue. "The fruit store has a few rotten apples, an old pear, dried plums and in the back they take wagers on the last few digits of the Treasury balance, numbers racket. Yet it all seems furtive, desperate, beleaguered swapping, the last jerk of a chicken's wings, its throat slit," he suggested. "As if the Jews had swept out of Dorchester in one blow. A thunderclap catastrophe the rabbi called upon our heads." By then, with only the shards of a community left behind, the Jewish exodus was over.[30]

Everywhere Jews had once lived and worshiped and shopped, African Americans now lived. For almost its full length—from Roxbury until the railroad bridge deep in Dorchester, just before Mattapan Square, where white Catholics continued to maintain a boundary at St. Angela's Church—Blue Hill Avenue was the central artery of Boston's black community. "Aaaah, what do they know, the map makers?" Alan Lupo wrote in 1969. "Blue Hill avenue stretches from the Don and the Volga and the Vistula to the Mississippi River. Once, it was a world peopled with the Yiddish and their offspring. Today, it is more Mississippi than Minsk." The citadel of Mattapan Jewry, the G&G delicatessen, had fallen. "Inside are maybe 20 Jews, most of them old. Some sit together, some, alone," Lupo noted. "Their world has moved to Milton, Newton, Brookline, Swampscott, and even if they joined that world, they might no longer recognize it." Catering to a new clientele, the G&G had begun serving bacon and eggs for breakfast.[31]

Catholic Exodus and Persistence

The example of Mattapan Jewry resonated: even in Neponset, the most secure of Dorchester's Catholic neighborhoods, old-time white residents feared an imminent stampede to the suburbs. "People are worried," Tom Stenson, the owner of a popular neighborhood bar, told a reporter in 1976. "People just aren't thinking or talking positive. They say this is the last of the good neighborhoods, and they wonder how long it will last." The question haunted Neponset residents. "Several times a week I'm asked how long I think the neighborhood will last," Stenson stated. "I say 10 years, and they tell me five." A large group of Neponset residents met that June to establish a neighborhood organization, which they called Stay in Neponset. According to its members, the organization was "designed to dissuade their neighbors from fleeing to the suburbs." Redlining, crime, arson, and court-ordered school desegregation all contributed to the growing fear that Dorchester's firmest Catholic bastions were vulnerable to rapid neighborhood change. "There's a sense of deja vu here," Alan Lupo observed in 1977. "Eight years ago in Mattapan. In a similar neighborhood of neat three-deckers, small yards and clean streets. A tight community also."[32]

Unlike Mattapan, Neponset and many other Catholic neighborhoods persisted unchanged through the 1970s. Racial change was generally more violent in Catholic districts than it had been in Jewish districts, but, in some Catholic neighborhoods, racial integration proved lasting and, in others, it was resisted altogether. Still, ethnic boundaries shifted quickly. Urban renewal, the continuing black migration to Boston, and the persistence of residential segregation contributed to an unrelenting demand for new districts of black housing. In the late 1960s and 1970s, as Catholics left Dorchester for the suburbs in ever-growing numbers, African Americans extended their neighborhoods into several former Catholic districts.

The number of white Catholics in Dorchester and upper Roxbury, which fell from 119,000 to 105,000 between 1960 and 1967, declined to 95,000 by 1970. By the early 1970s, as Map 16 shows, blacks had settled throughout St. Joseph's and St. John–St. Hugh's parishes, both in Roxbury, and throughout St. Leo's, whose church was physically separated from the once-Catholic section of the parish. "The demography of the parish is new: 75% black and 25% white," Rev. Joseph A. Gaudet wrote in June 1971, describing St. Leo's Parish. "Church attendance is sparse." Few English-speaking whites remained in St. Mary of the Angels' Parish and St. Paul's Parish, which had both attracted significant Hispanic communities as well as African-American residents. And nonwhites had begun moving onto white Catholic streets in St. Kevin's, St. Peter's, and St. Matthew's parishes, areas that bordered the large African-American district centered on Blue Hill Avenue.[33]

Many blacks were harassed or attacked when they moved into Catholic neighborhoods. William Curry and his wife purchased a three-decker on Hamilton Street, at the northwestern edge of St. Peter's Parish, in February 1967. "The Currys moved to an outpost on the frontier," according to a report written that winter. "There seem to be no other Negro families on Hamilton Street or in the immediate neighborhood." Soon after the Currys moved into their new home, vandals broke several windows. On a Monday night "a crowd of 15 or 20, who seemed to be teenagers, gathered by the house, drank beer, threw bottles at the windows, and jeered at the Currys with anti-Negro epithets," the report states. The Currys also received hate literature by mail, including "a representation of a 'ticket to Africa,'" with the typed message "Nigger get smart." Two years later, a black family who had recently moved into a home on Westville Street, at St. Peter's southern border, faced similar harassment from "a gang of youths who lived nearby." White teenagers broke three windows in the home, kicked in the apartment door, and struck a fifteen-year-old guest of the family with a brick.[34]

Dorchester High School erupted in violence in 1973. Located at the western edge of St. Matthew's Parish, the school stood on Dorchester's racial borderline. St. Mark's and St. Gregory's parishes, still Catholic bastions and both virtually all-white, extended east and south of the school. To its north and west lay the African-American neighborhoods that had recently emerged in St. Leo's Parish and in the districts near Blue Hill Avenue. In the last week of September 1973, black and white students engaged in sporadic confrontations. On Thursday morning, when black students staked out positions at the school entrance and white students gathered in the bleachers of the adjacent athletic field, classes were canceled for the rest of the week. "Bands of youths—armed with hockey sticks, broom handles, baseball bats and metal pipes—roamed Dorchester streets throughout the afternoon," the *Boston Globe* reported. "A constant complaint bitterly voiced by the young whites hanging around Dorchester," the *Boston Phoenix* stated, "is that 'the niggers are taking over the schools.'" The tension at Dorchester High School—and the controversy, two years before, over the assignment of white children to the nearby Lee Elementary School—proved a harbinger of the conflict to come. Court-ordered busing, which began in the fall of 1974, aggravated racial tensions and posed challenges to racial boundaries throughout the city. White resistance to busing was, in the main, Catholic resistance; few Jews remained in Dorchester in 1974.[35]

Parish institutions slowed but did not arrest the urban exodus. St. Matthew's and St. Angela's churches stood on the traditional border between Jewish and Catholic enclaves. In both parishes, the Jewish exodus brought the racial frontier to the parish center. St. Matthew's Catholic population began falling in the late 1960s and continued falling through the 1970s, and St. Angela's parishioners began leaving in large numbers in the middle 1970s. As blacks moved into these districts, they faced sporadic violence. "A black family in a predominantly white Mattapan neighborhood is repeatedly harassed," the *Boston Globe* stated in a 1977 editorial, "the youths going so far as to burn the family's car and garage."[36]

By the middle 1970s, blacks and Hispanics had settled in much of St. Peter's Parish. White parishioners, who had fiercely resisted racial change through the 1950s, had begun leaving outlying sections of the parish in the 1960s. The white exodus accelerated in the early and middle 1970s. Only the streets surrounding the church and the portions of the parish lying east and south of the church remained overwhelmingly white. "Those who could afford to, they've gone," one parishioner explained to the *Boston Globe* columnist Mike Barnicle in the fall of 1975. "The ones that have remained are here trying to hold it together: the neighborhood, the church, the parish school . . . all of it is important to them. They really want to hold it together." But St. Peter's Parish, three years into its second century, was disintegrating as a Catholic community. "Everything is burned on Bowdoin st. A drugstore where there were two fires in a week is closing, and a barber shop, five-and-ten, and a furniture store have closed. There are only a few businesses left," Rev. Robert G. Flynn, St. Peter's pastor, stated in the summer of 1976. "The feeling is, that if we don't make a stand here to stop the blight and everything that goes with it, all Dorchester will one day be gone . . . Savin Hill will go, and Fields Corner, and Neponset."[37]

But the white exodus was already slowing, and some stable, racially integrated neighborhoods were emerging. Since the late 1970s, racial boundaries in Dorchester have continued changing, but gradually. The area's white Catholic population, which fell sharply between 1970 and 1980, from 95,000 to 51,000, declined more moderately in the 1980s. In 1990, nearly 40,000 white Catholics still lived in Dorchester. Large Haitian communities developed in St. Leo's and St. Matthew's parishes in the 1980s. And, in the 1980s and 1990s, St. William's Parish, on Savin Hill— still home to a large white population—has been attracting many Asian residents. Parishes serving Roxbury and Dorchester's poorest neighborhoods sponsor latch-key programs, food pantries, and summer camps, explicitly responding to the needs of their predominantly non-Catholic districts. Stronger parishes, like St. William's and St. Brendan's, continue to support traditional parish social clubs and to attract large congregations for Sunday Masses. Parishes across Dorchester and Roxbury maintain their schools, with the assistance of the archdiocese.

Neponset's white residents have not fled en masse to the suburbs. "On a warm afternoon . . . a few elderly residents tend the narrow lawns and bright flower gardens that separate the mix of single-, two- and three-family houses," the *Globe* reported in 1987. "By early evening, parents sit on stoops and porches, enjoying the breezes off Dorchester Bay . . . and watching children riding bicycles and playing on the sidewalks." In the 1990s, St. Ann's Parish prospers. Led by their priests, the men and women of the Neponset parish raised $200,000 for a thoroughgoing renovation of the upper church; the work was completed in June 1991. "I was very, very familiar with the city and I watched the city change and the blight take hold and people pull up the stakes when they didn't care anymore. But this place remained stable," one resident stated.[38]

In 1978, when Rev. Timothy Murphy became the pastor of St. Angela's Parish, the exodus of white Catholics from Mattapan was steadily progressing. By the middle 1990s, when Murphy left the parish, few whites remained, and most of them were elderly. The majority of St. Angela's active parishioners were now Haitians and other Caribbeans. "Father Murphy was not only a priest, he was a community person. He was not only concerned about church issues, he was concerned about Blue Hill Avenue issues, he was concerned about Mattapan issues," one parishioner observed at a parish meeting in October 1994. Murphy had worked with local residents to combat crime, close down a crack house, limit the hours of a disruptive local business, and restore safe playgrounds and parks to the district. As Murphy later explained, "That's what the church is supposed to do—respond to the needs of the people in the parish." Representatives of the Office of Clergy Personnel attended the meeting, listened to the discussion, and took careful notes of the qualities parishioners were seeking in their new pastor. Later, the archdiocesan officials shared their notes with the cardinal.[39]

Outside a grocery store, stalks of sugarcane call to passersby in Grove Hall in the 1990s. The First Haitian Baptist Church, crowned by delicate Star-of-David finials, stands a block down Blue Hill Avenue. Dedicated in 1906 by Congregation Adath Jeshurun, the Blue Hill Avenue Synagogue was the district's pioneer Jewish institution. A century after Boston's Jews made it their first middle-class suburb and three decades after the neighborhood erupted in a riot, Grove Hall thrives anew. *(Photograph courtesy of Brett Miller.)*

Epilogue:
Return to the Church
and the Temple

I met Randi Donnis in downtown Boston. We hopped into her car, then drove out to Roxbury and Dorchester. She knew the way well. We made three stops, each in one of the city's poorest neighborhoods. First we stopped on Dudley Street, at the edge of upper Roxbury, where Donnis showed me some of the new, owner-occupied, two-family and four-family homes that have risen on vacant lots, fruits of the Dudley Street Neighborhood Initiative. Next we drove to the Bird Street Community Center, near Uphams Corner. Donnis and I walked into the building. Boys were playing basketball in the gym, and youth leaders were setting up tables in the social hall for an event later that day. Several people came over to Donnis, glad to see her. Finally, we drove to a large house in the Mount Bowdoin district, on a street that once straddled the Catholic districts of St. Peter's and St. Leo's parishes but now lies in a black neighborhood.

In the fall of 1996, during that visit, this house was being rebuilt and converted into a community center. Some of the upper rooms had been completed, but work was still going on in the basement, which would soon be a social center and lounge for local teenagers. This community center, the Ella Baker House, was the achievement of Rev. Eugene F. Rivers III and the Azusa Christian Community. Rivers had studied at Harvard but had left for Dorchester in the middle 1980s, without a college degree, convinced that nothing was more urgent than addressing the problems of inner-city black communities. He and other blacks, all sharing similar educations and convictions, created Azusa as an urban church. For a decade, the Pentecostal church had flourished without a building. Rivers held prayer meetings on sidewalks, disrupting the work of local drug dealers. He challenged blacks in the neighborhood—especially boys and young men—to assume responsibility for their lives and their decisions. And he preached relentlessly.

Soon after welcoming Donnis and me to the Ella Baker House, Rivers challenged the assumption that the white urban exodus contributed to the crisis of poor black communities. Rivers rejected with equal vigor the liberal, secular vision of an integrated society and the current black nationalist vision. "For more than 40 years, the integrationist conception of racial equality has dominated the nationalist alternative. But skin color still determines life-chances; millions of Blacks continue to be excluded from American life," Rivers had written in the summer of 1995. "Committed to racial equality, but faced with a segregated existence, we need to rethink our identification of racial equality with integration, and reopen debate about a sensible nationalist conception of racial equality." Rivers, however, had no sympathy for the black nationalism advocated by men like Louis Farrakhan and Leonard Jeffries. "They are cynically antisemitic, mean-spirited, and simply incompetent," Rivers wrote. "They are all demagoguery, uniforms, bow ties, and theater."[1]

As we spoke, Rivers contended that the long fight for integration had failed, at least for millions of poor blacks, and that any solution to the problems of the inner city required recognizing the permanence of segregation in American life. While he had little interest in the exodus of white people, Rivers spoke passionately about the central role played by churches like his in fighting crime, restoring parks and housing, extracting funds from government agencies, promoting local economic development, and strengthening schools. His battle was not to engage whites in the life of his community, but instead to obtain for his community the same resources and support from the government that whites enjoyed in their communities. Already his church was a national model. "Rivers's style of ministry represents a significant challenge to the political community beyond his neighborhood," Joe Klein observed in the *New Yorker* in 1997. "His message is that religious institutions are better equipped to deal with the problems of the poor than the government is, and that they should receive public support to do everything from crime prevention to welfare reform." To do his work, Rivers cooperates closely with other religious leaders. When he "needs access to Boston's power brokers, he dials the phone that rings beside the bed of Cardinal Bernard Law,"

Newsweek reported in a June 1998 cover story. "'He's my *patrone*,' says Rivers. 'I don't need an archdiocese because the cardinal already has one.'"[2]

Rev. John L. Doyle, the new pastor of St. Peter's Parish, had specifically sought assignment to an inner-city parish. Nearing retirement, he is a native of Dorchester who had previously served a Hispanic parish in a working-class Boston suburb and who had spent several years in Bolivia. "I started agitating. I wanted to spend the remaining days of my active ministry in a place that was needy. Little by little, I convinced Bishop [John P.] Boles that I was serious," Doyle told me, as we sat and talked in the reception room of St. Peter's rectory. The cardinal offered Doyle an assignment at St. Peter's. Few whites remained in the parish in the middle 1990s, and it struggled to serve its parishioners and pay its bills. The parish territory included large numbers of American-born blacks who did not identify with the church as well as many Cape Verdeans, Vietnamese, Hispanics, and immigrant blacks from the Caribbean. As soon as he arrived, Doyle began meeting with ministers and other priests to support efforts toward community organizing. "This parish is not viable right now. It is just a series of services. It runs a school, a dormitory, a women's shelter. But none of this is led by people in the parish. We have the shell, but the congregation is passive," Doyle explained. "Our instrument for making a difference is broad-based community organizing. That is how Catholics can affirm their faith."[3]

Doyle's skepticism regarding the relevance of many Catholic churches in the city's poorest neighborhoods is well founded. But the church—the Catholic parish, with its monumental, outdated structures—is at least still present in these neighborhoods, and its presence is a necessary precondition for Doyle's work. It is easy to mistake the relationship between this physical presence and the Catholic commitment to addressing urban problems. Catholic teaching emphasizes a concern for the poor, but this emphasis is no stronger than that in Protestant or Jewish teaching. Catholics are running soup kitchens, latch-key programs, and community-organizing workshops in Dorchester and Roxbury because of the rules that keep Catholic churches open in the inner city. The array of programs to assist the urban poor is not the cause of the Catholic institutional presence. Rather, it is the logical consequence.

In St. William's Parish, still home to a large white population as well as to a growing Vietnamese community, residents recognize the centrality of the institution to their district. Bill Walczak—the executive director of the Codman Square Health Center, itself a crucial community center in another part of Dorchester—lives in St. William's Parish and spends spare hours working with other laypersons and the pastor to build cross-ethnic links in the parish and to maintain the parish's financial health. "St. William's Parish is the core of the community," Walczak told me over lunch in a small sandwich shop. "It must be supported by everyone—even *non*-Catholics. We have now gotten political antagonists to sit down together on the parish census committee. We must get people to support the parish, to unify the community."[4]

Jews, except in a scattered way, no longer live in these neighborhoods. But Jews have begun returning to Dorchester and Roxbury. The afternoon that Randi Donnis and I drove to Roxbury had started with a meeting in a downtown office building. There I met with Nancy Kaufman, the executive director of the Jewish Community Relations Council (JCRC), and I learned about the work that Kaufman and Donnis had begun doing in Roxbury and Dorchester. "I came to JCRC in the fall of 1990. At the time, the Jewish community was doing nothing in the city," Kaufman said. "Then, that winter, I was invited by young Jewish leaders to talk on the subject, 'After Crown Heights, Could Boston Be Next?' It was a freezing cold night, in Brookline, but 250 people were there for the talk. All young adults. There's this thirsting, I realized, to do something. But what can we do?" For the next two years, with the support of the Boston Foundation, Kaufman worked with many others on the Boston Persistent Poverty Project. In its report, published early in 1994, the group called for "a new social contract which recognizes and honors the reciprocal rights, responsibilities and interdependence of all members of our community." By then, the Combined Jewish Philanthropies, Boston Jewry's central agency, had begun funding programs that were consistent with this broad, citywide initiative.[5]

Kaufman emphasized that the agenda and leadership for work in Dorchester and Roxbury could not be imposed by suburban Jews. "We can't send rabbis to do community organizing," she stated, but "we realized that we had these skills—institution-building, development, fundraising—that might be useful to others." Donnis, JCRC's director of domestic concerns, worked with Kaufman to identify institutions like the Bird Street Community Center and the Ella Baker House that would welcome assistance from members of the Jewish community. "We have *not* said that we're here to solve your problems. We know we're not in charge," Kaufman said. "We'll talk with anyone. We have this need, rooted in the Jewish imperative to *tikun olam,* to repair the world. We tell them that we feel isolated and disconnected. 'We need you,' we say, 'to help us to fix this need.'" Kaufman and Donnis have responded to specific requests from institutions in Dorchester and Roxbury, identifying Jews willing to offer legal assistance, fundraising skills, or help in navigating government bureaucracies. And college programs and leadership-training programs overseen by Boston's Jewish agencies now bring Jews back to Dorchester and Roxbury through a series of ongoing projects. "The tragedy of Dorchester is not that we left," Kaufman told me, "but that we're not still there."[6]

Each fall, a few days after Yom Kippur, Jews celebrate the festival of Sukkot. The holiday is a celebration of God's protection and bounty, recalling the temporary booths that Jews used for shelter in their forty years of wandering after the Exodus. It is a time to give thanks for ripe fruits and the harvest, and to recall the promise of a Jewish homeland. In ancient Israel, Jews made pilgrimage to the Temple in Jerusalem and offered sacrifices on the altar. But the Temple is destroyed, and there is no more altar. Jews now celebrate the festival by eating in open-air booths decorated with cranberries, flowers, gourds, and corn stalks. At night, observant Jews sleep in these booths, stars visible through the boughs covering the open roof. The booths are temporary homes, easily dismantled and stored away for the next year.

By the 1910s, the tradition of building these booths—these sukkot—was almost forgotten in the middle-class Jewish neighborhoods of upper Roxbury. "The Jewish Men's Club of Temple Mishkan Tefila built a Succah such as our grandfathers were wont to celebrate the Succoth holiday in," the *Jewish Advocate* reported in the fall of 1916. "To many of the guests it was the first real Succah they had ever seen." Mignon L. Rubenovitz, who had recently married Rabbi Herman H. Rubenovitz and settled in Roxbury, remembered that first sukkah on Moreland Street. "At 6:30 A.M. with our parishioners still snugly abed, the Rabbi and Rebbitzen could have been seen walking down Elm Hill Avenue and Warren Street, a goodly mile, each carrying a heavily loaded suitcase. For the old bare trestle, there was a shining white damask cloth, a carafe with wine, cookies for silver bowls (my wedding presents)," she later wrote. "Our members loved the little Sukkah, the older people remembered one in their youth, the children were taken with the gay decorations and the delicious smell of pine and spruce, not to mention the goodies." Every year since—on Moreland Street, on Seaver Street, in Newton—members of Mishkan Tefila have celebrated their fall festival in a sukkah. "How slight a protection it seems," Mignon Rubenovitz observed, "but this precarious haven has outlived our despoilers, has survived the destruction of the great Temple in Jerusalem."[7]

I drove out to Newton in the fall of 1996 to meet Michael Menitoff, the new rabbi of Mishkan Tefila, and I spent an hour or so roaming the temple and listening to its voices. The temple was growing and expanding. The office staff had just moved into their newly renovated offices, but the rabbi continued to work in temporary space as construction continued on his permanent office. Workers were painting walls with long roller brushes, and everywhere smelled of new carpet. I walked slowly through the temple's classroom wing. There are 240 children in the temple's Hebrew school, another 95 in the nursery school. In one classroom, young children were learning holiday songs. In other nursery-school classes that morning, boys and girls chattered and played. Outside the temple lobby, I watched two or three people building the sukkah, placing a few wooden boards across the top to provide support for hanging fruits and pine branches. As I watched these men work, Rabbi Menitoff explained that next year's sukkah would be built on a different part of the temple property. The congregation was about to break ground on this site for its museum, named in memory of Mignon L. Rubenovitz.[8]

There was so much else to do on this visit to Boston that I almost ran out of time before I made it back to the old temple building on Seaver Street. I drove there expecting to learn something new, but realized—abruptly, as soon as I had parked the car—that this building had already given up its secrets. It is a structure that inspires stubborn hope. The Seaver Street Temple nearly destroyed the congregation that built it and left it behind in their move to the suburbs. First an annex to a Lubavitcher day school, then the never-realized home of an African-American performing arts center, the building had been rotting for four decades. Deahdra Butler-Henderson, a Dorchester activist, had recently organized a campaign to restore the building as a community hall and arts center, as a testament to the ties binding Jews and blacks.[9]

One year after my visit, United House of Prayer, a national Pentecostal church, purchased the Seaver Street property for one million dollars. "The church plans to convert the Greek Revival temple into a 600-seat church, with the basement devoted to a 200-seat chapel alongside meeting rooms and a cafeteria," the *Boston Globe* reported in September 1997. "The adjacent school building will likely include elderly housing, job and entrepreneurial training facilities and other social services that are part of the church's ministry." The church's architect explained that contractors would begin by clearing trees and removing debris from the temple's interior. "It's completely gutted inside," the architect explained. "All the plaster is on the floor. It looks like a bomb went off."[10]

All I saw in the fall of 1996 was an empty building surrounded by wild grass, six-foot-tall weeds, and trees. The side entrance that I had once used—and the trash heaped in front of it—was now sealed in a dense thicket of vegetation. The weeds were so high that I could not even walk around the grounds. But the inscription, carved in limestone along the temple's side, was not obscured: "NOT BY MIGHT NOR BY POWER BUT BY MY SPIRIT, SAITH THE LORD." I read the words aloud and knew that this faith lives in many places—though not on Seaver Street, at least not on that day.

Abbreviations

AACC	Census Cards, RCAB
AAPB	Parish Boundary Files, RCAB
AAPC	Parish Correspondence Files, RCAB
AAPH	Parish History Files, RCAB
AJA	American Jewish Archives, Cincinnati
AJHS	American Jewish Historical Society, Waltham
BAdv	*Boston Advocate* (original name of the *Jewish Advocate)*
BHHC	Beth Hamidrash Hagadol Cemetery, West Roxbury
BHO	Boston Hebrew Observer
BPL	Boston Public Library
BPS	Department of Implementation, Boston Public Schools
BRA	Research Division, Boston Redevelopment Authority
BSB	*Bay State Banner*
Chron	*Boston Chronicle*
CJP	Combined Jewish Philanthropies Papers, AJHS
CMTA	Archives, Congregation Mishkan Tefila, Newton
CSHCA	Columbia–Savin Hill Civic Association Papers, UMBA
CSM	*Christian Science Monitor*
DorCN	*Dorchester Community News*
EDM	Archives, Episcopal Diocese of Massachusetts
FH	Freedom House, Roxbury
Glbpm	*Boston Evening Globe*
GlbSun	*Boston Sunday Globe*
Globe	*Boston Globe*
HC	Library, Hebrew College, Brookline
Her	*Boston Herald*
HerAm	*Boston Herald American*
HerTrv	*Boston Herald Traveler*
HH	Hecht Neighborhood House Papers, AJHS
HTrvSun	*Sunday Herald Traveler*
HUA	Harvard University Archives
HUL	Loeb Library, Harvard University

HUM	Map Collection, Harvard University
HUW	Widener Library, Harvard University
JAdv	*Jewish Advocate*
JCC	Jewish Community Council of Metropolitan Boston Papers, AJHS
JewH	*Jewish Herald*
Jrnl	*Boston Journal*
JTS	Special Collections, Jewish Theological Seminary, New York
JWB	Jewish Welfare Board Studies of Boston, AJHS
MSA	Massachusetts State Archives
MSL	Massachusetts State Library
NYT	*New York Times*
Post	*Boston Post*
RCAB	Archives, Roman Catholic Archdiocese of Boston
RCCP	Office of Clergy Personnel, Roman Catholic Archdiocese of Boston
RCSEC	*Roxbury Citizen and the South End Citizen*
RCSO	Catholic School Office, Boston
RecAm	*Boston Record-American*
Record	*Boston Record*
SJS	Library, St. John's Seminary
SPNEA	Society for the Preservation of New England Antiquities
TBC	Twelfth Baptist Church, Roxbury
Transcript	*Boston Evening Transcript*
Trav	*Boston Traveler*
UCPC	United Community Planning Corporation
UMBA	Archives, University of Massachusetts at Boston
URL	Rush Rhees Library, University of Rochester
WPA	Works Progress Administration, "Historical Records Survey," MSA

Notes

Prologue

1. *JAdv,* 11 Feb. 1926, 2:4.
2. "Roxbury an Area of Contrasts," section of a newspaper article, probably middle 1960s, CMTA.
3. St. Peter's Church Tower, capital expenditure authorization, 16 July 1980, St. Peter, AAPC; Most Rev. Thomas V. Daily to Rev. Robert G. Flynn, 24 July 1980, ibid.; *Globe,* letter to the editor, probably 18 Sept. 1980, in Rev. Frederick J. Ryan to Daily, 18 Sept. 1980, ibid.; St. Peter's Church Tower, capital expenditure authorization, 28 July 1981, ibid.; Daily to Flynn, 3 Aug. 1981, ibid.
4. St. Peter's School, School Survey, 1990–91, School Surveys and Reports, Office of Statistician, RCSO.
5. *JAdv,* 11 Feb. 1926, 2:4. See also Reevan Spiller to Benjamin B. Rosenberg and Howard Rubin, memorandum, 21 June 1968, box 175, CJP; Joshua Kastel, statement, 2 July 1968, ibid.; Rubin to Bernard D. Grossman, 2 July 1968, ibid.; Norman Leventhal to Grossman, 2 Aug. 1968, ibid.; "L'Dor V'Dor," *Mishkan Tefila News,* Dec. 1992.

1. Introduction

1. Catholic and Jewish families did not differ significantly in size. According to the 1950 census, the average household size in Jewish census tracts was 3.57 people; it was 3.66 people in Catholic census tracts. Children under the age of fourteen made up 20.8 percent of the population in Jewish tracts and 22.8 percent of the population in Catholic tracts. The following tracts in Dorchester and upper Roxbury were predominantly white and Jewish in 1950: T-6, T-7A, T-7B, T-8A, U-6A, U-6B, X-5A, X-5B, and X-6A. The following were predominantly white and Catholic: P-1C, P-2, P-3, P-4, P-6, T-1, T-2, T-3A, T-3B, T-4A, T-4B, T-5A, T-5B, T-8B, T-9, T-10, U-1, U-3, X-1, X-2, X-3A, X-3B, X-4A, X-4B, X-6B, and X-6C. See U.S. Department of Commerce, Bureau of the Census, *United States Census of Population,*

1950—Census Tract Statistics—Boston, Massachusetts, and Adjacent Area (Washington: Government Printing Office, 1952).

2. U.S. Census, *1950—Census Tract Statistics—Boston.* For the section of Mattapan that was heavily Jewish in 1950, I report data for census tract X-6A; for Savin Hill, I report data for census tracts T-1 and T-2. As the discussion in this chapter suggests, there appears to be no relationship between levels of segregation in former white-ethnic enclaves, like Mattapan and Savin Hill, and patterns of subsequent racial succession: though white Catholics and Jews maintained racially segregated neighborhoods for many years, their responses to the later entrance of African-American residents differed sharply. Census-based indexes of dissimilarity, such as those reported by Stanley Lieberson and Otis Dudley Duncan, measure only the extent to which two ethnic groups are segregated at a given time. Thus evidence that racial succession in later years would occur more quickly and peacefully in Chicago's Jewish than Irish neighborhoods is consistent with Lieberson and Duncan's finding that levels of residential dissimilarity between Jews and blacks were as high in 1930 and 1950 as those between Irish and blacks: see Duncan and Lieberson, "Ethnic Segregation and Assimilation," *American Journal of Sociology* 64 (1959), 374, also 373. See also Lieberson, *Ethnic Patterns in American Cities* (New York: Free Press of Glencoe, 1963), 120–132.

3. For the population of Dorchester and upper Roxbury in 1990, I combined the populations of census tracts 813, 815–821, 901–905, 907–924, and 1001–1011.02. See U.S. Department of Commerce, Bureau of the Census, *Census of Population and Housing, 1990,* machine-readable data file. Data from the federal census provide the basic framework for my analysis of racial, ethnic, and demographic change. In researching this book, I developed a separate computerized map of Boston for each census since 1940. Each of those six maps corresponds exactly to the six maps used by the federal census between 1940 and 1990 to report data at the level of the city block. To create each map, I had, first, to draw boundaries for each of more than 1,500 city blocks that matched block boundaries used by the census; then, second, to name each block with the name and number assigned to it by the census.

4. *NYT,* 15 Aug. 1971, 34. See also U.S. Senate Committee on the Judiciary, Subcommittee on Antitrust and Monopoly, *Competition in Real Estate and Mortgage Lending: Hearings—Part 1, Boston,* 92d Cong., 2d sess., 13–15 Sept. 1971; Ronald P. Formisano, *Boston against Busing: Race, Class, and Ethnicity in the 1960s and 1970s* (Chapel Hill: University of North Carolina Press, 1991), 73; Columbia–Savin Hill Civic Association, *The Neighbors* 163 (Nov. 1974), folder 33, box 3, CSHCA.

5. John A. McDermott, "Invitation to Leadership: The Parish and the Changing Neighborhood," *Interracial Review* 32 (Sept. 1959), 158, quoted in John T. McGreevy, *Parish Boundaries: The Catholic Encounter with Race in the Twentieth-Century Urban North* (Chicago: University of Chicago Press, 1996), 132. See also Peter Beinart, "Boston Diarist," *New Republic,* 24 Feb. 1997, 42.

6. Ernest W. Burgess, "Residential Segregation in American Cities," *Annals of the American Academy of Political and Social Science* 140 (Nov. 1928), 112; Malcolm X, with the assistance of Alex Haley, *The Autobiography of Malcolm X* (1965; rpt. New York: Ballantine, 1992), 408. See also Jonathan Rieder, *Canarsie: The Jews and Italians of Brooklyn against Liberalism* (Cambridge: Harvard University Press, 1985), 27; Harvey Luskin Molotch, *Managed Integration: Dilemmas of Doing Good in the City* (Berkeley and Los Angeles: University of California Press, 1972), 91, n.11; Yona Ginsberg, *Jews in a Changing Neighborhood: The Study of Mattapan* (New York: Free Press, 1975), 55, n.63.

7. McGreevy, *Parish Boundaries,* 103. See also Arnold R. Hirsch, *Making the Second Ghetto: Race and Housing in Chicago, 1940–1960* (Cambridge: Cambridge University Press, 1983), 84–99, 185–200; Thomas J. Sugrue, "Crabgrass-Roots Politics: Race, Rights, and the Reaction against Liberalism in the Urban North, 1940–1964," *Journal of American History* 82 (1995), 551–578; Sugrue, *The Origins of the Urban Crisis: Race and Inequality in Postwar Detroit* (Princeton: Princeton University Press, 1996), 241–246; J. Anthony Lukas, *Common Ground: A Turbulent Decade in the Lives of Three American Families* (New York: Knopf, 1985); Formisano, *Boston against Busing.*

8. Douglas S. Massey and Nancy A. Denton, *American Apartheid: Segregation and the Making of the Underclass* (Cambridge: Harvard University Press, 1993). But see also Stephan Thernstrom and Abigail Thernstrom, *America in Black and White: One Nation, Indivisible* (New York: Simon and Schuster, 1997).

9. Louis Wirth, *The Ghetto* (Chicago: University of Chicago Press, 1928), 245–246. See also Hirsch, *Making the Second Ghetto,* 195; John F. Stack, Jr., *International Conflict in an American City: Boston's Irish, Italians, and Jews, 1935–1944* (Westport, Conn.: Greenwood, 1979); Deborah Dash Moore, *At Home in America: Second Generation New York Jews* (New York: Columbia University Press, 1981), 12, 20–21.

10. In this section, I am referring to the rules that governed the Catholic parish before the reforms of the Second Vatican Council. The older rules governed everywhere into the 1960s and, even in the 1990s, are still largely respected in Dorchester's Catholic enclaves. The erosion of the

traditional territorial nature of the parish since the 1960s has undermined the ability of the Catholic parish to lend stability to neighborhoods: the institutional changes of the Second Vatican Council, like most institutional changes, have had unintended consequences.

11. As Jack Knight argues, the existence of a generally understood body of rules is fundamental to any definition of an institution: see Knight, *Institutions and Social Conflict* (Cambridge: Cambridge University Press, 1992), 2–3. While I consider the two sets of general rules defining congregations and churches to be institutions, I also consider each individual church and synagogue to be an institution; it is in this latter sense that I most often use the term in this book. Following Douglass C. North, of course, I could have referred to individual churches and synagogues as organizations: North, *Institutions, Institutional Change and Economic Performance* (Cambridge: Cambridge University Press, 1990), 4–5. But I have chosen to refer to them as institutions because each incorporates in its own constitutional framework a specific, unique form of the general rules, and its members operate within that specific understanding. This definition is consistent with Randall L. Calvert's theory of institutions as equilibria. He argues that "an equilibrium may represent a formally designed organization or an informal understanding about expected behavior, or any level of formality in between": see Calvert, "The Rational Choice Theory of Social Institutions: Cooperation, Coordination, and Communication," draft 1.2, paper originally prepared for presentation to the Inaugural Conference of the Wallis Institute for Political Economy, University of Rochester, Dec. 1992, 61. Knight argues that a church "can be conceptualized as both an institution and an organization": see Knight, *Institutions and Social Conflict*, 3.

12. H. Paul Douglass, *The Springfield Church Survey: A Study of Organized Religion with Its Social Background* (New York: George H. Doran, 1926), 282.

13. Claris Edwin Silcox and Galen M. Fisher, *Catholics, Jews, and Protestants: A Study of Relationships in the United States and Canada* (New York: Harper and Brothers, 1934), 69, as quoted in McGreevy, *Parish Boundaries,* 21; H. Paul Douglass, *The St. Louis Church Survey: A Religious Investigation with a Social Background* (New York: George H. Doran, 1924), 61. See also McGreevy, *Parish Boundaries,* 19–20.

14. Nancy Tatom Ammerman, *Congregation and Community* (New Brunswick, N.J.: Rutgers University Press, 1997), 330.

15. Thomas C. Schelling, "A Process of Residential Segregation: Neighborhood Tipping," in *Racial Discrimination in Economic Life,* ed. Anthony H. Pascal (Lexington, Mass.: Lexington Books, 1972), 175.

16. Albert O. Hirschman, *Exit, Voice, and Loyalty: Responses to Decline in*

Firms, Organizations, and States (Cambridge: Harvard University Press, 1970), 79.

17. The following parishes existed in Dorchester and upper Roxbury in the 1950s: St. Ambrose, St. Angela, St. Ann, St. Brendan, St. Christopher, St. Gregory, St. John (which included two churches, St. John's Church and the mission church of St. Hugh), St. Joseph, St. Kevin, St. Leo, St. Margaret, St. Mark, St. Mary of the Angels, St. Matthew, St. Paul, St. Peter, and St. William. Of the seventeen parishes, all but four supported schools: St. Christopher, St. Leo, St. Mary of the Angels, and St. Paul. St. John–St. Hugh's Parish, which supported two churches from its establishment at the turn of the century through the late 1960s, now maintains only one parish church; it is this same parish that closed its elementary school. In 1995, the parishes of St. Kevin and St. Paul merged, forming the new Holy Family Parish.

18. The Jewish Memorial Hospital, which is still located in upper Roxbury, was never a significant neighborhood institution.

19. Kenneth A. Shepsle, "Discretion, Institutions, and the Problem of Government Commitment," in *Social Theory for a Changing Society,* ed. Pierre Bourdieu and James S. Coleman (Boulder and New York: Westview Press and Russell Sage Foundation, 1991), 254.

20. Schelling, "A Process of Residential Segregation"; Thomas C. Schelling, "On the Ecology of Micromotives," in *The Corporate Society,* ed. Robin Marris (New York: John Wiley, 1974); Schelling, *Micromotives and Macrobehavior* (New York: Norton, 1978).

21. Robert Huckfeldt, Eric Plutzer, and John Sprague, "Alternative Contexts of Political Behavior: Churches, Neighborhoods, and Individuals," *Journal of Politics* 55 (1993), 365–381; Sidney Verba, Kay Lehman Schlozman, and Henry E. Brady, *Voice and Equality: Civic Voluntarism in American Politics* (Cambridge: Harvard University Press, 1995), 304–333; Robert D. Putnam, *Making Democracy Work: Civic Traditions in Modern Italy* (Princeton: Princeton University Press, 1993); Putnam, "Bowling Alone: America's Declining Social Capital," *Journal of Democracy* 6 (1995), 65–78. See also Ammerman, *Congregation and Community,* 362–367.

22. Robert E. Park, "Community Organization and the Romantic Temper," *Journal of Social Forces* 3 (1925), 674. See also Richard P. Taub, D. Garth Taylor, and Jan D. Dunham, *Paths of Neighborhood Change: Race and Crime in Urban America* (Chicago: University of Chicago Press, 1984), 182; Hirsch, *Making the Second Ghetto,* 135–170; Jennifer L. Hochschild, *The New American Dilemma: Liberal Democracy and School Desegregation* (New Haven: Yale University Press, 1984), 56; Molotch, *Managed Integration,* 90–91; S. Joseph Fauman, "Housing Discrimination, Changing Neighbor-

hoods, and Public Schools," *Journal of Social Issues* 13:4 (1957), 21–30; Brian J. L. Berry and John D. Kasarda, *Contemporary Urban Ecology* (New York: Macmillan, 1977), 52; Anthony Downs, *Neighborhoods and Urban Development* (Washington: Brookings, 1981), 19; Christine H. Rossell, "Desegregation Plans, Racial Isolation, White Flight, and Community Response," in *The Consequences of School Desegregation,* ed. Christine H. Rossell and Willis D. Hawley (Philadelphia: Temple University Press, 1983), 27; Christine H. Rossell, "Is It the Busing or the Blacks?" *Urban Affairs Quarterly* 24 (1988), 138–148; Formisano, *Boston against Busing,* 203–221; William Julius Wilson, *The Truly Disadvantaged: The Inner City, the Underclass, and Public Policy* (Chicago: University of Chicago Press, 1987).

23. William L. Yancey and Eugene P. Ericksen, "The Antecedents of Community: The Economic and Institutional Structure of Urban Neighborhoods," *American Sociological Review* 44 (1979), 255; Putnam, *Making Democracy Work,* 107–109; Verba, Schlozman, and Brady, *Voice and Equality,* 320–325. The most important work relating churches to communities emphasizes the effects of community change on religious institutions rather than the ways in which religious institutions shape patterns of residential mobility: see Douglass, *1000 City Churches: Phases of Adaptation to Urban Environment* (New York: George H. Doran, 1926); H. Paul Douglass, *The Church in the Changing City: Case Studies Illustrating Adaptation* (New York: George H. Doran, 1927); and Ammerman, *Congregation and Community.*

24. Hirsch, *Making the Second Ghetto,* 165; Hillel Levine and Lawrence Harmon, *The Death of an American Jewish Community: A Tragedy of Good Intentions* (New York: Free Press, 1992), 50, also 44–65, 201.

25. Eleanor K. Caplan and Eleanor P. Wolf, "Factors Affecting Racial Change in Two Middle Income Housing Areas," *Phylon* 21 (1960), 232; Albert J. Mayer, "Russel Woods: Change without Conflict—A Case Study of Neighborhood Racial Transition in Detroit," in *Studies in Housing and Minority Groups,* ed. Nathan Glazer and Davis McEntire (Berkeley and Los Angeles: University of California Press, 1960), 212. See also Chester Rapkin and William G. Grigsby, *The Demand for Housing in Racially Mixed Areas: A Study of the Nature of Neighborhood Change* (Berkeley and Los Angeles: University of California Press, 1960), 19.

26. McGreevy, *Parish Boundaries,* 15. See also Andrew M. Greeley, *Neighborhood* (New York: Seabury Press, 1977), 11; Jay P. Dolan, *The American Catholic Experience: A History from Colonial Times to the Present* (Notre Dame: University of Notre Dame Press, 1992), 196–197.

27. Marion Booth and Ordway Tead, "Dorchester, Ward 16," in *The Zone of Emergence: Observations of the Lower Middle and Upper Working Class Com-*

munities of Boston, 1905–1914, ed. Robert A. Woods and Albert J. Kennedy, abr. and ed. Sam Bass Warner, Jr., 2d ed. (Cambridge: MIT Press, 1969), 149.

28. Kenneth T. Jackson, *Crabgrass Frontier: The Suburbanization of the United States* (New York: Oxford University Press, 1985), 175. See also Sam Bass Warner, Jr., *Streetcar Suburbs: The Process of Growth in Boston, 1870–1900,* 2d ed. (Cambridge: Harvard University Press, 1978).

29. Marshall Sklare, *Conservative Judaism: An American Religious Movement* (Glencoe, Ill.: Free Press, 1955), 57; Wirth, *The Ghetto,* 254–255. See also Rapkin and Grigsby, *Demand for Housing,* 12–13; Steven A. Riess, *Touching Base: Professional Baseball and American Culture in the Progressive Era* (Westport, Conn.: Greenwood Press, 1980), 102–110; Harold X. Connolly, *A Ghetto Grows in Brooklyn* (New York: New York University Press, 1977), 55–58; Alter F. Landesman, *Brownsville: The Birth, Development and Passing of a Jewish Community in New York,* 2d ed. (New York: Bloch, 1971), 308; Egon Mayer, *From Suburb to Shtetl: The Jews of Boro Park* (Philadelphia: Temple University Press, 1979), 21–29; Moore, *At Home in America,* 22–31, 72, 78–80.

30. Hirsch, *Making the Second Ghetto,* 196, also 193; McGreevy, *Parish Boundaries,* 84. See also Levine and Harmon, *Death of an American Jewish Community,* chap. 1; Verlyn Klinkenborg, *The Last Fine Time* (New York: Knopf, 1991); Alan Ehrenhalt, *The Lost City: Discovering the Forgotten Virtues of Community in the Chicago of the 1950s* (New York: Basic Books, 1995); Sugrue, *Origins of the Urban Crisis;* Irving Cutler, *The Jews of Chicago: From Shtetl to Suburb* (Urbana and Chicago: University of Illinois Press, 1996), 209–233; Rieder, *Canarsie,* 52–53; Jim Sleeper, *The Closest of Strangers: Liberalism and the Politics of Race in New York* (New York: Norton, 1990), 142; Rapkin and Grigsby, *Demand for Housing,* 12–13.

31. Ehrenhalt, *Lost City;* Thomas Byrne Edsall with Mary D. Edsall, *Chain Reaction: The Impact of Race, Rights, and Taxes on American Politics* (New York: Norton, 1991); Rieder, *Canarsie;* Allen J. Matusow, *The Unraveling of America: A History of Liberalism in the 1960s* (New York: Harper and Row, 1984); Nicholas Lemann, *The Promised Land: The Great Black Migration and How It Changed America* (New York: Knopf, 1991); Wilson, *Truly Disadvantaged;* Hirsch, *Making the Second Ghetto;* Sugrue, "Crabgrass-Roots Politics"; Sugrue, *Origins of the Urban Crisis.*

32. The most prominent exception is the University of Massachusetts, Boston, which was built on Columbia Point, in Dorchester, in the 1970s. Not only is the university relatively new but it stands in an area that is physically detached and disconnected from the rest of Dorchester. Since the completion of the university, the John Fitzgerald Kennedy Library and Massa-

chusetts State Archives have been built nearby on Columbia Point. With the exception of a few small hospitals, there are not now and there have not been in the past any other major institutions in Dorchester or upper Roxbury.

2. Class, Crime, Homes, and Banks

1. Nathan Glazer and Daniel Patrick Moynihan, *Beyond the Melting Pot: The Negroes, Puerto Ricans, Jews, Italians, and Irish of New York City,* 2d ed. (Cambridge: MIT Press, 1970), 143. See also Anthony Downs, *Neighborhoods and Urban Development* (Washington: Brookings, 1981), 42–43; Robert Huckfeldt, *Politics in Context: Assimilation and Conflict in Urban Neighborhoods* (New York: Agathon, 1986), 87; Stephan Thernstrom, *The Other Bostonians: Poverty and Progress in the American Metropolis, 1880–1970* (Cambridge: Harvard University Press, 1973), 151–175.

2. The 1930 census does not report median or mean rents by census tracts. Instead, the 1930 census reports the number of dwelling units within each of ten rental categories (e.g., $20.00–29.99, 30.00–49.99, 50.00–74.99). To calculate an average rent for each census tract, I multiplied the number of homes within each category by that category's median rent (e.g., $25.00, 40.00, 62.50). For census data, see [U.S. Department of Commerce, Bureau of the Census, and] Boston Health Department, "Census Tract Data, [Boston,] 1930 Census," unpublished tables, UCPC, BRA, BPL; U.S. Department of Commerce, Bureau of the Census, *16th Census of the United States, 1940—Population and Housing—Statistics for Census Tracts, Boston, Mass.* (Washington: Government Printing Office, 1942); U.S. Department of Commerce, Bureau of the Census, *United States Census of Population, 1950—Census Tract Statistics—Boston, Massachusetts, and Adjacent Area* (Washington: Government Printing Office, 1952). See also Gerald H. Gamm, *The Making of New Deal Democrats: Voting Behavior and Realignment in Boston, 1920–1940* (Chicago: University of Chicago Press, 1989), 203–213.

3. U.S. Department of Commerce, Bureau of the Census, *U.S. Censuses of Population and Housing, 1960—Census Tracts—Boston, Mass. Standard Metropolitan Statistical Area* (Washington: Government Printing Office, 1962). I do not report data for census tracts whose populations in 1960 were majority nonwhite; thus most of the tracts in Roxbury are left blank on this map. The 1960 census reports data separately for nonwhites for census tracts that contained at least 400 nonwhites. For those tracts, I report data for the white population only. For other tracts, I report data for the whole population.

4. Morris Axelrod, Floyd J. Fowler, Jr., and Arnold Gurin, *A Community Survey for Long Range Planning: A Study of the Jewish Population of Greater Boston* (Boston: Combined Jewish Philanthropies of Greater Boston, 1967), 180.

5. *Glbpm,* 27 May 1970, 3. See also *Her,* 28 May 1970, 1, 3; *Globe,* 28 May 1970, 1; *JAdv,* 3 July 1969, 1, 11, 15; *HerTrv,* 4 July 1969, 8; *JAdv,* 10 July 1969, 1, 14, 2:2.

6. *Her,* 28 May 1970, 3.

7. Rev. Ernest P. Pearsall to Rt. Rev. Thomas J. Finnegan, Jr., 18 Oct. 1970, St. Ann, AAPC.

8. Kenneth T. Jackson, *Crabgrass Frontier: The Suburbanization of the United States* (New York: Oxford University Press, 1985), 213.

9. "Report on the Mattapan Organization," May 1968, box 76, JCC; Columbia–Savin Hill Civic Association, minutes of meeting, 1 May 1972, folder 6, box 1, CSHCA; *DorCN,* 1 Aug. [1974], 6; *DorCN,* May 1975, 3.

10. "Mattapan Report, (belated)," 5 July 1967, box 76, JCC; Steering Committee, Mattapan Organization, minutes of meeting, 6 July 1967, ibid.

11. Columbia Civic Association, minutes of meeting, 12 Jan. 1970, folder 4, box 1, CSHCA; *DorCN,* 15 Apr. [1974], 1, 9.

12. "Mattapan," 9 Aug. 1967, box 76, JCC.

13. Hillel Levine and Lawrence Harmon, "Profits and Prophets: Overcoming Civil Rights in Boston," *Tikkun* 3 (July/Aug. 1988), 45–48. See also *Globe,* 3 June 1971, 44; *Her,* 11 June 1971, 4; *NYT,* 15 Aug. 1971, 34; *Globe,* 15 Aug. 1971, 1, 21; *HerTrv,* 26 Aug. 1971, 1, 3; *JAdv,* 9 Sept. 1971, 1, 15; U.S. Senate Committee on the Judiciary, Subcommittee on Antitrust and Monopoly, *Competition in Real Estate and Mortgage Lending: Hearings—Part 1, Boston,* 92d Cong., 2d sess., 13–15 Sept. 1971; *HerTrv,* 14 Sept. 1971, 2; *Globe,* 15 Sept. 1971, 8; *Globe,* 16 Sept. 1971, 9; *JAdv,* 16 Sept. 1971, 5; Rachel G. Bratt, "A Home Ownership Survey: A Report on the Boston Banks Urban Renewal Group," report prepared for the Boston Model City Administration, Jan. 1972; *Globe,* 4 Apr. 1972, 1, 16; *Globe,* 5 Apr. 1972, 39; *Globe,* 29 Apr. 1972, 1, 6; Yona Ginsberg, *Jews in a Changing Neighborhood: The Study of Mattapan* (New York: Free Press, 1975), 38–43; Francis Russell, "How to Destroy a Suburb," *National Review,* 1 Oct. 1976, 1062–1064, 1081; "Jews in a New World," reprint of articles originally published in the *Globe,* 17–21 Feb. 1985, 6; *JAdv,* 13–19 Dec. 1991, 1, 24; Hillel Levine and Lawrence Harmon, *The Death of an American Jewish Community: A Tragedy of Good Intentions* (New York: Free Press, 1992); *JAdv,* 20–26 Dec. 1991, 11; *Globe,* 13 Jan. 1992, 13, 24; *JAdv,* 31 Jan.–6 Feb. 1992, 8; Nathan Glazer, "Goyz N the Hood," *New Republic,* 2 Mar. 1992, 38–40; Daniel J. Elazar, "Why the Neighborhood Went," *Jerusalem Report,*

21 May 1992, 57–58; Gerald H. Gamm, "Exploding Myths Surrounding Exodus of Boston Jewry," *JAdv,* 27 Mar.–2 Apr. 1992, 11; Lawrence Harmon and Hillel Levine, "A Response to Gerald Gamm," *JAdv,* 10–16 Apr. 1992, 11; Gerald H. Gamm, "Facts vs. Myth about Boston Jewish Exodus," *JAdv,* 1–7 May 1992, 9; Richard M. Valelly, "Democratic Dreams," *Boston Review* 17:5 (Sept./Oct. 1992), 20–21; Peter Beinart, "Boston Diarist," *New Republic,* 24 Feb. 1997, 42.

14. Glazer, "Goyz N the Hood," 38.

15. Levine and Harmon, *Death of an American Jewish Community,* 6.

16. Russell, "How to Destroy a Suburb," 1064; Levine and Harmon, "Profits and Prophets," 47, 46.

17. For a discussion of Jewish settlement in these neighborhoods, see Chapter 3.

18. Mark S. Israel, "Program for Neighborhood Stabilization in Mattapan-Dorchester," 6 Feb. 1967, box 76, JCC; Israel, "Program for Neighborhood Stabilization in Mattapan-Dorchester," 15 Mar. 1967, ibid.; Mattapan Organization, newsletter, unpublished draft, Mar. 1968, ibid.; *Globe,* 3 Aug. 1967, 8. See also Israel to Real Estate Committee, Mattapan Organization, 3 Aug. 1967, box 76, JCC; Mr. Y., Wellington Hill St., to Mattapan Homeowners and Residents, summer 1967, ibid.; Israel to James Bishop, 8 Aug. 1967, ibid.; "Mattapan," 9 Aug. 1967, ibid.; Israel to Sam Messina, 10 Aug. 1967, box 79, JCC.

19. In December 1967, the *Christian Science Monitor* reported that Mattapan "has a recently visible 5 percent Negro population": see *CSM,* 8 Dec. 1967, 10. In May 1968, the Mattapan Organization stated that 5 percent of Mattapan's population was black and estimated the total population of Mattapan at "about 20–25,000 persons": see "Report on the Mattapan Organization," May 1968, box 76, JCC. The Mattapan Organization defined Mattapan as a neighborhood covering a large territory: for the defined boundaries, see Constitution and By-laws of the Mattapan Organization, first draft, 19 Oct. 1967, box 76, JCC; *HTrvSun,* 5 Jan. 1969, 46. That area corresponded to the 1960 census tracts of X-6A, X-6B, and Z-1A, and to the 1970 tracts of 1010, 1011, and 1404. The total population of these three tracts rose from 25,313 in 1960 to 27,977 in 1970: U.S. Census, *1960—Census Tracts, Boston;* U.S. Department of Commerce, Bureau of the Census, *1970 Census of Population and Housing—Census Tracts—Boston, Mass. Standard Metropolitan Statistical Area* (Washington: Government Printing Office, 1972). If 5 percent of Mattapan's population was black in the winter of 1967–1968 and if the total population of Mattapan was at least 25,000, then about 1,250 blacks lived in Mattapan at the time. The *Sunday Herald Traveler* reported that blacks made up 5 percent of

Mattapan's entire population, but added that the figure was probably "closer to 20 per cent" in a "smaller subdivision" of Mattapan, apparently a reference to census tract X-6A/1011: see *HTrvSun,* 5 Jan. 1969, 46. The total population of that tract rose from 9,204 in 1960 to 9,428 in 1970: U.S. Census, *1960—Census Tracts, Boston;* U.S. Census, *1970—Census Tracts, Boston.* If the *Herald Traveler* was correct, more than 1,850 blacks lived in the tract. The *Herald Traveler*'s story appeared in January 1969, but I believe—given the continued use of the 5 percent estimate—that the numbers were outdated, more nearly approximating the racial composition of Mattapan in the winter of 1967–1968. Given these various sources, it seems reasonable to estimate that about 1,500 blacks lived in Mattapan by the end of 1967. If anything, this estimate may be low. The 1970 federal census reported that Mattapan already had a substantial black population in 1965: of 4,453 blacks who lived in tracts 1010 and 1011 in 1970 and who were at least five years of age, 534 had been living in the same house in 1965: see U.S. Census, *1970—Census Tracts, Boston,* P-166. That almost all of Mattapan's blacks lived in census tract X-6A/1011 in 1967 is evident not only from discussions of racial change and panic selling in the period 1967–1970 but from the 1970 census: almost 90 percent of all blacks in Mattapan in 1970 lived in that tract, and 94 percent of those living in the same house between 1965 and 1970 lived in that tract. The rate of African-American in-migration to Mattapan, at least through 1967, was slower than the rate of Jewish out-migration from Mattapan. Jews leaving Mattapan were replaced not just by blacks but by low-income white Catholics: see Mark S. Israel, "Program for Neighborhood Stabilization in Mattapan-Dorchester," 6 Feb. 1967, box 76, JCC; Israel, "Evelyn St., Mattapan," 8 Nov. 1967, ibid. See also Chapter 10, n.38.

20. "Tax assessor matter—Mattapan," 1 Apr. 1968, box 76, JCC.
21. "Report on the Mattapan Organization," May 1968, box 76, JCC.
22. Executive Board, Mattapan Organization, minutes of meeting, 5 Sept. 1968, box 76, JCC.
23. *NYT,* 15 Aug. 1971, 34; *Globe,* 4 Apr. 1972, 1; U.S. Senate Committee on the Judiciary, Subcommittee on Antitrust and Monopoly, *Competition in Real Estate and Mortgage Lending,* 26. See also Levine and Harmon, *Death of an American Jewish Community,* 6; Beinart, "Boston Diarist," 42.
24. *Globe,* 3 June 1971, 44; U.S. Senate Committee on the Judiciary, Subcommittee on Antitrust and Monopoly, *Competition in Real Estate and Mortgage Lending,* maps following pp. 340, 410, 490; Bratt, "Home Ownership Survey," map following p. 5; Levine and Harmon, *Death of an American Jewish Community,* 178–179.
25. U.S. Senate Committee on the Judiciary, Subcommittee on Antitrust and

Monopoly, *Competition in Real Estate and Mortgage Lending,* 284; Levine and Harmon, *Death of an American Jewish Community,* 176.

26. This assumption arose as people emphasized only the sections of Mattapan included within the BBURG line, in the process diverting attention from the rest of the BBURG territory. See, for example, *Globe,* 5 Apr. 1972, 39; Levine and Harmon, *Death of an American Jewish Community,* 178–179; U.S. Senate Committee on the Judiciary, Subcommittee on Antitrust and Monopoly, *Competition in Real Estate and Mortgage Lending,* 284–285.

27. U.S. Senate Committee on the Judiciary, Subcommittee on Antitrust and Monopoly, *Competition in Real Estate and Mortgage Lending,* 8–9; *NYT,* 15 Aug. 1971, 34.

28. Sydney Gale to Benjamin B. Rosenberg, memorandum, 11 Sept. 1969, box 77, JCC.

29. "Confessions of a Blockbuster," *Metropolitan Real Estate Journal,* May 1987, 5; Bratt, "Home Ownership Survey," 11, 14.

30. Thomas C. Schelling, "A Process of Residential Segregation: Neighborhood Tipping," in *Racial Discrimination in Economic Life,* ed. Anthony H. Pascal (Lexington, Mass.: Lexington Books, 1972), 175.

31. Levine and Harmon, *Death of an American Jewish Community,* 195, 208.

32. According to the 1960 block-level census data, 671 housing units were owner occupied and 1,480 units were renter occupied in the area bounded by Harvard, Morton, Norfolk, and Walk Hill streets: see U.S. Department of Commerce, Bureau of the Census, *U.S. Census of Housing, 1960—City Blocks—Boston, Mass.* (Washington: Government Printing Office, 1961).

33. John T. McGreevy, *Parish Boundaries: The Catholic Encounter with Race in the Twentieth-Century Urban North* (Chicago: University of Chicago Press, 1996), 18; Thomas J. Sugrue, *The Origins of the Urban Crisis: Race and Inequality in Postwar Detroit* (Princeton: Princeton University Press, 1996), 244. See also Arnold R. Hirsch, *Making the Second Ghetto: Race and Housing in Chicago, 1940–1960* (Cambridge: Cambridge University Press, 1983), 189–195.

34. Stanley Lieberson, *Ethnic Patterns in American Cities* (New York: Free Press of Glencoe, 1963), 206–218.

35. Ibid.

3. Institutions and Neighborhood Change

1. Jonathan Rieder, *Canarsie: The Jews and Italians of Brooklyn against Liberalism* (Cambridge: Harvard University Press, 1985), 22; *JAdv,* 10 July 1969, 2; *JAdv,* 4 Dec. 1969, 2.

2. *JAdv,* 2 Apr. 1970, 4.

3. *JAdv*, 10 July 1969, 2:2.
4. Sam Bass Warner, Jr., *Streetcar Suburbs: The Process of Growth in Boston, 1870–1900,* 2d ed. (Cambridge: Harvard University Press, 1978), 158, 159. See also Howard P. Chudacoff, "A New Look at Ethnic Neighborhoods: Residential Dispersion and the Concept of Visibility in a Medium-Sized City," *Journal of American History* 60 (1973), 87–89; Kathleen Neils Conzen, "Immigrants, Immigrant Neighborhoods, and Ethnic Identity: Historical Issues," *Journal of American History* 66 (1979), 603–615.
5. *JAdv*, 5 Aug. 1910, 1; Francis Russell, *The Great Interlude: Neglected Events and Persons from the First World War to the Depression* (New York: McGraw-Hill, 1964), 99–100.
6. Thomas C. Schelling, "On the Ecology of Micromotives," in *The Corporate Society,* ed. Robin Marris (New York: John Wiley, 1974), 53, 55.
7. For the term, see Gerald D. Suttles, *The Social Construction of Communities* (Chicago: University of Chicago Press, 1972).
8. Eleanor Collins, telephone interview with author, 24 May 1993; *JAdv*, 20 May 1920, 1; *JAdv*, 15 Sept. 1921, 1, 8; *JAdv*, 27 July 1922, 4; Anshey Ames, box 110, WPA.
9. St. Mark Congregational Church, "Souvenir—Fiftieth Anniversary, The St. Mark Congregational Church of Boston, Incorporated, 1895–1945; The Twenty-fifth of the St. Mark Social Center, Incorporated," Congregational Library, American Congregational Association, 43; "Learning from the Landscape of the Past: Talking with Robert C. Hayden," *The Boston Foundation Report,* Fall 1994, 6. See also St. Mark Congregational Church, untitled history, Personal Papers of Joan Allen; St. Mark Congregational Church, "Saint Mark Congregational Church, 1895," history, probably 1983, Personal Papers of Judge Harry J. Elam.
10. *Guardian,* 8 July 1939, 1, also 3, 5; *Guardian,* 10 June 1939, 4, also 1. See also *Guardian,* 24 June 1939, 1, 5; *Globe,* 14 Mar. 1991, calendar, 11; Chester Rapkin, "The Seaver-Townsend Urban Renewal Area" (Boston: Boston Redevelopment Authority, 1962), 42–43.
11. Lawrence F. Berry, *Greenwood Memorial Church (Methodist Episcopal), Dorchester, Massachusetts: Its Ancestry . . . and Growth with the Neighborhood* (Roxbury: Warren Press, 1936), BPL, 23–24, 27; Boston City Directory, 1893–1902; *BAdv*, 14 Dec. 1916, 1; *The American Jewish Year Book, 5680* (Philadelphia: Jewish Publication Society of America, 1919), 388; Richard Heath, "The House of the Flock of the Righteous: The Song of Synagogue Adath Jeshurun," unpublished paper, 1991, AJHS, 2; Aaron Pinkney, "Milestone in the Roxbury Jewish Community," *JAdv*, 26 Oct. 1950, 8.
12. Marion Booth and Ordway Tead, "Dorchester, Ward 16," in *The Zone of Emergence: Observations of the Lower Middle and Upper Working Class Com-*

munities of Boston, 1905–1914, ed. Robert A. Woods and Albert J. Kennedy, abr. and ed. Sam Bass Warner, Jr., 2d ed. (Cambridge: MIT Press, 1969), 152, 157. See also George W. Bromley and Walter S. Bromley, *Atlas of the City of Boston—Roxbury* (Philadelphia: Bromley, 1899), BPL, HUM; Aaron Pinkney, "Pioneer Congregations of the North End," *JAdv,* 14 Apr. 1949, B:9; Pinkney, "Milestone in the Roxbury Jewish Community," 8; Heath, "House of the Flock of the Righteous," 2; Adath Jeshurun, box 110, WPA.

13. Pinkney, "Milestone in the Roxbury Jewish Community," 8; *JAdv,* 17 Feb. 1931, 1. See also Heath, "House of the Flock of the Righteous," 2; Pinkney, "Pioneer Congregations of the North End," B:9; *American Jewish Year Book, 5661* (1900), 280; Adath Jeshurun, box 110, WPA.

14. Pinkney, "Milestone in the Roxbury Jewish Community," 8; *BAdv,* 26 May 1905, 2. See also Heath, "House of the Flock of the Righteous," 2–3, 8–9; Pinkney, "Pioneer Congregations of the North End," B:9–10; *JAdv,* 17 Feb. 1931, 1; *Jrnl,* 17 Sept. 1906, 3. To estimate the Jewish population of upper Roxbury and Dorchester, I examined 1905 state census data for wards 16, 20, 21, and 24. I assumed that the number of Jews in these wards included nearly all first- and second-generation Russians, most Poles, and small numbers of Germans, English, Canadians, and native-born Americans. See Commonwealth of Massachusetts, Bureau of Statistics of Labor, *Census of the Commonwealth of Massachusetts, 1905,* vol. 1, *Population and Social Statistics* (Boston: Wright and Potter, 1909), xcii–civ.

15. *Jrnl,* 14 Sept. 1906, 2; *BAdv,* 21 Sept. 1906, 1. See also *BAdv,* 14 Sept. 1906, 4; *Jrnl,* 17 Sept. 1906, 3; *BAdv,* 21 Sept. 1906, 1; Heath, "House of the Flock of the Righteous," 10–11.

16. *JAdv,* 3 Sept. 1915, 3. See also Bromley, *Atlas—Roxbury,* 1906; Bromley, *Atlas—Dorchester,* 1910; Bromley, *Atlas—Roxbury,* 1915; Bromley, *Atlas—Dorchester,* 1918; Shara Tfilo, box 110, WPA.

17. *JAdv,* 10 Oct. 1913, 1; *JAdv,* 5 Dec. 1913, 1; *JAdv,* 3 July 1914, 1, 8; *JAdv,* 27 Aug. 1915, 5; *JAdv,* 15 May 1924, 1, 3; *JAdv,* 6 Dec. 1928, 4; *JAdv,* 13 Dec. 1928, 3:1, 3:5; Congregation Beth Hamidrash Hagadol, *Tenth Anniversary Souvenir Book, 1914–1924* (Boston: Monroe Service, 1924), Congregation Beth Hamidrash Hagadol Papers, AJHS, 10; Congregation Beth Hamidrash Hagodol, *25th Anniversary Celebration, 1915–1940,* Congregation Beth Hamidrash Hagadol Papers, AJHS; lists of synagogues, box 110, WPA; Beth Hamidrash Hagadol, box 110, WPA; Suffolk County Deeds 3756:70–71, 3764:31–32, 3854:103–107, 4464:124, 4511:1; Warner, *Streetcar Suburbs,* 106–116; Richard Walden Hale, Jr., *Tercentenary History of the Roxbury Latin School, 1645–1945* (Cambridge, Mass.: Riverside Press, 1946), 137–138, 142, 145.

18. Congregation Beth Hamidrash Hagadol, *Tenth Anniversary Souvenir Book,*

1914–1924, 10–11. See also *JAdv*, 5 Oct. 1922, 1; *JAdv*, 28 Apr. 1921, 3; Hale, *Tercentenary History of the Roxbury Latin School*, 146, 148–151; Suffolk County Deeds 4464:124, 4511:1.

19. *JAdv*, 6 Jan. 1911, 7. Until the spring of 1911, Beth El was called Avath Achim. See also *JAdv*, 2 Sept. 1910, 1; *JAdv*, 6 Oct. 1911, 5; *JAdv*, 23 Aug. 1912, 2; *Her*, 2 Sept. 1912, 3; *JAdv*, 6 Sept. 1912, 8; Avath Achim, box 110, WPA; Beth El, box 110, WPA; Boston City Directory, 1909; Boston 200 Corporation, *Dorchester*, Boston 200 Neighborhood History Series (Boston: Boston 200 Corporation, 1976), 42–43; Suffolk County Deeds 3528:99; *JAdv*, 11 Apr. 1963, 4. The 1910 federal census reported 2,833 Russian-born residents of Ward 20 (which included the Mount Bowdoin–Franklin Park district and most of the Blue Hill Avenue–Grove Hall and Franklin Field districts). From 1905 ward data and 1910 citywide data, I estimate that there were about 2,125 second-generation Russians in the ward in 1905 (i.e., that, in Ward 20, there were three-quarters as many second-generation as first-generation Russians). Allowing for small numbers of native-born Americans, Germans, Canadians, and English—and noting that Poles were not reported separately from Russians in 1910—I estimate that about 6,000 Jews (or 1,300–1,400 families) lived in the ward in 1910. Most of those Jews lived in the Blue Hill Avenue–Grove Hall district. Having consulted a 1910 atlas of property owners in the ward, I estimate that about one-quarter of these Jews lived in the Mount Bowdoin–Franklin Park district. See U.S. Department of Commerce, Bureau of the Census, *Thirteenth Census of the United States, Taken in the Year 1910*, vol. 2, *Population, 1910—Reports by States* (Washington: Government Printing Office, 1913), 890; Massachusetts *Census, 1905*, xcii–civ; Bromley, *Atlas—Dorchester*, 1910.

20. *JAdv*, 10 Feb. 1921, 8. See also *JAdv*, 11 Oct. 1917, 2; *JAdv*, 6 Nov. 1919, 5; *JAdv*, 8 Jan. 1920, 2; *JAdv*, 17 Nov. 1921, 8; *JAdv*, 22 Dec. 1921, 6; *JAdv*, 26 Oct. 1922, 6. I estimate that 7,700 Jews lived in Ward 19 in 1920: for the sources I used in making this estimate, see Chapter 8, n.11. Having consulted a 1918 atlas of property owners in the ward, I estimate that about three-quarters of these Jews lived in the Mount Bowdoin–Franklin Park district: see Bromley, *Atlas—Dorchester*, 1918.

21. Until late 1915, Hadrath Israel was called Hadrath Kodesh. See *JAdv*, 1 Mar. 1912, 2; *JAdv*, 27 Sept. 1912, 2; Hadreth Israel, box 110, WPA; Hadrath Israel, box 110, WPA; *JAdv*, 12 Mar. 1915, 2; *JAdv*, 19 Mar. 1915, 2; *JAdv*, 25 June 1915, 3; *JAdv*, 13 Dec. 1917, 2; *JAdv*, 28 Nov. 1918, 4; Suffolk County Deeds 3928:193, 4181:72. I estimate that 900 Jews lived in Ward 24 in 1910: for the sources I used in making this estimate, see n.19. I estimate that 11,000 Jews lived in Ward 21 in 1920: see Chapter 8, n.11.

22. I have located three accounts of Chai Odom's founding, two of which report that the congregation was organized in 1902. The WPA Historical Records Survey states that Chai Odom was organized in 1902 by "a group of members of the Congregation Adruth Israel" and began worshiping that year on Nightingale Street. And a recent history of the congregation, based entirely on an oral tradition, states that Chai Odom had been organized by a group of men worshiping "in a private home on Lorne St." who in 1902 applied for a charter to establish a synagogue on Nightingale Street. But neither of these sources can be accurate: first, no congregation called "Adruth Israel" (or "Hadrath Israel") existed in Boston in 1902; second, Lorne Street, originally called Lena Park, had not yet been laid out in 1902; third, Hadrath Israel, which had been worshiping on Lorne Street, moved to Mattapan in 1915; and fourth, the building and land on Nightingale Street were not acquired for Chai Odom until May 1917. Consequently, I reject the founding date offered in these two sources and instead follow a chronology published in a congregational news bulletin in the middle 1950s. This chronology states that Chai Odom had been organized in 1915 on Lorne Street and moved in 1917 to Nightingale Street. Chai Odom was first listed in the Boston City Directory in 1918. For sources on Chai Odom, see Congregation Chai Odom, chronology of congregation from Chai Odom news bulletin, probably 1956, Personal Papers of Esther Epstein; Chevra Chai Odom, box 110, WPA; Sylvia M. Widershien, "History of Chai Odom," in Congregation Chai Odom, *Banquet Program: Jan. 27, 1991,* Personal Papers of Rabbi Shloma Margolis, 6; Sylvia M. Widershien, telephone interviews with author, 3 Nov. 1991 and 23 Mar. 1992; Rabbi Shloma Margolis, interview with author, Brighton, Mass., 26 June 1991; Marvin Gorodetzer, telephone interviews with author, 23 Mar. 1992 and 24 Mar. 1992; Bromley, *Atlas—West Roxbury,* 1905; Boston City Directory, 1904, 1917–1918; Suffolk County Deeds 4040:159, 4108:84–88. For sources on Agudath Israel, see Agudath Israel, box 110, WPA; *JAdv,* 27 Oct. 1921, 1; *JAdv,* 3 Nov. 1921, 8; *JAdv,* 30 Aug. 1923, 3; *JAdv,* 17 Apr. 1924, 1; *JAdv,* 15 Apr. 1926, 3:4.

23. *JAdv,* 25 May 1922, 1; *JAdv,* 2 Nov. 1922, 3; *JAdv,* 31 May 1923, 1; *JAdv,* 22 Nov. 1923, 4, 5; *JAdv,* 20 Nov. 1924, 1.

24. Rev. Francis J. Butler to Abp. William O'Connell, 6 Nov. 1907, St. Leo, AAPC.

25. St. Angela's Parish, *St. Angela's, 1907–1982, Mattapan, Massachusetts: Anniversary Book, 75 Years,* 1983, St. Angela, AAPH; Robert H. Lord, John E. Sexton, and Edward T. Harrington, *History of the Archdiocese of Boston in the Various Stages of Its Development, 1604 to 1943* (New York: Sheed and Ward, 1944), iii:685; *Pilot,* 31 May 1919, 1.

26. St. John–St. Hugh's Parish, *Golden Jubilee Reunion, 1891–1941: St. John's–St. Hugh's Parish, Roxbury, Mass.,* 1941, Personal Papers of Rev. Laurence McGrath. See also Lord et al., *History of the Archdiocese of Boston,* iii:252–253, 686; *Globe,* 25 Nov. 1907, 3; Boston Catholic Directory, 1900–1902; "Parish Boundary Lines, 1871–1906," notebook, RCAB; *Pilot,* 13 June 1903, 5; Pulpit announcements, 15 Oct. 1911, 14 Apr. 1912, in St. Hugh's Church, Pulpit Announcements, 1911–1914, RCAB; Pulpit announcements, 35, 64, 79, 178, in St. Mary of the Angels' Parish, pulpit announcement book, St. Mary of the Angels' Rectory; *Pilot,* 12 Oct. 1907, 5; *Pilot,* 29 Feb. 1908, 5; *Pilot,* 14 Mar. 1908, 5.

27. Parish records, 1907, in St. Mary of the Angels' Parish, finance book, 1907–1930, St. Mary of the Angels' Rectory; St. John and St. Angela, 1908, AACC.

28. Rev. Francis J. Butler to Abp. William O'Connell, 21 July 1908, St. Leo, AAPC. See also letter dated 26 Aug. 1908, ibid.; Commission to Redistrict the Parishes of Dorchester and Roxbury, report, 14 Dec. 1908, "Parish Boundary Lines, 1871–1906," notebook, RCAB; St. John, 1908, 1912, AACC.

29. "Parish Boundary Lines, 1871–1906." See also Susan L. Emery, *A Catholic Stronghold and Its Making: A History of St. Peter's Parish, Dorchester, Massachusetts, and of Its First Rector, the Rev. Peter Ronan, P.R.* (Boston: Geo. H. Ellis, 1910), BPL, 31; Lord et al., *History of the Archdiocese of Boston,* iii:251, 683; St. Paul, 1908, AACC.

30. Rev. Francis J. Butler to Abp. William O'Connell, 6 Nov. 1907 and 21 July 1908, St. Leo, AAPC. See also "Parish Boundary Lines, 1871–1906."

31. "Parish Boundary Lines, 1871–1906." The only significant matter in the report unrelated to the Blue Hill Avenue area was the recommendation to create St. William's Parish, in Savin Hill.

32. Booth and Tead, "Dorchester," 156; Pulpit announcement, 3 June 1917, in St. Hugh's Church, Pulpit Announcements, 1914–1917, RCAB.

33. Rev. Charles A. Finnigan to Card. William O'Connell, 12 Nov. 1919, St. Mary of the Angels, AAPC. See also *Pilot,* 15 Nov. 1913, 1; *Globe,* 17 Nov. 1913, 8; Lord et al., *History of the Archdiocese of Boston,* iii:686; St. John–St. Hugh's Parish, *Golden Jubilee Reunion, 1891–1941.*

34. Rev. John E. O'Connell to Card. William O'Connell, probably Oct. 1932, St. John, AAPC.

35. Rev. Francis A. Cunningham to Card. William O'Connell, 13 Oct. 1915, St. Leo, AAPC; Cunningham to Rev. Richard J. Haberlin, 23 Nov. 1916, ibid. See also Cunningham to Haberlin, 27 Nov. 1916, ibid.

36. St. Leo's Catholic population declined sharply in size after the middle 1920s: see St. Leo, 1920–1935, AACC. For sources on Chai Odom, see

n.22. For sources on Linas Hazedek, see Linas Hazedek, box 110, WPA; lists of synagogues, box 110, WPA; *JAdv,* 3 Sept. 1925, 6.

37. Theodore H. White, *In Search of History: A Personal Adventure* (New York: Harper and Row, 1978), 28.

38. Ibid.; Rev. Leo J. Knapp to Card. William O'Connell, 20 Nov. 1925, St. Matthew, AAPC. See also Mrs. K., Tremlett St., to Card. Richard J. Cushing, 13 Apr. 1960, St. Mark, AAPB.

39. "Mattapan," 9 Aug. 1967, box 76, JCC. See also Ben Rosen, "The Trend of Jewish Population in Boston: A Study to Determine the Location of a Jewish Communal Building," *Monographs of Federated Jewish Charities of Boston* 1:1 (Jan. 1921), 11, 24–25; Hecht Neighborhood House, "Material Relative to Moving Hecht Neighborhood House from 22 Bowdoin Street, Boston to Home for Jewish Children, Canterbury Street, Dorchester," 19 June 1935, box 1, HH.

40. Rev. Charles A. Finnigan to Card. William O'Connell, 1 Sept. 1928, St. Mary of the Angels, AAPB. See also U.S. Department of Commerce, Bureau of the Census, *16th Census of the United States, 1940—Housing—Block Statistics, Boston* (Washington: Government Printing Office, 1942).

41. Abraham Weinstein, "Old Roxbury—A Reply to Barney Glazer," *JAdv,* 30 Aug. 1962, 9; Barney Glazer, "Barney Glazer's Glazed Bits: Recalling His Boston Youth," *JAdv,* 16 Aug. 1962, 15.

42. Yona Ginsberg, *Jews in a Changing Neighborhood: The Study of Mattapan* (New York: Free Press, 1975), 55, n.63.

43. St. Hugh's was a mission church, not a parish church. Also, unlike St. Leo's Parish, where Catholics maintained a geographically distinct enclave, the entire territory assigned to St. Hugh's was populated by Jews.

44. Rev. Richard Craig, comments on parish data form submitted to Personnel Board, Nov. 1968, St. Leo's Parish, Parish Files, RCCP.

45. Rev. Joseph A. Gaudet, brief description, St. Leo's Parish, 22 June 1971, St. Leo's Parish, Parish Files, RCCP.

46. St. Leo, 1962–1970, AACC.

47. Thomas J. Sugrue, e-mail to the author, 2 Jan. 1996. See also Sugrue, *The Origins of the Urban Crisis: Race and Inequality in Postwar Detroit* (Princeton: Princeton University Press, 1996), 214, 235–241, 247; Gerald Gamm, "City Walls: Neighborhoods, Suburbs, and the American City," paper prepared for presentation to the annual meeting of the American Political Science Association, New York, Sept. 1994; Peter H. Rossi and Robert A. Dentler, *The Politics of Urban Renewal: The Chicago Findings* (New York: Free Press, 1961); Arnold R. Hirsch, *Making the Second Ghetto: Race and Housing in Chicago, 1940–1960* (Cambridge: Cambridge University Press, 1983), 135–170.

48. The 1960 federal census reports the total number of elementary school children as well as the number attending public school. I summarized data for the following census tracts, which made up the white Catholic sections of Dorchester with parochial schools: P-1C, P-2, T-2, T-3A, T-3B, T-4A, T-4B, T-5A, T-9, T-10, X-1, X-2, X-3A, X-3B, X-4A, X-4B, X-5C, and X-6C. In this area, 6,895 of 12,901 schoolchildren attended public school. See U.S. Department of Commerce, Bureau of the Census, *U.S. Censuses of Population and Housing, 1960—Census Tracts—Boston, Mass. Standard Metropolitan Statistical Area* (Washington: Government Printing Office, 1962).

49. Isaac Leeser, "The Jews and Their Religion," in I. Daniel Rupp, ed., *An Original History of the Religious Denominations in the U.S.* (Philadelphia, 1844), 368: quoted in Abraham J. Karp, "Overview: The Synagogue in America—A Historical Typology," in *The American Synagogue: A Sanctuary Transformed,* ed. Jack Wertheimer (Cambridge: Cambridge University Press, 1987), 7–8. See also Jay P. Dolan, "Patterns of Leadership in the Congregation," in *American Congregations,* vol. 2: *New Perspectives in the Study of Congregations* (Chicago: University of Chicago Press, 1994), 240.

50. All Jews recognize that ten men constitute a minyan. In recent years, Reform and most Conservative congregations have regarded any ten adults, women as well as men, as a minyan.

51. Jay P. Dolan, *The American Catholic Experience: A History from Colonial Times to the Present* (Notre Dame: University of Notre Dame Press, 1992), 172. See also Dolan, "Patterns of Leadership," 241–250.

52. John T. McGreevy, *Parish Boundaries: The Catholic Encounter with Race in the Twentieth-Century Urban North* (Chicago: University of Chicago Press, 1996), 10, 19. See also Edward Kantowicz, "Church and Neighborhood," *Ethnicity* 7 (1980), 349.

53. William G. Tachau, "The Architecture of the Synagogue," *American Jewish Year Book,* 5687 (1926), 164–165. See also *Jewish Encyclopedia,* s.v. "synagogue"; *Encyclopaedia Judaica,* s.v. "synagogue"; Tachau, "Architecture of the Synagogue," 162; Abraham P. Bloch, "How Do You Sell a Synagogue?" *Jewish Digest,* Nov. 1966, 75–78.

4. Jubilee Celebrations, 1910

1. The title of the anniversary publication is Temple Mishkan Tefila, *Our Golden Jubilee, 1860–1910* (Boston: Congregation Mishkan Tefila, 1910), CMTA. The source of the 1860 date is not clear: in his history, which is featured in the publication, Abraham G. Daniels stated that the congregation of Mishkan Israel was formed on 18 August 1858. See Abraham G.

Daniels, "From Ghetto to Temple: Scraps of History in the Evolution of Mishkan Israel," in Temple Mishkan Tefila, *Our Golden Jubilee,* 7.

2. Through most of its twenty-year history, Shaaray Tefila was known as "Gates of Prayer," the English translation of its Hebrew name.

3. Daniels, "From Ghetto to Temple," 9, also 7. See also Gerald H. Gamm, "In Search of Suburbs: Boston's Jewish Districts, 1843–1994," in *The Jews of Boston: Essays on the Occasion of the Centenary (1895–1995) of the Combined Jewish Philanthropies of Greater Boston,* ed. Jonathan D. Sarna and Ellen Smith (Boston: Combined Jewish Philanthropies, 1995), 132–134. For the date of Mishkan Israel's founding, see Gerald H. Gamm, "Neighborhood Roots: Exodus and Stability in Boston, 1870–1990" (Ph.D. diss., Harvard University, 1994), 72, n.4.

4. Daniels, "From Ghetto to Temple," 11, also 9; *Post,* 28 Aug. 1871, 3. See also Suffolk County Deeds 888:20; *Her,* 25 Aug. 1871, 1.

5. Solomon Schindler, "Israelites in Boston: A Tale Describing the Development of Judaism in Boston" (1889; rpt. *JAdv,* 26 June 1952), A:11. See also Arthur Mann, ed., *Growth and Achievement: Temple Israel, 1854–1954* (Cambridge, Mass.: Riverside Press, 1954), 50–51; Albert Ehrenfried, "A Chronicle of Boston Jewry: From the Colonial Settlement to 1900," unpublished, 1963, AJHS, 359–363, 388–389; "Israel Cohen," in *History of the Jews of Boston and New England* (Boston: Jewish Chronicle Publishing Co., 1892), AJHS; Abraham P. Spitz, "How the Pioneer Jews of Boston Started First Congregation: History of Temple Ohabei Shalom and Subsequent Houses of Worship Recounted," *JAdv,* 26 June 1952, 3:19; Temple Ohabei Shalom, *The By-Laws of Temple Ohabei Shalom, Boston, Mass., Prefaced with an Historical Sketch* (Boston: Daniels Printing Company, 1907), HUW, 12–13; *JAdv,* 30 Sept. 1943, 6.

6. *BHO,* 27 Feb. 1885, 4; *Her,* 24 Feb. 1885, 2. See also Daniels, "From Ghetto to Temple," 13; Boston City Directory, 1877–1885; Shaaray Tefila, box 110, WPA.

7. *BHO,* 27 Feb. 1885, 4; *Her,* 24 Feb. 1885, 2; *Trav,* 16 Sept. 1854, as quoted in Ehrenfried, "Chronicle of Boston Jewry," 372–373, and Mann, *Growth and Achievement,* 27.

8. First Parish in Dorchester, *Dedication of the Sixth Meeting-House* (1897), 9. See also Dorchester Tercentenary Committee, *Dorchester Old and New: Tercentenary, 1630–1930* (Dorchester: Chapple Publishing Company, 1930), 10, 18–20, 37, 53, 63; First Church and Parish of Dorchester, *Proceedings of the Two Hundred and Fiftieth Anniversary of the Gathering in England, Departure for America, and Final Settlement in New England* (Boston: Geo. H. Ellis, 1880), HUW, 9, 61, 98; Mary Fifield King, *First Parish Church in Dorchester, Tercentenary Celebration, 1630–1930: The Story of the*

Church (1930), BPL, 1–2, 6–7; Boston 200 Corporation, *Dorchester,* Boston 200 Neighborhood History Series (Boston: Boston 200 Corporation, 1976), 15; Sam Bass Warner, Jr., *Streetcar Suburbs: The Process of Growth in Boston, 1870–1900,* 2d ed. (Cambridge: Harvard University Press, 1978), 43, 81, 158–159, 163; Sam Bass Warner, Jr., "Residential Development of Roxbury, West Roxbury and Dorchester, Massachusetts, 1870–1900" (Ph.D. diss., Harvard University, 1959), 10–11.

9. South Boston is a district distinct from Boston's South End, which is in Boston proper.

10. Susan L. Emery, *A Catholic Stronghold and Its Making: A History of St. Peter's Parish, Dorchester, Massachusetts, and of Its First Rector, the Rev. Peter Ronan, P.R.* (Boston: Geo. H. Ellis, 1910), BPL, 11, 13–14, 89; William H. Marnell, "The Parish," in William H. Marnell and Douglass Shand Tucci, *Saint Peter's Church, 1872–1972* (Boston: Fandel Press, 1972), 10; Michael Parise, *The History of Saint Gregory's Parish, Lower Mills, Dorchester and Milton, 1862–1987* (1987), St. Gregory's Rectory, 19.

11. Emery, *Catholic Stronghold,* 14, also 13, 90. See also Parise, *History of Saint Gregory's Parish,* 24, 29; James S. Sullivan, ed., *The Catholic Church of New England* (Boston: Boston and Portland Illustrated Publishing Company, 1895), RCAB, 72–73; Robert H. Lord, John E. Sexton, and Edward T. Harrington, *History of the Archdiocese of Boston in the Various Stages of Its Development, 1604 to 1943* (New York: Sheed and Ward, 1944), iii:246–247, 260, 714; Marnell, "The Parish," 10; *Pilot,* 30 Aug. 1873, 4.

12. Emery, *Catholic Stronghold,* 15, also 8. See also Marnell, "The Parish," 10–11; *Pilot,* 30 Aug. 1873, 4; Lord et al., *History of the Archdiocese of Boston,* iii:248. For a description of St. Gregory's Church as it stood in 1872, see Parise, *History of Saint Gregory's Parish,* 24–29.

13. Emery, *Catholic Stronghold,* 16, also 15. See also *Pilot,* 30 Aug. 1873, 4; Marnell, "The Parish," 10–12; Douglass Shand Tucci, "The Church," in Marnell and Tucci, *Saint Peter's Church, 1872–1972,* 36–38; Tucci, *The Second Settlement, 1875–1925: A Study in the Development of Victorian Dorchester* (Boston: Trustees of St. Margaret's Hospital, 1974), I:4.

14. *Pilot,* 23 Feb. 1884, 5. See also *Pilot,* 30 Aug. 1873, 4; Lord et al., *History of the Archdiocese of Boston,* iii:249; *Jrnl,* 18 Feb. 1884, 1; Emery, *Catholic Stronghold,* 9, 17–18; Marnell, "The Parish," 12; St. Peter's Parish, *Annual Reunion of St. Peter's Parish and Reception to the Pastor, Rev. Peter Ronan, P.R.* (1908), St. Peter, AAPH, 41.

15. Emery, *Catholic Stronghold,* 18, also 22; Sullivan, *Catholic Church of New England,* 175, also 179.

16. Schindler, "Israelites in Boston," A:18. See also Boston City Directory,

1885–1890; Daniels, "From Ghetto to Temple," 13; "Rabbi Jacob Feuer-licht," in *History of the Jews of Boston and New England.*

17. *Boston Jewish Chronicle,* Aug. 1891, as cited in David Kaufman, "Syna-gogues of Boston," draft dated 7 June 1993; Daniels, "From Ghetto to Temple," 13. The Massachusetts General Court authorized the consolida-tion in May 1895: see copy of the act in Jacob L. Sieve, *L'dor Vodor: From Generation to Generation—Congregation Mishkan Tefila, 1858–1983* (New-ton: Congregation Mishkan Tefila, 1983). The certificate of union issued by the Secretary of the Commonwealth is dated 23 August 1895: see Suffolk County Deeds 2481:43. A marble tablet placed in the Moreland Street Synagogue recorded the merger date as 1895: see Atereths Israel, box 110, WPA. Daniels, "From Ghetto to Temple," 13, stated that the merger took place in 1894. Subsequent congregational histories have gen-erally relied on Daniels and repeated the incorrect date: see, for example, Temple Mishkan Tefila, *Temple Mishkan Tefila: A History, 1858–1958* (New-ton: Temple Mishkan Tefila, 1958), CMTA, 16; Sieve, *L'dor Vodor,* 115.

18. Suffolk County Deeds 2481:40; Sanborn-Perris Map Co., *Insurance Maps of Boston, Massachusetts,* vol. 2 (New York: Sanborn-Perris Map Co., 1897), HUM; George W. Bromley and Walter S. Bromley, *Atlas of the City of Boston—Roxbury* (Philadelphia: Bromley, 1899), BPL, HUM; *Globe,* 6 Sept. 1898, 8; Boston City Directory, 1895–1899.

19. William I. Cole, "Introductory," in *The City Wilderness: A Settlement House Study,* ed. Robert A. Woods (Boston: Houghton Mifflin, 1898), 6.

20. *Globe,* 6 Sept. 1898, 8. See also *Her,* 6 Sept. 1898, 3; *Jrnl,* 6 Sept. 1898, 4; Daniels, "From Ghetto to Temple," 13.

21. *JAdv,* 11 June 1909, 1. See also Gamm, "In Search of Suburbs," 141; Daniels, "From Ghetto to Temple," 13–15; *GlbSun,* 12 May 1907, 17; John Daniels, *In Freedom's Birthplace: A Study of the Boston Negroes* (1914; rpt. New York: Arno Press and the New York Times, 1969), 143–148, 238–240, 250, 262; George Cary and Ordway Tead, "Roxbury Crossing, Wards 18 and 19," in *The Zone of Emergence: Observations of the Lower Middle and Upper Working Class Communities of Boston, 1905–1914,* ed. Robert A. Woods and Albert J. Kennedy, abr. and ed. Sam Bass Warner, Jr., 2d ed. (Cambridge: MIT Press, 1969), 127; Twelfth Baptist Church, *Dedicatory Programme: The New Twelfth Baptist Church, Corner Madison Street and Shawmut Ave., Boston, Massachusetts, Nov. 11 to Dec. 31, '06* (1906), TBC, 22; *JAdv,* 30 Sept. 1943, 6; *Globe,* 7 June 1903, 13; *Globe,* 8 June 1903, 12; *BAdv,* 23 Mar. 1906, 1; *BAdv,* 24 May 1907, 5.

22. This statement is based on a telephone conversation I had on 27 January 1992 with Noah Feldman and confirmed by a conversation I had on 11 August 1992 with Ely Razin.

23. *JAdv*, 11 June 1909, 3, also 1. See also Daniels, "From Ghetto to Temple," 13; Boston City Directory, 1904–1905.

24. Daniels, "From Ghetto to Temple," 15. See also Twelfth Baptist Church, *Dedicatory Programme* (1906), 22–23, 25, 27–29, 31–32; Suffolk County Deeds 3153:130; *BAdv*, 5 Oct. 1906, 6; *BAdv*, 12 Oct. 1906, 6; *BAdv*, 19 Oct. 1906, 6.

25. *JAdv*, 4 Sept. 1924, 5. See also Atereths Israel, box 110, WPA.

26. Daniels, "From Ghetto to Temple," 15. See also Suffolk County Deeds 3194:273; Bromley, *Atlas—Roxbury*, 1906. A marble tablet placed by Mishkan Tefila in the Moreland Street Temple stated that the building was purchased in March 1907 and dedicated in May: see Atereths Israel, box 110, WPA. The finest illustration of the structure is a sketch entitled "Moreland St Congregational Church" and dated, in pencil, "1886," Roxbury Engraving, SPNEA. Before moving into the Moreland Street Temple, the congregation leased space in a hall at 24 Warren Street, near Dudley Street in upper Roxbury: see *BAdv*, 19 Oct. 1906, 6; *BAdv*, 22 Mar. 1907, 6.

27. Temple Mishkan Tefila, *Dedication Souvenir of the Temple Mishkan Tefila, Moreland and Copeland Sts., Roxbury, Mass., Sunday, May 12th, 1907* (1907), box 7, Herman H. Rubenovitz Papers, JTS; *Globe*, 13 May 1907, 6. See also *GlbSun*, 12 May 1907, 17; *Post*, 12 May 1907, 11; *Her*, 13 May 1907, 3; *Jrnl*, 13 May 1907, 7.

28. Temple Mishkan Tefila, *Dedication Souvenir* (1907); Daniels, "From Ghetto to Temple," 15, also 13; *BAdv*, editorial, probably 17 May 1907, CMTA. See also Boston City Directory, 1905–1910; *Jrnl*, 13 May 1907, 7; *Her*, 13 May 1907, 3.

29. *JAdv*, 26 Aug. 1910, 4; Edward J. Bromberg to Herman H. Rubenovitz, 12 Sept. 1910, box 7, Herman H. Rubenovitz Papers, JTS; *JAdv*, 11 Nov. 1910, 1. See also *JAdv*, 7 Oct. 1910, 8; Joseph S. Phillips to Rubenovitz, 23 Oct. 1910, box 7, Herman H. Rubenovitz Papers, JTS.

30. Herman H. Rubenovitz, "My Rabbinate at Temple Mishkan Tefila: A History from 1910 to 1946," in Temple Mishkan Tefila, *Temple Mishkan Tefila: A History, 1858–1958* (Newton: Temple Mishkan Tefila, 1958), CMTA, 19–20. See also *JAdv*, 11 Nov. 1910, 1; *JAdv*, 18 Nov. 1910, 1; *JAdv*, 30 Dec. 1910, 1, 8; Sieve, *L'dor Vodor*, 10.

31. Daniels, "From Ghetto to Temple," 15, also 7. See also Temple Mishkan Tefila, *Our Golden Jubilee, 1860–1910*, "Roll of Members."

32. *JAdv*, 30 Dec. 1910, 1.

33. Ibid. See also *JAdv*, 16 Dec. 1910, 1; *JAdv*, 6 Jan. 1911, 7; Daniels, "From Ghetto to Temple."

34. Emery, *Catholic Stronghold*, 92–93. See also St. Peter's Parish, *Annual Reunion* (1908), 42.

35. Emery, *Catholic Stronghold*, 32. See also St. Peter, 1911, AACC. The territory originally assigned to St. Peter's Parish included St. Peter's, St. Margaret's, St. Leo's, St. Paul's, and St. William's parishes in 1910 as well as portions of St. John's and St. Ann's parishes.

36. Emery, *Catholic Stronghold*, 75, also 31, 40, 42. See also Marnell, "The Parish," 14–15.

5. Membership

1. *JAdv*, 2 May 1913, 1. See also Joseph S. Phillips to Herman H. Rubenovitz, 23 Oct. 1910, box 7, Herman H. Rubenovitz Papers, JTS; Edward J. Bromberg to Rubenovitz, 28 Apr. 1913, ibid. A full membership list, with addresses, is included in Congregation Mishkan Tefila, *Constitution and By-Laws of the Congregation Mishkan Tefila, Boston, Massachusetts* (Boston, 1913), CMTA.

2. Susan L. Emery, *A Catholic Stronghold and Its Making: A History of St. Peter's Parish, Dorchester, Massachusetts, and of Its First Rector, the Rev. Peter Ronan, P.R.* (Boston: Geo. H. Ellis, 1910), BPL, 75. See also St. Peter, 1911–1916, AACC.

3. T. Lincoln Bouscaren and Adam C. Ellis, *Canon Law: A Text and Commentary*, 3d rev. ed. (Milwaukee: Bruce Publishing Company, 1957), 76, also 735.

4. *Code of Canon Law: Latin-English Edition* (Washington: Canon Law Society of America, 1983), 197. See also R. Stephen Warner, "The Place of the Congregation in the Contemporary American Religious Configuration," in *American Congregations*, vol. 2: *New Perspectives in the Study of Congregations* (Chicago: University of Chicago Press, 1994), 77–80.

5. *JAdv*, 17 Sept. 1925, 2:6. See also *JAdv*, 12 Nov. 1925, 2; Horace Stern, "The Synagogue and Jewish Communal Activities," *The American Jewish Year Book, 5694* (Philadelphia: Jewish Publication Society of America, 1933), 162. Five of the congregation's directors lived in Dorchester, one man lived in a suburb north of Boston, and two men are listed in neither the Boston nor the Brookline directory. For the membership of the board of directors, see dedication plaque placed in the Seaver Street Temple, photograph, CMTA; "Dedication—Temple Mishkan Tefila, Seaver Street and Elm Hill Avenue, Roxbury, Massachusetts—Sunday, the Thirteenth of Sept., Nineteen hundred and twenty-five," booklet, CMTA. For the home address of each director, see Brookline Directory, 1925; Boston City Directory, 1925. I am grateful to Dan Gamm, who looked up all of these addresses.

6. William I. Cole, "The Church and the People," in *The City Wilderness: A Settlement House Study*, ed. Robert A. Woods (Boston: Houghton Mifflin,

1898), 204; *JAdv*, 7 Apr. 1927, 10. See also Hecht Neighborhood House, "Report on West End Population Trends," Jan. 1935, chart III, box 3, HH.

7. Albert J. Kennedy, "Roxbury, Ward 17," in *The Zone of Emergence: Observations of the Lower Middle and Upper Working Class Communities of Boston, 1905–1914*, ed. Robert A. Woods and Albert J. Kennedy, abr. and ed. Sam Bass Warner, Jr., 2d ed. (Cambridge: MIT Press, 1969), 145; Agudath Achim, box 110, WPA. See also *JAdv*, 29 Aug. 1913, 1; Boston City Directory, 1912–1919; Congregation Beth Hamidrash Hagadol, *Tenth Anniversary Souvenir Book, 1914–1924* (Boston: Monroe Service, 1924), Congregation Beth Hamidrash Hagadol Papers, AJHS, 94–99.

8. *JAdv*, 1 Apr. 1938, 5.

9. Rt. Rev. Walter J. Furlong to Rev. Ralph W. Farrell, 22 Oct. 1953, St. Margaret, AAPC.

10. Residents of Mattapan District, Milton, to Abp. William O'Connell, petition, probably early 1908, St. Angela, AAPC.

11. Mrs. C., Leahaven Rd., to the Chancellor, 29 May 1953, St. Gregory, AAPB.

12. James T. Cotter to Mrs. C., Leahaven Rd., 2 June 1953, St. Gregory, AAPB.

13. St. Mark's Parish, *75th Anniversary, St. Mark the Evangelist Parish, Dorchester, Mass., 1905–1980: An Illustrated History*, St. Mark, AAPH, 36.

14. Miss M., Dakota St., to Card. Richard J. Cushing, 20 Mar. 1959, St. Peter, AAPB.

15. Miss P., Bloomfield St., to Rt. Rev. Robert J. Sennott, 1 May 1959, St. Peter, AAPB.

16. Rt. Rev. Francis J. Sexton to Miss P., Bloomfield St., 4 May 1959, St. Peter, AAPB.

17. Mrs. L., Dakota St., to Card. Richard J. Cushing, Wednesday of Holy Week 1959, St. Peter, AAPB.

18. Bouscaren and Ellis, *Canon Law*, 149; Roman Catholic Archbishop of Boston, *Acta et Statuta Synodi Bostoniensis Septimae* (1953), §74; Rt. Rev. Francis J. Sexton to Miss P., Bloomfield St., 4 May 1959, St. Peter, AAPB. See also Wolfgang L. Grichting, *Parish Structure and Climate in an Era of Change: A Sociologist's Inquiry* (Washington: Center for Applied Research in the Apostolate, 1969), 2–4; Archdiocese of Boston, Eighth Synod, *Pastoral Plan for Mission* (Boston: Archdiocese of Boston, 1989), 18; *Code of Canon Law*, 195.

19. Roman Catholic Archbishop of Boston, *Acta et Statuta Synodi Bostoniensis Septimae*, §151, §53, §54, also §16, §73; Bouscaren and Ellis, *Canon Law*, 208, also 188, 197–198, 213. See also Joseph H. Fichter, *Social Relations in the Urban Parish* (Chicago: University of Chicago Press, 1954), 11–12; *Code of Canon Law*, 201–203.

20. Rt. Rev. Edward F. Hurley to Card. William O'Connell, 5 May 1926, St.

Matthew, AAPC; Hurley to O'Connell, 28 June 1926, ibid. See also Rev. Richard J. Haberlin to Hurley, 6 May 1926, ibid.

21. Douglass Shand Tucci, "The Church," in William H. Marnell and Douglass Shand Tucci, *Saint Peter's Church, 1872–1972* (Boston: Fandel Press, 1972), 35; *Pilot,* 31 May 1919, 1.

22. *New Catholic Encyclopedia,* s.v. "parish."

23. Rev. James Flavin, interview with author, St. William's Rectory, Dorchester, 10 Aug. 1991; Emery, *Catholic Stronghold,* 31, also 30; Chancellor to Rev. Charles N. Cunningham, 20 Sept. 1945, St. Paul, AAPC. See also Robert H. Lord, John E. Sexton, and Edward T. Harrington, *History of the Archdiocese of Boston in the Various Stages of Its Development, 1604 to 1943* (New York: Sheed and Ward, 1944), iii:251; Cunningham to the Chancery, 13 Nov. 1946, description of parish boundaries, St. Paul, AAPB; Chancellor to Cunningham, 24 Sept. 1945, St. Paul, AAPC; Cunningham to Chancellor, 25 Sept. 1945, ibid.

24. Congregation Beth Hamidrash Hagadol, *Tenth Anniversary Souvenir Book, 1914–1924,* 11; Congregation Beth Hamidrash Hagadol, *Year Book, 5683 (1922–1923)* (Boston: Monroe Service, n.d.), Congregation Beth Hamidrash Hagadol Papers, AJHS, 10.

25. Congregation Beth Hamidrash Hagadol, *Tenth Anniversary Souvenir Book, 1914–1924,* 16; *JAdv,* 31 May 1923, 4; *JAdv,* 7 June 1923, 4.

26. Congregation Beth Hamidrash Hagadol, *Year Book, 5683 (1922–1923),* 29. See also *JAdv,* 25 June 1925, 6. The congregation remodeled the frame structure that stood on the land that had been purchased for the new school: see *JAdv,* 31 Dec. 1925, 8; *JAdv,* 21 Jan. 1926, 6; *JAdv,* 13 Dec. 1928, 3:3.

27. Gerald H. Gamm, "Neighborhood Roots: Exodus and Stability in Boston, 1870–1990" (Ph.D. diss., Harvard University, 1994), 183, nn.85,86; 184, nn.87,88,89; and 185, n.90.

28. *JAdv,* 31 May 1923, 4. See also *Encyclopaedia Judaica,* s.v. "community"; Stern, "The Synagogue and Jewish Communal Activities," 160; Albert I. Gordon, *Jews in Suburbia* (Boston: Beacon Press, 1959), 88.

29. *JAdv,* 26 May 1911, 8.

30. Marshall Sklare, *Conservative Judaism: An American Religious Movement* (Glencoe, Ill.: Free Press, 1955), 42. See also Marshall Sklare and Joseph Greenblum, *Jewish Identity on the Suburban Frontier: A Study of Group Survival in the Open Society,* 2d ed. (Chicago: University of Chicago Press, 1979), 179–180; Cole, "The Church and the People," 225–227; Stern, "The Synagogue and Jewish Communal Activities," 158–160.

31. The following are the synagogues, with their locations in 1929: Hadrath Israel, Woodrow Avenue at the corner of Ashton Street; Agudath Israel,

Woodrow Avenue at the corner of Lucerne Street; Beth Hamedrosh Hago-
dol Adath Jacob, Woodrow Avenue at the corner of Don Street; Chevra
Shas, Ashton Street near Woodrow Avenue; and Anshi Volin, Harwood
Street at the corner of Lucerne Street. The Dorchester-Mattapan Hebrew
School was located at 170 Woodrow Avenue, at the corner of Willowood
Street.

32. *BAdv,* 23 Oct. 1908, 8; *BAdv,* 31 Aug. 1906, 8.

33. *JAdv,* 12 Sept. 1929, 2:2; *JAdv,* 5 Sept. 1930, 4. See also Deborah Dash
    Moore, *At Home in America: Second Generation New York Jews* (New York:
    Columbia University Press, 1981), 140–141; Beth S. Wenger, *New York
    Jews and the Great Depression: Uncertain Promise* (New Haven: Yale Univer-
    sity Press, 1996), 175–176.

34. *JAdv,* 27 Aug. 1915, 5; *JAdv,* 23 Aug. 1923, 1; *JAdv,* 29 Aug. 1930, 1. See
    also Abraham J. Karp, "Overview: The Synagogue in America—A Histori-
    cal Typology," in *The American Synagogue: A Sanctuary Transformed,* ed.
    Jack Wertheimer (Cambridge: Cambridge University Press, 1987), 14–15,
    18–19; Jeffrey S. Gurock, "The Orthodox Synagogue," in *The American
    Synagogue,* ed. Jack Wertheimer, 49–50.

35. *Jrnl,* 28 Sept. 1908, 1; *BAdv,* 23 Oct. 1908, 1. See also *BAdv,* 2 Oct. 1908, 1;
    BAdv, 16 Oct. 1908, 1.

36. *BAdv,* 16 Oct. 1908, 8, 1; *BAdv,* 23 Oct. 1908, 1; *BAdv,* 2 Oct. 1908, 1.

6. Rootedness

1. Susan L. Emery, *A Catholic Stronghold and Its Making: A History of St.
   Peter's Parish, Dorchester, Massachusetts, and of Its First Rector, the Rev. Peter
   Ronan, P.R.* (Boston: Geo. H. Ellis, 1910), BPL, 2, 92, 79, 94–95. See also St.
   Peter's Parish, *Annual Reunion of St. Peter's Parish and Reception to the
   Pastor, Rev. Peter Ronan, P.R.* (1908), St. Peter, AAPH, 41.

2. Emery, *Catholic Stronghold,* 2, caption for photograph following p. 92, also
   21, 79, 84, 85. See also *Pilot,* 23 Feb. 1884, 5.

3. *New Catholic Encyclopedia,* s.v. "churches, canon law of," "parish"; Ignazio
   M. Calabuig, "The Dedication of a Church and an Altar: A Theological
   Commentary," booklet reprinted from *The Roman Pontifical: The Dedication of a Church and an Altar* (Washington: United States Catholic Conference, 1980), 25.

4. T. Lincoln Bouscaren and Adam C. Ellis, *Canon Law: A Text and Commentary,* 3d rev. ed. (Milwaukee: Bruce Publishing Company, 1957), 648,
   637, also 649. See also *New Catholic Encyclopedia,* s.v. "churches, dedication of."

5. *New Catholic Encyclopedia,* s.v. "churches, dedication of"; Calabuig, "Ded-

ication of a Church and an Altar," 32. See also Bouscaren and Ellis, *Canon Law,* 634.

6. Bouscaren and Ellis, *Canon Law,* 695, 634, 639, 644, 649–650, also 637. See also *New Catholic Encyclopedia,* s.v. "churches, dedication of."

7. Fragment, *Globe,* probably 18 July 1910, the Boston Herald Library. See also St. William's Parish, *Souvenir Golden Jubilee Program of Saint William's Parish, Dorchester, Massachusetts, 1909–1959* (Dorchester: St. William's Parish, 1959), St. William's Rectory; Robert H. Lord, John E. Sexton, and Edward T. Harrington, *History of the Archdiocese of Boston in the Various Stages of Its Development, 1604 to 1943* (New York: Sheed and Ward, 1944), iii:684.

8. Emery, *Catholic Stronghold,* 50.

9. *Encyclopaedia Judaica,* s.v. "ark," "synagogue." See also Mishna Berurah 153:1–6; William S. Green, "Romancing the Tome: Rabbinic Hermeneutics and the Theory of Literature," *Semeia* 40: *Text and Textuality,* ed. Charles Winquist (1987), 156. For the reference to Mishna Berurah, I am grateful to Ely Razin.

10. Green, "Romancing the Tome," 155–156.

11. *Jewish Encyclopedia,* s.v. "consecration or dedication."

12. *GlbSun,* 22 Oct. 1972, magazine, 34.

13. Abraham G. Daniels, "From Ghetto to Temple: Scraps of History in the Evolution of Mishkan Israel," in Temple Mishkan Tefila, *Our Golden Jubilee, 1860–1910* (Boston: Congregation Mishkan Tefila, 1910), CMTA, 15.

14. *BHO,* 6 Feb. 1885, 4; *Globe,* 8 June 1903, 12. See also Arthur Mann, ed., *Growth and Achievement: Temple Israel, 1854–1954* (Cambridge, Mass.: Riverside Press, 1954), 31; *JAdv,* 19 Jan. 1928, 2:5.

15. *BHO,* 6 Feb. 1885, 4.

16. Jack Wertheimer, "The Conservative Synagogue," in *The American Synagogue: A Sanctuary Transformed,* ed. Jack Wertheimer (Cambridge: Cambridge University Press, 1987), 114; Daniel J. Elazar and Stephen R. Goldstein, "The Legal Status of the American Jewish Community," *American Jewish Year Book* 73 (1972), 53; W. Lloyd Warner and Leo Srole, *The Social Systems of American Ethnic Groups,* Yankee City Series, vol. 3 (New Haven: Yale University Press, 1945), 205–217.

17. *BAdv,* 26 May 1905, 2; *BAdv,* 23 Mar. 1906, 1, 7; *JAdv,* 19 Jan. 1928, 2:5; *JAdv,* 30 Sept. 1943, 6.

18. *JAdv,* 2 Dec. 1920, 1. See also Chapter 4. For sources on Adath Israel's Commonwealth Avenue Temple and Ohabei Shalom's Beacon Street Temple, see *BAdv,* 6 Sept. 1907, 1; *JAdv,* 18 May 1916, 1; *JAdv,* 28 Feb. 1918, 1, 8; *JAdv,* 23 Sept. 1920, 4; *JAdv,* 3 Mar. 1921, 1; *JAdv,* 24 Mar. 1921, 1; *JAdv,*

6 Apr. 1922, 1, 8; *JAdv,* 21 May 1925, 1, 5; *JAdv,* 4 June 1925, 6; *JAdv,* 22 Nov. 1928, 2:1; *JAdv,* 6 Dec. 1928, 2:1, 2:2.

19. *JAdv,* 8 Feb. 1917, 1; *JAdv,* 2 Nov. 1916, 1, also 9; Temple Mishkan Tefila, "An Appeal to Thinking Jews," brochure, ca. 1917, box 7, Herman H. Rubenovitz Papers, JTS.

20. Temple Mishkan Tefila, "An Appeal to Thinking Jews"; *JAdv,* 8 Feb. 1917, 1; *JAdv,* 5 Sept. 1918, 1. See also Suffolk County Deeds 4108:315; *JAdv,* 28 Nov. 1918, 1, 5.

21. *JAdv,* 9 Oct. 1919, 1.

22. *Transcript,* 26 Sept. 1922, CMTA; *JAdv,* 17 Apr. 1924, 3. See also *JAdv,* 11 Dec. 1919, 1, 5; *JAdv,* 25 Dec. 1919, 1; Suffolk County Deeds 4208:273; *JAdv,* 5 Feb. 1920, 1; *JAdv,* 28 Sept. 1922, 1; *JAdv,* 5 Oct. 1922, 1, 8; A. A. Bloome, "The New Temple," in Temple Mishkan Tefila, *The Jewish Center,* Jan. 1923, Mishkan Tefila Papers, AJHS; Harry I. Kessler to Louis Mazur, 16 Feb. 1924, financial report for year ending 31 Dec. 1923, CMTA; Congregation, minutes of meeting with attached document, 13 May 1924, Mishkan Tefila Papers, AJA; Board of Directors, minutes of meeting, 3 June 1924, Mishkan Tefila Papers, AJA; *JAdv,* 24 July 1924, 4.

23. *Her,* 14 Sept. 1925, 6; *JAdv,* 17 Sept. 1925, 2:6, also 1. See also "Tentative Program—To be carried out at DEDICATION of Temple Mishkan Tefila—Sunday, Sept. 13th, 1925 at 7:30 P.M.," 14 Aug. 1925, box 7, Herman H. Rubenovitz Papers, JTS; "Dedication—Temple Mishkan Tefila, Seaver Street and Elm Hill Avenue, Roxbury, Massachusetts—Sunday, the Thirteenth of Sept., Nineteen hundred and twenty-five," booklet, CMTA; *JAdv,* 12 Sept. 1929, 1; *JAdv,* 19 Sept. 1929, 4:6.

24. Barbara Miller Solomon, "Pioneers in Service: The History of the Associated Jewish Philanthropies of Boston," feature section, *JAdv,* 27 June 1957, 24, 31, 34; History of Boston YMHA, untitled, circa 1948, box 16, HH; *BAdv,* 26 May 1905, 2; *JAdv,* 26 May 1911, 1; *JAdv,* 22 Dec. 1911, 2; *JAdv,* 17 May 1912, 1; *JAdv,* 24 May 1912, 1; *JAdv,* 13 Dec. 1935, 1, 5; *JAdv,* 17 Jan. 1936, 1, 2; *JAdv,* 28 Jan. 1936, 2; *JAdv,* 6 Oct. 1939, 4; Jewish Welfare Board, "Study of the Jewish Community of Greater Boston, Massachusetts, with Special Reference to Needs for Jewish Center Work," unpublished, 1940, JWB, and box 131, CJP, 446; Sibyl Soroker, "Historical Sketch of Growth and Progress of the Jewish Hospital Movement," *JAdv,* 26 July 1928, 2:1, 2:2; *JAdv,* 26 Oct. 1916, 1; *JAdv,* 3 Apr. 1924, 1; *JAdv,* 9 Aug. 1928, 1.

25. *JAdv,* 29 Aug. 1913, 1; George Cary and Ordway Tead, "Roxbury Crossing, Wards 18 and 19," in *The Zone of Emergence: Observations of the Lower Middle and Upper Working Class Communities of Boston, 1905–1914,* ed.

Robert A. Woods and Albert J. Kennedy, abr. and ed. Sam Bass Warner, Jr., 2d ed. (Cambridge: MIT Press, 1969), 127. See also Suffolk County Deeds 3753:5, 4128:518; Agudath Achim, box 110, WPA; Edith Arnold, "Agudas Achim Synagogue, 1890–1960," unpublished, AJHS; Boston City Directory, 1913–1919; Shepetovka Volin Nusach Sfard, box 110, WPA; *JAdv,* 24 July 1924, 4; *JAdv,* 4 Sept. 1924, 1, 5; *JAdv,* 11 Sept. 1924, 1, 3; Atereths Israel, box 110, WPA; Chevra Mishnaeth Shomreh Shabas, ibid.; Anshe Volin, ibid.; *JAdv,* 4 May 1967, 2; *JAdv,* 21 Feb. 1929, 2:6; Beth Jacob Anshi Sfard, box 110, WPA; Nevah Zedeck, ibid.; *JAdv,* 10 Jan. 1936, 2:1; Machseke Torah Rabbi Horowitz, box 110, WPA; *JAdv,* 8 Mar. 1945, 18; *JAdv,* 21 May 1953, 4; *JAdv,* 27 Apr. 1961, 4; *JAdv,* 9 Nov. 1961, 1, 15.

26. *JAdv,* 29 Dec. 1927, 2:2.
27. *New Catholic Encyclopedia,* s.v. "parish."
28. *Globe,* 24 Dec. 1977, 7; *Globe,* 4 Sept. 1971, 7. The identification of parish and neighborhood has characterized Catholic life in many cities: see Kathleen Gavigan, "The Rise and Fall of Parish Cohesiveness in Philadelphia," *Records of the American Catholic Historical Society of Philadelphia* 86 (1975), 107; Edward Kantowicz, "Church and Neighborhood," *Ethnicity* 7 (1980), 349; *New Yorker,* 22 Mar. 1993, 33; John T. McGreevy, *Parish Boundaries: The Catholic Encounter with Race in the Twentieth-Century Urban North* (Chicago: University of Chicago Press, 1996), 21–22.
29. Boston 200 Corporation, *Dorchester,* Boston 200 Neighborhood History Series (Boston: Boston 200 Corporation, 1976), 14.
30. Fragment, *Globe,* probably 18 July 1910, the Boston Herald Library; *Globe,* 25 Sept. 1980, 4.

7. Authority

1. *New Bedford Mercury,* early Oct. 1872, undated article, reprinted in *Pilot,* 19 Oct. 1872, 3. See also Susan L. Emery, *A Catholic Stronghold and Its Making: A History of St. Peter's Parish, Dorchester, Massachusetts, and of Its First Rector, the Rev. Peter Ronan, P.R.* (Boston: Geo. H. Ellis, 1910), BPL, 5–7.
2. Emery, *Catholic Stronghold,* 8, 90–91.
3. *JAdv,* 26 Aug. 1910, 1, 4. See also Edward J. Bromberg to Herman H. Rubenovitz, 12 Sept. 1910, box 7, Herman H. Rubenovitz Papers, JTS.
4. Joseph S. Phillips to Herman H. Rubenovitz, 1 Nov. 1910, box 7, Herman H. Rubenovitz Papers, JTS. See also Phillips to Rubenovitz, 23 Oct. 1910, ibid.; *JAdv,* 11 Nov. 1910, 1; *JAdv,* 18 Nov. 1910, 1.
5. Congregation Mishkan Tefila, *Constitution and By-Laws of the Congregation Mishkan Tefila, Boston, Massachusetts* (Boston, 1913), CMTA, 9, 16.

6. All Jews recognize that ten men constitute a minyan. In recent years, Reform and most Conservative congregations have regarded any ten adults, women as well as men, as a minyan.

7. Emanuel Rackman, "From Synagogue toward Yeshiva: Institutionalized Cult or Congregations of the Learned?" *Commentary* 21 (Apr. 1956), 354.

8. *NYT,* 19 Aug. 1877, 7.

9. Jay P. Dolan, *The American Catholic Experience: A History from Colonial Times to the Present* (Notre Dame: University of Notre Dame Press, 1992), 180; *Handbook for Parishioners of the Archdiocese of Milwaukee,* 23–24, originally quoted in Anthony J. Kuzniewski, "The Catholic Church in the Life of the Polish-Americans," in *Poles in America,* ed. Frank Mocha (Stevens Point, Wisc.: Worzalla Publishing, 1978), 413: quoted in Dolan, *The American Catholic Experience,* 180–181; T. Lincoln Bouscaren and Adam C. Ellis, *Canon Law: A Text and Commentary,* 3d rev. ed. (Milwaukee: Bruce Publishing Company, 1957), 93.

10. Bouscaren and Ellis, *Canon Law,* 636, also 644; H. Paul Douglass, *The Springfield Church Survey: A Study of Organized Religion with Its Social Background* (New York: George H. Doran, 1926), 73. See also *Code of Canon Law: Latin-English Edition* (Washington, D.C.: Canon Law Society of America, 1983), 195, 437–439; Rev. James McCarthy, interviews with author, Tribunal Building, Archdiocese of Boston, Brighton, 15 July 1991 and 23 July 1991.

11. *Pilot,* 22 Nov. 1913, 1. See also *Globe,* 17 Nov. 1913, 8; Dolan, *The American Catholic Experience,* 222.

12. Mrs. Q., Elmer Rd., to Abp. Richard J. Cushing, 12 Sept. 1950, St. Brendan, AAPB. See also Residents of Mattapan District, Milton, to Abp. William O'Connell, petition, probably early 1908, St. Angela, AAPC; Mrs. K., Tremlett St., to Card. Richard J. Cushing, 13 Apr. 1960, St. Mark, AAPB.

13. This account is based on three interviews with Frieda Cooper, 3 Nov. 1991, 23 Mar. 1992, and 2 Apr. 1992, all by telephone. In researching the origins of Chevra Shas, I also consulted Boston City Directory, 1928; *JAdv,* 12 Jan. 1928, 3:5; *JAdv,* 6 Sept. 1928, 2:1; *JAdv,* 13 Sept. 1928, 1st supp., 7; Suffolk County Deeds 5018:511–512, 4929:532; Richard Heath, "The House of the Flock of the Righteous: The Song of Synagogue Adath Jeshurun," unpublished paper, 1991, AJHS, 5; Chevra Shaas, box 110, WPA; Hadreth Israel, ibid.; Hadrath Israel, ibid. For a full discussion of the Cooper interviews and the other sources, see Gerald H. Gamm, "Neighborhood Roots: Exodus and Stability in Boston, 1870–1990" (Ph.D. diss., Harvard University, 1994), 198, n.14.

14. Boston City Directory, 1928; Frieda Cooper, telephone interviews with author, 3 Nov. 1991, 23 Mar. 1992, and 2 Apr. 1992.

15. Jonathan D. Sarna, "Introduction," in *American Synagogue History: A Bibliography and State-of-the-Field Survey,* ed. Alexandra Shecket Korros and Jonathan D. Sarna (New York: Markus Wiener, 1988), 14. See also Suffolk County Deeds 5018:511–512; *JAdv,* 6 Sept. 1928, 2:1; *JAdv,* 13 Sept. 1928, 1st supp., 7; *JAdv,* 13 Sept. 1928, 8; Abraham J. Karp, "Overview: The Synagogue in America—A Historical Typology," in *The American Synagogue: A Sanctuary Transformed,* ed. Jack Wertheimer (Cambridge: Cambridge University Press, 1987), 7; Marshall Sklare, *Conservative Judaism: An American Religious Movement* (Glencoe, Ill.: Free Press, 1955), 42.

16. Daniel J. Elazar, "The Development of the American Synagogue," in *American Synagogue History: A Bibliography and State-of-the-Field Survey,* ed. Alexandra Shecket Korros and Jonathan D. Sarna (New York: Markus Wiener, 1988), 33; *Transcript,* 11 Dec. 1858, reproduction of article, CMTA.

17. Chevra Mishnaeth Shomreh Shabas, box 110, WPA; *JAdv,* 15 June 1916, 2. See also *JAdv,* 2 Nov. 1916, 2; Boston City Directory, 1918–1920; *The American Jewish Year Book, 5680* (Philadelphia: Jewish Publication Society of America, 1919), 388. For sources on Roxbury's Hadrath Israel, see *BAdv,* 11 Sept. 1908, 4; Suffolk County Deeds 3753:1–5, 3818:382; *BAdv,* 14 May 1909, 1; *JAdv,* 11 June 1909, 1, 3; *JAdv,* 23 Sept. 1910, 6; *JAdv,* 28 Mar. 1913, 2; *JAdv,* 29 Aug. 1913, 1; Shara Tfilo, box 110, WPA; Boston City Directory, 1911–1916. I have located no evidence suggesting a connection between this congregation and the Mattapan congregation of the same name.

18. Heath, "House of the Flock of the Righteous," 8–9. See also Suffolk County Deeds 3467:377, 3920:397, 4040:159, 4108:85–88, 4485:358, 7598:348; Shara Tfilo, box 110, WPA; Congregation Chai Odom, chronology of congregation from Chai Odom news bulletin, probably 1956, Personal Papers of Esther Epstein.

19. *JAdv,* 4 Sept. 1924, 5. See also *JAdv,* 23 Aug. 1923, 1, 8; *JAdv,* 30 Aug. 1923, 6; Congregation, minutes of meeting, 10 Jan. 1924, Mishkan Tefila Papers, AJA; *JAdv,* 27 Mar. 1924, 3; *JAdv,* 18 Sept. 1924, 1, 4.

20. Congregation Kehillath Jacob, "Record of First Meeting of the Incorporators of the Kehillath Jacob of Mattapan," AJHS, 7–8. See also Daniel J. Elazar and Stephen R. Goldstein, "The Legal Status of the American Jewish Community," *American Jewish Year Book* 73 (1972), 53.

21. *BAdv,* 11 Sept. 1908, 4; *JAdv,* 29 Aug. 1913, 1; Boston City Directory, 1904–1914, 1918–1919; Suffolk County Deeds 3753:5; Hebrew Teachers College, box 110, WPA; *JAdv,* 30 Sept. 1943, 6; *JAdv,* 18 Aug. 1921, 1; *Hebrew Teachers College Bulletin,* Nov. 1951, HC, 4; *Hebrew College Bulletin,* June 1975, HC, 19; *Hebrew College Bulletin,* June 1979, HC, 21.

22. *JAdv,* 1 May 1924, 1. See also *JAdv,* 3 July 1914, 1, 8; *JAdv,* 4 Sept. 1914, 5; *JAdv,* 18 Sept. 1914, 2; *JAdv,* 26 Mar. 1915, 2; *JAdv,* 11 June 1915, 2; *JAdv,* 27 Aug. 1915, 5; *JAdv,* 24 Sept. 1915, 2; *JAdv,* 8 Oct. 1915, 2; *JAdv,* 25 May 1916, 2; *JAdv,* 6 Dec. 1928, 4, 2:1; *JAdv,* 13 Dec. 1928, 3:1; *Post,* 2 June 1947, 11; Jewish Welfare Board, "Recreational, Social and Cultural Resources and Activities of the Jewish Community of Boston," unpublished, June 1930, JWB, 2, 6; *JAdv,* 18 Oct. 1928, 1; *JAdv,* 12 Jan. 1928, 3; *JAdv,* 9 Feb. 1967, 1.

23. *JAdv,* 8 Dec. 1927, 1. See also Jewish Welfare Board, "Recreational, Social and Cultural Resources and Activities of the Jewish Community of Boston," June 1930, 8; *JAdv,* 17 Dec. 1925, 1; Harry I. Kessler, balance sheet, 1 Sept. 1942, CMTA; Board of Directors, minutes of meeting, 6 Oct. 1925, Mishkan Tefila Papers, AJA; Board of Directors, minutes of meeting, 19 Jan. 1926, Mishkan Tefila Papers, AJA; *JAdv,* 11 Feb. 1926, 1, 2:1; Board of Directors, minutes of meeting, 31 Mar. 1926, Mishkan Tefila Papers, AJA; Board of Directors, minutes of meeting, 6 Apr. 1926, Mishkan Tefila Papers, AJA; Board of Directors, minutes of meeting, 14 Feb. 1928, Mishkan Tefila Papers, AJA; Executive Committee, minutes of meeting, 9 Nov. 1930, Mishkan Tefila Papers, AJA; Report to Finance and Audit Committee, 20 Dec. 1934, CMTA; "A. A. Bloom," 24 Feb. 1948, CMTA; Report of Executive Committee, 19 May 1949, Mishkan Tefila Papers, AJA; Myer H. Slobodkin, "A Review of Our Bonded Indebtedness," 29 Dec. 1949, Mishkan Tefila Papers, AJA.

24. Board of Directors, minutes of meeting, 16 Feb. 1927, Mishkan Tefila Papers, AJA; Congregation, minutes of meeting, 13 Jan. 1927, ibid.; Board of Directors, minutes of meeting, 20 Jan. 1927, ibid.; "Emergency Banquet," 2 June 1927, booklet, CMTA; *JAdv,* 8 Dec. 1927, 1; Congregation, minutes of meeting, 17 Jan. 1929, Mishkan Tefila Papers, AJA. See also Executive Committee, minutes of meeting, 9 Nov. 1930, ibid.; Board of Directors, minutes of meeting, 1 Feb. 1927, ibid.; Congregation, minutes of meeting, 23 Feb. 1927, ibid.; *JAdv,* 24 Feb. 1927, 1; *JAdv,* 10 Mar. 1927, 3:1; *JAdv,* 9 June 1927, 3.

25. Board of Directors, minutes of meeting, 9 June 1931, Mishkan Tefila Papers, AJA; Board of Directors, minutes of meeting, 1 Oct. 1931, ibid.; Board of Directors, minutes of meeting, 20 June 1935, ibid.; Board of Directors, minutes of meeting, 29 Aug. 1935, ibid.; Board of Directors, minutes of meeting, 28 May 1936, ibid.; Rabbi Herman H. Rubenovitz to the Chairman and Members of the Board of Directors, 3 Dec. 1936, ibid. For additional sources, see Gamm, "Neighborhood Roots," 211, n.57.

26. Executive Committee, minutes of meeting, 26 Sept. 1937, Mishkan Tefila Papers, AJA; Board of Directors, minutes of meeting, 28 May 1936, ibid.;

"Tribute to Myer H. Slobodkin on His Birthday at Board Meeting," 22 Sept. 1949, ibid. See also Report to Finance and Audit Committee, 20 Dec. 1934, CMTA; Special Bondholders Committee, minutes of dinner meeting, 16 June 1937, Mishkan Tefila Papers, AJA; Executive Committee, minutes of meeting, 28 Dec. 1937, ibid.; Congregation, minutes of meeting, 24 Jan. 1943, ibid.; Annual Report of Executive Committee, 30 Dec. 1945, ibid.; Report of Executive Committee, 19 May 1949, ibid.; Myer H. Slobodkin, "A Review of Our Bonded Indebtedness," 29 Dec. 1949, ibid.

27. *JAdv,* 11 Feb. 1926, 2:1.

28. Jack Wertheimer, "The Conservative Synagogue," in *The American Synagogue: A Sanctuary Transformed,* ed. Jack Wertheimer (Cambridge: Cambridge University Press, 1987), 121, also 122; *JAdv,* 3 Oct. 1929, 5:4. See also Deborah Dash Moore, *At Home in America: Second Generation New York Jews* (New York: Columbia University Press, 1981), 129–147; Beth S. Wenger, *New York Jews and the Great Depression: Uncertain Promise* (New Haven: Yale University Press, 1996), 168–173; David Kaufman, "'Shul with a Pool': The Synagogue-Center in American Jewish Life, 1875–1925" (Ph.D. diss., Brandeis University, 1993).

29. *JAdv,* 3 Oct. 1929, 5:4.

30. Bouscaren and Ellis, *Canon Law,* 783; Roman Catholic Archbishop of Boston, *Acta et Statuta Synodi Bostoniensis Septimae* (1953), §197; *Her,* 17 Feb. 1969, 37. See also Dolan, *The American Catholic Experience,* 171–172; Wolfgang L. Grichting, *Parish Structure and Climate in an Era of Change: A Sociologist's Inquiry* (Washington: Center for Applied Research in the Apostolate, 1969), 2–3; W. Lloyd Warner and Leo Srole, *The Social Systems of American Ethnic Groups,* Yankee City Series, vol. 3 (New Haven: Yale University Press, 1945), 172.

31. Roman Catholic Archbishop of Boston, *Acta et Statuta Synodi Bostoniensis Septimae,* §192; Office of Planning and Research, Archdiocese of Boston, "Planning Guide 2000: Addressing the Challenges Facing the Church of Boston," draft discussion guide, Mar. 1997, iv.

32. Letter from a committee in St. William's Parish, untitled, probably Jan. 1982, St. William's Parish, Boston Churches, the Boston Herald Library; *Globe,* 20 Jan. 1982, 20.

33. Dolan, *The American Catholic Experience,* 170–171. See also Joseph H. Fichter, *Social Relations in the Urban Parish* (Chicago: University of Chicago Press, 1954), 130.

34. *Globe,* 20 Jan. 1982, 20. See also Bouscaren and Ellis, *Canon Law,* 804, 808–809; *Globe,* 20 Apr. 1981, 23; St. William's Parish, capital expenditure authorization, 11 May 1981, St. William, AAPC; Most Rev. Thomas V.

Daily to Rev. Francis J. Crowley, 11 May 1981, ibid.; St. William's Parish, capital expenditure authorization, 2 Nov. 1981, ibid.; Daily to H. et al., Dorchester, 12 Nov. 1981, ibid.

35. Card. William O'Connell to Rev. Michael J. Cuddihy, 25 Nov. 1932, St. Matthew, AAPC; Roman Catholic Archbishop of Boston, *Acta et Statuta Synodi Bostoniensis Septimae,* §217, §201, §216, §200, also §§211–212. See also Bouscaren and Ellis, *Canon Law,* 807–809.

36. Bouscaren and Ellis, *Canon Law,* 636; James W. Sanders, "Boston Catholics and the School Question, 1825–1907," chap. 4 in *From Common School to Magnet School* (Boston, 1979), reprinted in *Building the American Catholic City: Parishes and Institutions,* ed. Brian C. Mitchell (New York: Garland, 1988), 56. See also *Code of Canon Law,* 437; Edward Kantowicz, "Church and Neighborhood," *Ethnicity* 7 (1980), 355–356; Robert H. Lord, John E. Sexton, and Edward T. Harrington, *History of the Archdiocese of Boston in the Various Stages of Its Development, 1604 to 1943* (New York: Sheed and Ward, 1944), iii:686.

37. Rev. Francis A. Cunningham to Card. William O'Connell, 13 Oct. 1915, St. Leo, AAPC; Cunningham to Rev. Richard J. Haberlin, 27 Nov. 1916, ibid. See also O'Connell to Cunningham, 15 Oct. 1915, ibid.; Cunningham to Haberlin, 23 Nov. 1916, ibid.; Cunningham to Haberlin, 5 Nov. 1917, ibid.

38. *JAdv,* 13 Dec. 1928, 3:5; James S. Sullivan, ed., *The Catholic Church of New England* (Boston: Boston and Portland Illustrated Publishing Company, 1895), RCAB, 179; Emery, *Catholic Stronghold,* 77. See also *JAdv,* 22 Nov. 1928, 2:1; *JAdv,* 6 Dec. 1928, 4; Rev. John A. Donnelly to Card. William O'Connell, 6 Aug. 1915, St. Matthew, AAPC; O'Connell to Donnelly, 9 Aug. 1915, ibid.; St. Matthew's Parish, *Golden Jubilee, 1900–1950: Saint Matthew's Parish, Dorchester* (1950), St. Matthew, AAPH; Lord et al., *History of the Archdiocese of Boston,* iii:685; Rev. Richard J. Haberlin to Donnelly, 20 Jan. 1920, St. Matthew, AAPC; Donnelly to Haberlin, 13 Sept. 1921, ibid.

39. Roman Catholic Archbishop of Boston, *Acta et Statuta Synodi Bostoniensis Septimae,* §60, §5, §6. See also *New Catholic Encyclopedia,* s.v. "liturgy."

40. Bouscaren and Ellis, *Canon Law,* 687, also 733–735; Roman Catholic Archbishop of Boston, *Acta et Statuta Synodi Bostoniensis Septimae,* §120, §117, appendix 12, also §§108–123, §181.

41. Bouscaren and Ellis, *Canon Law,* 751, also 750–772.

42. *Transcript,* 28 Sept. 1908, 16; Roman Catholic Archbishop of Boston, *Acta et Statuta Synodi Bostoniensis Septimae,* §78, §6. See also Rev. Richard J. Haberlin to Rt. Rev. Patrick J. Supple, 14 Dec. 1916, St. John, AAPC; Rev. James J. McCafferty to Card. William O'Connell, 8 Apr. 1917, ibid.

43. Rev. John A. Daly to Card. William O'Connell, 3 Dec. 1921, in St. Mark's Parish, *75th Anniversary, St. Mark the Evangelist Parish, Dorchester, Mass., 1905–1980: An Illustrated History,* St. Mark, AAPH, 5; Rt. Rev. Edward F. Hurley to O'Connell, 5 May 1926, St. Matthew, AAPC. See also Bouscaren and Ellis, *Canon Law,* 746.

44. *Code of Canon Law,* 201, also 205–207; Archdiocese of Boston, Eighth Synod, *Parish Pastoral Councils* (Boston: Archdiocese of Boston, 1989), 10, also 7–14. See also Archdiocese of Boston, Eighth Synod, *Pastoral Plan for Mission* (Boston: Archdiocese of Boston, 1989), 18–19.

45. St. Mark's Parish, *75th Anniversary, St. Mark the Evangelist Parish,* 19, 36, also 27, 41; *Code of Canon Law,* 207. See also Archdiocese of Boston, Eighth Synod, *Parish Pastoral Councils,* 9; E. Brooks Holifield, "Toward a History of American Congregations," in *American Congregations,* vol. 2: *New Perspectives in the Study of Congregations* (Chicago: University of Chicago Press, 1994), 46.

46. Albert Ehrenfried, "A Chronicle of Boston Jewry: From the Colonial Settlement to 1900," unpublished, 1963, AJHS, 360–369, 387–389, 395–396; Solomon Schindler, "Israelites in Boston: A Tale Describing the Development of Judaism in Boston" (1889; rpt. *JAdv,* 26 June 1952), A:5, A:11; *JAdv,* 19 Jan. 1928, 2:5; Temple Ohabei Shalom, *The By-Laws of Temple Ohabei Shalom, Boston, Mass., Prefaced with an Historical Sketch* (Boston: Daniels Printing Company, 1907), HUW, 12–13, 15, 18; Abraham P. Spitz, "How the Pioneer Jews of Boston Started First Congregation: History of Temple Ohabei Shalom and Subsequent Houses of Worship Recounted," *JAdv,* 26 June 1952, 3:19; "Israel Cohen" and "Directory of Jewish Institutions in Boston," in *History of the Jews of Boston and New England* (Boston: Jewish Chronicle Publishing Co., 1892), AJHS; Menahem M. Eichler, "Factions in Judaism," in Temple Mishkan Tefila, *Our Golden Jubilee, 1860–1910* (Boston: Congregation Mishkan Tefila, 1910), CMTA, 31; *JAdv,* 18 May 1916, 1; *JAdv,* 8 Jan. 1920, 2; *JAdv,* 25 Mar. 1920, 1; Arthur Mann, *Yankee Reformers in the Urban Age: Social Reform in Boston, 1880–1900* (Cambridge: Belknap Press of Harvard University Press, 1954), 56–57.

47. *BAdv,* editorial, probably 17 May 1907, CMTA. See also chapter 4; Temple Mishkan Tefila, *Dedication Souvenir of the Temple Mishkan Tefila, Moreland and Copeland Sts., Roxbury, Mass., Sunday, May 12th, 1907* (1907), box 7, Herman H. Rubenovitz Papers, JTS; Abraham G. Daniels, "From Ghetto to Temple: Scraps of History in the Evolution of Mishkan Israel," in Temple Mishkan Tefila, *Our Golden Jubilee,* 15; Herman H. Rubenovitz and Mignon L. Rubenovitz, *The Waking Heart: Adventure in Achievement* (Cambridge, Mass.: Nathaniel Dame, 1967), 31–32.

48. Rubenovitz and Rubenovitz, *The Waking Heart*, 32, also 31; Congregation Mishkan Tefila, *Constitution and By-Laws* (1913), 19; Herman H. Rubenovitz, "My Rabbinate at Temple Mishkan Tefila: A History from 1910 to 1946," in Temple Mishkan Tefila, *Temple Mishkan Tefila: A History, 1858–1958* (Newton: Temple Mishkan Tefila, 1958), CMTA, 21–22.

49. Rubenovitz and Rubenovitz, *The Waking Heart*, 34, also 32–33; Rubenovitz, "My Rabbinate," 22, also 21; *JAdv*, 14 May 1915, 1. See also Congregation Mishkan Tefila, *Constitution and By-Laws* (1913), 8; Temple Mishkan Tefila, *A History, 1858–1958*, 98; Jacob L. Sieve, *L'dor Vodor: From Generation to Generation—Congregation Mishkan Tefila, 1858–1983* (Newton: Congregation Mishkan Tefila, 1983), 115; Wertheimer, "The Conservative Synagogue," 115.

50. *JAdv*, 14 May 1915, 1; *JAdv*, 13 Aug. 1915, 1. See also Rubenovitz, "My Rabbinate," 22; Rubenovitz and Rubenovitz, *The Waking Heart*, 34; *JAdv*, 3 Sept. 1915, 3. For Magidson's first name, see Board of Directors, minutes of meeting, 8 July 1924, Mishkan Tefila Papers, AJA.

51. Congregation Kehillath Jacob, "Record of First Meeting of the Incorporators of the Kehillath Jacob of Mattapan," AJHS, 7–8. See also Chapter 9; *JAdv*, 5 Feb. 1925, 4; Karp, "Overview: The Synagogue in America," 11–13. Only when a majority violates a specific provision in a bequest or a fundamental doctrine embedded in the congregation's own charter or by-laws might an American court recognize a minority position: see Elazar and Goldstein, "Legal Status," 54–64.

52. Sklare, *Conservative Judaism*, 41. Even the small group of Orthodox rabbis who denounced Reform and Conservative Judaism in 1997 as "not Judaism at all, but another religion," did not question the status of most Jews who identified with the non-Orthodox movements. "We never said, God forbid, that a person born to a Jewish mother is not a Jew," Rabbi Hersh Ginsberg "was overheard shouting into the telephone receiver," according to a report in the *Washington Post*. "A Jew is a Jew is a Jew! What we said is that Reform and Conservative as a religion is not Judaism!": see *Washington Post*, 1 Apr. 1997, A3.

53. Congregation Kehillath Jacob, "Record of First Meeting of the Incorporators of the Kehillath Jacob of Mattapan," AJHS, 7. See also Kehillath Jacob, box 110, WPA.

54. *Globe*, 2 Apr. 1972, B:36.

55. *JAdv*, 19 May 1927, 2:2; *JAdv*, 22 Apr. 1926, 4. For the employment of rabbis at Adath Jeshurun, see *JAdv*, 25 Dec. 1924, 6; *JAdv*, 29 July 1926, 1; *JAdv*, 7 Oct. 1926, 1; *JAdv*, 14 Oct. 1926, 1. For Beth Hamidrash Hagadol, see *JAdv*, 8 Jan. 1925, 3; *JAdv*, 25 June 1925, 8; *JAdv*, 2 July 1925, 2; *JAdv*, 19

Apr. 1928, 4; *JAdv*, 30 Aug. 1928, 3; *JAdv*, 6 Sept. 1928, 3; *JAdv*, 13 Dec. 1928, 3:3. For Beth El, see *JAdv*, 12 Nov. 1925, 3; *JAdv*, 19 Sept. 1929, 2:5; *JAdv*, 20 June 1930, 1.

56. Congregation, minutes of meeting, 27 Dec. 1944, Mishkan Tefila Papers, AJA; *JAdv*, 28 Apr. 1966, 6. See also *JAdv*, 14 Apr. 1966, 1, 13, 2:2; *JAdv*, 21 Apr. 1966, 4.

57. *JAdv*, 11 Nov. 1910, 1; J. S. Phillips to Herman H. Rubenovitz, 23 Oct. 1910, box 7, Herman H. Rubenovitz Papers, JTS; *JAdv*, 2 May 1913, 1; Edward J. Bromberg to Rubenovitz, 28 Apr. 1913, box 7, Herman H. Rubenovitz Papers, JTS; Rubenovitz to the President and Members, 26 Dec. 1929, Mishkan Tefila Papers, AJA; Harry I. Kessler to Louis Mazur, 16 Feb. 1924, financial report for year ending 31 Dec. 1923, CMTA; Cash disbursements, Jan. 1924, Mishkan Tefila Papers, AJA; Congregation, minutes of meeting, 10 Jan. 1924, ibid.; *JAdv*, 17 Jan. 1924, 1, 8.

58. Board of Directors, minutes of meeting, 18 Sept. 1929, Mishkan Tefila Papers, AJA; Rabbi Herman H. Rubenovitz to the President and Members, 26 Dec. 1929, ibid. See also Board of Directors, minutes of meeting, 8 Dec. 1929, ibid.; Congregation, minutes of meeting, 26 Dec. 1929, ibid.; *JAdv*, 27 June 1930, 1; *JAdv*, 19 Sept. 1946, 13.

59. Board of Directors, minutes of meeting, 9 June 1931, Mishkan Tefila Papers, AJA; Executive Committee, minutes of meeting, 30 Oct. 1930, ibid.; Congregation, minutes of meeting, 8 Oct. 1931, ibid. See also Board of Directors, minutes of meeting, 10 Sept. 1930, ibid.; *JAdv*, 12 Sept. 1930, 1; Board of Directors, minutes of meeting, 29 Sept. 1930, Mishkan Tefila Papers, AJA; Board of Directors, minutes of meeting, 9 Apr. 1931, ibid.; Board of Directors, minutes of meeting, 9 May 1931, ibid.

60. Congregation, minutes of meeting, 16 Aug. 1932, first draft with corrections, Mishkan Tefila Papers, AJA; Board of Directors, minutes of meeting, 11 Jan. 1932, ibid.; Board of Directors, minutes of meeting, 6 Oct. 1932, ibid. See also Rabbi Herman H. Rubenovitz to the Chairman and Members of the Board of Directors, 8 Nov. 1932, ibid.; Board of Directors, minutes of meeting, 9 Nov. 1932, ibid.; Executive Committee, minutes of meeting, 1 Nov. 1933, ibid. By 1944, Rubenovitz's salary had increased only to $5,500: see Harry I. Kessler to Board of Directors, 16 Dec. 1943, financial report for year ending 31 Aug. 1943, CMTA; Board of Directors, minutes of meeting, 24 Dec. 1944, Mishkan Tefila Papers, AJA; Congregation, minutes of meeting, 27 Dec. 1944, ibid.

61. Congregation, minutes of meeting, 16 May 1933, Mishkan Tefila Papers, AJA.

62. Emery, *Catholic Stronghold*, 90. See also William H. Marnell, "The Parish," in William H. Marnell and Douglass Shand Tucci, *Saint Peter's Church,*

1872–1972 (Boston: Fandel Press, 1972), 10–11, 20–23, 27; *Trav,* 2 May 1967, 3; Rev. Robert G. Flynn to Most Rev. Thomas V. Daily, 9 June 1975, St. Peter, AAPC; Daily to Flynn, 11 June 1975, ibid.; *Globe,* 20 Oct. 1975, 22.

63. Bouscaren and Ellis, *Canon Law,* 107, also 187, 193, 196, 208–209; Warner and Srole, *The Social Systems of American Ethnic Groups,* 171. See also *Code of Canon Law,* 199; Roman Catholic Archbishop of Boston, *Acta et Statuta Synodi Bostoniensis Septimae,* §43.

64. This paragraph is based on an interview with Rt. Rev. Thomas J. Finnegan, Jr., St. Elizabeth's Rectory, Milton, Mass., 14 Aug. 1991.

65. This paragraph is based on interviews with two people: Rev. James McCarthy, Tribunal Building, Archdiocese of Boston, Brighton, 15 July 1991 and 23 July 1991, and telephone, 3 June 1997; and Rt. Rev. Thomas J. Finnegan, Jr., St. Elizabeth's Rectory, Milton, Mass., 14 Aug. 1991.

66. *Globe,* 18 Mar. 1972, 7; Bouscaren and Ellis, *Canon Law,* 187, also 191–193. See also *Globe,* 2 Apr. 1972, B:29; *Glbpm,* 27 June 1972, 3; *Globe,* 2 July 1972, 26; Rev. James McCarthy, interviews with author, Tribunal Building, Archdiocese of Boston, Brighton, 15 July 1991 and 23 July 1991, and telephone, 3 June 1997; *Code of Canon Law,* 195–213.

67. Mr. O'C., Park View St., to Card. William O'Connell, 18 May 1928, St. Mary of the Angels, AAPC; Anonymous parishioner to the Chancellor, 10 Feb. 1937, ibid. See also J. McC. to O'Connell, 1929?, ibid.; Rev. Charles A. Finnigan to O'Connell, 22 Sept. 1929, ibid.; Rev. Timothy M. Howard to O'Connell, 18 Feb. 1935, ibid.

68. Letter from a committee in St. William's Parish, untitled, probably Jan. 1982, St. William's Parish, Boston Churches, the *Boston Herald* Library. See also *Globe,* 20 Jan. 1982, 19, 20; Columbia–Savin Hill Civic Association, *The Neighbors,* 5–12 Apr. 1982, folder 34, box 3, CSHCA.

69. *Globe,* 20 Jan. 1982, 19, also 20. This account of the meeting is based on a telephone interview with Joe Burnieika, 4 June 1997. Crowley resigned in the spring of 1986, probably owing to difficulties in managing the parish's finances and running the parish school: see *Globe,* 13 July 1986, 28.

70. *GlbSun,* 15 Oct. 1995, metro/region, 33.

71. "Committee Report," in St. Matthew's Parish, *Visitation Committee Report, St. Matthew Parish, Dorchester, MA* (1990), St. Matthew's Rectory; St. Mark's Parish, *Come Together in Me,* parish visitation report, 1991, St. Mark's Rectory, 9; *Code of Canon Law,* 201. See also Jay P. Dolan, "Patterns of Leadership in the Congregation," in *American Congregations,* vol. 2, 242–243.

72. Dolan, "Patterns of Leadership," 243. See also Bouscaren and Ellis, *Canon Law,* 95, 101, 212; *Code of Canon Law,* 203, 403; Dolan, *The American*

Catholic Experience, 224–225; Fichter, *Social Relations in the Urban Parish,* 125–126.

73. Fichter, *Social Relations in the Urban Parish,* 123.

74. Rackman, "From Synagogue toward Yeshiva," 354. See also Warner and Srole, *The Social Systems of American Ethnic Groups,* 171, 194; Sklare, *Conservative Judaism,* 49; *JAdv,* 26 Mar. 1953, B:16; *Jewish Encyclopedia,* s.v. "liturgy"; *Encyclopaedia Judaica,* s.v. "synagogue."

75. *Encyclopaedia Judaica,* s.v. "minyan"; *Jewish Encyclopedia,* s.v. "community, organization of," also "minyan." See also Warner and Srole, *The Social Systems of American Ethnic Groups,* 167; Elazar and Goldstein, "Legal Status," 56; Dolan, "Patterns of Leadership," 240; Marshall Sklare and Joseph Greenblum, *Jewish Identity on the Suburban Frontier: A Study of Group Survival in the Open Society,* 2d ed. (Chicago: University of Chicago Press, 1979), 180.

8. Towns, Suburbs, and Neighborhoods

1. Dorchester Board of Trade, *Dorchester Prospectus and Map: Facts of Interest Profitable to Manufacturers, Investors, and Home Seekers* (Dorchester: Dorchester Board of Trade, probably 1916). See also Sam Bass Warner, Jr., *Streetcar Suburbs: The Process of Growth in Boston, 1870–1900,* 2d ed. (Cambridge: Harvard University Press, 1978); Sam Bass Warner, Jr., "Residential Development of Roxbury, West Roxbury and Dorchester, Massachusetts, 1870–1900" (Ph.D. diss., Harvard University, 1959).

2. Warner, *Streetcar Suburbs,* 110; Richard Walden Hale, Jr., *Tercentenary History of the Roxbury Latin School, 1645–1945* (Cambridge, Mass.: Riverside Press, 1946), 1, 7.

3. Warner, *Streetcar Suburbs,* 40.

4. Ibid., 42.

5. *Picturesque Boston Highlands, Jamaica Plain, and Dorchester* (New York: Mercantile Illustrating Co., 1895), Bostonian Society, 3; Warner, *Streetcar Suburbs,* 108, 107, 111, 41.

6. James Howard Means, *An Historical Discourse on Occasion of the Fiftieth Anniversary of the Gathering of the Second Church, Dorchester,* delivered 3 Jan. 1858 (Boston: T. R. Marvin and Son, 1858), HUW, 12; Boston 200 Corporation, *Dorchester,* Boston 200 Neighborhood History Series (Boston: Boston 200 Corporation, 1976), 6; Warner, *Streetcar Suburbs,* 43, also 70. See also William Irvin Lawrance, *A History of the Third Religious Society in Dorchester, 1813–1888* (Boston: Third Religious Society, 1888), HUW, 9; First Church and Parish of Dorchester, *Proceedings of the Two*

Hundred and Fiftieth Anniversary of the Gathering in England, Departure for America, and Final Settlement in New England (Boston: Geo. H. Ellis, 1880), HUW, 117; James Howard Means, *An Historical Discourse on Occasion of the Seventieth Anniversary of the Gathering of the Second Church, Dorchester,* delivered 6 Jan. 1878 (Boston: Frank Wood, 1878), 3–4; Dorchester Tercentenary Committee, *Dorchester Old and New: Tercentenary, 1630–1930* (Dorchester: Chapple Publishing Company, 1930), 13, 31–33; Warner, "Residential Development," 5, 10.

7. Second Church, Dorchester, *Sermon and Addresses Commemorative of the Twenty-fifth Anniversary of the Ordination of Rev. James H. Means as Pastor of the Second Church, Dorchester, July 13th and 14th, 1873* (Boston: Congregational Publishing Society, 1873), HUW, 23; Justin Winsor, ed., *The Memorial History of Boston, Including Suffolk County, Massachusetts, 1630–1880* (Boston: James R. Osgood, 1881), iii:600, 595; Warner, *Streetcar Suburbs,* 22, also 69. See also Kenneth T. Jackson, *Crabgrass Frontier: The Suburbanization of the United States* (New York: Oxford University Press, 1985), 114–120.

8. Warner, *Streetcar Suburbs,* 75, 43, 45. See also U.S. Department of the Interior, Census Office, *Twelfth Census of the United States, Taken in the Year 1900,* vol. 1, *Population,* pt. 1 (Washington: Census Office, 1901); Warner, "Residential Development," 5.

9. Marion Booth and Ordway Tead, "Dorchester, Ward 16," in *The Zone of Emergence: Observations of the Lower Middle and Upper Working Class Communities of Boston, 1905–1914,* ed. Robert A. Woods and Albert J. Kennedy, abr. and ed. Sam Bass Warner, Jr., 2d ed. (Cambridge: MIT Press, 1969), 146, 152; Warner, *Streetcar Suburbs,* 115, also 62, 74, 76. See also *Dorchester Day: Celebration of the Two Hundred and Seventy-seventh Anniversary of the Settlement of Dorchester, June 8th, 1907* (Boston: Municipal Printing Office, 1907), URL, 104.

10. These population figures are based on three sources: U.S. Department of Commerce, Bureau of the Census, *Fourteenth Census of the United States, Taken in the Year 1920,* vol. 3, *Population, 1920* (Washington: Government Printing Office, 1922); probably U.S. Department of Commerce, Bureau of the Census, and Boston Council of Social Agencies, "Census Tract Population—Boston—1910, 1920, 1930, 1934, 1940," typed table, 5 pp., UCPC; Ben Rosen, "The Trend of Jewish Population in Boston: A Study to Determine the Location of a Jewish Communal Building," *Monographs of Federated Jewish Charities of Boston* 1:1 (Jan. 1921). For the 1920 population of Dorchester, I added together the population of Precinct 2 in Ward 24, the populations of Wards 17–21, and two-thirds of the population of Ward 11:

see Rosen, "The Trend of Jewish Population in Boston," 25; U.S. Census, *Fourteenth Census, 1920,* 457–458. For the 1920 population of upper Roxbury, I combined the populations of census tracts U-1, U-2, U-3, U-4, U-5, U-6, and V-1: see U.S. Census, "Census Tract Population—Boston—1910, 1920, 1930, 1934, 1940."

11. To establish the area's Jewish population, I began with three estimates. Ben Rosen offers two different estimates of the Jewish population in 1920, both for areas that corresponded generally to Ward 21. He presents estimates for the "circular area" and for the Roger Wolcott School District. Though his two estimates differ, the Jewish populations of those two districts were in fact roughly equivalent to each other and to the Jewish population of Ward 21: that the estimates differ is not evidence that the true populations differed in size. The third estimate is mine. I assume that the number of Jews in Ward 18 was roughly equivalent to the total population of census tract T-6: that is, I believe that in 1920 census tract T-6 was predominantly Jewish and that the number of Jews in Ward 18 who lived outside the tract was approximately equal to the number of non-Jews who lived inside the tract. Using these three separate estimates, I derived three separate sets of figures for the entire Jewish population in upper Roxbury and Dorchester. The 1920 census reports the country of birth of foreign-born whites. For Wards 21 and 18, I calculated the relationship between the three estimates of Jewish population and the total number of persons born in Austria, Germany, Lithuania, Poland, and Russia. I then applied those ratios to the populations in the other Roxbury and Dorchester wards born in those five countries. The number reported in the text reflects a composite of the three estimates, which do not vary widely. See Rosen, "The Trend of Jewish Population in Boston"; U.S. Census, *Fourteenth Census, 1920,* pp. 457–458; U.S. Census, "Census Tract Population—Boston—1910, 1920, 1930, 1934, 1940." This number differs from that offered in Gerald H. Gamm, *The Making of New Deal Democrats: Voting Behavior and Realignment in Boston, 1920–1940* (Chicago: University of Chicago Press, 1989), 51–52, which I now believe overestimates the true size of the area's Jewish population.

12. Booth and Tead, "Dorchester," 155.

13. Ibid., 151.

14. The exception is St. Christopher's Parish, Dorchester, which was set off from St. Margaret's Parish and thus received no territory directly from St. Peter's.

15. Booth and Tead, "Dorchester," 149.

16. *Pilot,* probably late Nov. 1904, as reproduced in St. Margaret's Parish, *A*

Little Story of Growth and Heavenly Blessings during Forty Years, 1893–1933: St. Margaret's Parish, Dorchester, Mass., St. Margaret's Rectory. See also Robert H. Lord, John E. Sexton, and Edward T. Harrington, *History of the Archdiocese of Boston in the Various Stages of Its Development, 1604 to 1943* (New York: Sheed and Ward, 1944), iii:250; *Trav*, 28 Feb. 1967, 3; St. Margaret's Parish, *St. Margaret's First Parish Reunion: October 4, 1980*, St. Margaret's Rectory.

17. Booth and Tead, "Dorchester," 156, 150.

18. *BAdv*, 27 Sept. 1907, 7.

19. Booth and Tead, "Dorchester," 163, 158, 157; Kaplan diary, 16 Mar. 1915, Mordecai M. Kaplan Diaries, JTS.

20. *JAdv*, 2 Sept. 1910, 1.

21. Warner, *Streetcar Suburbs*, 114.

22. *JAdv*, 15 May 1924, 1; Congregation Beth Hamidrash Hagadol, *Tenth Anniversary Souvenir Book, 1914–1924* (Boston: Monroe Service, 1924), Congregation Beth Hamidrash Hagadol Papers, AJHS, 16, also 12, 48–51, 77. See also Abraham J. Karp, "The Conservative Rabbi—'Dissatisfied But Not Unhappy,'" in *The American Rabbinate: A Century of Continuity and Change, 1883–1983*, ed. Jacob Rader Marcus and Abraham J. Peck (Hoboken, N.J.: Ktav Publishing House, 1985), 98; *JAdv*, 8 Jan. 1925, 3.

23. The structure was razed in the middle 1960s: see *JAdv*, 14 Jan. 1965, 1. In addition to photographs of the structure that appeared in the *Jewish Advocate* and in Yearbook and Souvenir Books, Congregation Beth Hamidrash Hagadol, 1922–1940, AJHS, I located excellent photographs in two other locations. The Archives of Congregation Mishkan Tefila, Newton, contain a pair of framed photographs, an interior view, showing the ark in the Crawford Street Synagogue, and an exterior view of the building. The Beth Hamidrash Hagadol Cemetery, West Roxbury, is the depository for a set of exterior views of the building, photographs probably taken in the summer of 1964 by the Boston Redevelopment Authority. The photographs at the cemetery are in an envelope addressed to Abraham Close postmarked 5 August 1964. Elsewhere at the cemetery I located a letter, addressed to Close and dated 4 August 1964, that stated, "The enclosed photographs were taken by a member of my staff"; the letter was written by Robert B. McGilvray, of the Boston Redevelopment Authority. See McGilvray to Close, 4 Aug. 1964, Papers, 1963–1964, BHHC.

24. Congregation Beth Hamidrash Hagadol, *Tenth Anniversary Souvenir Book, 1914–1924*, 11, also 13, 15, 16, 18, 19, 53. See also Congregation Beth Hamidrash Hagadol, *Year Book, 5683 (1922–1923)* (Boston: Monroe Service, n.d.), Congregation Beth Hamidrash Hagadol Papers, AJHS, 28–31;

JAdv, 3 July 1914, 1; *JAdv,* 4 Sept. 1914, 5; Sumner Greenberg, telephone interview with author, 1 Oct. 1992; *JAdv,* 15 May 1924, 3; *JAdv,* 31 May 1923, 4; *JAdv,* 7 June 1923, 4.

9. Membership and Mobility

1. Ben Rosen, "The Trend of Jewish Population in Boston: A Study to Determine the Location of a Jewish Communal Building," *Monographs of Federated Jewish Charities of Boston* 1:1 (Jan. 1921), 18.
2. Kenneth T. Jackson, *Crabgrass Frontier: The Suburbanization of the United States* (New York: Oxford University Press, 1985), 162. According to the 1920 federal census, 162,000 persons lived in Dorchester and 45,000 persons lived in upper Roxbury: see Chapter 8, n.10. According to the 1930 census, 192,000 persons lived in Dorchester and 48,000 persons lived in upper Roxbury. For the 1930 population of Dorchester, I combined the populations of census tracts P-2, P-3, P-4, P-5, P-6, T-1, T-2, T-3, T-4, T-5, T-6, T-7, T-8, T-9, T-10, X-1, X-2, X-3, X-4, X-5, and X-6 and portions of census tracts P-1 and W-3. For the 1930 population of upper Roxbury, I combined the populations of census tracts U-1, U-2, U-3, U-4, U-5, U-6, and V-1. For 1930 census tract data, see [U.S. Department of Commerce, Bureau of the Census, and] Boston Health Department, "Census Tract Data, [Boston,] 1930 Census," unpublished tables, UCPC, BRA, BPL. For 1930 census tract maps, see Boston Council of Social Agencies, Bureau of Research and Studies, *Social Statistics by Census Tracts in Boston: A Method of Neighborhood Study* (Boston: Boston Council of Social Agencies, 1933); Boston Health League, *Alphabetical Street Index and Basic Demographic Data for the City of Boston by Census Tracts,* compiled for the Boston Health Department (Boston: City Printing Department, 1931). For the 1920 and 1930 populations of Brookline and Newton, see U.S. Department of Commerce, Bureau of the Census, *Fourteenth Census of the United States, Taken in the Year 1920,* vol. 3, *Population, 1920* (Washington: Government Printing Office, 1922), 445–446; U.S. Department of Commerce, Bureau of the Census, *Fifteenth Census of the United States, 1930,* vol. 3, pt. 1, *Population* (Washington: Government Printing Office, 1932), 1091, 1094.
3. Theodore H. White, *In Search of History: A Personal Adventure* (New York: Harper and Row, 1978), 26–27.
4. *JAdv,* 13 Dec. 1928, 3:1. *Miketz* is Genesis 41:1–44:17. Four years later, Steinberg wrote that he had heard *Miketz* in January or February 1924, "on the first Saturday after taking office": see *JAdv,* 13 Dec. 1928, 3:1. He was wrong. *Miketz* was read on 8 December 1923 and was next read on 27 December 1924: see *The American Jewish Year Book, 5684* (Philadelphia:

Jewish Publication Society of America, 1923), 7; *American Jewish Year Book, 5685* (1924), 7. The Crawford Street Synagogue elected its officers each year in late December or early January, installing them in January: see *JAdv,* 10 Jan. 1918, 2; *JAdv,* 1 Jan. 1925, 4; *JAdv,* 31 Dec. 1925, 8; *JAdv,* 21 Jan. 1926, 6; *JAdv,* 20 Jan. 1927, 1, 7; *JAdv,* 13 Dec. 1928, 3:1. Steinberg specifically noted that he had been elected and installed as president before the day on which he was impressed by the lesson of *Miketz.* On that Saturday morning, Steinberg recalled, "I stood at my place on the Altar": see *JAdv,* 13 Dec. 1928, 3:1. The first time *Miketz* was read after Steinberg's installation was 27 December 1924.

5. The translation is from *Tanakh—The Holy Scriptures: The New JPS Translation According to the Traditional Hebrew Text* (Philadelphia: Jewish Publication Society, 1985).

6. *JAdv,* 25 Dec. 1924, 1, also 6. See also Congregation Beth Hamidrash Hagadol, *Tenth Anniversary Souvenir Book, 1914–1924* (Boston: Monroe Service, 1924), Congregation Beth Hamidrash Hagadol Papers, AJHS, 10, 94, 98, 100, 104; *JAdv,* 13 Dec. 1928, 3:5; Beth Hamidrash Hagadol, box 110, WPA; *JAdv,* 10 Oct. 1913, 1; *JAdv,* 5 Dec. 1913, 1; *JAdv,* 3 July 1914, 1, 8; *JAdv,* 1 May 1924, 1, 2; *JAdv,* 21 May 1925, 1, 5; *JAdv,* 4 June 1925, 6; *JAdv,* 10 Jan. 1918, 2; Congregation Beth Hamidrash Hagadol, *Year Book, 5683 (1922–1923)* (Boston: Monroe Service, n.d.), Congregation Beth Hamidrash Hagadol Papers, AJHS, 52; *JAdv,* 4 Oct. 1923, 1; *JAdv,* 18 Oct. 1923, 11; *JAdv,* 8 Jan. 1925, 4.

7. *JAdv,* 13 Dec. 1928, 3:1.

8. Ibid., 3:3.

9. Ibid., 3:1, also 3:3, 3:5. See also Congregation Beth Hamidrash Hagadol, *Tenth Anniversary Souvenir Book, 1914–1924,* 11, 14–19, 48–51; *JAdv,* 1 Jan. 1925, 4; *JAdv,* 8 Jan. 1925, 3.

10. *JAdv,* 13 Dec. 1928, 3:1, also 3:3. See also *JAdv,* 6 June 1918, 4; *JAdv,* 8 Aug. 1918, 2; *JAdv,* 21 Nov. 1918, 2; *JAdv,* 12 Dec. 1918, 2; *JAdv,* 6 Nov. 1919, 5; *JAdv,* 9 Dec. 1920, 5; *JAdv,* 28 Apr. 1921, 3; *JAdv,* 26 May 1921, 7; Congregation Beth Hamidrash Hagadol, *Year Book, 5683 (1922–1923),* 31, 110; Congregation Beth Hamidrash Hagadol, *Tenth Anniversary Souvenir Book, 1914–1924,* 12–13, 15, 17–18, 48–51; *JAdv,* 25 June 1925, 8; *JAdv,* 2 July 1925, 2; *JAdv,* 12 Nov. 1925, 6; *JAdv,* 13 Jan. 1927, 1, 2.

11. *JAdv,* 1 Jan. 1925, 4. See also *JAdv,* 3 July 1914, 1, 8; *JAdv,* 10 Jan. 1918, 2; *JAdv,* 6 June 1918, 4; *JAdv,* 8 Aug. 1918, 2; Congregation Beth Hamidrash Hagadol, *Tenth Anniversary Souvenir Book, 1914–1924,* 10–11, 13, 16, 18, 19, 53, 80; *JAdv,* 25 June 1925, 6, 8; *JAdv,* 2 July 1925, 2; *JAdv,* 20 Aug. 1925, 2; *JAdv,* 31 Dec. 1925, 8; *JAdv,* 21 Jan. 1926, 6; *JAdv,* 20 Jan. 1927, 1, 7; *JAdv,* 19 May 1927, 2:2; *JAdv,* 15 Nov. 1928, 1; *JAdv,* 22 Nov. 1928, 2:1;

JAdv, 29 Nov. 1928, 8; *JAdv,* 6 Dec. 1928, 4; *JAdv,* 13 Dec. 1928, 3:1, 3:3, 3:4, 3:5, 5:2; *JAdv,* 20 Dec. 1928, 6; *JAdv,* 19 Sept. 1929, 2:1; Congregation Beth Hamidrash Hagodol, *25th Anniversary Celebration, 1915–1940,* Congregation Beth Hamidrash Hagadol Papers, AJHS.

12. *JAdv,* 8 Jan. 1925, 3. See also *JAdv,* 25 June 1925, 8; *JAdv,* 13 Jan. 1927, 1, 2; *JAdv,* 20 Jan. 1927, 1, 7; *JAdv,* 2 July 1925, 2; *JAdv,* 19 Apr. 1928, 4; *JAdv,* 30 Aug. 1928, 3; *JAdv,* 6 Sept. 1928, 3; *JAdv,* 15 Nov. 1928, 1; *JAdv,* 22 Nov. 1928, 2:1; *JAdv,* 29 Nov. 1928, 8; *JAdv,* 6 Dec. 1928, 4; *JAdv,* 13 Dec. 1928, 3:1, 3:3, 3:4, 3:5; Congregation Beth Hamidrash Hagadol, *25th Anniversary Celebration, 1915–1940.*

13. *JAdv,* 12 Nov. 1925, 1; *JAdv,* 13 Jan. 1927, 1; *JAdv,* 14 Apr. 1966, 2:2. See also *JAdv,* 25 June 1925, 8; *JAdv,* 2 July 1925, 2; *JAdv,* 3 Sept. 1925, 8; *JAdv,* 19 Nov. 1925, 1; *JAdv,* 30 Dec. 1926, 1; *JAdv,* 18 Dec. 1942, 1, 14; *JAdv,* 21 Nov. 1946, 5; *JAdv,* 4 Dec. 1947, 9; David Kaufman, "'Shul with a Pool': The Synagogue-Center in American Jewish Life, 1875–1925" (Ph.D. diss., Brandeis University, 1993).

14. *JAdv,* 2 July 1925, 2; *JAdv,* 25 June 1925, 8. See also Congregation Beth Hamidrash Hagadol, *Tenth Anniversary Souvenir Book, 1914–1924,* 11; *JAdv,* 7 Nov. 1918, 2; *JAdv,* 20 Feb. 1919, 1, 5; *JAdv,* 12 Nov. 1925, 3.

15. *Transcript,* 15 Feb. 1907, 1. See also *BAdv,* 6 Sept. 1907, 1.

16. *JAdv,* 18 Dec. 1942, 1, 14; *JAdv,* 25 May 1922, 1; *JAdv,* 1 June 1922, 10; *JAdv,* 4 Oct. 1923, 1; lists of synagogues, box 110, WPA; *JAdv,* 2 Nov. 1916, 1, 9; *JAdv,* 8 Feb. 1917, 1; *JAdv,* 9 Oct. 1919, 1; *JAdv,* 6 Nov. 1919, 5; *JAdv,* 5 Feb. 1920, 1; Suffolk County Deeds 4208:273; *JAdv,* 8 Nov. 1923, 11; Cash Disbursements, Jan.–Feb. 1924, Mishkan Tefila Papers, AJA; *JAdv,* 12 Nov. 1925, 2; *JAdv,* 26 Aug. 1926, 5; Rabbi Herman H. Rubenovitz to the Chairman and Members of the Board of Directors, 16 Nov. 1926, Mishkan Tefila Papers, AJA; Simon Finberg to the President and Members of the Congregation, 28 Dec. 1926, ibid.; Board of Directors, minutes of meeting, 1 Feb. 1927, ibid.; *JAdv,* 10 Mar. 1927, 3:1; Board of Directors, minutes of meeting, 29 Sept. 1927, Mishkan Tefila Papers, AJA; Board of Directors, minutes of meeting, 9 Nov. 1927, ibid.; School Committee, annual report, 30 Jan. 1928, ibid.; *JAdv,* 7 Feb. 1929, 5; *JAdv,* 12 Sept. 1929, 1, 2, 2:5.

17. To make these population estimates, I relied on several sources. For the number of Russian-born residents in Brookline and the total population of that town in 1920, see U.S. Census, *Fourteenth Census, 1920,* 445, 455–456. For the number of Russian-born residents in, number of school-age children in, and total population of Brookline in 1930, see U.S. Census, *Fifteenth Census, 1930,* 1091, 1098–1099. For the number of Brookline children absent from school on Yom Kippur in 1929, see Bureau of Jewish

Social Research, "Summary—Jewish Communal Survey of Boston," unpublished, Oct. 1930, JWB, 1–2.

18. Rabbi Herman H. Rubenovitz to the Chairman and Members of the Board of Directors, 8 Nov. 1932, Mishkan Tefila Papers, AJA. See also Jewish Welfare Board, "Study of the Jewish Community of Greater Boston, Massachusetts, with Special Reference to Needs for Jewish Center Work," unpublished, 1940, JWB, and box 131, CJP, 193–194; Albert I. Gordon, *Jews in Suburbia* (Boston: Beacon Press, 1959), 25–27, 106–107. For the number of Russian-born residents and the total population of Newton in 1920, see U.S. Census, *Fourteenth Census, 1920,* 446, 455–456. To estimate the Jewish population of Newton in 1930, I analyzed the following sources: U.S. Census, *Fifteenth Census, 1930,* 1094, 1098–1099; Bureau of Jewish Social Research, "Summary—Jewish Communal Survey of Boston," Oct. 1930, 1–2.

19. Rabbi Herman H. Rubenovitz to the Chairman and Members of the Board of Directors, 8 Nov. 1932, Mishkan Tefila Papers, AJA; School Committee, minutes of meeting, 7 Nov. 1932, ibid.; School Committee, minutes of meeting, 29 Oct. 1935, ibid.

20. *JAdv,* 13 Dec. 1935, 2:6; *JAdv,* 13 Apr. 1950, 1, 7. See also *JAdv,* 20 Sept. 1935, 2; Gordon, *Jews in Suburbia,* 27, 107–109; Jewish Welfare Board, "Study of the Jewish Community of Greater Boston," 1940, 193–194; *JAdv,* 23 Feb. 1950, 1; *JAdv,* 23 Mar. 1950, 1; *JAdv,* 8 June 1950, 4; *JAdv,* 21 Feb. 1952, 18; *JAdv,* 27 Mar. 1952, 16; *JAdv,* 15 May 1952, 1, 9; *JAdv,* 4 Sept. 1952, 20. To estimate the 1950 Jewish population of Newton, I examined the following data at the census-tract level: number of whites, number of foreign-born whites, number of whites born in U.S.S.R., and number of whites born in Central or Eastern Europe: see U.S. Department of Commerce, Bureau of the Census, *United States Census of Population, 1950—Census Tract Statistics—Boston, Massachusetts, and Adjacent Area* (Washington: Government Printing Office, 1952).

21. To make these population estimates, I examined the following data at the census-tract level: number of persons, number of whites, number of foreign-born whites, number of whites born in U.S.S.R., and number of whites born in Central or Eastern Europe: see U.S. Census, *1950—Census Tract Statistics—Boston.* For the 1950 population of Brighton and Allston, I combined the populations of census tracts Y-1, Y-2, Y-3A, Y-3B, Y-4, Y-5A, Y-5B, and Y-5C.

22. *JAdv,* 6 Dec. 1945, 1, also 8, 10. See also Board of Trustees, Jewish Centers Association of Greater Boston, minutes of meeting, 11 Dec. 1945, box 25, HH; Board of Trustees, Jewish Centers Association of Greater Boston, min-

utes of meeting, 3 Apr. 1946, ibid.; Executive Committee, Associated Jewish Philanthropies, minutes of meeting, 28 Jan. 1948, box 6, CJP; *JAdv,* 20 May 1948, 1, 11; *JAdv,* 3 June 1948, 13.

23. Saul Bernstein, Report of Executive Director, Jewish Centers Association of Greater Boston, Sept. 1946, box 25, HH, 10. See also *JAdv,* 11 Jan. 1945, 1, 18; Recommendations to the Board, Jewish Centers Association of Greater Boston, with cover letter by Saul Bernstein, 25 Oct. 1945, box 25, HH.

24. To make this population estimate, I relied on several sources. I examined the following data at the census-tract level: number of persons, number of whites, number of foreign-born whites, number of native-born whites of foreign-born parentage, number of whites born in Russia and number of native-born whites with a parent born in Russia, number of whites born in Central or Eastern Europe and number of native-born whites with a parent born in Central or Eastern Europe, and number of native-born whites of native-born parentage. Also at the census-tract level, I examined the percentage of school-age children in the population of various Jewish districts. For the 1930 population of Dorchester and Roxbury, I combined the populations of census tracts P-2, P-3, P-4, P-5, P-6, T-1, T-2, T-3, T-4, T-5, T-6, T-7, T-8, T-9, T-10, U-1, U-2, U-3, U-4, U-5, U-6, V-1, X-1, X-2, X-3, X-4, X-5, and X-6 and portions of census tracts P-1 and W-3. For 1930 census-tract data, see U.S. Census, "Census Tract Data, [Boston,] 1930 Census." For 1930 census-tract maps, see Boston Council of Social Agencies, *Social Statistics by Census Tracts;* Boston Health League, *Alphabetical Street Index.* For the number of children absent from Dorchester and Roxbury schools on Yom Kippur in 1929, which I organized according to the actual location of each school, see Bureau of Jewish Social Research, "Summary—Jewish Communal Survey of Boston," Oct. 1930, 1; Jewish Welfare Board, "Study of the Jewish Community of Greater Boston," 1940, 2–10, 33–34, 37.

25. To make these population estimates, I relied on several sources. I examined the following data at the census-tract level: number of persons, number of whites, number of foreign-born whites, number of whites born in U.S.S.R., and number of whites born in Central or Eastern Europe. Also at the census-tract level, I examined the percentage of school-age children and voting-age adults in the population of various Jewish districts. For the 1940 and 1950 populations of Dorchester and Roxbury, I combined the populations of census tracts P-1C, P-2, P-3, P-4, P-5, P-6, T-1, T-2, T-3A, T-3B, T-4A, T-4B, T-5A, T-5B, T-6, T-7A, T-7B, T-8A, T-8B, T-9, T-10, U-1, U-2, U-3, U-4, U-5, U-6A, U-6B, V-1, X-1, X-2, X-3A, X-3B, X-4A, X-4B, X-5A, X-5B, X-5C, X-6A, X-6B, and X-6C. For 1940 and 1950 census-tract

data, see U.S. Department of Commerce, Bureau of the Census, *16th Census of the United States, 1940: Population and Housing—Statistics for Census Tracts, Boston, Mass.* (Washington: Government Printing Office, 1942); U.S. Census, *1950—Census Tract Statistics—Boston.* For the number of children absent from Dorchester and Roxbury schools on Yom Kippur in 1938, which I organized according to the actual location of each school, see Jewish Welfare Board, "Study of the Jewish Community of Greater Boston," 1940, 2–10, 33–34, 37. For an estimate of the numbers of Jews and non-Jews in the voting-age populations of Wards 12 and 14, based on names recorded in the 1940 police lists, see Jewish Welfare Board, "Study of the Jewish Community of Greater Boston," 1940, 17–23. For other contemporary studies of the Jewish population of Dorchester and Roxbury in the 1940s and early 1950s, see "Estimates of the Metropolitan Boston Population: Statistics (1,000 & Over)," 10 Jan. 1944, box 14, CJP; S. C. Kohs, for the National Jewish Welfare Board, "Boston Jewish Population Count, May 1945," Apr. 1946, JWB; [Erich Rosenthal?], "Distribution of Jewish Population in Roxbury, Dorchester North and Dorchester South (including Mattapan) According to Age Ranges," probably 1946, box 20, CJP; Jewish Centers Association of Greater Boston, "Report of Center Planning Committee for Dorchester-Mattapan-Roxbury," unpublished, 1946, box 131, CJP, and box 33, JCC; "Comparative Report of Greater Boston Jewish and General Population," 27 Nov. 1957, including estimates of Jewish populations in 1945–1946 and 1957, box 14, CJP; Associated Jewish Philanthropies, Committee on Leisure-Time Services, with the assistance of the National Jewish Welfare Board, "Survey and Recommendations on Social, Cultural, and Recreational Activities of the Jewish Community of Greater Boston," unpublished, June 1950, JWB.

26. In referring to the Jewish population of Roxbury, I include not only Elm Hill and the rest of upper Roxbury (which is west of Blue Hill Avenue) but also the Grove Hall–Blue Hill Avenue district (the area, physically located in Dorchester, that lies just east of upper Roxbury). Boston's Jews regarded this entire area as Roxbury. That Boston's Jews regarded a section of Dorchester as part of Roxbury led to great confusion among contemporaries measuring the area's population: professional researchers, with little direct knowledge of the community, included the Grove Hall–Blue Hill Avenue district in Dorchester, while local Jewish leaders naturally included the district in Roxbury. Thus, for the 1930 population of Jewish Roxbury, I combined the populations of census tracts P-3, P-4, P-5, P-6, T-6, U-1, U-2, U-3, U-4, U-5, U-6, and V-1 and a portion of census tract T-7. For the 1940 and 1950 populations of Jewish Roxbury, I combined the populations of census tracts P-3, P-4, P-5, P-6, T-6, T-7A, U-1, U-2, U-3, U-4, U-5,

U-6A, U-6B, and V-1. See the two previous notes for sources of population estimates.

27. Saul Bernstein, "Summary and Interpretation of Roxbury-Dorchester-Mattapan Jewish Population Study—1946," in Jewish Centers Association, "Report of Center Planning Committee for Dorchester-Mattapan-Roxbury," 1946, 3.

28. Judge Harry J. Elam, telephone interview with author, 1 June 1993.

29. For the 1920 population of upper Roxbury, I combined the populations of Ward 16 and a portion of Ward 15. For 1920 ward data, see U.S. Census, *Fourteenth Census, 1920,* 458. For the 1930 population of upper Roxbury, I combined the populations of census tracts U-1, U-2, U-3, U-4, U-5, U-6, and V-1. For 1930 census-tract data, see U.S. Census, "Census Tract Data, [Boston,] 1930 Census." For 1930 census-tract maps, see Boston Council of Social Agencies, *Social Statistics by Census Tracts;* Boston Health League, *Alphabetical Street Index.* For the 1940 and 1950 populations of upper Roxbury, I combined the populations of census tracts U-1, U-2, U-3, U-4, U-5, U-6A, U-6B, and V-1. For 1940 and 1950 census-tract data, see U.S. Census, *16th Census, 1940: Statistics for Census Tracts, Boston;* U.S. Census, *1950—Census Tract Statistics—Boston.* As late as 1950, only 833 blacks lived in all of Dorchester (including the Grove Hall–Blue Hill Avenue district).

30. *Guardian,* 16 Sept. 1939, 3.

31. Nat Hentoff, *Boston Boy* (New York: Knopf, 1986), 5. See also Suffolk County Deeds 4865:506–507; St. Mark Congregational Church, untitled history, Personal Papers of Joan Allen; St. Mark Congregational Church, "Saint Mark Congregational Church, 1895," history, probably 1983, Personal Papers of Judge Harry J. Elam; St. Mark Congregational Church, "Souvenir—Fiftieth Anniversary, the St. Mark Congregational Church of Boston, Incorporated, 1895–1945; The Twenty-fifth of the St. Mark Social Center, Incorporated," Congregational Library, American Congregational Association, 19, 43.

32. Board of Directors, Greater Boston Council of Jewish Centers, minutes of meeting, 11 Dec. 1947, box 25, HH; "Roxbury," enclosed in George I. Samansky to Joseph Bower, 9 June 1950, box 16, HH; Associated Jewish Philanthropies, "Jewish Center Developments in Greater Boston: A Special Report," Apr. 1949, box 10, CJP, 15.

33. "Dorchester-Mattapan," enclosed in George I. Samansky to Edward Sidman, 9 June 1950, box 25, HH; Rev. Waldo C. Hasenfus to Rt. Rev. Walter Furlong, 12 Dec. 1946, St. Matthew, AAPB.

34. *GlbSun,* 7 Mar. 1971, A:3. See also *JAdv,* 8 Apr. 1954, 15.

35. Francis Russell, "How to Destroy a Suburb," *National Review*, 1 Oct. 1976, 1064.
36. *JAdv*, 9 Oct. 1919, 1; *JAdv*, 11 Dec. 1919, 1, 5; *JAdv*, 25 Dec. 1919, 1, 8; Herman H. Rubenovitz, "My Rabbinate at Temple Mishkan Tefila: A History from 1910 to 1946," in Temple Mishkan Tefila, *Temple Mishkan Tefila: A History, 1858–1958* (Newton: Temple Mishkan Tefila, 1958), CMTA, 24; Suffolk County Deeds 4208:273; *JAdv*, 5 Feb. 1920, 1. Jacob L. Sieve, *L'dor Vodor: From Generation to Generation—Congregation Mishkan Tefila, 1858–1983* (Newton: Congregation Mishkan Tefila, 1983), 12, mistakenly states that the banquet was in Dec. 1918.
37. For the membership of the board of directors in 1919, see "Attendance, 1919," Mishkan Tefila Papers, AJA. For the home address of each director, see Brookline Directory, 1919; Boston City Directory, 1919. I am grateful to Dan Gamm, who looked up all of these addresses.
38. *JAdv*, 9 Oct. 1919, 1.
39. For the membership of the board of directors in 1925, see Dedication Plaque placed in the Seaver Street Temple, photograph, CMTA; "Dedication—Temple Mishkan Tefila, Seaver Street and Elm Hill Avenue, Roxbury, Massachusetts—Sunday, the Thirteenth of Sept., Nineteen hundred and twenty-five," booklet, CMTA. For the home address of each director, see Brookline Directory, 1925; Boston City Directory, 1925.
40. Rev. John E. O'Connell to Card. William O'Connell, probably Oct. 1932, St. John, AAPC. For 1930 census-tract data, see U.S. Census, "Census Tract Data, [Boston,] 1930 Census." For 1930 census-tract maps, see Boston Council of Social Agencies, *Social Statistics by Census Tracts*; Boston Health League, *Alphabetical Street Index*. For the Elm Hill district, I report data for census tract U-6. I do not report data for tract U-5, which is also on Elm Hill, because a large section of the tract was occupied by blacks rather than by Jews. For Dorchester and upper Roxbury, I report data for all tracts beginning with suffixes P, T, U, and X, as well as tract V-1.
41. Rabbi Herman H. Rubenovitz to the Chairman and Members of the Board of Directors, 25 Feb. 1926, Mishkan Tefila Papers, AJA; Simon Finberg to the President and Members, 28 Dec. 1926, ibid. See also Rubenovitz to the President and Members, 29 Dec. 1932, ibid.
42. Rabbi Herman H. Rubenovitz to the President and Members, 29 Dec. 1932, Mishkan Tefila Papers, AJA. See also Rubenovitz to the Chairman and Members of the Board of Directors, 27 Nov. 1935, ibid.
43. For a list of members in 1913, see Congregation Mishkan Tefila, *Constitution and By-Laws of the Congregation Mishkan Tefila, Boston, Massachusetts* (Boston, 1913), CMTA, 25–29. For a list of members in 1950, see Mem-

bership List, Congregation Mishkan Tefila, 2 Nov. 1950, CMTA. Both the 1913 and the 1950 lists include home addresses. I located only one list of members' names for the period 1914–1949. Prepared in the winter of 1923–1924, it gives only surnames, first initials, and account balances with the congregation; lacking home addresses and full first names, the list is not useful for identifying and locating individual members: see Harry I. Kessler to Louis Mazur, 16 Feb. 1924, financial report for year ending 31 Dec. 1923, CMTA.

44. Board of Directors, Temple Mishkan Tefila, 24 May 1950, CMTA.

45. According to the 1950 membership list, 372 families lived in the Roxbury-Dorchester area, 257 families lived in the Brookline-Brighton-Newton area, and 36 families lived elsewhere: see Membership List, Congregation Mishkan Tefila, 2 Nov. 1950, CMTA.

46. Harry Cushing, "Fifty Years of Faith: A History of the Religious Institutions of Greater Boston," *JAdv*, 26 June 1952, 3:6.

47. *JAdv*, 6 Dec. 1935, 5; *JAdv*, 20 Dec. 1935, 4.

48. Helen Saftel, "Hecht Neighborhood House: Report, June 1935–June 1937," box 3, HH. See also Jewish Welfare Board, "Study of the Jewish Community of Greater Boston," 1940, 332; Hecht House, untitled three-page report that begins, "The problems concerning the building and the facilities of Hecht House may be divided into three parts . . . ," 12 May 1949, box 147, CJP; Board of Directors, 1951–1952, Hecht House, 1 May 1951, box 1, HH.

49. Barbara Miller Solomon, "Pioneers in Service: The History of the Associated Jewish Philanthropies of Boston," feature section, *JAdv*, 27 June 1957, 24, 31; Jewish Welfare Board, "Study of the Jewish Community of Greater Boston," 1940, 229. See also *JAdv*, 17 May 1912, 1; *JAdv*, 26 May 1911, 1, 8; *JAdv*, 2 June 1911, 8; *JAdv*, 22 Dec. 1911, 2; *JAdv*, 24 May 1912, 1; History of Boston YMHA, untitled, circa 1948, box 16, HH.

50. Melvin S. Cohen, "Factors Concerned in the Decline of Membership," 17 Mar. 1941, box 21, HH.

51. Probably Rabbi Israel J. Kazis, untitled notes that begin, "Statistics on local Temples," 2 pp., 9 Dec. 1953, CMTA. See also Board of Directors, minutes of meeting, 20 Dec. 1953, CMTA.

52. *BAdv*, editorial, probably 17 May 1907, CMTA; Kaplan diary, 29 Dec. 1914, Mordecai M. Kaplan Diaries, JTS. See also *BAdv*, 10 Jan. 1908, 2; *JAdv*, 17 Jan. 1913, 2; *JAdv*, 4 Nov. 1915, 2; *JAdv*, 14 Dec. 1916, 1; *JAdv*, 3 Jan. 1918, 1; *JAdv*, 8 Aug. 1918, 2; *JAdv*, 7 Nov. 1918, 2; *JAdv*, 12 Dec. 1918, 2; *JAdv*, 20 Feb. 1919, 1; *JAdv*, 6 Nov. 1919, 5; *JAdv*, 8 Jan. 1920, 2; *JAdv*, 25 Nov. 1920, 2; *JAdv*, 9 Dec. 1920, 5; Congregation Beth Hamidrash Hagadol,

Tenth Anniversary Souvenir Book, 1914–1924, 12, 17–18, 48–51, 77; *JAdv,* 8 Jan. 1925, 3; *JAdv,* 25 June 1925, 8; *JAdv,* 30 Dec. 1926, 2:3; *JAdv,* 13 Jan. 1927, 1.

53. *JAdv,* 17 Nov. 1911, 8; Kaplan diary, 2 Feb. 1917, Mordecai M. Kaplan Diaries, JTS.

54. *JAdv,* 24 Sept. 1925, 5; Rabbi Herman H. Rubenovitz to the President and Members, 13 Jan. 1927, Mishkan Tefila Papers, AJA. See also Congregation Beth Hamidrash Hagadol, *Tenth Anniversary Souvenir Book, 1914–1924,* 48; *JAdv,* 12 Nov. 1925, 6.

55. Marshall Sklare, "Response," *American Jewish History* 74 (Dec. 1984), 162; Jack Wertheimer, "The Conservative Synagogue Revisited," *American Jewish History* 74 (Dec. 1984), 122, also 119–123. See also Marshall Sklare, *Conservative Judaism: An American Religious Movement* (Glencoe, Ill.: Free Press, 1955), 47–82, 262, n.11; Jack Wertheimer, "The Conservative Synagogue," in *The American Synagogue: A Sanctuary Transformed,* ed. Jack Wertheimer (Cambridge: Cambridge University Press, 1987), 114–123, 142, n.8; Deborah Dash Moore, *At Home in America: Second Generation New York Jews* (New York: Columbia University Press, 1981), 138–139, 236–237; Kaufman, "'Shul with a Pool.'"

56. Rabbi Herman H. Rubenovitz to the President and Members, 29 Dec. 1932, Mishkan Tefila Papers, AJA; Rubenovitz to the Chairman and Members of the Board of Directors, 25 Feb. 1926, ibid. Temple Beth Hillel, the only other Conservative congregation in Dorchester and Roxbury, was not organized until 1944: see *JAdv,* 15 June 1944, 2; *JAdv,* 31 Aug. 1944, 1.

57. *JAdv,* 12 Sept. 1929, 1, 2; *JAdv,* 19 Sept. 1929, 4:6; *JAdv,* 17 Mar. 1939, 6.

58. *JAdv,* 13 May 1926, 1; *JAdv,* 29 Sept. 1927, 2:4; Jewish Welfare Board, "Recreational, Social and Cultural Resources and Activities of the Jewish Community of Boston," unpublished, June 1930, JWB, 10, 108. See also *JAdv,* 10 June 1926, 2; *JAdv,* 12 Sept. 1930, 1; *JAdv,* 4 Nov. 1930, 5.

59. Jewish Welfare Board, "Study of the Jewish Community of Greater Boston," 1940, 77.

60. *JAdv,* 11 Oct. 1928, 6; *JAdv,* 21 Feb. 1929, 2:1. See also *JAdv,* 15 Dec. 1927, 5; White, *In Search of History,* 21–22; *JAdv,* 20 June 1930, 1; *JAdv,* 22 Oct. 1935, 5; *JAdv,* 6 Dec. 1935, 5; *JAdv,* 31 Jan. 1930, 5; *JAdv,* 30 Jan. 1931, 3; *JAdv,* 23 Apr. 1943, 10; Congregation Adath Jeshurun, annual report for year ending 23 Dec. 1938, box 110, WPA.

61. Bureau of Jewish Education, "Memorandum on Community Responsibility for Jewish Education," 6 June 1950, box 10, CJP. See also AJP Budget Committee on Education, minutes of meeting, 12 June 1950, ibid.

62. Executive Committee, Associated Jewish Philanthropies, minutes of meet-

ing, 1 July 1949, box 136a, CJP; Bureau of Jewish Education, "Memorandum on Community Responsibility for Jewish Education," 6 June 1950,
box 10, CJP. See also Executive Committee, Associated Jewish Philanthropies, minutes of meeting, 8 June 1949, box 136a, CJP; *JAdv,* 4 May 1950, 1,
9, 14; *JAdv,* 26 Oct. 1950, 4; AJP Budget Committee on Jewish Education,
minutes of meeting, 2 Jan. 1952, box 10, CJP.

63. For sources, see Gerald H. Gamm, "Neighborhood Roots: Exodus and
Stability in Boston, 1870–1990" (Ph.D. diss., Harvard University, 1994),
366, n.234.

64. Congregation Adath Jeshurun, annual report for year ending 23 Dec.
1938, box 110, WPA.

65. Sumner Greenberg, telephone interview with author, 15 Apr. 1992.
(Greenberg's father-in-law is Abraham Close.) See also Congregation Beth
Hamidrash Hagodol, financial report, 1 Dec. 1944–31 Oct. 1945, Finan-
cial Reports, 1944–1960, BHHC; Congregation Beth Hamidrash Hagodol,
financial report for year ended 31 Oct. 1947, ibid.; Congregation Beth
Hamidrash Hagodol, financial report for year ended 31 Oct. 1949, ibid.;
Congregation Beth Hamidrash Hagodol, financial report for year ended 31
Oct. 1951, ibid.; Congregation Beth Hamidrash Hagadol, *Tenth Anniver-
sary Souvenir Book, 1914–1924,* 11.

66. Stephan Thernstrom, *The Other Bostonians: Poverty and Progress in the
American Metropolis, 1880–1970* (Cambridge: Harvard University Press,
1973), 145–175; Gerald H. Gamm, *The Making of New Deal Democrats:
Voting Behavior and Realignment in Boston, 1920–1940* (Chicago: University of Chicago Press, 1989), 49–55, 76–80, 139–146.

67. According to various sources, Catholics made up a very large majority of
Dorchester's non-Jewish white population. Msgr. Patrick Lydon, the pastor
of St. Mark's Parish, noted in 1954 that "the population in this area is over
90% Catholic": Rt. Rev. Patrick J. Lydon, 14 Nov. 1954, description of
parish boundaries, St. Mark, AAPB. See notes 24 and 25 for my estimates
of Dorchester's Jewish population. For 1930 census-tract data, see U.S.
Census, "Census Tract Data, [Boston,] 1930 Census." For 1930 census-
tract maps, see Boston Council of Social Agencies, *Social Statistics by
Census Tracts;* Boston Health League, *Alphabetical Street Index.* For 1940
and 1950 census-tract data, see U.S. Census, *16th Census, 1940: Statistics
for Census Tracts, Boston;* U.S. Census, *1950—Census Tract Statistics—Boston.* To check the accuracy of these estimates, which rely on estimating the
number of Jews in Dorchester and the proportion of Dorchester's non-Jewish population that was Catholic, I made a second set of estimates that rely
on an entirely separate body of data. For this second set of population

estimates, I examined census data to determine what proportion of an area's population was composed of persons born in the preceding year, then drew on annual parish records of infant baptisms to calculate the area's total Catholic population. These calculations support the figures that I present in the text.

68. St. Joseph, 1925–1951, AACC.

69. Rt. Rev. Thomas J. Finnegan, Jr., interview with author, St. Elizabeth's Rectory, Milton, Mass., 14 Aug. 1991; Robert H. Lord, John E. Sexton, and Edward T. Harrington, *History of the Archdiocese of Boston in the Various Stages of Its Development, 1604 to 1943* (New York: Sheed and Ward, 1944), iii:686; St. Mark's Parish, *75th Anniversary, St. Mark the Evangelist Parish, Dorchester, Mass., 1905–1980: An Illustrated History*, St. Mark, AAPH, 9, also 10–12. See also St. John–St. Hugh's Parish, *Golden Jubilee Reunion, 1891–1941: St. John's–St. Hugh's Parish, Roxbury, Mass.*, 1941, Personal Papers of Rev. Laurence McGrath.

70. The other four parishes were St. Gregory, St. Joseph, St. Margaret, and St. Peter. For the completion of St. Mark's Convent, see St. Mark's Parish, *75th Anniversary, St. Mark the Evangelist Parish*, 5–6.

71. Chancellor to Rev. Charles N. Cunningham, 20 Sept. 1945, St. Paul, AAPC; *Post*, 14 Apr. 1947, 5. See also Lord et al., *History of the Archdiocese of Boston*, iii:685–686; St. Brendan's Parish, *Golden Anniversary*, probably 1979, St. Brendan's Rectory; *Pilot*, 4 Nov. 1933, 1, 2; *Pilot*, 11 Nov. 1933, 1; Rev. Joseph M. White, telephone interviews with author, 5 Jan. 1993, 13 Jan. 1993, and 17 May 1993; Rev. J. Joseph Kierce, "To a Prospective Lay Volunteer . . . ," St. Kevin's Rectory; "General Data Form," St. Kevin, School Profiles, RCSO; Chancellor to Cunningham, 24 Sept. 1945, St. Paul, AAPC; St. Kevin, 1946, AACC.

72. St. Mark's Parish, *75th Anniversary, St. Mark the Evangelist Parish*, 14, 10. See also Annual Parish and Cemetery Reports, 1947–1951, RCAB, for the following parishes: St. Ann, St. John–St. Hugh, St. Leo, St. Mary of the Angels, St. Matthew, St. William, St. Peter, and St. Mark.

73. St. Mark's Parish, *75th Anniversary, St. Mark the Evangelist Parish*, 13; Rev. James McCarthy, interview with author, Tribunal Building, Archdiocese of Boston, Brighton, 23 July 1991. See also Rt. Rev. Thomas J. Finnegan, Jr., interview with author, St. Elizabeth's Rectory, Milton, Mass., 14 Aug. 1991; St. Matthew, 1953, Annual Parish and Cemetery Reports, RCAB.

74. Cushing, "Fifty Years of Faith," 3:6.

75. Report of Executive Committee, 29 Apr. 1951, CMTA.

76. *JAdv*, 14 June 1951, 5; *JAdv*, 24 Apr. 1958, feature section, 2; Report of Executive Committee, 23 May 1950, Mishkan Tefila Papers, AJA. See also

JAdv, 21 June 1951, 16; Congregation, minutes of meeting, 23 May 1950, Mishkan Tefila Papers, AJA; Paula E. Hyman, "From City to Suburb: Temple Mishkan Tefila of Boston," in *The American Synagogue,* 189.

77. Congregation, minutes of meeting, 23 May 1950, Mishkan Tefila Papers, AJA.

10. The Uprooted and the Rooted

1. Susan L. Emery, *A Catholic Stronghold and Its Making: A History of St. Peter's Parish, Dorchester, Massachusetts, and of Its First Rector, the Rev. Peter Ronan, P.R.* (Boston: Geo. H. Ellis, 1910), BPL, 89, also 12–14; Douglass Shand Tucci, "The Church," in William H. Marnell and Douglass Shand Tucci, *Saint Peter's Church, 1872–1972* (Boston: Fandel Press, 1972), 35. See also Weekly Attendance Record, First Parish Church Services, 1951–1991. Elizabeth Allen, who has been compiling the First Parish attendance record by hand each week since February 1951, generously shared it with me when I met with her at the First Parish Church on 5 October 1991. And see also St. Peter, 1958, AACC. While I did not locate a schedule of Sunday Masses for the late 1950s, I did locate a schedule of Masses for 1964, when the parish was no larger than it had been in 1958: see St. Peter's Church, weekly parish bulletin, 5 Apr. 1964, St. Peter, Parish Materials, RCAB.

2. Tucci, "The Church," 35; St. Peter, 1958, AACC; Annual Parish and Cemetery Reports, St. Peter, 1959, RCAB; William H. Marnell, "The Parish," in Marnell and Tucci, *Saint Peter's Church, 1872–1972,* 17; Miss M., Dakota St., to Card. Richard J. Cushing, 20 Mar. 1959, St. Peter, AAPB; Mrs. L., Dakota St., to Cushing, Wednesday of Holy Week 1959, ibid.; Miss P., Bloomfield St., to Rt. Rev. Robert J. Sennott, 1 May 1959, ibid.; Rt. Rev. Francis J. Sexton to Miss P., Bloomfield St., 4 May 1959, ibid.

3. Temple Mishkan Tefila, *Temple Mishkan Tefila: A History, 1858–1958* (Newton: Temple Mishkan Tefila, 1958), CMTA, 100; Jacob L. Sieve, *L'dor Vodor: From Generation to Generation—Congregation Mishkan Tefila, 1858–1983* (Newton: Congregation Mishkan Tefila, 1983), 16; Suffolk County Deeds 7321:163; Congregation, minutes of meeting, 30 Apr. 1958, CMTA; President, annual report, 30 Apr. 1958, CMTA.

4. Israel J. Kazis, "A History of Temple Mishkan Tefila: From 1946," in Temple Mishkan Tefila, *Temple Mishkan Tefila: A History, 1858–1958* (Newton: Temple Mishkan Tefila, 1958), CMTA, 38; *JAdv,* 11 Dec. 1958, 2:2. See also *JAdv,* 1 May 1958, 5; Sieve, *L'dor Vodor,* 14.

5. Temple Mishkan Tefila, *A History, 1858–1958,* 54; Board of Directors, minutes of meeting, 20 Dec. 1953, CMTA. See also Paula E. Hyman, "From

City to Suburb: Temple Mishkan Tefila of Boston," in *The American Syna-gogue: A Sanctuary Transformed,* ed. Jack Wertheimer (Cambridge: Cambridge University Press, 1987), 192–194; Hillel Levine and Lawrence Harmon, *The Death of an American Jewish Community: A Tragedy of Good Intentions* (New York: Free Press, 1992), 44–53, 58–65.

6. *JAdv,* 14 Apr. 1966, 2:2.

7. Conference between a special committee of the Jewish Community Council and representatives of the YMHA, YMHA headquarters, minutes of meeting, 9 Dec. 1951, box 61, JCC; NCRAC Committee on Overt Anti-Semitism, minutes of meeting, 18 Dec. 1951, ibid.

8. Evelyn N. Rossman [Sylvia Rothchild], "The Community and I: Two Years Later—The Wine, or the Blessing?" *Commentary* 21 (Mar. 1956): 230. See also Boston Redevelopment Authority, Planning Department, "Housing in Boston" (Boston: Boston Redevelopment Authority, 1967), 29; *CSM,* 27 Aug. 1962, 12. For estimates of the Jewish population in Dorchester, including the Grove Hall–Blue Hill Avenue district (which Jews regarded as part of Roxbury), see National Jewish Welfare Board, "Survey of the Jewish Community of Dorchester-Mattapan," 26 Mar. 1956, box 147, CJP. For an estimate of the 1955 Jewish population in upper Roxbury (not including the Grove Hall–Blue Hill Avenue district), see National Jewish Welfare Board survey, cited in Albert I. Gordon, *Jews in Suburbia* (Boston: Beacon Press, 1959), 27, 252, n.5. See also "Comparative Report of Greater Boston Jewish and General Population," 27 Nov. 1957, including estimates of Jewish populations in 1945–1946 and 1957, box 14, CJP. The population figures presented in the text rely primarily on these sources but also on 1950 and 1960 census data and various assessments in the 1950s of changes in the area's population.

9. *GlbSun,* 7 Mar. 1971, A:3; National Jewish Welfare Board, "Survey of the Jewish Community of Dorchester-Mattapan," 26 Mar. 1956, box 147, CJP.

10. *CSM,* 17 Mar. 1954, 2; Gordon, *Jews in Suburbia,* 27.

11. National Jewish Welfare Board, "Survey of the Jewish Community of Dorchester-Mattapan," 26 Mar. 1956, box 147, CJP; Gordon, *Jews in Suburbia,* 27; *GlbSun,* 7 Mar. 1971, A:3.

12. *GlbSun,* 7 Mar. 1971, A:3, A:8. See also "Comparative Report of Greater Boston Jewish and General Population," 27 Nov. 1957, including estimates of Jewish populations in 1945–1946 and 1957, box 14, CJP.

13. *JAdv,* 29 Sept. 1911, 1; Wallace Stegner, "Who Persecutes Boston?" *Atlantic Monthly,* July 1944, 45–46, also 47–52; Daniel Rudsten, "Problem of Hoodlum Riots in Dorchester," 3 July 1951, box 61, JCC. See also *Newsweek,* 22 Nov. 1943, 47–48; *JAdv,* 20 July 1944, 4; "Letters to and from the Editor," *Atlantic Monthly,* Sept. 1944. Evidence of these confrontations

exists in letters, memoranda, minutes of meetings, and reports, as well as in newspaper and journal articles: see especially boxes 61 and 62, JCC.

14. Public meeting to discuss the Dorchester situation, Workmen's Circle, minutes of meeting, 24 Oct. 1951, box 61, JCC. See also minutes of meetings, memoranda, and letters in boxes 61, 67, and 202, JCC; Lloyd Randolph to Mr. T., 16 May 1947, box 1, HH; Muriel Snowden, "People as Partners in Urban Renewal (The Story of Washington Park)," 17 Dec. 1962, HUL; Muriel Snowden, "Planning with People: Finding the Formula," paper presented at Boston College Seminar, 23 Apr. 1963, HUL; Otto and Muriel Snowden, letter to Freedom House annual meeting, 28 June 1963, HUL; *CSM,* 17 Mar. 1954, 2; *JAdv,* 25 Sept. 1958, 2; *GlbSun,* 12 June 1988, 1, 30; Lewis G. Watts, *The Middle-Income Negro Family Faces Urban Renewal* (Massachusetts Department of Commerce and Development, 1964), 18; Langley Carleton Keyes, Jr., *The Rehabilitation Planning Game: A Study in the Diversity of Neighborhood* (Cambridge: MIT Press, 1969), 155; Chester Rapkin, "The Seaver-Townsend Urban Renewal Area" (Boston: Boston Redevelopment Authority, 1962), 43–44.

15. *Globe,* 3 Jan. 1953, 1.

16. The murder was never solved: see *JAdv,* 14 Jan. 1965, 1.

17. *Glbpm,* 2 Jan. 1953, 1, also 22, 23; *Glbpm,* 6 Jan. 1953, 15, also 1; Robert E. Segal to Isadore Zack, memorandum, 26 June 1956, box 67, JCC. See also *Glbpm,* 3 Jan. 1953, 1, 2; *Globe,* 9 Jan. 1953, 5.

18. *JAdv,* 8 Jan. 1953, 8; Freedom House, press release, 5 Jan. 1953, box 175, JCC; Statement to *Boston Globe* that begins, "I believe we make a serious error . . . ," one paragraph, 7 Jan. 1953, ibid. See also *Globe,* 5 Jan. 1953, 3; Robert E. Segal to Thomas C. Heffernan, 5 Jan. 1953, box 175, JCC; *JAdv,* 8 Jan. 1953, 1, 15; *Globe,* 8 Jan. 1953, 1, 5; United Community Services, "Progress Report of Group Work Division Planning on 'Teen-Age Gang Problems,'" 13 Jan. 1953, box 61, JCC; *JAdv,* 15 Jan. 1953, 1, 9; *JAdv,* 5 Feb. 1953, 4, 14; *JAdv,* 12 Feb. 1953, 7.

19. *Hebrew Teachers College Bulletin,* Nov. 1951, HC, 2; *Hebrew College Bulletin,* June 1976, HC, 22, 23; *Hebrew Teachers College Bulletin,* Jan. 1953, HC, 5, also 3. See also *JAdv,* 22 Nov. 1951, 1, 8; *JAdv,* 31 Jan. 1952, 1, 11.

20. *JAdv,* 12 Nov. 1959, 2:10; George Halzel, telephone interview with author, 13 May 1992; Murray Block, telephone interview with author, 3 May 1992. See also Bureau of Jewish Education, "Memorandum on Community Responsibility for Jewish Education," 6 June 1950, box 10, CJP; *JAdv,* 26 Oct. 1950, 4; AJP Budget Committee on Jewish Education, minutes of meeting, 2 Jan. 1952, box 10, CJP; AJP Budget Committee on Jewish Education, minutes of meeting, 6 Nov. 1952, ibid.; *JAdv,* 2 June 1955, 11; AJP Budget Committee on Jewish Education, minutes of meeting, 7 Feb.

1955, box 10, CJP; *JAdv,* 27 Mar. 1958, 13; *JAdv,* 12 Nov. 1959, 2:10; *JAdv,* 30 June 1955, 1, 4; *JAdv,* 28 July 1955, 4; *JAdv,* 3 Nov. 1955, 2:8; *Glbpm,* 3 Jan. 1956, 52; *Record,* 6 Jan. 1956, 5; *JAdv,* 12 Jan. 1956, 1, 11; *JAdv,* 16 Feb. 1956, 2:11; *JAdv,* 19 Apr. 1956, 4; *JAdv,* 31 May 1956, 9; *JAdv,* 6 Sept. 1956, 2; *JAdv,* 29 Aug. 1957, 12; *JAdv,* 19 Sept. 1957, 2, 2:12; *JAdv,* 31 Oct. 1957, 2:5, 2:7; Murray Kesselman, telephone interview with author, 30 Aug. 1991; Rob Schneider, interview with author, Newton, Mass., 14 July 1991.

21. *JAdv,* 1 Apr. 1948, 11; Rabbi Moses J. Cohn, telephone interview with author, 8 June 1992; *JAdv,* 22 Dec. 1955, 14; *JAdv,* 17 Oct. 1957, 2. See also Maimonides School Dedication Commemorative Edition, 2, in *JAdv,* 13 Sept. 1962; *JAdv,* 25 Aug. 1939, 2; *JAdv,* 1 Sept. 1939, 10; *JAdv,* 14 June 1951, 5; *JAdv,* 18 Sept. 1952, A:13–14; *JAdv,* 4 Dec. 1952, 1, 9; *JAdv,* 18 Dec. 1952, 13; *JAdv,* 15 Jan. 1953, 15; *JAdv,* 24 Dec. 1953, 5; *JAdv,* 17 June 1954, 2:1; *JAdv,* 10 May 1956, 3; *JAdv,* 29 Nov. 1956, 4; Bernard Short to Board Member, 16 Aug. 1954, CMTA; Special committee from suburban and local areas regarding Temple finances, minutes of meeting, 10 Feb. 1955, CMTA; Special finance committee, minutes of meeting, 10 Mar. 1955, CMTA; AJP Social Planning and Budget Committee on Jewish Education, minutes of meeting, 26 Dec. 1955, box 10, CJP; *JAdv,* 3 May 1956, 2; *JAdv,* 7 Aug. 1958, 1, 17; *JAdv,* 14 Aug. 1958, 2; *JAdv,* 21 Aug. 1958, 3; *JAdv,* 4 Dec. 1958, 2; Norfolk County Deeds 3468:581; Frieda Cooper, telephone interviews with author, 3 Nov. 1991, 23 Mar. 1992, and 2 Apr. 1992; Mrs. Moses J. Cohn, interview with author, Brighton, Mass., 19 May 1992; Reuven Cohn, telephone interview with author, 21 Apr. 1992. Levine and Harmon argue that Maimonides School "wanted to stay in Roxbury [*sic*]" and hoped to purchase the Crawford Street building; they suggest that it was because "liberal Jewish philanthropists" were willing to donate funds to Freedom House but not to Maimonides that Maimonides could not (and thus did not) purchase the structure. Except for references to interviews with Muriel and Otto Snowden, who were not involved in Maimonides' internal deliberations, Levine and Harmon offer no evidence for these assertions: see Levine and Harmon, *The Death of an American Jewish Community,* 55–57.

22. Minutes of meeting at home of Henry G. Cohen, 13 Apr. 1953, CMTA; Executive Board, tape recording of meeting, 8 Sept. 1954, as cited in paper by Faye Yudkin, CMTA; President, annual report, 1962, CMTA; President, annual report, 1963, CMTA. See also Myer H. Slobodkin to Bernard Short, 6 Mar. 1950, CMTA; Board of Directors, minutes of meeting, 13 May 1951, Mishkan Tefila Papers, AJA; Board of Directors, minutes of meeting, 24 Feb. 1952, ibid.; "Membership," for years 1946–1953, 9 Dec. 1953,

CMTA; "Cash Statement, Sept. 1, 1952 (fiscal date) to Apr. 1, 1953," 26 Apr. 1953, CMTA; President, annual report, 28 Apr. 1955, CMTA; Henry G. Cohen to Rabbi Herman H. Rubenovitz, 8 Apr. 1953, CMTA; Harry L. Katz, letter, 14 Apr. 1953, CMTA; Abraham A. Bloom and Harry L. Katz, "'Call Them Your Builders . . . ,'" in Temple Mishkan Tefila, *Temple Mishkan Tefila: A History, 1858–1958* (Newton: Temple Mishkan Tefila, 1958), CMTA, 48; Board of Directors, minutes of meeting, 28 Apr. 1954, CMTA; Land Site Committee, minutes of meeting, 9 June 1954, CMTA; Board of Directors, minutes of meeting, 27 July 1954, CMTA; *JAdv*, 26 Aug. 1954, 1, 2; *JAdv*, 30 Sept. 1954, 2; Congregation, minutes of meeting, 14 Nov. 1954, CMTA; Temple Mishkan Tefila, *A History, 1858–1958*, 52–58; Executive Committee, minutes of meeting, 8 Nov. 1954, CMTA; *JAdv*, 16 Dec. 1954, 1, 15; *JAdv*, 13 Jan. 1955, 2:4; *JAdv*, 28 Apr. 1955, 2; *JAdv*, 10 Nov. 1955, 1; Kazis, "A History of Temple Mishkan Tefila," 38; President, annual report, 30 Apr. 1956, CMTA; President, annual report, 30 Apr. 1957, CMTA; *JAdv*, 16 May 1957, 14; *JAdv*, 13 June 1957, 7; Congregation, minutes of meeting, 30 Apr. 1958, CMTA; President, annual report, 30 Apr. 1958, CMTA; *JAdv*, 1 May 1958, 5; "Information for Treasurer's Report," 9 May 1962, CMTA; *JAdv*, 12 Dec. 1963, 2:3; President, annual report, 1964, CMTA; Hyman, "From City to Suburb."

23. Temple Mishkan Tefila, *A History, 1858–1958*, 51; Minutes of meeting at home of Henry G. Cohen, 13 Apr. 1953, CMTA. See also Leon Steinberg to Robert Goldstein, 26 May 1953, CMTA; Probably Rabbi Israel J. Kazis, untitled notes that begin, "Statistics on local Temples," 2 pp., 9 Dec. 1953, CMTA; Board of Directors, minutes of meeting, 20 Dec. 1953, CMTA; Rabbi Simon Greenberg to Kazis, 30 Dec. 1953, CMTA; Board of Directors, minutes of meeting, 10 Jan. 1954, CMTA; "Report of the Decision of the Rabbinical Assembly Committee Involving the Differences That Arose as a Result of the Intention of Congregation Mishkan Tefila to Build a School and Eventually a Synagogue in the Newton Area," copy dated 18 Jan. 1954, CMTA; Temple Mishkan Tefila, *A History, 1858–1958*, 51–52; Hyman, "From City to Suburb," 189–191.

24. For evidence, see minutes of meetings, memoranda, and reports in box 10, CJP.

25. Bureau of Jewish Education, "Subventions to Hebrew Schools," report enclosed in AJP Budget Committee on Jewish Education, minutes of meeting, 3 Feb. 1955, box 10, CJP; Congregation Beth Hamidrash Hagodol, financial report for year ended 31 Oct. 1951, Financial Reports, 1944–1960, BHHC; Congregation Beth Hamidrash Hagodol, financial report for year ended 31 Oct. 1956, ibid.

26. William Zakon and Edward L. Weisberg, letter beginning "Dear Friend," 4

Nov. 1955, box 136a, CJP; AJP Budget Committee on Jewish Education, 26 May 1955, minutes of meeting, box 10, CJP. See also minutes of meetings and memoranda in boxes 10 and 136a, CJP; *JAdv*, 23 June 1955, 2:7; *JAdv*, 25 Aug. 1955, 3, 14; *JAdv*, 28 June 1956, 5; President, annual report, 28 Apr. 1955, CMTA; *JAdv*, 29 Aug. 1957, 1, 7.

27. *JAdv*, 28 June 1956, 2:4; *Glbpm*, 26 Apr. 1960, 32. See also *JAdv*, 18 Sept. 1924, 3; *Globe*, 14 Sept. 1925, 5; *Her*, 14 Sept. 1925, 6; *JAdv*, 17 Sept. 1925, 1, 2:3, 2:6; Suffolk County Deeds 7298:218, 7352:348, 3753:5; *JAdv*, 10 Aug. 1961, 4; *JAdv*, 4 July 1963, 2; *JAdv*, 13 Mar. 1958, 3; *JAdv*, 20 Mar. 1958, 8; *JAdv*, 29 Aug. 1913, 1; Boston City Directory, 1912–1919; Agudath Achim, box 110, WPA; Edith Arnold, "Agudas Achim Synagogue, 1890–1960," unpublished, AJHS; *JAdv*, 12 Mar. 1959, 14; *JAdv*, 26 Mar. 1959, 7; Captain Dennis F. Dalton to Deputy Superintendent Francis M. Tiernan, Boston Police Department, memorandum, 11 May 1960, box 66, JCC.

28. Rabbi Benjamin L. Grossman left Beth Hamidrash Hagadol in the spring of 1956: see *JAdv*, 10 May 1956, 2:4; *JAdv*, 17 May 1956, 2:8. Rabbi Eliezer Berkovits left Adath Jeshurun in the fall of 1956: see *JAdv*, 6 Sept. 1956, 4. Neither congregation would again be served by a full-time rabbi, though Rabbi Isaac J. Levine served Beth Hamidrash Hagadol in a limited capacity from the middle 1950s until his death in 1963: see Gerald H. Gamm, "Neighborhood Roots: Exodus and Stability in Boston, 1870–1990" (Ph.D. diss., Harvard University, 1994), 413, n.126.

29. *JAdv*, 6 Sept. 1956, 4.

30. Frieda Cooper, telephone interviews with author, 3 Nov. 1991 and 2 Apr. 1992.

31. St. Brendan's Parish, *Golden Anniversary*, probably 1979, St. Brendan's Rectory; "Brief History of St. Brendan School," St. Brendan, School Profiles, RCSO; St. Mark's Parish, *75th Anniversary, St. Mark the Evangelist Parish, Dorchester, Mass., 1905–1980: An Illustrated History*, St. Mark, AAPH, 12; "History of Saint Mark School, 1923–1983," St. Mark, School Profiles, RCSO; Michael Parise, *The History of Saint Gregory's Parish, Lower Mills, Dorchester and Milton, 1862–1987* (1987), St. Gregory's Rectory, 85; Abp. Richard J. Cushing to Rev. Ralph W. Farrell, 18 Apr. 1957, St. Margaret's Rectory; "Columbia Pt," notes, 25 Apr. 1957, St. Christopher, AAPC; Rev. Francis J. Mosley to Cushing, 6 May 1957, ibid.; Rev. James T. Cotter to Farrell, 3 Feb. 1954, St. Margaret, AAPC; Rt. Rev. Lawrence J. Riley to Farrell, 7 Feb. 1956, St. Christopher, AAPC; Cushing to Sister Mary Jogues, 23 Apr. 1956, ibid.; Notes that begin, "at the television studio," 12 Aug. 1956, ibid.; St. Margaret's Parish, *St. Margaret's First Parish Reunion: Oct. 4, 1980*, St. Margaret's Rectory.

32. Rev. John J. Watson to Rt. Rev. Robert J. Sennott, 5 Feb. 1955, St. Leo, AAPC; Rev. Francis X. Turke, interview with author, St. Agatha's Rectory, Milton, Mass., 2 Sept. 1991; Letter from Watson, 25 Oct. 1957, in St. Leo's Parish, selections from 55th anniversary celebration book, 1957, Personal Papers of Rev. Francis X. Turke. See also St. Leo, 1949–1959, AACC; Watson to Rt. Rev. Walter J. Furlong, 30 Sept. 1952, St. Leo, AAPC; Watson to Furlong, 10 Nov. 1952, ibid.; Watson to Furlong, 28 Nov. 1952, ibid.; Furlong to Watson, 5 Dec. 1952, ibid.; Watson to Furlong, 12 Jan. 1953, ibid.; Notes that begin, "4300 people," on sheet of paper from Office of the Chancellor, undated, ibid.; Edward Sidman to George I. Samansky, 10 June 1952, box 147, CJP; Staff, minutes of meeting, Hecht House, 24 Apr. 1953, box 3, HH; Note dated 29 Nov. 1954, St. Leo, AAPB.

33. St. Joseph, 1950–1957, AACC.

34. *Globe,* 14 Dec. 1977, 3.

35. These estimates are based on the assumption that Catholics made up a substantial majority of Dorchester and upper Roxbury's non-Jewish white population. For the population of Dorchester, I combined the populations of census tracts P-1C, P-2, P-3, P-4, P-5, P-6, T-1, T-2, T-3A, T-3B, T-4A, T-4B, T-5A, T-5B, T-6, T-7A, T-7B, T-8A, T-8B, T-9, T-10, X-1, X-2, X-3A, X-3B, X-4A, X-4B, X-5A, X-5B, X-5C, X-6A, X-6B, and X-6C. For the population of upper Roxbury, I combined the populations of census tracts U-1, U-2, U-3, U-4, U-5, U-6A, U-6B, and V-1. For sources of data, see notes 37, 38, and 42.

36. *Trav,* 28 Feb. 1967, 3. See also St. Margaret, 1959–1967, AACC.

37. To make the 1960 population estimate, I relied on several sources. I examined the following data at the census-tract level: number of persons, number of whites, number of foreign-stock persons, number of persons born in U.S.S.R., and number of persons born in Central or Eastern Europe. For the population of Dorchester and Roxbury, I combined the populations of census tracts P-1C, P-2, P-3, P-4, P-5, P-6, T-1, T-2, T-3A, T-3B, T-4A, T-4B, T-5A, T-5B, T-6, T-7A, T-7B, T-8A, T-8B, T-9, T-10, U-1, U-2, U-3, U-4, U-5, U-6A, U-6B, V-1, X-1, X-2, X-3A, X-3B, X-4A, X-4B, X-5A, X-5B, X-5C, X-6A, X-6B, and X-6C. For 1960 census-tract data, see U.S. Department of Commerce, Bureau of the Census, *U.S. Censuses of Population and Housing, 1960—Census Tracts—Boston, Mass. Standard Metropolitan Statistical Area* (Washington: Government Printing Office, 1962). For other contemporary reports and evidence regarding the Jewish population of Dorchester and Roxbury in the late 1950s and early 1960s, see "Comparative Report of Greater Boston Jewish and General Population," 27 Nov. 1957, including estimates of Jewish populations in 1945–46 and 1957, box 14, CJP; Administrative Staff, minutes of meeting, Hecht House, 1

Feb. 1957, box 3, HH; Mrs. Carl Spector to Simon J. Helman, memorandum, 25 Nov. 1959, box 10, CJP; Staff, minutes of meeting, Boston YMHA–Hecht House, 15 Jan. 1960, box 23, HH; AJP Jewish Education Committee, "1960–61 Budgeting," box 10, CJP; Helman to Judge Lewis Goldberg, 16 Jan. 1961, box 136a, CJP.

38. Previous researchers have offered widely varying estimates of the 1967 Jewish population. In its 1967 study of Greater Boston's Jewish population, the Combined Jewish Philanthropies estimated that 14,000–15,000 Jews lived in Dorchester and Roxbury in 1965: see Morris Axelrod, Floyd J. Fowler, Jr., and Arnold Gurin, *A Community Survey for Long Range Planning: A Study of the Jewish Population of Greater Boston* (Boston: Combined Jewish Philanthropies of Greater Boston, 1967), 16, 20–21, 180. Harmon and Levine, in contrast, argue that 40,000 Jews still lived in Dorchester and Roxbury in 1967: see Lawrence Harmon and Hillel Levine, "A Response to Gerald Gamm," *JAdv,* 10–16 Apr. 1992, 11. To estimate the 1967 population, I examined data from the 1960 and 1970 federal censuses as well as from several other reports. The total population of each census tract was documented in the 1960 and 1970 censuses; contemporary observers all agreed which tracts were nearly all-black, which were nearly all-white, and which were racially integrated in 1967; and observers generally offered similar estimates of the racial breakdown of each integrated tract in 1967. On the basis of these data—as well as the reports and anecdotes cited by other scholars—I estimate the area's Jewish population. See U.S. Census, *1960—Census Tracts, Boston;* U.S. Department of Commerce, Bureau of the Census, *1970 Census of Population and Housing—Census Tracts—Boston, Mass. Standard Metropolitan Statistical Area* (Washington: Government Printing Office, 1972); Meeting on Jewish-Negro Cooperation, minutes, 13 Nov. 1963, box 79, JCC; Visit to Boston YMHA–Hecht House by Group Work Services Committee, 9 Mar. 1964, box 148, CJP; Robert E. Segal to Joshua Guberman, 21 July 1964, box 79, JCC; "Relationship between Jews and Negroes, Especially in the Boston Area," notes dated 8 Nov. 1964, box 79, JCC; Untitled notes that begin, "Mar. 30, 1965: Hubie . . . ," 1 pg., box 76, JCC; Board of Directors, minutes of meeting, Boston YMHA–Hecht House, 16 Nov. 1965, box 22, HH; "Report for Special Meeting of Executive Committee—Sept. 13, 1966," Combined Jewish Philanthropies, box 77, CJP; Mark S. Israel, "Program for Neighborhood Stabilization in Mattapan-Dorchester," 6 Feb. 1967, box 76, JCC; Israel, "Jewish People in Roxbury," probably 23 Mar. 1967, box 202, JCC; *Globe,* 3 Aug. 1967, 8; "Mattapan," 9 Aug. 1967, box 76, JCC; *Glbpm,* 15 Sept. 1967, 50; "Program ideas for the Jewish Community Council," 10 Nov. 1967, box 79, JCC; *CSM,* 8 Dec. 1967, 10; "Tax assessor

matter—Mattapan," 1 Apr. 1968, box 76, JCC; "Report on the Mattapan Organization," May 1968, ibid.; Board of Directors, minutes of meeting, Boston YMHA–Hecht House, 19 Sept. 1968, box 22, HH. See also Chapter 2, n.19.

39. *Glbpm,* 7 Feb. 1967, 22.
40. Untitled notes that begin, "I. Increasing Negro frustration, hostility and militancy," 2 pp., undated, box 79, JCC.
41. *GlbSun,* 11 Apr. 1965, 70; *Globe,* 3 Aug. 1967, 8; *Globe,* 16 Oct. 1967, 5, also 1. See also Chapter 2, n.19; Steering Committee, Mattapan Organization, minutes of meeting, 6 July 1967, box 76, JCC; Mark S. Israel to Real Estate Committee, Mattapan Organization, 3 Aug. 1967, ibid.; Mr. Y., Wellington Hill St., to Mattapan Homeowners and Residents, summer 1967, ibid.; Israel to James Bishop, 8 Aug. 1967, ibid.; "Mattapan," 9 Aug. 1967, ibid.; *Glbpm,* 15 Sept. 1967, 50; *Mattapan Tribune,* 21 Sept. 1967, box 76, JCC; *CSM,* 6 Oct. 1967, 1; Executive Board, Mattapan Organization, minutes of meeting, 7 Dec. 1967, box 76, JCC; *CSM,* 8 Dec. 1967, 10.
42. To make this estimate, I examined data from the 1960 and 1970 federal censuses: see U.S. Census, *1960—Census Tracts, Boston;* United States Census, *1970—Census Tracts, Boston.* For the population of Dorchester and upper Roxbury in 1960, I combined the populations of census tracts P-1C, P-2, P-3, P-4, P-5, P-6, T-1, T-2, T-3A, T-3B, T-4A, T-4B, T-5A, T-5B, T-6, T-7A, T-7B, T-8A, T-8B, T-9, T-10, U-1, U-2, U-3, U-4, U-5, U-6A, U-6B, V-1, X-1, X-2, X-3A, X-3B, X-4A, X-4B, X-5A, X-5B, X-5C, X-6A, X-6B, and X-6C. For the population of Dorchester and upper Roxbury in 1970, I combined the populations of census tracts 813, 815–821, 901–905, 907–924, and 1001–1011. For evidence of the extent of racial succession in the middle 1960s, see note 38.
43. Rapkin, "Seaver-Townsend Urban Renewal Area," 44, 41, 45–46.
44. Rev. Thomas C. Burns to Rt. Rev. Robert J. Sennott, 13 Feb. 1964, St. John, AAPC; Burns to Rt. Rev. Francis J. Sexton, 16 Jan. 1965, ibid. See also St. John's School, 1966–1967, in folder titled "Negro Enrollment 1965–71," School Surveys and Reports, Basement Files, RCSO.
45. Rt. Rev. Francis F. McElroy to Rt. Rev. Francis J. Sexton, memorandum, 13 May 1965, St. Paul, AAPC.
46. Rev. George H. Callahan to Rt. Rev. Francis J. Sexton, 19 Apr. 1966, St. Leo, AAPC; Callahan to Sexton, 23 June 1966, ibid.; *Globe,* 12 Feb. 1967, 63; Rev. Shawn G. Sheehan to Sexton, 1 June 1967, St. Leo, AAPC. See also Callahan to Sexton, 19 May 1966, ibid.; Rt. Rev. Thomas J. Finnegan, Jr., to Callahan, 7 June 1966, ibid.
47. Rev. Francis X. Turke, interview with author, St. Agatha's Rectory, Milton, Mass., 2 Sept. 1991; Mr. C., Spencer St., to Card. Richard J. Cushing, 16

Sept. 1962, St. Leo, AAPC. See also Rev. James Lyons, telephone interview with author, 28 Apr. 1992.

48. Rev. Thomas C. Burns to Rt. Rev. Robert J. Sennott, 14 Dec. 1961, St. John, AAPC; Burns to Sennott, 22 May 1963, ibid.; Rt. Rev. Francis F. McElroy, report to the Chancery, 7 July 1960, St. Paul, AAPC; McElroy to Sennott, 5 July 1961, ibid. See also Rev. George H. Callahan to Rt. Rev. Francis J. Sexton, 19 Apr. 1966, St. Leo, AAPC; Callahan to Sexton, 19 May 1966, ibid.; Rt. Rev. Thomas J. Finnegan, Jr., to Callahan, 7 June 1966, ibid.; Burns to Sennott, 2 Oct. 1961, St. John, AAPC; Burns to the Chancery, 25 Oct. 1961, ibid.; Burns to Sexton, 16 Jan. 1965, ibid.; Sexton to Burns, 18 Jan. 1965, ibid.; Rev. Thomas A. Dwyer to Sexton, 20 Apr. 1966, ibid.

49. Rev. Thomas C. Burns to Rt. Rev. Robert J. Sennott, 13 Feb. 1964, St. John, AAPC. See also Parish Assignments, 31 July 1960, St. Paul, Parish Files, RCCP; Chancery to Burns, 6 Feb. 1962, St. John, AAPC; Parish Assignments, 31 Dec. 1964, St. John, Parish Files, RCCP.

50. Rt. Rev. Francis F. McElroy to Rt. Rev. Francis J. Sexton, memorandum, 13 May 1965, St. Paul, AAPC; *Globe,* 3 Aug. 1967, 8; *Globe,* 12 Feb. 1967, 63; probably Mark S. Israel, notes that begin, "Ward 14 Betterment Association, Salvation Army Nursing Home," 15 Feb. 1967, box 76, JCC.

51. Staff, minutes of meeting, Boston YMHA–Hecht House, 15 Jan. 1960, box 23, HH.

52. The synagogue was Chai Odom's Nightingale Street Synagogue. The school was the New England Hebrew Academy (formerly called the Lubavitz Yeshiva), which occupied the old Mishkan Tefila structures on Seaver Street and Elm Hill Avenue.

53. Saul Bernstein, Report of Executive Director, Jewish Centers Association of Greater Boston, Sept. 1946, box 25, HH, 21; Executive Committee, Associated Jewish Philanthropies, minutes of meeting, 11 June 1954, box 147, CJP; George J. Arafe, "President's Annual Report—1955/56," Boston YMHA, 22 Apr. 1956, box 17, HH. See also minutes of meetings, memoranda, letters, and reports in boxes 1, 3, 17, 22, 23, 25, and 26, HH; minutes of meetings, maps, reports, memoranda, contracts, and letters in boxes 6, 10, 136a, and 147, CJP; *JAdv,* 11 Jan. 1945, 1, 18; Associated Jewish Philanthropies, "Jewish Center Developments in Greater Boston: A Special Report" (Boston, Apr. 1949), box 10, CJP; *JAdv,* 6 May 1954, 1, 11; *JAdv,* 3 Mar. 1955, 5; *JAdv,* 10 Mar. 1955, 1, 11; *JAdv,* 12 May 1955, 1, 11; *JAdv,* 26 Jan. 1956, 1, 6; *JAdv,* 29 Mar. 1956, 1, 6; *JAdv,* 31 May 1956, A:16; *JAdv,* 21 Nov. 1957, 2:12; *JAdv,* 14 May 1959, 1, 14; *JAdv,* 11 June 1959, 4; *JAdv,* 8 Oct. 1959, 2:5; *JAdv,* 17 Mar. 1960, 3.

54. Bernie Hyatt, interview with author, Boston, 13 Mar. 1992; *JAdv,* 9 Nov. 1961, 1, also 15. See also *JAdv,* 27 Apr. 1961, 4; *JAdv,* 18 May 1961, 3; *JAdv,*

29 June 1961, 2; *JAdv,* 6 July 1961, 4; *JAdv,* 20 July 1961, 14; *JAdv,* 27 July 1961, 3; *JAdv,* 10 Aug. 1961, 20; *JAdv,* 19 Oct. 1961, 15; Suffolk County Deeds 7610:245.

55. Mogain Moshe Lebet David, box 110, WPA; lists of synagogues, ibid.; *JAdv,* 29 Apr. 1926, 2:3; *JAdv,* 1 June 1972, 1, 4; *JAdv,* 15 Mar. 1973, 14; Suffolk County Deeds 4882:295, 7530:366, 7540:484–489; Boston City Directory, 1960–1961.

56. *JAdv,* 4 Feb. 1960, 16; *JAdv,* 20 Sept. 1962, 4. See also Rabbi Moses J. Cohn, telephone interview with author, 8 June 1992; Mrs. Moses J. Cohn, interview with author, Brighton, Mass., 19 May 1992; Reuven Cohn, telephone interview with author, 21 Apr. 1992; Frieda Cooper, telephone interviews with author, 3 Nov. 1991 and 23 Mar. 1992; Norfolk County Deeds 3468:581, 3729:592, 3934:138; *JAdv,* 28 Jan. 1960, 1, 12; *JAdv,* 9 June 1960, 14; *JAdv,* 23 June 1960, 1, 14; *JAdv,* 16 Aug. 1962, 3; *JAdv,* 6 Sept. 1962, 1, 12; *JAdv,* 13 Sept. 1962, 1, 16, 2:2; Maimonides School Dedication Commemorative Edition, in *JAdv,* 13 Sept. 1962; *JAdv,* 6 Dec. 1962, 9; *JAdv,* 20 June 1963, 1, 5; *JAdv,* 26 Sept. 1963, 3; *JAdv,* 27 Aug. 1964, 14; *JAdv,* 8 Oct. 1964, 1, 8; *JAdv,* 15 Oct. 1964, 3; *JAdv,* 2 Sept. 1965, 17; *JAdv,* 21 Oct. 1965, 2:9; *JAdv,* 16 Dec. 1965, 3; *JAdv,* 24 Mar. 1966, 18.

57. Congregation Toras Moshe, "1961/5722—Important High Holiday Notice!" Hebrew Educational Alliance and Congregation Toras Moshe Papers, AJHS; Toras Moshe Brotherhood, Seventeenth Annual Banquet, 27 May 1962, program, Hebrew Educational Alliance and Congregation Toras Moshe Papers, AJHS; Congregation Kadimah–Toras Moshe, *Kadimah–Toras Moshe Bulletin,* Sept. 1964, Personal Papers of Gertrude Markson, 4; *JAdv,* 19 Nov. 1964, 2:13. See also Toras Moshe, box 110, WPA; *JAdv,* 7 Dec. 1916, 1; *JAdv,* 20 May 1920, 1; *JAdv,* 15 Sept. 1921, 1, 8; *JAdv,* 27 July 1922, 4; *JAdv,* 14 Sept. 1922, 3; Robert Cohen, interview with author, Brighton, Mass., 22 Aug. 1991; Hebrew Educational Alliance and Congregation Toras Moshe, financial records, 1958–1964, Hebrew Educational Alliance and Congregation Toras Moshe Papers, AJHS; Max Walter and Israel Lichtman to Member, notice of meeting on 7 June 1964, ibid.; Congregation Kadimah–Toras Moshe, *Kadimah–Toras Moshe Bulletin,* various bulletins, 1964–1965, Personal Papers of Gertrude Markson; *JAdv,* 22 Oct. 1964, 3; *JAdv,* 5 Nov. 1964, 3.

58. *JAdv,* 29 Dec. 1966, 12. See also *JAdv,* 24 June 1965, 9; *JAdv,* 16 Sept. 1965, 18; *JAdv,* 24 Feb. 1966, 7; *JAdv,* 2 June 1966, 15; *Glbpm,* 7 Feb. 1967, 22; Norfolk County Deeds 4469:310.

59. *JAdv,* 16 June 1966, 4. See also *JAdv,* 31 Aug. 1961, 5; Suffolk County Deeds 7598:348, 7742:451, 4691:473, 8041:549, 8097:007; Rapkin, "Seaver-Townsend Urban Renewal Area," 39; Arthur E. Paris, *Black Pente-*

costalism: Southern Religion in an Urban World (Amherst: University of Massachusetts Press, 1982), 37–43; *JAdv,* 13 Sept. 1962, 2:1; *JAdv,* 16 Apr. 1964, 14; *JAdv,* 3 Sept. 1964, 2:1; *JAdv,* 23 Sept. 1965, 2:1; Nusach Hoari Anshei Libavitz, box 110, WPA; lists of synagogues, ibid.

60. Board of Directors, Beth Hamidrash Hagodol, minutes of meeting, probably 8 Dec. 1963, minutes dated 13 Dec. 1963, Papers, 1963–1964, BHHC; *JAdv,* 14 Jan. 1965, 1, also 6; "The Congregation Beth Hamidrash Hagodol of Crawford St. Roxbury," 4 pp., enclosed in Rabbi Samuel I. Korff to Abraham Close, 14 Jan. 1965, Papers, 1963–1964, BHHC; Korff to John D. Hewitt, 24 June 1964, ibid.; Sumner Greenberg, telephone interview with author, 15 Apr. 1992. See also *JAdv,* 12 Dec. 1963, 2:19; Mr. M. to Close, 13 Dec. 1963, Papers, 1963–1964, BHHC; Congregation Beth Hamidrash Hagodol, income and expenses, 1961–1964, ibid.; Boston City Directory, 1964–1965; Suffolk County Deeds 7875:001; Robert B. McGilvray to Close, 4 Aug. 1964, Papers, 1963–1964, BHHC; *JAdv,* 21 Jan. 1965, 2; Congregation Beth Hamidrash Hagadol, financial statement, 1 Apr. 1967–1 June 1969, Papers, 1963–1964, BHHC; Mr. K. to Close, 20 Dec. 1965, ibid.

61. *JAdv,* 24 Jan. 1963, 2; *GlbSun,* 8 May 1966, 42; Isadore Zack to Robert E. Segal, memorandum, 15 Aug. 1966, box 202, JCC; Zack to Sol Kolack, memorandum, 22 Aug. 1966, dictated 19 Aug. 1966, ibid. See also Note to Kolack, 27 July 1962, box 66, JCC; Zack to Kolack, memorandum, 15 June 1964, ibid.; Note to Zack, 8 July 1964, ibid.; *JAdv,* 16 June 1966, 1; *Trav,* 27 June 1966, 1, 11; Segal, "Emergency Request," 28 June 1966, box 202, JCC; *JAdv,* 30 June 1966, 1, 2; *JAdv,* 7 July 1966, 1; Jewish Community Council, press release, 7 July 1966, box 202, JCC.

62. Robert E. Segal to George Frank, 8 Dec. 1966, box 202, JCC; Frank to Segal, 22 Dec. 1966, ibid. See also Segal to Albert Schlossberg, 23 Aug. 1966, ibid.; "Conversation with Benjamin Trustman," 3 Oct. 1966, ibid.; Segal to Bernard D. Grossman, 10 Oct. 1966, ibid.; Minutes of meeting regarding Adath Jeshurun Synagogue, 9 Nov. 1966, ibid.; Rudolph H. Wyner to Leslie A. Pike, 14 Dec. 1966, ibid.; "Blue Hill Avenue Shule," probably 29 Mar. 1967, ibid.; "Blue Hill Avenue Shul," probably Aug. 1967, ibid.; Richard Heath, "The House of the Flock of the Righteous: The Song of Synagogue Adath Jeshurun," unpublished paper, 1991, AJHS, 20–22; Marshall Dana, telephone interview with author, 26 Apr. 1992; Justin Wyner, telephone interview with author, 10 May 1992.

63. *Glbpm,* 7 Feb. 1967, 22.

64. George Halzel, telephone interview with author, 13 May 1992; *JAdv,* 10 Dec. 1964, 2:2, also 1, 15. See also *JAdv,* 8 Sept. 1960, 2:9; *JAdv,* 16 Aug. 1962, 6; *JAdv,* 17 Dec. 1964, 14; *JAdv,* 17 June 1965, 14; *JAdv,* 26 Aug.

1965, 1, 5; *JAdv,* 2 Sept. 1965, 5; *JAdv,* 3 Mar. 1966, 16; *JAdv,* 5 May 1966, 2:9; *JAdv,* 19 May 1966, 11; Suffolk County Deeds 8132:064; Murray Block, telephone interview with author, 3 May 1992.

65. *Glbpm,* 7 Feb. 1967, 1, 22.

66. Ibid.

67. AJP Jewish Education Committee, "1960–61 Budgeting," box 10, CJP; "Enrollment Trends, 1956–66: CJP Supported Schools," 20 June 1966, box 136a, CJP.

68. Probably Mark S. Israel, "Program Ideas for the Jewish Community Council," 10 Nov. 1967, box 79, JCC.

69. U.S. Department of Commerce, Bureau of the Census, *United States Census of Housing, 1950—Block Statistics—Boston, Massachusetts* (Washington: Government Printing Office, 1952); U.S. Department of Commerce, Bureau of the Census, *U.S. Census of Housing, 1960—City Blocks—Boston, Mass.* (Washington: Government Printing Office, 1961).

70. *Trav,* 2 May 1967, 3; Card. Richard J. Cushing to James O. Dunn, memorandum, 14 Oct. 1968, St. Peter, AAPC. See also Dorchester and Roxbury parishes, 1967, AACC; St. Peter's School, 1966–1967, in folder entitled "Negro Enrollment 1965–71," School Surveys and Reports, Basement Files, RCSO; St. Peter's Church, weekly parish bulletin, 22 Oct. 1967, St. Peter, Parish Materials, RCAB; *Globe,* 7 Nov. 1969, 52.

71. Probably Rev. John J. Philbin, Report to Chancellor, 12 Mar. 1968, St. John, AAPC.

72. *Glbpm,* 7 Feb. 1967, 22; "Roxbury an Area of Contrasts," section of a newspaper article, probably middle 1960s, CMTA. See also Isadore Zack to Robert E. Segal, memorandum, 7 Aug. 1964, box 66, JCC.

11. Authority in an Age of Crisis

1. This account is based on interviews with Rev. John J. Philbin, Wellesley, Mass., 20 Aug. 1991; Philbin, telephone, 31 July 1995; Rev. Gerald Osterman, telephone, 4 Aug. 1995; and Harriet White, telephone, 4 Aug. 1995.

2. St. John–St. Hugh, 1956–1968, AACC; probably Rev. John J. Philbin, "Report to Chancellor," 12 Mar. 1968, St. John–St. Hugh, AAPC.

3. Rev. John J. Philbin, interview with author, Wellesley, Mass., 20 Aug. 1991.

4. Thomas D. Corrigan, "Boston Priests at Grips with the Diaspora," *Catholic World* 212 (Oct. 1970), 36, also 35. See also Rev. John J. Philbin, interview with author, Wellesley, Mass., 20 Aug. 1991; *Globe,* 12 Mar. 1968, 1, 28; *Her,* 17 Sept. 1968, 3.

5. Rt. Rev. Thomas J. Finnegan, Jr., interview with author, St. Elizabeth's Rectory, Milton, Mass., 14 Aug. 1991. See also Priest Assignment Cards,

RCAB, for Rev. John J. Philbin, Rev. William F. Calter, Rev. Maurice J. Mahoney, Rev. Paul J. McManus, and Rev. Leonard J. Burke.

6. Rt. Rev. Thomas J. Finnegan, Jr., interview with author, St. Elizabeth's Rectory, Milton, Mass., 14 Aug. 1991.

7. Rev. John J. Philbin, interview with author, Wellesley, Mass., 20 Aug. 1991. See also Rt. Rev. Thomas J. Finnegan, Jr., interview with author, St. Elizabeth's Rectory, Milton, Mass., 14 Aug. 1991; probably Philbin, Report to Chancellor, 12 Mar. 1968, St. John, AAPC; Philbin, pulpit announcement, 24 Mar. 1968, ibid.; "A 'Small Miracle' in Roxbury," newspaper article, 1968, Parish Materials, St. John, RCAB; Arthur Melville to Finnegan, memorandum, 16 May 1968, St. John, AAPC; Finnegan to James O. Dunn, memorandum, 20 May 1968, ibid.; Finnegan to Philbin, 11 June 1968, ibid.; Melville to Finnegan, 10 Dec. 1968, ibid.

8. Rev. John J. Philbin to Rt. Rev. Thomas J. Finnegan, Jr., 5 July 1968, St. John, AAPC; Philbin to Card. Richard J. Cushing, 2 May 1969, ibid.; Finnegan to Philbin, 1 Oct. 1970, ibid.

9. *Pilot,* 22 July 1972, 7. See also Rev. Thomas V. Daily to Card. Humberto Medeiros, memorandum, 10 Feb. 1973, St. Ambrose, AAPC; James O. Dunn to Daily, memorandum, 22 June 1973, ibid.; Rt. Rev. Henry J. O'Connell to Daily, 12 Sept. 1973, ibid.

10. Abp. Humberto S. Medeiros, "Man's Cities and God's Poor," pastoral letter (Boston: Daughters of St. Paul, 1972), 9, 5.

11. *Globe,* 2 Feb. 1977, 1; *Globe,* 6 Feb. 1978, 1. See also *GlbSun,* 6 Feb. 1977, 1, 4.

12. Rev. John L. Doyle, interview with author, St. Peter's Rectory, Dorchester, Mass., 16 Sept. 1996. See also James Walsh, fax to author, 7 May 1997; Rev. William Schmidt, interview with author, Chancery Building, Archdiocese of Boston, Brighton, 8 Aug. 1991; Rev. James McCarthy, interviews with author, Tribunal Building, Archdiocese of Boston, Brighton, 15 July 1991 and 23 July 1991; Rev. Robert McMillan, telephone interview with author, 15 Dec. 1995; Office of Planning and Research, Archdiocese of Boston, "Planning Guide 2000: Addressing the Challenges Facing the Church of Boston," Mar. 1997; *GlbSun,* 8 Mar. 1998, B:1; *Globe,* 9 Mar. 1998, B:1.

13. Robert E. Segal to Ellis Ash, 22 Mar. 1967, box 76, JCC. See also "Roxbury–North Dorchester Problem Areas," 10 Mar. 1966, box 79, JCC; Segal, telephone interview with author, 31 Mar. 1992.

14. Probably Mark S. Israel, "Mattapan," 4 Apr. 1967, box 76, JCC.

15. *JAdv,* 15 June 1967, 2:2.

16. See letters, memoranda, and minutes of meetings in boxes 76, 79, and 202, JCC.

17. Probably Mark S. Israel, "Report on the Mattapan Organization," May 1968, box 76, JCC; Executive Board, Mattapan Organization, minutes of meeting, 6 June 1968, ibid.

18. Notes that begin, "Dist. 3 Police Community Relations Workshop . . . ," 14 Feb. 1967, box 76, JCC; "Meeting with Mildred Kaufman," 31 Oct. 1968, box 79, JCC; Robert E. Segal to Benjamin B. Rosenberg, memorandum, 25 July 1969, ibid.

19. Communal Property Committee, minutes of meeting, 13 Jan. 1970, box 37, CJP. See also *Mattapan Tribune*, 3 Sept. 1970, 1; Suffolk County Deeds 8384:123.

20. Stephen R. Morse to David R. Pokross and Benjamin B. Rosenberg, memorandum, 12 Aug. 1969, box 37, CJP; Rabbi Samuel I. Korff to Albert Silverman, memorandum, 12 Aug. 1969, box 79, JCC; Korff to Morse, 8 Dec. 1969, ibid. See also Sydney Gale to Rosenberg, memorandum, 14 Oct. 1969, box 142, CJP; Dorchester-Mattapan Committee, Combined Jewish Philanthropies, minutes of meeting, 17 Dec. 1969, box 77, JCC; Dorchester-Mattapan Committee, Combined Jewish Philanthropies, minutes of meeting, 13 Jan. 1970, ibid.; Dorchester-Mattapan Committee, Combined Jewish Philanthropies, minutes of meeting, 18 Mar. 1970, ibid.

21. Letter to Combined Jewish Philanthropies, 19 Apr. 1968, box 175, CJP. See also Elma Lewis, telephone interview with author, 20 Aug. 1995; New England Hebrew Academy and Combined Jewish Philanthropies, purchase and sale agreement, 5 Apr. 1968, box 175, CJP; *Globe,* 18 Apr. 1968, 1, 21; Board of Trustees, Combined Jewish Philanthropies, minutes of meeting, 2 May 1968, box 175, CJP.

22. Robert M. Segal to Benjamin Rosenberg, memorandum, 1 Aug. 1969, box 37, CJP. See also Dorchester-Mattapan Committee, Combined Jewish Philanthropies, minutes of meeting, 5 Sept. 1969, ibid.; *JAdv,* 3 July 1969, 1, 11, 15.

23. Stephen R. Morse to David R. Pokross and Benjamin B. Rosenberg, memorandum, 12 Aug. 1969, box 37, CJP; Dorchester-Mattapan Committee, Combined Jewish Philanthropies, minutes of meeting, 5 Sept. 1969, ibid.; Yona Ginsberg, *Jews in a Changing Neighborhood: The Study of Mattapan* (New York: Free Press, 1975), 105–106. See also *Glbpm,* 20 Aug. 1969, 1, 27; *Mattapan Tribune,* 2 Apr. 1970, 1; Temple Hillel B'nai Torah and the Associated Communities Hebrew School, *Dedication* (1970), AJHS.

24. Dorchester-Mattapan Committee, Combined Jewish Philanthropies, minutes of meeting, 5 Sept. 1969, box 37, CJP. See also *JAdv,* 6 Aug. 1970, 1, 8; Rev. Shawn G. Sheehan, comments on parish data form submitted to Personnel Board, Nov. 1968, St. Leo, Parish Files, RCCP.

25. *JAdv,* 10 Dec. 1970, 5; *JAdv,* 19 Nov. 1970, 19. See also *Glbpm,* 27 May 1970, 3; *HerTrv,* 3 June 1970, 3; *Globe,* 3 June 1970, 36; *Glbpm,* 20 June 1970, 3; *JAdv,* 20 Aug. 1970, 2; *Globe,* 22 June 1970, 3; *JAdv,* 24 Dec. 1970, 2; Suffolk County Deeds 8493:026; Rabbi Samuel I. Korff to Albert Silverman, memorandum, 12 Aug. 1969, box 79, JCC.

26. *HerTrv,* 4 Aug. 1972, 1, also 7; *GlbSun,* 13 Aug. 1972, B:6, also B:1. See also *Globe,* 1 Sept. 1971, 3; *JAdv,* 17 June 1971, in Congregation Kehillath Jacob Papers, AJHS; Dan Mariaschin to Herman Brown, memorandum, 29 Dec. 1973, box 78a, JCC; Mariaschin to Brown, memorandum, 28 Jan. 1974, ibid.

27. Mrs. B. to Rabbi Samuel I. Korff, 10 May 1968, box 76, JCC; Note that begins, "On Sept 19 the Admin. Com. voted to endorse efforts . . . ," box 76, JCC.

28. Sydney Gale to file, "Mattapan Survey," preliminary draft of memorandum, 12 Sept. 1972, box 78a, JCC.

29. *Morgan v. Hennigan,* 379 F. Supp. 410 (D. Mass. 1974), 451, also 481; *JAdv,* 15 June 1967, 2:2. See also *JAdv,* 12 Dec. 1930, 1; Notes that begin, "Mar. 30, 1965: Hubie Jones phoned . . . ," box 76, JCC; *GlbSun,* 11 Apr. 1965, 70; *HTrvSun,* 5 Jan. 1969, 46–47; *GlbSun,* 16 Nov. 1969, 7; Stephen R. Morse to Robert E. Segal, memorandum, 17 Nov. 1969, box 76, JCC; *Glbpm,* 19 Nov. 1969, 28; *HerTrv,* 24 Nov. 1969, 7; *HerTrv,* 27 Nov. 1969, 3; *HerTrv,* 28 Nov. 1969, 13.

30. Mark Mirsky, *Blue Hill Avenue* (Indianapolis: Bobbs-Merrill, 1972), 3.

31. Alan Lupo, "The Blue Hill Avenue Story," *GlbSun,* 4 May 1969, magazine, 36. See also *Globe,* 24 Jan. 1972, 11; *GlbSun,* 7 Mar. 1971, A:8.

32. *Her,* 9 Aug. 1976, 12; *Globe,* 16 June 1976, 3; *Glbpm,* 31 May 1977, 3.

33. Rev. Joseph A. Gaudet, brief description, St. Leo's Parish, 22 June 1971, St. Leo's, Parish Files, RCCP. See also *Glbpm,* 29 Apr. 1970, 18.

34. Mark S. Israel, "Open Housing; American Nazi Party," 15 Mar. 1967, box 76, JCC; *GlbSun,* 29 June 1969, in box 175, JCC.

35. *Globe,* 28 Sept. 1973, 1; *Boston Phoenix,* 2 Oct. 1973, 5. See also *Globe,* 27 Aug. 1971, 6; *Globe,* 22 Sept. 1971, 1, 12; *GlbSun,* 30 Sept. 1973, 1, 14, 15; Alan Lupo, *Liberty's Chosen Home: The Politics of Violence in Boston* (Boston: Little, Brown, 1977); J. Anthony Lukas, *Common Ground: A Turbulent Decade in the Lives of Three American Families* (New York: Knopf, 1985); Ronald P. Formisano, *Boston against Busing: Race, Class, and Ethnicity in the 1960s and 1970s* (Chapel Hill: University of North Carolina Press, 1991).

36. *GlbSun,* 13 Nov. 1977, A:6. See also St. Matthew, 1964–1978, AACC; St. Angela, 1972–1984, AACC.

37. *Globe,* 20 Oct. 1975, 22; *Her,* 9 Aug. 1976, 12, also 1.
38. *Globe,* 19 June 1987, 20. See also Rev. Stephen Madden, interview with author, St. Ann's Rectory, Dorchester, Mass., 9 July 1991.
39. *Globe,* 15 Jan. 1995, city weekly, 9, also 1.

Epilogue

1. Eugene F. Rivers III, "Beyond the Nationalism of Fools: Toward an Agenda for Black Intellectuals," *Boston Review* 20:3 (Summer 1995), 16–17.
2. Joe Klein, "In God They Trust," *The New Yorker,* 16 June 1997, 40; Kenneth L. Woodward, "The New Holy War," *Newsweek,* 1 June 1998, 27. See also Rev. Eugene F. Rivers III, discussion with author, Ella Baker House, Dorchester, Mass., 17 Sept. 1996; George F. Will, "Reaching 'Escape Velocity,'" *Washington Post,* 12 Dec. 1996, A:21; John J. DiIulio, Jr., "The Lord's Work: The Church and the 'Civil Society Sector,'" *Brookings Review* 15:4 (Fall 1997), 27–31.
3. Rev. John L. Doyle, interview with author, St. Peter's Rectory, Dorchester, Mass., 16 Sept. 1996. See also *GlbSun,* 22 Mar. 1998, city weekly, 2.
4. Bill Walczak, interview with author, Dorchester, Mass., 16 Sept. 1996.
5. Nancy Kaufman, interview with author, Boston, 17 Sept. 1996; *To Make Our City Whole: A Report on the Work of the Strategy Development Group of the Boston Persistent Poverty Project* (Boston: Boston Foundation, 1994), vii.
6. Nancy Kaufman, interview with author, Boston, 17 Sept. 1996.
7. *JAdv,* 19 Oct. 1916, 1; Mignon L. Rubenovitz, "Jewishness Made Beautiful," in Temple Mishkan Tefila, *Temple Mishkan Tefila: A History, 1858–1958* (Newton: Temple Mishkan Tefila, 1958), CMTA, 70; Herman H. Rubenovitz and Mignon L. Rubenovitz, *The Waking Heart: Adventure in Achievement* (Cambridge, Mass.: Nathaniel Dame, 1967), 191.
8. Rabbi Michael Menitoff, interview with author, Temple Mishkan Tefila, Newton, Mass., 19 Sept. 1996.
9. Deahdra Butler-Henderson, telephone interview with author, 18 Aug. 1995; *DorCN,* 3 Nov. 1995, 1, 25–26; *Globe,* 4 Dec. 1995, metro/region, 21; *Globe,* 6 Jan. 1996, 10.
10. *GlbSun,* 21 Sept. 1997, real estate, 61. See also *Globe,* 27 Sept. 1997, A:14.

Acknowledgments

I had been thinking about Boston neighborhoods for a while, but it was in a few exchanges with Tim Burnieika that this book actually began. I lived in Greenough Hall as a proctor during my second year in graduate school, and Tim, a Harvard freshman, lived down the hall from me. With a habit of forgetting when I have previously asked a question and already know the answer, I asked Tim two or three times where he had grown up. His family had since moved, but Tim hailed originally from Dorchester. I asked him which part of Dorchester he was from, and each time he answered, "St. William's." Like any stubborn researcher, I ignored the answer and asked him to give me a neighborhood name that I could find on a map. Tim, obliging, explained that St. William's was in Dorchester's Savin Hill neighborhood. I rested easy with that answer: I could find Savin Hill on a map.

It took three years for me to realize that I was looking for Tim's old home on the wrong map. While many Dorchester residents had grown up in a world mapped according to neighborhood names like Savin Hill and Ashmont and Mattapan, many others had grown up in a world mapped according to parishes. Those two worlds and two maps were fundamentally different, and each world took its identity from a distinct set of institutions. Understanding those maps, those worlds, those institutional networks—understanding that Tim had grown up in a place called St. William's—proved crucial as I set out to examine patterns of neighborhood stability and change. I had not seen Tim much after his freshman year, but I remember calling him just a few weeks before he graduated to tell him that I had finally found St. William's.

A year or two after that phone call, I learned from my research that the original St. William's Church had burned down in the fall of 1980. On Christmas Day, a large group of parishioners had gathered at the site of their church to celebrate Mass. The vacant lot was covered with snow;

363

the temperature was seven degrees below zero. "Strategically placed bricks from the gutted church kept the altar cloth from being carried down Dorchester avenue by bitter 20-mph winds," the *Boston Globe* reported the next day. "Maureen Burnieika cradled her young son Jeffrey in her arms through the first half of the Mass but headed for her car after another son, Timothy, completed his Biblical reading. 'It is just too cold for him,' she said, gesturing to the faceless bundle of clothes in her arms. 'We've lived here all our lives. It was a lovely church. We had to come.'"

This book brought me to several archives and libraries. I am very grateful to Congregation Mishkan Tefila, especially to Michael R. Hart, Martin Hoffman, Charlotte Kaitz, and Rabbi Michael Menitoff. I am also grateful to several other persons and institutions for their assistance with this project: John Cronin and Tom Clark, the *Boston Herald* Library; Roger Cunningham, Department of Implementation of the Boston Public Schools; Anne Reed, Brookline Public Library; Sister Mary Jude Waters and Diane Noonan, Catholic School Office of the Archdiocese of Boston; Harold F. Worthley, Congregational Library of the American Congregational Association; John Baldisserotto, Government Documents and Microforms Department of the Harvard College Library; Christopher Pederson, Harvard University Map Collection; Mary Bicknell, Special Collections of the Massachusetts State Library; Lorna Condon, Society for the Preservation of New England Antiquities; Betsy Friedman Abrams, Temple Israel Archives; and Elizabeth R. Mock, Archives of the University of Massachusetts at Boston. I owe special thanks to the staffs of two institutions that became second homes for me: Phyllis Danehy, Beth Lindblom, Ron Patkus, and Sandra Sudak, at the Archives of the Roman Catholic Archdiocese of Boston; and Gina Hsin, Ellen Smith, and the late Nathan Kaganoff, at the American Jewish Historical Society.

The search for documents was a treasure hunt. I found many of my most valuable sources tucked away in forgotten drawers, carefully written out in ink in the sacramental records of urban churches, in school basements, in cemetery chapels, in rectories, and in private homes. I discovered that the buildings of Dorchester and Roxbury were themselves a precious historical record. And, in the process of this search, I discovered how much I could learn just by keeping quiet and listening. For their time and guidance, I am grateful to Joseph Abelow, Elizabeth Allen, Joan Allen, Murray Block, Jim Brett, Rose Bronstein, Rev. Anthony

Buchette, Joe Burnieika, Tim Burnieika, Deahdra Butler-Henderson, Rev. Arthur Calter, Rabbi Chaim Ciment, Esther Ciment, Abraham Close, Robert Cohen, Rabbi and Mrs. Moses Cohn, Reuven Cohn, Eleanor Collins, Frieda Cooper, Herman Cooper, Marshall Dana, Randi Donnis, Rev. John L. Doyle, Barbara Clark Elam, Judge Harry J. Elam, Esther Epstein, Lillian Feinstein, Louis Feinstein, Lewis Finfer, Rev. Msgr. Thomas J. Finnegan, Jr., Mary Lou Flaherty, Rev. James Flavin, Dorothy Gamm, Louis Gamm, Sandra Gamm, Stephen Gamm, Bette Gladstone, Marvin Gorodetzer, Sumner Greenberg, Barbara Greene, George Halzel, Richard Heath, Rev. Joseph Hennessey, Bernie Hyatt, Nathaniel Jacobson, Rabbi Shamai Kanter, David Kaufman, Maurice Kaufman, Nancy Kaufman, Steve Kellerman, Thomas Kelly, Murray Kesselman, Rev. J. Joseph Kierce, Sister M. Christine Kleponis, Norman Kristal, Marvin Lampert, Rev. James H. Lane, Rev. James Larner, Hillel Levine, Ruth Levitan, Elma Lewis, Rev. James Lyons, Rev. James McCarthy, Sister Katherine McGrath, Rev. Laurence McGrath, Rev. Robert McMillan, Rev. Craig W. McMullen, Ed Madden, John Madden, Rev. Stephen Madden, Rev. Paul Mahan, Rabbi Shloma Margolis, Gertrude Markson, Israel Mindick, Mark Mirsky, Rev. Thomas Oates, Rev. Paul O'Brien, Brian Wright O'Connor, Rev. John F. O'Donnell, Dorothy Olson, Rev. Gerald Osterman, Rev. Paul C. Peterson, Rev. John J. Philbin, Rev. Robert P. Reed, Rev. Eugene F. Rivers III, Michael Rosenberg, Rev. John Roussin, Rev. Paul P. Rynne, Rev. William Schmidt, Rob Schneider, Bob Segal, Bill Sicord, Betty Singer, Ernest Singer, Andrew Sullivan, Rev. Eugene Sullivan, Rev. Francis X. Turke, Rev. Edward O. Waldron, Jim Walsh, Lewis Weinstein, Harriet White, Rev. Joseph M. White, Sylvia M. Widershien, Carrye Williams, Laval Wilson, Herbert Woolf, Rabbi and Mrs. Walter S. Wurzburger, and Justin Wyner. I owe an extra measure of thanks to Bill Walczak, who has introduced me to half the restaurants and bars in Dorchester and always makes me eager to get back for another visit.

Many colleagues, at conferences and at seminars at various universities, have strengthened this book with their questions, criticisms, and suggestions. Above all, I thank Jo Ann Argersinger, Sarah Binder, Henry Brady, Amy Bridges, Nancy Burns, Randy Calvert, Rui de Figueiredo, Philip Ethington, Dick Fenno, Bill Green, Arnold Hirsch, Eric Lawrence, Eileen McDonagh, Forrest Maltzman, John McGreevy, David O'Brien, Bill Riker, Curt Signorino, Ellen Smith, Renée Smith, Tom Sugrue, Cynthia Verba, Barry Weingast, and the students in my urban seminar at the

University of Rochester and Nancy Burns's urban seminar at the University of Michigan. Mike Aronson, my editor at Harvard University Press, has done yeoman's work in encouraging me to keep this book short, tight, and readable. Christine Thorsteinsson, my manuscript editor, has been exemplary.

To work on this book, I received research support from the University of Rochester, a dissertation completion fellowship from the Mellon Foundation, and a grant from the Irish American Cultural Institute (through the Irish Research Fund endowment given by the Irish Institute of New York). I wrote the final draft of the text while I was in Washington, D.C., as a fellow at the Woodrow Wilson International Center for Scholars. All this support came at crucial stages in this project and provided me with vital resources and time.

I started this book in Mather House, at Harvard. I am finishing it in Harkness Hall, at Rochester. A group of Matherites helped me identify relevant news stories from old, hand-compiled indexes, then copied those news stories from microfilm onto paper: Brian Buckley, Brian Enge, Sean Koscho, and Michael Zimmerman. Another group, including persons not only at Harvard and Rochester but also at the Boston Redevelopment Authority and the City of Rochester's Bureau of Data Processing, assisted me in creating computerized block-level maps and data records for every census since 1940: John Bauerschmidt, Josh Blatt, Anjan Chaklader, Rolf Goetze, Sean Koscho, and Michael Zazzaro. And three people, each with a Mather affiliation, together produced hundreds of photographs of buildings and neighborhood life in Roxbury and Dorchester, which I consulted constantly as I wrote this book: Elsa Dorfman, Jamie Rosen, and, above all, Brett Miller. Others helped me with additional research tasks: Colin Chant, Barbara Cohen, Damon D'Arienzo, David Finkelstein, Dan Gamm, Neil Mello, Jamie Reilly, Christopher Rezendes, Brian Roraff, and Matthew Walker. Aaron Wicks created the index.

Mather and Harkness are special places. At the long wooden tables in Mather Dining Hall, students and colleagues and friends listened to me over dinner as I worked to define my thesis question. Then every night, as I returned from another day's research, they listened to me talk excitedly about my latest discovery. I am lucky to have them around—and, now, to have the couches to sleep on when I find myself away from home. They fill the Harkness lounge with brown bags at lunchtime and feign interest in my maps in the evening. They question, talk, and listen. And they tell their own stories.

When I was a senior in college, Sid Verba shared with me The Three Rules of Research. On that particular day, I was in the midst of writing my senior honors thesis; I had arrived at his office in Wadsworth House, concerned that I would not be able to complete the whole thesis that I had planned to submit, not knowing how he would react to the news. Sid's three rules were reassuring. First, he said, all research will take longer than you initially expect. Second, the project will cost more than you had foreseen. And third, what you wind up writing in the end is not what you had set out to write in the beginning. It has been a few years since Sid told me about those three rules, so I hope that I am remembering them correctly. Whether or not my memory is accurate, I have been reassured by his words many times and now I have begun to share this wisdom with students of my own.

Ken Shepsle, Stephan Thernstrom, and Sid Verba were the pillars of my graduate education. They, with Ernest May, supervised my doctoral program in history and political science. And they supervised the dissertation that became this book. They showed me unwavering patience. It was in a meeting with them in January 1991 that I began to consider the different experiences of Dorchester's Jews and Catholics and to ask if those differences were rooted in local institutions. They have not hesitated to criticize and they have offered me constant, unyielding support and encouragement. They have shown me what research and teaching are all about.

Although I am a child of a Boston suburb, I had nearly no personal knowledge of Dorchester or Roxbury when I began this project. And though my parents lived in Dorchester when they were children and for the first two years of their marriage, their days in Dorchester seemed almost as distant as the Exodus itself to a boy growing up in Sharon. What I know about Dorchester and Roxbury I have learned from others, from documents, and from visits in the last few years. But I have enjoyed sharing my stories with and asking questions of my father and grandmothers and, while they lived, my mother and grandfathers. They, like Tim Burnieika, remind me that I write about real people, about a world that most city people inhabit today or were inhabiting just yesterday. My father has listened many nights on the telephone as I tell him one story after another, though he, like my friends, knows that my stories are seldom brief. I am grateful to him, Celia, and the rest of my family for shepherding me through to this day.

I have one childhood memory of Dorchester. More than once, I stood as a little boy in a butcher shop on Blue Hill Avenue as my mother walked up to the counter to purchase meat. I remember the butcher shop as an exotic place, unlike any of the places that we shopped near our suburban home. I remember the chickens laid out by the window, their beaks and eyes and feathers and claws giving them an animated appearance. I remember the sawdust that covered the floors. Nowhere else had I seen floors covered in sawdust. And I remember my mother was there with me in the shop. Always, I remember her by my side.

Index

Abrams, Rabbi Samuel J., 160. *See also* Ohabei Shalom, Congregation

ABUP. *See* Association of Boston Urban Priests

Adath Israel, Congregation, 99, 101, 105, 138, 147, 181; building plans, 124, 152; financial difficulties, 149; move to Columbus Avenue, 100, 135–136; move to Commonwealth Avenue, 136, 192–193; Reform Judaism in, 100, 108, 159, 192–193, 195; sale of temple to black church, 105, 135

Adath Jeshurun, Congregation, 66, 70, 71, 127, 254; Blue Hill Avenue Synagogue, 75, 125, 139, 147–148, 149, 180, 181, 280; building of Menorah Institute, 123, 124, 149, 152; Conservative Judaism in, 161–162, 208–212; dissolution of congregation and physical deterioration of Blue Hill Avenue Synagogue, 252–253, 263; Dudley Street Synagogue, 63; financial difficulties of congregation and Menorah Institute, 149, 214, 215, 234, 235, 247; High Holy Day services, 127; move to Blue Hill Avenue and dedication of synagogue, 63, 65–66, 75, 107; Orthodox Judaism in, 161–162, 208–212; rabbis in, 163, 209, 215, 235–236, 351n28; sale of Menorah Institute, 232

African Americans: crime against, 276–277, 278; general settlement in Dorchester and Roxbury, 60–63, 83–92, 185, 186, 196, 217, 224–229, 241, 259, 292n2; prejudice against by Catholic institutions, 239; settlement along Blue Hill Avenue, 37–39, 49, 50, 52–55, 83, 89, 90, 242, 255–256;

settlement in Catholic areas, 39, 60, 83, 85–91, 197, 217, 238–239, 242–244, 246–247, 257–258, 263–264, 275–279, 283; settlement in Elm Hill district, 60, 83, 196–197, 224–226, 242; settlement in Franklin Field district, 91, 226, 243–244; settlement in Mattapan, 44–45, 50, 83, 241–242, 255–257, 268, 273; tensions with Catholics and Jews, 15, 25, 224, 228–229, 274, 276–277

Agudath Achim, Congregation, 116, 138, 149, 235

Agudath Israel, Congregation, 270, 272; crime against, 39; dissolution of, 273; religious reform debate in, 162; Woodrow Avenue Synagogue, 70, 139, 198, 234, 255

AJP. *See* Associated Jewish Philanthropies

Allston, 137, 184, 192–195, 200, 204, 220. *See also* Brighton; Brookline

Altar: immobility of, 18, 131, 132; in St. Peter's Church, 5, 129, 133, 258; in St. William's Church, 132. *See also* Canon law; Catholicism

Ammerman, Nancy Tatom, 19

Anderson, Rev. Joseph G., 166. *See also* St. Peter's Church; St. Peter's Parish

Ansel, Julius, 173

Anshe Shepetovka, Congregation, 138, 235

Anshey Amis, Congregation, 60

Anshi Volin, Congregation, 138, 255

Anti-Defamation League, 252

Arafe, George J., 248

Archdiocese of Boston, 219; arrangement of parishes in early 1900s, 71–78, 117, 179–180; Catholic School Office, 5; Clergy Personnel Board, 167; funding of parishes, 21, 153, 155, 217–219, 237,

369